Prelude to Independence

PRELUDE TO INDEPENDENCE

THE NEWSPAPER WAR
ON BRITAIN
1764-1776

by Arthur M. Schlesinger

with a prefatory note by
ARTHUR SCHLESINGER, JR.
and a new foreword by
CHARLES W. AKERS

A Northeastern Classics Edition

NORTHEASTERN UNIVERSITY PRESS
Boston

First Northeastern Edition, 1980

NORTHEASTERN UNIVERSITY PRESS

© Copyright, 1957, by Arthur M. Schlesinger
Reprinted by arrangement with Alfred A. Knopf, Inc.

Library of Congress Cataloging in Publication Data

Schlesinger, Arthur Meier, 1888-1965.
    Prelude to independence.
Reprint of the 1958 ed. published by Knopf, New York.
Bibliography: p.   Includes index.
1. Press—United States—History—18th century.
2. United States—History—Revolution, 1775-1783
—Causes. I. Title.
[PN4861.S3   1980]   071'.3   80-22830
                ISBN 0-930350-13-8

Manufactured in the United States of America
86 85 84 83   5 4 3 2

T O

THE NIEMAN FELLOWS

OF

HARVARD UNIVERSITY

PAST AND PRESENT

Prefatory Note

BY ARTHUR SCHLESINGER, JR.

PRELUDE TO INDEPENDENCE is first of all an expression of my father's lifelong interest in the origins of the American Revolution. The struggle for national identity was the subject of his first book, *Colonial Merchants and the American Revolution* in 1918, and of his last book, *The Birth of the Nation* half a century later. At the same time, *Prelude to Independence* reflected another of his lifelong interests—newspapers and newspapermen.

In fact my father came rather close to being a newspaperman himself. As a high school senior in a small Ohio town, he wrote student news for the *Xenia Gazette* and served as an occasional Xenia correspondent for the paper in neighboring Springfield. Richard Harding Davis's reporting of the Spanish–American and Boer Wars had made journalism, my father later recalled, "seem a glamorous calling," so when he went to Ohio State University in the autumn of 1906, his aim—inasmuch as he had one—was to prepare for a journalistic career.

At Ohio State he did become editor-in-chief of the *Lantern*, the undergraduate paper, and spent nearly as much of his senior year on the paper as on his classes. "I wrote all the editorials, revised stories assigned to reporters, and put together a regular column of news of other universities. . . . I learned more about writing from this practical experience than from all my English courses combined." But the direction of his life changed as he encountered professors of history and political science "whose teaching and example cured me for all time of the half-formed idea of entering journalism." So my father became a professional historian and never looked back.

Yet, as the dedication of this book to the Nieman Fellows of Harvard attests, he retained a lively interest in the press. The Nieman Foundation, established at Harvard just before the Second World

War, brought a group of bright young newspapermen and women to Cambridge every fall for a year of academic refreshment. Louis M. Lyons, the Foundation's director for so many productive years, later wrote that my father was "a friend to all of them from the beginning. He has often said that he placed his activity for the Nieman Foundation second only to his profession of history." He served on the selection committees, attended the monthly dinners and entertained the Fellows at Sunday afternoon teas. "The personal relationships thus begun have carried down the years and across the land," Lyons added—a fact to which I can testify from the fond and respectful remembrances of my father that I have heard from so many Nieman alumni during my own travels.

In 1944 my father, along with Reinhold Niebuhr, Archibald MacLeish, Robert M. Hutchins and others, was named a member of the Commission on Freedom of the Press, established, but not controlled, by Time, Inc. The Commission's three-year labor produced the well-known report *A Free and Responsible Press* and a series of valuable supporting studies. "The predominant editorial reaction," my father later noted with some wryness, "ranged from derision to denunciation." But the Commission had impact nonetheless, and the establishment twenty years later of the National News Council carried one of the report's major recommendations into effect.

The role of the press in preparing the way for American independence thus represented a felicitous union of two of the author's abiding concerns. And the continuing vitality of *Prelude to Independence* comes not only from its meticulous scholarship but from the fact that my father saw the colonial editors and journalists with personal immediacy as if they were, in a way, the Nieman Fellows of their time.

Foreword

BY CHARLES W. AKERS

ON THE EVE of World War I, while preparing his doctoral dissertation, *The Colonial Merchants and the American Revolution, 1763-1776*, Arthur M. Schlesinger (1888-1965) became convinced of the collective importance of the colonial newspapers in generating resistance to Great Britain. While a young professor at the University of Iowa in the early 1920s, he lectured to several colleges in that state on the role of the newpaper press. But not until after his retirement in 1954 from a distinguished career of teaching and research at Harvard University did he find time to return to this study of his youth. *Prelude to Independence: The Newspaper War on Britain, 1764-1776*, appeared in 1957 as the first major product of an active retirement. Now, a generation later, it remains the most useful single treatment of the entire newspaper press in the twelve years before independence.

Schlesinger's achievement resulted from his long familiarity with all the newspapers from New Hampshire to Georgia, a total of thirty-eight at the outbreak of the War of Independence. Previous general studies had catalogued the papers and provided biographies of their printers; but these, along with a few monographs on limited aspects, failed to offer an all-colonial perspective. Even today, when nearly all the colonial newspapers are conveniently available in microform in single university libraries, few historians can muster the fortitude or find the time required to read each issue of every paper for even a decade. Considering the magnitude of the task, it is all the more remarkable that *Prelude to Independence* is succinct and readable. No serious reader can miss its three main conclusions.

First, Schlesinger maintained that "although a multitude of factors from the Sugar Act onward pushed the colonists along the road to Independence, the movement could hardly have succeeded without an ever alert and dedicated press.'' This conclusion, though incorporating Schlesinger's interpretation of the coming of the Revolution set forth in his *Colonial Merchants*, was informative and stimulating without being confining. It pointed scholars to both the necessity and the difficulty of making a more thorough use of the newspapers. Whatever one's view of the origin of the Revolution, ''the newspaper war on Britain'' had to be taken into account. For example, Schlesinger saw the masses as having ''little grasp of constitutional subtleties'' and consequently easily propagandized by radical Whigs. Yet he acknowledged that the newspaper printers belonged to the artisan class, thus providing an opening for the contrary view of those later historians who have stressed the direction given the resistance movement by large numbers of patriotic workingmen with a mind of their own and separate goals from the elite.

Second, Schlesinger concluded that ''in fostering a revolution in politics'' the printers ''also fostered a revolution in journalism.'' They made newspaper reading an American habit, created a market for more papers, and established themselves as opinion makers. Some recent historians have shifted the emphasis from the success of propaganda to the widespread politicizing of ordinary citizens by the importance of the issues at stake in throwing off British rule and creating new American governments. In this view the newspaper press was more of the platform on which debate was staged than the tool of a few radicals who pushed a reluctant populace into rebellion. Other colonial historians have raised questions concerning the control of the Revolutionary press, for then, as now, publishers were dependent on advertisers as well as subscribers. Whatever the reservations and new questions, Schlesinger correctly described the ''revolution in journalism'' taking place in the years from the Stamp Act to Independence. Benjamin Franklin, who rose from printer to newspaper publisher to founding father stands as the most dramatic symbol of this ''revolution.''

Schlesinger's third major conclusion has raised considerable controversy. ''Next to Independence itself,'' he maintained, ''the Revolutionary generation's greatest legacy to the American people'' was the ''conviction that freedom of utterance ranks unique among human rights as the protector and promoter of all the others.'' But how could the Whig patriots who denied freedom of the press to American loyalists be hailed as champions of this fundamental liberty? Schlesinger acknowledged that the Whigs seemed to accept the doctrine that "liberty of speech belonged solely to those who spoke the speech of liberty." With this acknowledgment the *Prelude* raised the issue and helped to define the terms of the continuing debate.

It is particularly fortunate that a new edition of the *Prelude* should appear at this time. In the last decade investigative journalism helped to force the resignation of a President of the United States; the private lives of public figures are considered by the courts to be public information; judges have recently jailed reporters for refusing to disclose their sources; and questions concerning the limits of a free press are frequently heard. In such an age, a reaffirmation of the importance of the freedom of the press and an examination of the responsibilities that should accompany that freedom are equally vital. A thoughtful reading of the *Prelude* can contribute to that end.

Since publication of the *Prelude*, a number of specialized studies have amplified topics that Schlesinger treated more generally. Several of the best of these appear in *The Press and the American Revolution* (Worcester: American Antiquarian Society, 1980), an anthology edited by Bernard Bailyn and John B. Hench. This handsome volume contains chapters on the printers and the Revolution, freedom of the press, the newspapers in the southern colonies, the German language-press, the reporting of news from England, the loyalist press, and the statistics of printing in the Revolutionary era. Leonard W. Levy expressed serious doubts concerning the commitment of American Whigs to freedom of the press in *Legacy of Suppression: Freedom of Speech and Press in Early American History* (Cambridge: Harvard University Press, 1960). Stephen Botein expanded knowledge of the "revolution in journalism" in " 'Meer Mechanics' and an Open Press: The Business and Political Strategies of Colonial American Printers," in *Perspectives in American History* 9 (1975): 127–225. The value of studying the control of newspapers became clear in Mary Ann Yodelis' "Who Paid the Piper? Publishing Economics in Boston, 1763–1775," *Journalism Monographs* 38(1975): 1–49. Richard L. Merritt made a pioneer effort to apply the social scientific methodology of content analysis to the colonial newspapers in *Symbols of American Community, 1735–1775* (New Haven: Yale University Press, 1966).

Two useful books survey the entire Revolutionary press from different perspectives: Philip Davidson, *Propaganda and the American Revolution, 1763–1775* (Chapel Hill: University of North Carolina

Press, 1941); and Bruce Ingham Granger, *Political Satire in the American Revolution, 1763-1783* (Ithaca: Cornell University Press, 1960). Sooner or later all students of the subject turn to the classic by Isaiah Thomas, *The History of Printing in America,* first published in 1810, which is now available in a modern edition (New York: Weathervane Books, 1970). Clarence S. Brigham's *History and Bibliography of American Newspapers, 1690-1820* (Worcester: American Antiquarian Society, 1947) remains the indispensable reference work.

No one interested in the Revolutionary newspapers should fail to sample them directly. One major newspaper, *The Pennsylvania Gazette*, 1728-1789, started by Benjamin Franklin, is available in a letterpress edition of twenty-five volumes (Philadelphia: Microsurance, Inc., 1968). The *Virginia Gazette* on microfilm with an index was issued by the Institute of Early American History and Culture. Most of the other newspapers can be read on microcards supplied by the Readex Microprint Corporation. In *The South Carolina Gazette, 1732-1775* (Columbia: University of South Carolina Press, 1953), Hennig Cohen provided an account of this paper with numerous excerpts classified according to subject. America's "first syndicated newspaper column" has been republished in *Boston under Military Rule, 1768-1769, as Revealed in A Journal of the Times*, Oliver Morton Dickerson, ed. (Boston: Mount Vernon Press, 1936). Solomon Lutnick, *The American Revolution and the British Press, 1775-1783* (Columbia: University of Missouri Press, 1967) made possible an informative comparison of English and American newspapers.

Professor Schlesinger's life and historical viewpoints are fascinatingly detailed in his autobiography, *In Retrospect: The History of a Historian* (New York: Harcourt, Brace & World, 1963), and in a volume of essays, *Nothing Stands Still* (Cambridge: Belknap Press of Harvard University Press, 1969).

The accumulation of specialized research on the Revolutionary press will in time, no doubt, make possible a general study superceding the *Prelude*. Its republication will both contribute to that end and refresh our memory of Schlesinger's major contributions to American historiography. In the meantime, the *Prelude* remains the work with which to begin an investigation of the subject.

Preface

In establishing American independence, the pen and the press had a merit equal to that of the sword.

DAVID RAMSAY, The History of the American Revolution (Phila., 1789), II, 319.

I saw the small seed of sedition, when it was implanted; it was, as a grain of mustard. I have watched the plant until it has become a great tree; the vilest reptiles that crawl upon the earth, are at the root; the foulest birds of the air rest upon its branches. I would now induce you to go to work immediately with axes and hatchets, and cut it down, for a twofold reason: because it is a pest to society, and lest it be felled by a stronger arm and crush its thousands in the fall.

"MASSACHUSETTENSIS" (DANIEL LEONARD) in the Massachusetts Gazette and Boston Post-Boy, Jan. 1, 1775.

THESE QUOTATIONS, one from a Whig contemporary, the other from a Tory, point up the purpose of this book, which is to assess the role of the newspaper in undermining loyalty to the mother country and creating a demand for separation. The first two chapters set the stage by portraying the conditions which bred colonial discontent following the Seven Years' War, the agencies other than the press that stimulated and organized resistance, and the methods they employed. Then after a review of American journalism prior to the crisis the bulk of the volume details the part played by the newspaper. The evidence fully sustains Dr. Ramsay's conclusion, in the passage just cited, that "the exertions of the army would have been insufficient to effect the revolution, unless the great body of the people had been prepared for it, and also kept in a constant disposition to oppose Great Britain." Incidentally, the editors, who from the very start had acted in many communities as postmasters, performed a further service in pioneering the United States post office.

In fostering a revolution in politics they also fostered a revolution in journalism. New occasions taught new duties, transforming routine vehicles of news and miscellany into engines of opinion. Bristling controversial articles and striking typographical innovations signaled the change and inevitably brought the patriot prints into head-on collision with the English common law of seditious libel. Some of the most vigorous discussions of liberty of the press in our history resulted, with the Whigs themselves finding as time went on that what suited them as means did not suit them as ends. In fact, unmitigated intolerance of Tory organs marked the final stages of the dispute. Nonetheless the eventual outcome was a decisive reaffirmation of the right of untrammeled publication in both law and custom.

The term "propaganda" in these pages carries no opprobrious overtones. It is used in the strict dictionary sense of "any organized or concerted effort or movement to spread a particular doctrine or system of doctrines or principles." Not only did both sides employ the device, but each, feeling it sought only the higher good, resorted at times to unconscionable distortion and misrepresentation. The Whig exponents, however, were the more numerous and proficient and, thanks partly to the unwitting help of bungling Ministries in London, they enjoyed the additional advantage of addressing a more receptive audience.

My interest in the Revolutionary press goes back many years, and from time to time I have published articles on aspects of it. These have been assimilated into the present work with such revision as later research required. In writing this over-all treatment I am deeply indebted to a critical reading of the manuscript by my wife Elizabeth Bancroft Schlesinger, my son Arthur M. Schlesinger, Jr., my friend and publisher Alfred A. Knopf, my colleague Louis M. Lyons, Curator of the Nieman Foundation at Harvard, and, at every stage of the preparation, to my secretary Elizabeth F. Hoxie.

A. M. S.

Contents

PART I

"The Real American Revolution"

Chapter I

The Sources of Disaffection

THE AMERICANS REJOICED as wildly as the mother country over France's defeat in the Seven Years' War. Not only had their arms hastened the event, but the Peace of 1763, concluding a century-long rivalry of the two great powers for North America, rid King George's overseas subjects of the haunting fear of an aggressor on their borders. Their delight, however, quickly faded when the victory wrought an unexpected change in the colonies' relations with the homeland. The conflict had saddled an enormous debt on Britain and created fresh territorial responsibilities in two hemispheres. In the Ministry's view the need to protect these new domains as well as the older ones against future attack rendered obsolete the traditional policy of "salutary neglect." The colonies must henceforth be attached more closely to the Empire, contribute to the cost of imperial defense and obey more faithfully the Acts of Trade and Navigation.

Britain inaugurated the new system with the Sugar Act of 1764 and the Stamp Act of 1765. These measures proving abortive, the Townshend Acts followed in 1767, with the establishment of a Customs Board in the colonies shortly after. When renewed American opposition forced Parliament in 1770 to revise the Townshend imposts, the Ministry next concentrated upon a single duty on tea. As the King said, "there must always be a tax to keep up the right." [1] Then in 1774, after Boston's destruction of the East India Company shipments, came the vengeful legislation against Massachusetts, ever

[1] Letter of Sept. 11, 1774, to Lord North, George III, *Correspondence with Lord North* (W. B. Donne, ed., London, 1867), I, 202.

since known as the Intolerable or Coercive Acts. Within another
year America flamed into open rebellion.

This was the backdrop against which the colonists moved falter-
ingly toward Independence. Twelve rasping years of irritation, incident and propaganda converted an unquestioning love of the parent
state first into distrust and foreboding, then into hatred and repudia-
tion. In John Adams's words, too often forgotten by historians, "The
Revolution was effected before the war commenced. The Revolution was in the hearts and minds of the people. . . . *This radical
change in the principles, opinions, sentiments, and affections of the
people was the real American Revolution.*"² The military ordeal
merely served to test the depth and tenacity of a conviction which
had been slow to form.

I

When the troubles started in 1764 probably none of the colonists
even dreamed of Independence. Pride in being Englishmen bridged
any feeling of estrangement due to geographic remoteness. Moreover, under Britain's lenient sway of a century and a half they had
transformed the wilderness into thriving communities, developed
representative institutions, carried on a far-flung overseas trade and
come to consider themselves, in Adams's expression, as "brethren
and fellow subjects with those in Britain, only under a somewhat
different method of legislation, and a totally different method of taxation." ³ No matter when they had first settled in America, "home"
remained for them as well as their children the land of their fore-
bears. They gloried in belonging to the world's mightiest empire,
and they were linked to the mother country by economic bonds as
well as by the impalpable strands of a common history and culture.

Indeed, as Benjamin Franklin attested, the colonies felt closer to
England than they did to one another.⁴ For one thing travel condi-

² Letter to Hezekiah Niles, Feb. 13, 1818, Adams, *Works* (C. F. Adams, ed.,
Boston, 1850–56), X, 282–283. Nevertheless, L. H. Gipson's recent scholarly account of the years 1763–75 is called *The Coming of the Revolution* (N. Y.,
1954), and J. R. Alden's follow-up volume on the war bears the title *The American Revolution* (N. Y., 1954).

³ "A Dissertation on the Canon and Feudal Law" (1765), Adams, *Works,* III,
461.

⁴ Cited in Richard Frothingham, *The Rise of the Republic of the United States*
(Boston, 1872), 153.

tions discouraged interprovincial contacts. Even the political leaders soon to become prominent had seldom or ever met their counterparts elsewhere. It took two days to ride by stage from Philadelphia to New York, as much as four or five to go from New York to Boston. In the South the roads were so wretched that except for short distances people usually went by water. Clashing interests further impeded intercourse. In many respects the colonies were like thirteen separate nations, each nursing its own ambitions and jealously eying its rivals; when boundary quarrels embittered relations, the outcome sometimes proved explosive. As late as 1769–72 settlers from Connecticut warred intermittently with Pennsylvanians over lands claimed by both provinces in the Susquehanna River basin, and about the same time New Yorkers fought with Hampshiremen over similarly disputed tracts. Occasionally the discord divided a province against itself. In North Carolina in 1770 the friction between tidewater and back country provoked a pitched battle.

Yet the colonies, joined by affection and interest to Britain and relatively isolated from one another, overcame their internal differences to unite against the new ministerial program. A number of factors, however, explain this seeming paradox. Basic to all of them was the ousting of France from North America by the Peace of 1763. By eliminating England's ancient enemy as an ever-present danger it not only weakened the colonists' sense of military dependence on the homeland but also their sense of political dependence. As a Tory sadly observed a decade later, "I am now convinced that if it [Canada] had remained to the French none of this spirit of opposition to the mother country would have yet appeared, and I think the effects of it worse than all we had to fear from French or Indians." [5]

This British partisan ignored other scarcely less vital influences. One of these was the prolonged economic eclipse that darkened men's lives following the Seven Years' War. The depression was occasioned by the banning of certain wartime traffic with the West Indies simultaneously with the reduction of British military expenditures in America and the stiffer enforcement of the Acts of Trade, and the hard times persisted with little abatement till 1770. Unsalable surpluses piled up in the hands of merchants, unemployment

[5] Thomas Hutchinson to Lord Dartmouth, Dec. 14, 1773, *New-England Chronicle,* July 6, 1775.

became rife, and bankruptcies drove even substantial businessmen to the wall.[6] In these dismal circumstances the imposition of further commercial and revenue controls by Parliament seemed intolerably oppressive.

At the same time the rise of cities to a pivotal position in colonial society gave strength and direction to the movement of resistance. From 1760 to the eve of the war with Britain in 1775, Philadelphia grew from 23,750 inhabitants to 40,000; New York from 18,000 to 25,000; Charleston (then Charles Town) from 8000 to 12,000; Newport from 7500 to 11,000. Boston alone marked time, increasing only from 15,630 to 16,000.[7] These seaports, with their low skylines of brick and frame buildings pierced with church steeples and shipmasts, plied a brisk domestic and transatlantic commerce and served as the political as well as the economic nerve centers of their respective regions. Although small by modern standards, they rivaled many British municipalities in size. Indeed, Philadelphia with its 40,000 souls surpassed every English city but London.

On these urban dwellers the blows of the depression fell hardest, and the ease of taking common action facilitated measures of redress. In fact, throughout the dozen years of controversy the cities headed the forces of opposition, furnishing most of the militant leaders, providing press support, organizing mass demonstrations and economic reprisals, and mobilizing farmer resistance. Boston's primacy as the "Cradle of Liberty" may well have sprung from her lagging progress in relation to the other ports, inciting her at any cost to remove the obstacles that Parliament was thrusting in her way. And, besides these major centers, places like Providence, New Haven, Hartford, Annapolis, Baltimore and, during legislative sessions, Williamsburg fervidly seconded the cause.

Another circumstance also furthered co-operation among the scattered communities. Benjamin Franklin, owner of the *Pennsylvania Gazette*, and William Hunter of the *Virginia Gazette*, jointly appointed to the office of Deputy Postmaster General for the colonies in 1753, greatly enlarged the system of postroads and otherwise quickened the mails. For example, in lieu of dispatching letter

---

[6] Carl Bridenbaugh, *Cities in Revolt* (N. Y., 1955), 250–255; A. M. Schlesinger, *The Colonial Merchants and the American Revolution, 1763–1776* (N. Y., 1918), 56–57, 241–243; E. S. and Helen M. Morgan, *The Stamp Act Crisis* (Chapel Hill, 1953), 31–32.

[7] Bridenbaugh, *Cities in Revolt,* 216–217.

bags once a week between Philadelphia and Boston with only a fort-
nightly service during the winter, they extended the faster schedule
throughout the year. Indeed, by 1764 the mail moved three times
weekly each way between Philadelphia and New York, so that with
good luck a writer could obtain an answer from his correspondent
the next day. Soon afterward, thanks to additional reforms, New
Yorkers and Bostonians could exchange letters within four days,
thus enabling a Philadelphian to receive a reply from Boston in six
days. South of Pennsylvania, where population centers were scarce,
the service continued slow, varying from weekly deliveries in the
region between Philadelphia and Charleston to monthly ones beyond. Even this, however, marked an improvement over former
years. Naturally the better facilities resulted in greatly increased in-
tercommunication.[8]

The final condition that lowered intercolonial barriers was perhaps the most significant of all. Till almost the end of the dispute the
patriot party sought merely to safeguard provincial home rule—to
restore the relations with the mother country that had subsisted before the Peace of 1763. As George Mason of Virginia wrote in
words echoing those of John Adams, "We claim nothing but the liberty and privileges of Englishmen, in the same degree, as if we had
still continued among our brethren in Great Britain . . . ."[9] Their
object was not to disrupt the Empire but only to ensure what today
would be called a dominion status. Having enjoyed greater freedom
than any other European colonists, they strove to preserve the blessing intact. This common political faith cut horizontally across ver-
tical provincial differences. It constituted a platform broad enough
to accommodate all Americans, including at the outset the bulk of
those who subsequently became Tories.

II

In addition to these matters of universal application nearly every
section of the population discovered special grievances as the min-

[8] Postal receipts rose from less than £938 during 1753–56 to nearly £3369
during 1757–60, and though Parliament in 1765 reduced mail rates by about a
third, the revenue for fiscal 1768–69 totaled £3285. W. E. Rich, *The History of
the United States Post Office to the Year 1829* (Cambridge, 1924), 31–41.

[9] Letter of June 6, 1766, to the Committee of Merchants in London, Kate M.
Rowland, *The Life and Correspondence of George Mason* (N. Y., 1892), I, 387.

isterial program unfolded. The powerful merchants of New England and the Middle colonies, feeling the initial impact of the commercial and fiscal policies, fomented the original protests and never afterward relaxed their vigilance. Allied in interest were the small tradesmen, artisans, mechanics, day laborers, longshoremen and mariners, who depended upon a flourishing mercantile class for their livelihood. These, as a contemporary said, constituted "that numerous portion of the community in republics, styled *The People*; in monarchies, *The Populace*; or still more irreverently, *The Rabble or Canaille*." [10] From their ranks also came practically all the printers, whom certain of the enactments directly affected and who struck back with newspaper, pamphlet and broadside. This collaboration of rich and poor proved an uneasy one, though, for the masses lacked the businessman's innate respect for law and order. But by the time some of the more substantial merchants decided to drop out of the coalition, events had passed irreparably beyond their control.[11]

In the North the small farmers followed the lead of the urban dweller. Not only did their welfare in part hinge on his, but the sheer loneliness of rural life predisposed them toward collective demonstrations, even if this involved going some distance for the purpose. These occasions in fact afforded an emotional release comparable to the later frontier camp meetings. Moreover, in New England, where the people were accustomed to run their town affairs, they instinctively resented Britain's desire to interfere in provincial affairs. Little wonder that the Northern press scolded a South Carolina Tory parson for "impudently saying, that *Mechanicks* and Country *Clowns* had no Right to dispute about Politics, or what King, Lords and Commons had done or might do!—All such Divines should be taught to know that Mechanicks and Country Clowns (infamously so called) are the real and absolute Masters of Kings, Lords, Commons, and Priests . . . ." [12]

[10] Alexander Grayson, *Memoirs of His Own Time* (J. S. Littell, ed., Phila., 1846), 122.

[11] Schlesinger, *Colonial Merchants*, esp. 91–93, 240–241, 591–606.

[12] *Newport Mercury*, Sept. 26, 1774, and *N.–H. Gazette*, Oct. 7; similarly, *N.–Y. Journal*, Jan. 26, 1775, and *Mass. Spy*, Feb. 2. Edward McCrady, *The History of South Carolina under the Royal Government* (N. Y., 1899), 752–755, relates this incident at length. For a detailed discussion of rural attitudes in Massachusetts, see L. N. Newcomer, *The Embattled Farmers* (N. Y., 1953), chaps. i–iii, whose analysis should be qualified by R. J. Taylor, *Western Massachusetts in the Revolution* (Providence, 1954), chaps. i–iv.

The Southern ruling class, aside from the Charleston merchants, felt less aggrieved by the direct than by the indirect effects of the new imperialism. Already heavily in debt to British creditors for luxuries and other goods, the great landholders viewed any further financial burdens with a feeling of outrage. Of his own Virginia, Thomas Jefferson said, "These debts had become hereditary from father to son for many generations, so that the planters were a species of property, annexed to certain mercantile houses in London." Oliver Wolcott indeed went so far in after years as to allege that "the *whiggism* of Virginia was chiefly owing to the *debts of the planters*." [13] It is revealing that when Parliament overreached itself in the Intolerable Acts all the provincial conventions of the South retaliated with some form of debt moratorium.[14] In any case the self-sufficiency and rooted habit of governing bred by a baronial type of life made the gentry oppose on principle any enlarging of British power, and in lawyer-planters like Jefferson, Patrick Henry, George Mason and William Henry Drayton they possessed tribunes who phrased their sentiments with telling effect.

Another element of the population, less defined geographically, consisted of the colonists of non-English stock. The bulk of the French Huguenots had settled in the coastal towns during the late seventeenth century and were by the 1760's indistinguishable from their Anglo-American neighbors. Such individuals as James Bowdoin (Baudouin) and Paul Revere (Rivoire) in Boston, John Jay in New York and Henry Laurens in Charleston figured prominently in the patriot movement. No less zealous was the far greater number of Scotch-Irish who, coming in the eighteenth century, scattered along the seaboard as well as through the interior. Their animus against the parent state harked back to sufferings in Ulster at the hands of Parliament and absentee English landlords. As a contemporary put it, "They had fled from oppression in their native country, and could not brook the idea that it should follow them." [15]

[13] Jefferson, *Writings* (P. L. Ford, ed., N. Y., 1892–99), IV, 155; Wolcott as quoted in C. A. Beard, *Economic Origins of Jeffersonian Democracy* (N. Y., 1915), 297–298. See also "A Planter" in the *Va. Gazette* (Purdie and Dixon), April 13, 1774. Washington's economic embarrassments included difficulties with the British government over his land speculations. C. P. Nettels, *George Washington and American Independence* (Boston, 1951), chap. iv.

[14] Schlesinger, *Colonial Merchants*, chaps. xiii–xiv, *passim*.

[15] David Ramsay, *The History of the American Revolution* (Phila., 1789), II, 311.

Only the Germans dwelling clannishly in the Pennsylvania back country remained for the most part aloof from the agitation; many of them were religious pacifists. Their compatriots elsewhere, however, generally supported the patriots. Thus, apart from the "Pennsylvania Dutch," the presence of these and other ethnic groups created no political problem for the Whigs. Of the fifty-six signers of the Declaration of Independence, eighteen were of non-English blood, nearly half of them immigrants.

The legal profession and the clergy provided the most articulate spokesmen for the cause. Lawyers had long taken the lead in public affairs; the art of special pleading, refined in the courtroom, proved equally successful in the political arena. They nearly always dominated the legislatures, and, whether trained in local law offices or at the famous London Inns of Court, they had drunk deep of English constitutional theory as well as of the natural-rights philosophy. "Nothing is too wicked for them to attempt which serves their purposes—the Press is to them what the Pulpit was in times of Popery," asserted New York's Lieutenant Governor Cadwallader Colden.[16] The Stamp Act, levying taxes on important legal documents and imposing a £10 fee for admission to the bar (much higher than in England), aroused their initial ire against Britain. To John Adams, who "had but just become known and had gained a small degree of reputation" as a Massachusetts attorney, it seemed that "this execrable project was set on foot for my own ruin as well as that of America in general, and of Great Britain"; and from New York, General Thomas Gage reported that "The Lawyers are the Source from whence the Clamors have flowed in every Province." [17] Each successive crisis repeated the story. Advocates of the caliber of Adams, James Otis, John Dickinson, James Iredell and Thomas Jefferson

[16] Colden, *Letter Books* (N.–Y. Hist. Soc., *Colls.*, IX–X, 1876–77), II, 71. Two other contemporaries, a Briton and an American, emphasize this political role of the colonial lawyer: Edmund Burke, *Speeches and Letters on American Affairs* (*Everyman's Library*, London, n.d.), 94–95, and Ramsay, *American Revolution*, I, 134. Dorothy R. Dillon, *The New York Triumvirate* (N. Y., 1949), singles out William Livingston, John Morin Scott and William Smith, Jr., in this respect. For more general accounts, see Charles Warren, *A History of the American Bar* (Boston, 1911), chaps. ii–ix, *passim*, and R. B. Morris, *Studies in the History of American Law* (N. Y., 1930), esp. 65–68.

[17] Adams, *Works*, II, 156; Gage to H. S. Conway, Dec. 21, 1765, Gage, *Correspondence with the Secretaries of State* (C. E. Carter, ed., New Haven, 1931), I, 79. The *N.–Y. Gazette or Weekly Post-Boy*, Feb. 20, 1766, confirmed the view that "some of the Lawyers in the several Provinces have been, and continue, the principal Writers on the Side of American Liberty."

analyzed the issues with legal and philosophical acumen, and their prestige in the community further aided the cause. It is not surprising that the profession furnished over half the members of the First Continental Congress as well as a like proportion of the signers of the Declaration of Independence.

The clergy carried hardly less weight. The New England Congregational divines larded their nonconformist theology with the precepts of Sidney, Milton, Locke and other revered English liberals, knowing from long practice how to insinuate politics into sermons and sermons into prayers. In short, they emulated their brethren of the bar in vaunting the colonists' natural and constitutional rights and the bounden duty to resist oppression. As a friendly contemporary wrote, they "represented the cause of America as the cause of heaven," or, as a British sympathizer said, they sounded "the Yell of Rebellion in the Ears of an ignorant & deluded People." [18] And in the Middle colonies, where the Presbyterians predominated, the clerics proclaimed similar doctrines.

This concern of religionists for political home rule gained strength from their concern for ecclesiastical home rule. The much mooted but never consummated project of a colonial Anglican episcopate conjured up the specter of a return to conditions which had driven many of the original settlers to the New World. Capping this alarm, the Quebec Act of 1774, which accompanied the Intolerable Acts, officially established Catholicism in French Canada, frightening the Americans as to what awaited them, for to the Calvinist mind the difference between the Church of Rome and the Church of England was negligible. The Tory, Joseph Galloway, taking into account merely the two major dissenting sects, estimated that only 12 out of the 550 New England parsons and "a still smaller number" else-

---

[18] Ramsay, *American Revolution*, I, 199; Peter Oliver, The Origin and Progress of the American Rebellion to the Year 1776 (Gay Transcripts, Mass. Hist. Soc.), 39. The abundant writings on the political role of the clergy include A. P. Stokes, *Church and State in the United States* (N. Y., 1950), I, 231–240, 258–264; W. W. Sweet, *Religion in the Development of American Culture, 1765–1840* (N. Y., 1952), chaps. i–ii; E. F. Humphrey, *Nationalism and Religion in America, 1774–1789* (Boston, 1924), chaps. ii–vi; Alice M. Baldwin, *The New England Clergy and the American Revolution* (Durham, 1928); M. C. Tyler, *The Literary History of the American Revolution* (N. Y., 1897), I, 121–140, II, 278–294, 302–306; C. H. Van Tyne, *The Causes of the War of Independence* (Boston, 1922), chap. xiii; F. D. Gifford, "The Influence of the Clergy on American Politics from 1763 to 1776," Protestant Episcopal Church, *Hist. Mag.*, X (1941), 104–123; Frank Moore, ed., *The Patriot Preachers of the American Revolution* (N. Y., 1862); and J. W. Thornton, ed., *The Pulpit of the American Revolution* (Boston, 1860).

where "declined the rebellious talk." [19] The Congregational divine, John Cleaveland of Ipswich, among others, blasted England in the press; and the Presbyterian minister, John Witherspoon, president of the College of New Jersey at Princeton, besides writing for the newspapers, became a member of the Second Continental Congress and signed the Declaration of Independence. In fact, the Anglican clergy itself was to a degree rent politically, with some in the South siding with the laymen who appointed and paid them, while the Northern ones, mostly English-supported missionaries, championed the mother country.

The Ministry kindled further popular wrath by markedly increasing royal appointees in the colonies. "Are not pensioners, stipendiaries, and salary-men (unknown before,) hourly multiplying on us, to riot in the spoils of miserable America?" raged Boston's Josiah Quincy, Jr.[20] Blatant nepotism in some provinces aggravated the resentment. In New Hampshire, for example, all but one of the Executive Council were related to Governor John Wentworth by blood or marriage, as were also one of the judges and the clerk of the Superior Court.[21] Moreover, the Crown officers, having favors to bestow, commanded a large following of "little tools and creatures"— stationers, aspirants for minor customs posts, informers, wharfingers, carters and the like.[22]

The conviction grew that Britain was deliberately restricting the opportunities for official preferment in America to political toadies. As one who spoke from personal knowledge attested, "The active and spirited part of the community, who felt themselves possessed of talents, that would raise them to eminence in a free government, longed for the establishment of independent constitutions." And on the same score a London commentator warned the Ministry three months before the Declaration of Independence that it was too late to patch up the quarrel. Already the wheel of fortune had elevated "shop-keepers, tradesmen, and attorneys" to "statesmen and legislators," with each filling "a station superior not only to what he had ever filled before, but to what he had ever expected to fill." And be-

[19] *Historical and Political Reflections on the Rise and Progress of the American Rebellion* (London, 1780), 110–111.

[20] *Boston Gazette,* Oct. 3, 1768.

[21] *Boston Evening-Post,* June 16, 1770. For the comparable situation in Massachusetts, see Ellen E. Brennan, *Plural Office-Holding in Massachusetts, 1760– 1780* (Chapel Hill, 1945), 32–34, 48–49, 59–60, 179–180.

[22] The quoted phrase is John Adams's. Adams, *Works,* II, 154.

sides, he went on, "Five hundred different people, perhaps, who in different ways act immediately under the Continental Congress; and five hundred thousand, perhaps, who act under those five hundred, all feel, in the same manner, a proportionable rise in their own importance." [23] The Declaration itself cited the "swarms of officers to harass our people, and eat our substances," as a reason for separation.

III

From the very beginning the patriots in every colony unhesitatingly challenged the ministerial program and strove, in John Adams's phrase, to make the thirteen clocks strike as one.[24] The efforts displayed a complex and evolving pattern which varied with the occasion and gained cohesion and strength as the crisis mounted. One flank of the movement consisted of a maze of volunteer agencies; the other, of the popularly controlled organs of the local and provincial governments; and, significantly, both forged intercolonial connections. Which type of organization had the greater effect it would be impossible to say, but it is certain that neither could have succeeded alone.

The unofficial bodies sought in most cases to safeguard the interests of special groups. As early as 1763 and 1764 the merchants of the major ports began to form committees of correspondence to ensure common action in such matters as remonstrating to Parliament and suspending British imports; and in these exertions the artisans and petty tradesmen eagerly co-operated with pledges of nonconsumption.[25] The masses, however, worked more characteristically through loosely knit, semisecret societies called Sons of Liberty, which issued fiery manifestoes, engineered tumultuous demonstrations, and exchanged vows of mutual assistance with their counterparts in other colonies. The Sons of Liberty ceased to exist as a clearly identifiable group by the early 1770's only to reappear in the guise of so-called mechanics' committees. But the original name

[23] Ramsay, *American Revolution*, II, 314; *Middlesex Journal*, April 6, 1776, quoted in Frank Moore, ed., *Diary of the American Revolution* (N. Y., 1860), I, 228–229.

[24] Letter to Hezekiah Niles, Feb. 13, 1818, Adams, *Works*, X, 283.

[25] Schlesinger, *Colonial Merchants, passim*, and, for a close-up of a single city from 1763 to 1770, C. M. Andrews, "The Boston Merchants and the Non-Importation Agreement," Colonial Soc. of Mass., *Pubs.*, XIX (1917), 159–259.

continued to be used, as it had earlier in many parts of the South, as a generic designation of uncompromising patriots.[26]

The lawyers, having contact with all walks of society, participated in most types of agencies with no need for one of their own, while the nonconforming clergy restricted themselves to instilling their political maxims in their parishioners until the bugbear of an Anglican episcopate aroused them to intercolonial organization. In 1766 the General Association of Congregational Ministers of Connecticut and the United Presbyterian Synod of New York and Pennsylvania entered into such a union "for preserving their religious liberty." Active up to the onset of war in 1775, this body repeatedly warned the public against the dreaded ecclesiastical "tyranny." In 1769 a Society of Dissenters, based in New York City, took up the task of spreading the alarm by correspondence with still other denominations.[27] So closely linked were the fears for theological and political freedom that in 1775, after the passage of the Quebec Act, four Philadelphia Presbyterian ministers addressed an open letter on the subject to their coreligionists in North Carolina; and a few months later the Continental Congress itself employed two preachers to tour the North Carolina back country with a similar message.[28]

The colleges emulated the nonconformist churches as "seminaries of sedition." The students may have imbibed their libertarianism from courses in classical history or from the politics of admired instructors; and undoubtedly both teachers and taught bridled at the £2 tax prescribed by the Stamp Act for matriculation and for graduation. In any event the undergraduates flaunted their views in declamations, forensic disputes and commencement theses, discoursing on such themes as "Oppression and Tyranny," "The Pernicious Practice of Drinking Tea" and "All Men Are Free by the Law of Nature." The Princeton boys in the aftermath of the Boston Tea Party burned the college steward's supply of the obnoxious herb. At

---

[26] The best accounts are Philip Davidson, *Propaganda and the American Revolution* (Chapel Hill, 1941), 68–80, and, for a single city, H. M. Morais, "The Sons of Liberty in New York," R. B. Morris, ed., *The Era of the Revolution* (N. Y., 1939), 269–289.

[27] Stokes, *Church and State*, I, 235–238; H. L. Osgood, ed., "The Society of Dissenters Founded at New York in 1769," *Am. Hist. Rev.*, VI (1900–01), 498–507.

[28] W. L. Saunders, ed., *The Colonial Records of North Carolina* (Raleigh, 1886–90), X, 86, 222–228, 338.

Rhode Island College (later Brown University) the seniors in 1775 persuaded the governing board to omit the public commencement festivities as unbefitting their Spartan mood. And the same year Yale undergraduates went so far as to advertise a fellow student in the press for criticizing the American cause.[29] As a friendly observer said of the Harvard lads, "They have catched the spirit of the times," to such a degree indeed, he continued, that "it has been difficult to keep them within due bounds. But their tutors are fearful of giving too great a check to a disposition which may hereafter fill the country with patriots . . . ." Moreover, coming from all parts of the country, college youths carried the flame back to their home communities. The Virginian, James Madison, for example, who studied under President Witherspoon at Princeton, where he helped form the American Whig Society, had as fellow graduates in 1771 Philip Freneau of New York and Hugh H. Brackenridge of Pennsylvania.[30]

Dr. David Ramsay, another son of Princeton, testified that upwards of 2000 alumni of Harvard and Yale strove to "influence and direct the great body of the people to a proper line of conduct" and that the 300 of his own alma mater, a much younger seat of learning, were hardly less "active and useful." [31] If these institutions set the pace, the six other colleges were not far behind, if allowance be made for the fact that three of them came into being after the troubles arose. Of the 56 signers of the Declaration of Independence, 19 held degrees from colonial colleges and 8 (including Witherspoon) from abroad.

[29] David Potter, *Debating in the Colonial Chartered Colleges* (N. Y., 1944), 44–46, 131–145; E. J. Young, "Subjects for Master's Degree in Harvard College," Mass. Hist. Soc., *Procs.*, ser. 1, XVIII (1880–81), 125–127; Richard Hofstadter and W. P. Metzger, *The Development of Academic Freedom in the United States* (N. Y., 1955), 203–205; S. E. Morison, *Three Centuries of Harvard* (Cambridge, 1936), 135–151; T. J. Wertenbaker, *Princeton* (Princeton, 1946), 55–58; Peter Force, comp., *American Archives*, ser. 4 (Wash., 1837–46), II, 935–936, regarding Rhode Island College; *Conn. Journal*, Aug. 30, 1775, regarding Yale; E. P. Cheyney, *History of the University of Pennsylvania* (Phila., 1940), 114–119; Alice M. Baldwin, "Sowers of Sedition," *William and Mary Quar.*, ser. 3, V (1948), 59–63.

[30] Andrew Eliot to Thomas Hollis, Dec. 25, 1769, Mass. Hist. Soc., *Colls.*, ser. 4, IV (1858), 447; Michael Kraus, *Intercolonial Aspects of American Culture on the Eve of the Revolution* (N. Y., 1928), 119–124.

[31] *American Revolution*, II, 320–321. In 1775 President Eleazar Wheelock of Dartmouth excited "public and loud clamour" for allegedly having "said and done many things disrespectfully of the Congress and the colonies," but the Committees of Safety of Hanover and Lebanon after "a most critical and thorough enquiry" unanimously gave him a clean bill of health, citing in rebuttal his many affirmative services. *Conn. Courant*, March 25, 1775.

IV

Rounding out this elaborate machinery of organization were the duly constituted legal instrumentalities.[32] In so free a society the people possessed abundant means of official expression. Massachusetts usually led the way at both the local and provincial levels. At every emergency the town meetings wheeled into line, adopting fierce resolves and inciting their legislative representatives to greater boldness. Of the Boston town meeting Governor Thomas Hutchinson bitterly remarked that despite the property qualification for membership "anything with the appearance of a man" voted, so that "the lowest class" prevailed "under the influence of a few of the higher class." [33]

To step up the agitation Samuel Adams in 1772, taking his cue from the volunteer agencies, induced Boston to establish a standing committee of correspondence for airing "the Rights of the Colonists and of this Province" between town meetings and to invite all the other towns to do likewise. Soon nearly eighty of these furnaces of propaganda were ablaze. "This," railed a Tory, "is the foulest, subtlest, and most venomous serpent that ever issued from the eggs of sedition." [34] Meanwhile the parent committee also exchanged views with Whig groups outside Massachusetts. To curb such "dangerous and unwarrantable" doings the Intolerable Acts belatedly forbade the calling of town meetings henceforth (except for the indispensable purpose of elections) without the Governor's written consent; but the move proved vain. Under the legal fiction of repeatedly adjourning the meetings held just before the ban took effect, the citizens continued to assemble and the committees continued to function. The only result was a more strident note of defiance.

[32] The principal references are E. D. Collins, "Committees of Correspondence of the American Revolution," Am. Hist. Assoc., *Report for 1901*, I, 243–271; R. V. Harlow, *The History of Legislative Methods in the Period before 1825* (New Haven, 1917), chaps. ii–iii; J. M. Leake, *The Virginia Committee System and the American Revolution* (Balt., 1917); Morgans, *Stamp Act Crisis*, 103–112; E. C. Burnett, *The Continental Congress* (N. Y., 1941), chaps. i–iii.
[33] Letter to Lord Hillsborough, March 29, 1772, J. K. Hosmer, *The Life of Thomas Hutchinson* (Boston, 1896), 231.
[34] "Massachusettensis" (Daniel Leonard) in the *Mass. Gazette and Boston Post-Boy*, Jan. 2, 1775.

The universal indignation at the Intolerable Acts caused the Massachusetts plan to spread before the end of 1774 to every colony but Georgia, always a laggard in the patriot movement. The Middle and Southern provinces, lacking New England's town-meeting system, proceeded through informal popular gatherings which appointed committees of correspondence, sometimes for a city or village, sometimes for an entire county. Voluntary action thus filled the void created by the absence of official means. To Samuel Adams this was all a dream come true. "Colony communicates freely with Colony," he exulted to Benjamin Franklin in London, adding that "the whole continent is now become united in sentiment and in opposition to tyranny." [35] Though he undoubtedly overrated a single type of organization, his famous kinsman John, looking back from the vantage point of some forty years, feelingly exclaimed, "What an engine! France imitated it, and produced a revolution." [36]

Inasmuch as every province elected at least one branch of its legislature, these bodies co-operated from the outset across colonial lines. "They none of them choose to be foremost in sedition," a Crown official sneered, "and endeavour to excite each other to take the lead in opposition." [37] The overriding motive, however, was to impress upon the Ministry the solidarity of American opinion at the very highest deliberative level. In 1764 Massachusetts, Rhode Island, New York and North Carolina named legislative committees of correspondence to deal on a common basis with the emergency occasioned by the Sugar Act and the impending Stamp Act. The next year the Bay Colony initiated the Stamp Act Congress of delegates from the several Assemblies. Then in 1768, trying still another device, it appealed directly in a Circular Letter to the lawmakers elsewhere to "harmonize" in assailing the Townshend duties. At this point, however, the Ministry, finally taking notice, ordered the Massachusetts House to disavow its action on pain of instant dissolution, and it admonished all the other provinces under like penalty to ac-

[35] W. V. Wells, *The Life and Public Services of Samuel Adams* (Boston, 1865), II, 146–147. Since this letter was dated March 31, 1774, Adams somewhat anticipated the course of events.

[36] But the old revolutionary, having learned much in the interval, cautioned that "committees of secret correspondence are . . . . incision knives, to which recourse should never be had but in the last extremities of life, in the last question between life and death." Letter to Jedidiah Morse, Dec. 22, 1815, *Works*, X, 197.

[37] Lieutenant Governor William Bull of South Carolina to Lord Hillsborough, Sept. 10, 1768, British Papers Relating to the American Revolution (Sparks MSS., Harvard College Library), III, 125.

cord it "the contempt it deserves." The Bay Colony legislators refused by a thunderous 92 to 17—a vote which was to supply the patriots everywhere with a potent rallying cry—and the Assemblies
that had not already answered the Circular Letter now defiantly proceeded to do so.

In 1773 came the next move. The Virginia Burgesses, angered by
the royal inquiry into the burning of the revenue schooner *Gaspee*
by a Providence, R. I., mob, created a standing—not temporary—
legislative committee of correspondence on American grievances
and asked the other provinces to set up counterparts. Presently a
whole network was functioning. Construing their mandates liber-
ally, they operated not only in the intervals between sessions but
even when the Assemblies suffered dissolution. Governor Hutchinson with reason interpreted this maneuver as a "glaring attempt to
alter the constitution of the colonies" and to unite "a number of
bodies, which, by their constitutions, were intended to be kept separate and unconnected." [38] This time, however, the Ministry chose to
do no more than express disapproval. Thus, as the opposition to Britain neared its climax, corresponding committees forwarded the popular movement at both provincial and town levels.

The Assemblies evidenced their growing insubordination in other
actions. The Massachusetts House of Representatives, violating im-
memorial precedent, opened a spectators' gallery in 1766 in order
to ventilate their views before a wider audience; soon, to the horror
of the Crown authorities, the members were terming themselves
"his majesty's commons," their debates "parliamentary debates,"
and the imperial enactments "acts of the British Parliament." [39] Outraged governors learned that even dissolution could not gag the
popular branches. After the Bay Colony lawmakers lost their seats
in 1768 for reaffirming the Circular Letter, the Boston town meeting sponsored a province-wide convention which, with the late
Speaker of the House in the chair, protested the sending of troops
to that city. The next year the disbanded legislators of both Virginia and North Carolina reassembled in their private capacities to
adopt nonimportation resolutions. Such transactions, unauthorized
by law, paved the way for the self-constituted bodies which in 1774

[38] Thomas Hutchinson, *The History of the Province of Massachusetts Bay*,
III (London, 1828), 397.
[39] *Ibid.*, III, 165–166, 413 *n.*

and thereafter superseded the regular provincial regimes and evolved into the first state governments.

For nine years after the Stamp Act Congress, however, the patriots avoided another intercolonial parley. That meeting, summoned in a blaze of excitement, had brought together an ill-assorted crew from nine Assemblies, "some of the members," according to one attendant, being "as timid as if engaged in a traitorous conspiracy." Two of the three from Massachusetts had indeed gone expressly to head off "undutiful and improper" proceedings. In the end the chairman (one of the Bay Colony conservatives) and a New Jersey representative declined on principle to sign the resolutions.[40]

By 1774, however, the Whig leaders, enraged by the Intolerable Acts and supported by the legal and extralegal agencies enmeshing the land, felt certain of an essentially like-minded gathering. The Virginia Burgesses, acting after dissolution by the Governor, issued the formal call. The Continental Congress, convening at Philadelphia in the autumn, consisted of members selected by Assemblies in five colonies and by popular conventions or the equivalent in seven others, with Georgia the only absentee. Practically all the attendants had served on committees of correspondence or similar bodies. And, significantly, they conducted their deliberations in Carpenters' Hall, a choice "highly agreeable to the mechanics and citizens in general." [41]

The delegates, besides framing remonstrances, declared a sweeping economic boycott of the mother country, and to implement it they took over the whole mechanism of local committees. In short, they exercised what amounted to legislative and coercive powers, going far toward erecting a government within the government. Moreover, they arranged for a follow-up meeting in May of the next year in case the Ministry should prove adamant. It was this Second Continental Congress which, assembling in May, 1775, after the bloodshed at Lexington and Concord, formed an intercolonial army and in due course proclaimed Independence. A dozen years of organizational activity had loaded the gun; the Second Continental Congress pulled the trigger. An apparatus of resistance instituted for limited objectives ended by creating an American nation.

[40] Thomas McKean to John Adams, Aug. 20, 1813, Adams, *Works*, X, 61; Hutchinson, *Massachusetts Bay*, III, 118 *n.*

[41] Silas Deane to his wife, Sept. 8, 1774, Conn. Hist. Soc., *Colls.*, II (1870), 172.

Chapter II

The
Levers of Propaganda

ROM THE INCEPTION of the controversy the patriots exhibited
extraordinary skill in manipulating public opinion, playing upon the
emotions of the ignorant as well as the minds of the educated.
Though they had never before faced a like situation and were un-
accustomed to co-operate across provincial lines, no disaffected element in history has ever risen more splendidly to the occasion. Indeed, the French revolutionists a generation later could do no
better than employ many of the same devices.[1]

Everywhere men threw themselves wholeheartedly into the movement, often at great personal risk; and some, like Samuel Adams in
Boston, Alexander McDougall in New York, John Dickinson in
Philadelphia and Christopher Gadsden in Charleston, achieved intercolonial prominence. No central board of strategy, however, su-
perintended the agitation, no long-range plan guided it, and no campaign chest paid for spellbinders, publicity or mass demonstrations.
But despite the absence of unified direction the propaganda in the
different provinces revealed striking similarities. In part this was an
automatic response to common grievances, but, even more, it
stemmed from the unceasing correspondence of Whig committees
and, perhaps most of all, from the imitation excited in one community by newspaper accounts of activities in other places.

The main elements of the offensive appeared in the opposition to
the Stamp Act. As John Adams summarized the reaction, "In every
colony, from Georgia to New Hampshire inclusively, the stamp dis-

[1] C. C. Brinton, *The Jacobins* (N. Y., 1930), chap. iv; Huntley Dupre, "Some
French Revolutionary Propaganda Techniques," *Historian*, II (1940), 156–164;
Charles Hughes, "Music of the French Revolution," *Science and Society*, IV (1940),
193–210.

tributers and inspectors have been compelled by the unconquerable rage of the people to renounce their offices. . . . Our presses have groaned, our pulpits have thundered, our towns have voted; the crown officers have everywhere trembled," and "innumerable have been the monuments of wit, humor, sense, learning, spirit, patriotism, and heroism, erected in the several colonies and provinces in the course of this year." [2] Later crises showed, however, that the Americans' virtuosity had not been exhausted.

I

At every stage the propaganda of the fist reinforced the propaganda of the word. As a Tory commentator testified from personal experience, "mobs were a necessary ingredient" of the Whig program.[3] Some of these disturbances were deliberately contrived by the party higher-ups; others came about more or less spontaneously; but, whatever their origin, they furthered patriot purposes in several essential ways. They high-lighted grievances as mere language could never have done, they struck terror into the hearts of British adherents, and, as notoriously in the case of the Boston Massacre, they fashioned folk heroes out of street loafers and hoodlums.

At the very outset the Whig leaders directed calculated violence against the Stamp Act. In explaining the outbreaks in New York, General Gage in effect explained them in all the colonies. "The Plan of the People of Property," he informed the Ministry, "has been to raise the lower Class to prevent the Execution of the Law," and he stated on good authority that many of the instigators had themselves

[2] Diary entry, Dec. 18, 1765, John Adams, *Works* (C. F. Adams, ed., Boston, 1850–56), II, 154. For a snarling Tory account of Whig propaganda methods from the Stamp Act onward, see "Massachusettensis" (Daniel Leonard) in the *Mass. Gazette and Boston Post-Boy*, Dec. 19, 1774.

[3] *Ibid.* The discussion which follows is condensed from A. M. Schlesinger, "Political Mobs and the American Revolution, 1765–1776," Am. Phil. Soc., *Procs.*, XCIX (1955), 244–250. Another over-all treatment is Carl Bridenbaugh, *Cities in Revolt* (N. Y., 1955), 305–314. For more particular accounts, see E. S. and Helen M. Morgan, *The Stamp Act Crisis* (Chapel Hill, 1953), chaps. viii–xi; H. M. Morais, "The Sons of Liberty in New York," R. B. Morris, ed., *The Eve of the American Revolution* (N. Y., 1939); and, for Massachusetts, R. S. Longley, "Mob Activities in Revolutionary Massachusetts," *New England Quar.*, VI (1933), 98–130; Albert Matthews, "Joyce Junior," Colonial Soc. of Mass., *Pubs.*, VIII (1902–04), 90–104, and "Joyce Junior Once More," *ibid.*, XI (1906–07), 280–294; and G. P. Anderson, "Ebenezer Mackintosh: Stamp Act Rioter and Patriot," *ibid.*, XXVI (1924–26), 15–64, 348–361.

joined in the tumults.[4] In Boston, in fact, the Whig politicians took little pains to conceal their participation, for some forty substantial citizens, thinly disguised in the trousers and jackets of mechanics, headed the marchers who wrecked the stampmaster's abode. Lieutenant Governor Hutchinson, one of the later victims, described the local chain of command. The "rabble," he said, took their cue from "a superior set consisting of master-masons, carpenters, &c.," who in turn took theirs from the merchants' committee in certain matters and from the "mob-high eloquence" of the town meeting in still others.[5]

Another glaring instance of planned lawlessness, though on a more limited scale, was the arson of the British revenue craft *Gaspee* near Providence, R. I., at midnight of June 9, 1772. John Brown, one of the town's leading merchants, not only organized the destruction but took part in it personally.[6]

The supreme example, however, was the so-called Boston Tea Party toward the end of the following year. For six weeks before the event the town meeting and various unofficial gatherings, augmented by people from neighboring communities, had protested the importation of dutied tea by the East India Company. When the vessels arrived and the Crown authorities refused to let them depart without payment of the tax, Samuel Adams, rising to his feet in the densely packed Old South Church, gave the prearranged signal: "This meeting can do nothing more to save the country." At once a war whoop at the door started a lurking band of make-believe Mohawk Indians to Griffin's Wharf, where they cast the 342 chests into the harbor while a crowd on shore looked silently on. History has never beheld a more superbly disciplined mob. Despite the intense excitement the despoilers hurt no one aboard and were so respectful of personal property that they afterward replaced a padlock that they had accidentally broken.[7]

[4] Letter to H. S. Conway, Dec. 21, 1765, Thomas Gage, *Correspondence with the Secretaries of State* (C. E. Carter, ed., New Haven, 1931–33), I, 78.

[5] Thomas Hutchinson, *The History of the Province of Massachusetts Bay*, III (London, 1828), 120–121; J. K. Hosmer, *The Life of Thomas Hutchinson* (Boston, 1896), 103–104.

[6] J. R. Bartlett, *A History of the Destruction of His Britannic Majesty's Schooner Gaspee* (Providence, 1861), 17, 19, 23; J. B. Hedges, *The Browns of Providence Plantations: Colonial Years* (Cambridge, 1952), 209–210.

[7] A. M. Schlesinger, *The Colonial Merchants and the American Revolution* (N. Y., 1918), 281–290; *Barrington-Bernard Correspondence* (Edward Channing

In bald contrast were the countless headstrong mobs. An early instance was the pillaging of Hutchinson's mansion in Boston on August 26, 1765, during the Stamp Act disorders. Not content with gutting the structure from ground to roof, the "hellish crew" scattered abroad the Lieutenant Governor's historical papers and the manuscript of the second volume of his *History of Massachusetts Bay*. Another outstanding disturbance was the so-called Battle of Golden Hill in New York in January, 1770, the climax of a series of collisions with the redcoats that had been going on ever since they were stationed there at the close of the Seven Years' War. In this culminating brawl the soldiers fought back with bayonets and cutlasses, killing one of the crowd and wounding others.[8]

But the pre-eminent impromptu commotion was the clash with the military in Boston some weeks later. A British garrison had been sent there two years earlier following a daring riot over the seizure of John Hancock's sloop *Liberty* by the revenue authorities for alleged smuggling. Bad blood had quickly developed between the troops and "the inhabitants of the lower class," who openly insulted the intruders, beat them up in lonely neighborhoods and haled them into court on every possible pretext.[9] Popular resentment mounted dangerously when a customs informer inadvertently killed a boy while firing into a mob. A great throng ostentatiously accompanied the corpse to the cemetery in imitation of a recent procession in London for a child slain during a riot in St. George's Field. The demonstration was, as the incensed Hutchinson observed, designed further "to raise the passions of the people." [10] Soon afterward, on the night of March 5, 1770, a file of regulars, provoked beyond endurance, shot into a crowd of their tormentors, killing five and injuring others. The Whig chieftains at once labeled the unhappy affair the "Boston Massacre" and acclaimed the fallen—whose very names had heretofore been unknown to most of the townsfolk—as martyrs to the cause of American liberty.[11] A casual street fight thus came to be regarded as a premeditated slaughter of innocents.

and A. C. Coolidge, eds., Cambridge, 1912), 294–302; F. S. Drake, ed., *Tea Leaves* (Boston, 1884), pp. lxv, lxviii.

[8] Hutchinson to Richard Jackson, Aug. 30, 1765, Colonial Soc. of Mass., *Pubs.*, XXVI (1924–26), 33; H. B. Dawson, *The Sons of Liberty in New York* (N. Y., 1859), 112–118.

[9] The quoted phrase is John Adams's. *Works*, II, 230.

[10] Hutchinson, *Massachusetts Bay*, III, 269–270.

[11] Frederic Kidder, ed., *History of the Boston Massacre* (Albany, 1870).

Not every patriot, it is true, approved of strong-arm methods. Men like James Otis and John Dickinson maintained that such acts not only degraded the cause, but were more likely to alienate Britain than to wring concessions from her. Moreover, as General Gage noted at the time of the Stamp Act, politically motivated mobs tended to become mobs with a roving commission. For that reason, he wrote the Ministry, the well-to-do citizens, who had unleashed the terror, drew back when the rioters began pursuing objects of their own. In fact, John Adams and Josiah Quincy, Jr., both sterling Whigs, went so far as to act as counsel for the soldiers accused of the Boston Massacre and, by exhorting the jury against "brutal rage or wanton rashness" under "pretence of patriotism," helped clear the defendants of the charge of murder. It is revealing in another way that none of the "Mohawks" of the Boston Tea Party publicly admitted his identity until more than half a century had passed.[12]

Indeed, political mobs, though they had long plagued England and were never more rampant than during the 1760's, had hitherto been rare in America; the principal exception was resistance to navy press gangs. The pacific attitude of earlier times had doubtless arisen from general contentment with things as they then were and from the success of the legislatures in preventing undue British interference in American affairs. But now, with Parliament bent on "enslaving" the colonies, mobs roared into action on the slightest excuse all the way from New Hampshire to Georgia. Though the coastal cities set the pace, inland towns and villages were seldom far behind.

The royal officials stood well-nigh helpless before the anarchy. The colonial law-enforcement agencies usually winked at the disorders, and if the culprits were brought into court, juries quickly acquitted them. Sometimes both the magistrates and individual jurors had themselves been involved, and in any event they did not dare defy community sentiment; in New England, indeed, the town meetings elected the jurors. General Gage reported from New York that "the Officers of the Crown grow more timid, and more fearfull

---

[12] Richard Frothingham, *Life and Times of Joseph Warren* (Boston, 1865), 38–39 *n.* (for Otis's attitude); John Dickinson, *Writings* (P. L. Ford, ed.; Hist. Soc. of Pa., *Memoirs*, XIV, 1895), I, 323–325; Gage to H. S. Conway, Dec. 21, 1765, Gage, *Correspondence*, I, 78–79; Josiah Quincy, *Memoir of the Life of Josiah Quincy Junior* (Eliza S. Quincy, ed., rev. ed., Boston, 1874), 39–40; Adams, *Works*, II, 230–236; Drake, *Tea Leaves*, p. xcii.

of doing their Duty every Day." And in similar strain Governor Hutchinson declared that during the tea commotions, "There was not a justice of peace, sheriff, constable, or peace officer in the province, who would venture to take cognizance of any breach of law, against the general bent of the people." [13]

Behind this "bent of the people" lay the fact that the masses saw nothing morally wrong in nullifying legislation which they considered oppressive and to which they had never consented. Few Americans could accept the British view that the tumults were criminal proceedings, and those who did ordinarily kept silent from fear for their own persons and property. Outside Massachusetts, to be sure, there was widespread Whig criticism of the Boston Tea Party as sheer vandalism, but this ceased when Parliament committed the even greater error of perpetrating the Intolerable Acts. Moreover, a singular self-restraint characterized the disturbances: the participants invariably stopped short of murder, relying on horror rather than homicide. Though they occasionally brandished cutlasses and muskets, usually they employed less lethal weapons such as clubs, rocks, brickbats and clods of dung. This doubtless made it easier for the more law-abiding Whigs to condone the affairs, but it afforded cold comfort to the victims, who never knew when a mob, fortified perhaps with alcoholic as well as patriotic spirits, might go further. Still, the greater stigma, that of actually killing, fell alone on the British "tyrants" and their hirelings.[14] Considering the repeated provocations the only wonder is that they did not yield to the impulse more often, but this naturally failed to impress the colonists.

While the rioters did not inflict death, they had no compunction about ruthlessly destroying property, roughing the unfortunates, tar-and-feathering them and lynching them in effigy. The tar brush was the favorite discipline for those of low degree. The mob after applying a "suit of the modern mode" carted the victim through the town as an object lesson to others as well as himself. In one instance the

---

[13] Gage to Lord Barrington, July 22, 1769, Gage, *Correspondence,* II, 518; Hutchinson, *Massachusetts Bay,* III, 437; R. D. Younger, "Grand Juries and the American Revolution," *Va. Mag. of History,* LXIII (1955), 257–268.

[14] William Gordon, *The History of the Rise, Progress, and Establishment of the United States* (London, 1788), I, 321; "Novanglus" (John Adams) in the *Boston Gazette,* Feb. 13, 1775; "Lucius" in the *Mass. Spy,* March 9, 1775. There were, however, some near-fatalities, notably the wounding of the commander of the *Gaspee* and of a soldier in the brawls preceding the Boston Massacre.

vigilantes even set fire to the feathers.[15] Hanging in effigy was reserved for offenders of higher station. Royal governors, stampmasters, revenue collectors, contumacious importers, East India Company consignees and the like suffered this indignity, sometimes in
company with their official superiors in London—Lord Bute,
George Grenville, Lord North and so on—or with their alleged infernal chief, the Devil. After the passage of the Quebec Act in 1774
the Pope too sometimes figured in the cast of characters thus symbolizing the people's religious as well as political bias. Indeed, the
overzealous townsfolk of Newport, R. I., on one occasion exhibited two Popes.[16] The accepted ritual was to display the grotesque
images for a while in some public place, then carry them through the
streets to the gallows or to a funeral pyre. As in the case of tar-and-
feathering, the proceedings, whether or not terrifying to the persons
concerned, effectively advertised their misconduct to the community.

The representatives of the Crown continually sent home pathetic
accounts of their impotence in face of these excesses, but the London authorities were too far away and too immersed in their own
concerns to give the situation more than offhand attention. Governor Bernard of Massachusetts, Hutchinson's predecessor in that
office, complained that "the indifference" had "so effectually discouraged the Friends of Government, that they have been gradually
falling off, 'till at length the Cause is become desperate." [17] Yet,
even when the imperial government tried to help, the outcome
proved disappointing. Upon the repeal of the Stamp Act, for example, the Ministry, at the behest of the House of Commons, instructed
the American governors to require their Assemblies to indemnify
all who had lost property in the disturbances; but only three colonies
responded. Of these, Maryland alone voted full damages; New York
recompensed one of the two major sufferers but not the other; and
Massachusetts after delaying fifteen months reimbursed Hutchinson for his looted mansion, but only on condition that nobody be
punished for this or any other of the tumults that had taken place in
the province.[18]

[15] E. A. Jones, *The Loyalists of Massachusetts* (London, 1930), 243.
[16] *Newport Mercury*, Nov. 7, 1774.
[17] Francis Bernard to Lord Barrington, July 30, 1768, *Barrington-Bernard Correspondence*, 170.
[18] *Annual Register for the Year 1766* (London, 1767), 46; Horatio Sharpe

Three years later, in 1769, the home government moved to prevent the thwarting of justice by biased juries in the prosecution of rioters. With this chiefly in mind Parliament proposed that colonists charged with treasonable conduct be conveyed to England for trial under an old statute of Henry VIII; and following the *Gaspee* affair, the Ministry set up a royal commission to do just that. Though the tribunal conducted its inquiry on the spot and fully a thousand people must have known the incendiaries, it could not obtain sufficient evidence to apprehend a single suspect.[19] The proceeding resulted only in shooting a flame of indignation through every part of America.

Nor did the presence of British troops in New York and Boston, the chronic trouble centers, have a pacifying effect. On the contrary, the enforced association, irksome to both parties, only intensified the friction that normally exists between garrisons and civilians. To the townsfolk the "Bloody Backs" were visible reminders of English "tyranny," hence proper subjects for verbal and physical harassment; and not unnaturally the soldiers repaid in kind. The Battle of Golden Hill and the Boston Massacre were merely extreme examples of what happened.

It was a preconcerted riot, however, not a spontaneous disturbance, that finally drove Britain to drastic punitive action. The Intolerable Acts, passed in retaliation for the Boston Tea Party, permanently deprived the entire province of cherished democratic rights, while the particular law known as the Boston Port Act closed that city to seaborne commerce till the East India Company should be reimbursed and the King convinced that the Bostonians would henceforth behave. Parliament further withdrew from the Whig-controlled town meetings the cherished privilege of choosing juries, giving it instead to the sheriffs, who were creatures of the royal Governor. Then, for double assurance, Parliament specified that anyone accused of murder in quelling an outbreak might be tried in another colony or in England.[20] This last provision, coming after the exem-

---

to Hugh Hamersley, Dec. 8, 1766, Sharpe, *Correspondence* (W. H. Browne, ed.; *Archives of Maryland*, XIV, Balt., 1895), III, 358; Alice M. Keys, *Cadwallader Colden* (N. Y., 1906), 330–331; E. F. Brown, *Joseph Hawley* (N. Y., 1933), 107–110; L. H. Gipson, *The Coming of the Revolution* (N. Y., 1954), 165–169. The Privy Council disallowed the Massachusetts enactment because of the rider, but not in time to stop payment of the £3194 to Hutchinson.

[19] Bartlett, *Destruction of His Britannic Majesty's Schooner Gaspee*, 55–140.
[20] 14 George III, c. 19, c. 39, c. 45.

plary trial accorded the soldiers in the Boston Massacre, seemed to the patriots a blanket warrant to slay rioters at will.

These stringent measures, prompted by a particular act of mobbing, dealt with conditions in Massachusetts that had actually been long out of hand. Even so, they fell short of the need by ignoring the commotions in the other colonies, though the Ministry by singling out the worst offender intended the penalties as a sort of Damoclean sword. In any event the legislation came far too late. Instead of intimidating the Americans it only spurred them to greater violence with the result that they drove the more intractable British sympathizers into exile.

II

Just as the fomenters of direct action traded on the fact that "the bulk of mankind are more led by their senses than by their reason," [21] so also did the planners of orderly demonstrations. By accenting rites rather than rights they influenced minds untouched by constitutional and economic issues. As stage properties they employed flags, lanterns, fireworks, transparencies and bonfires and, to engage the ear as well as the eye, added drums, guns and the town's bells. The drums and guns evoked the desired martial spirit, while the bells churned the emotions by being put to hitherto unfamiliar uses. Before, they had announced the outbreak of fires or the approach of church services and the opening and closing of markets; now, they also called the citizens together in defense of their liberties, caroled the repeal of hated legislation and dirged fresh acts of aggression. For the greatest effect these devices were used in combination. Thus, when Boston learned of the repeal of the Stamp Act, "the Dawn was ushered in by the Ringing of all the Bells in Town, Guns Firing, Drums Beating, and all Sorts of Musick.—Besides a Display of Colours on board the Shipping in the Harbour, and on the Tops of Houses, &c." No less typical was Philadelphia's mourning on the day the Boston Port Act went into force: "The bells were rang muffled all the day, and the ships in the port had their colours half hoisted." [22]

[21] David Ramsay, *The History of the American Revolution* (Phila., 1789), I, 69.

[22] *Boston Gazette*, May 19, 26, 1766; Philadelphia news in the *Mass. Spy*, June 23, 1774. For the most famous of Philadelphia's bells, see J. B. Stoudt, *The*

As a continuing symbol of the need for vigilance the Boston Sons of Liberty early dedicated a giant elm near the Common as "Liberty Tree." From the Stamp Act onward it served as their rendezvous, as well as an ever-present warning to Tories to repent if they did not wish to hang in effigy from its branches or be brought in person to confess their errors. It was at the "sacred elm" that the procession formed to escort the body of the child slain by the customs informer, and there too the mobs usually forgathered to set out on their excursions. Boston's example excited much of New England and even far-off Charleston to emulation, while other communities, no less zealous, attested their devotion with Liberty Poles. Indeed, one observer derided the much vaunted American patriotism as the *"Happiness of Assembling in the open Air,* and performing *idolatrous* and *vociferous* Acts of Worship, *to a Stick of Wood."* These emblems, of course, bred constant friction with British adherents. It was the redcoats' pertinacity in pulling down four successive Liberty Poles between 1766 and 1770 which finally resulted in New York's Battle of Golden Hill; but in this as in most other cases the Sons of Liberty had the last word: the fifth one survived until eighteen months after Lexington and Concord. Whether Trees or Poles, however, the mute sentinels had an electrifying effect on "the inconsiderate people." [23]

As still another way of rendering the masses "fond of their leaders, and averse and bitter against all opposers," the Whigs staged community anniversaries of dramatic moments in the struggle.[24] The Bostonians, besides commemorating the tumults of August 14 that had panicked the stamp agent into resigning, joined with their brethren in the other colonies every March 18 to celebrate the Stamp Act's repeal. Parades signalized these occasions, cannons boomed, bells pealed, Liberty Trees and Liberty Poles blossomed with decorations, and the affairs usually culminated in civic banquets seasoned with patriotic toasts and singing. The exuberant

---

Liberty Bells of Pennsylvania (Pa. German Soc., *Procs. and Addresses*, XXXVII, 1930), esp. chap. iii.

[23] "The Dougliad," *N.–Y. Gazette and Weekly Mercury*, April 23, 1770: "The Liberty Pole on the Commons," N.–Y. Hist. Soc., *Quar. Bull.*, III (1919–20), 109–127; "Bellisarius" in the *N.–Y. Gazetteer*, March 9, 1775. For a detailed discussion, see A. M. Schlesinger, "Liberty Tree: a Genealogy," *New England Quar.*, XXV (1952), 435–452.

[24] Adams, *Works*, II, 218; similarly, "Consideration" in the *N.–H. Gazette*, March 1, 1771.

trenchermen evidenced their ardor—and capacity—by drinking endless bumpers to such inspiriting sentiments as "A speedy Repeal of unconstitutional Acts of Parliament," "Strong Halters, firm Blocks, and sharp Axes, to Such as deserve Either," "The Sons of Liberty throughout the World," and, with an eye cocked at ethnic minorities, "The German Protestants" and "Prosperity to Ireland." These toasts, moreover, had an impact beyond the immediate audience inasmuch as the press reported them far and wide.[25]

The Boston Massacre lit a fuse of observances of a different and grimmer sort. None other than Josiah Quincy, Jr., one of the soldiers' lawyers, proposed in the press "an annual & solemn remembrance of the 5th of March" to protest Britain's "aspiring lust of domination" and "imprint on the mind of the rising youth" the dire consequences to America.[26] The town meeting, ruled by Samuel Adams, instituted the series at the first anniversary in 1771. On each occasion bells tolled at intervals through the day, and in the evening lighted transparencies near the site of the tragedy displayed tableaux of the "murderers" and the "martyred," with perhaps a symbolic America trampling a supine redcoat under foot. Versified screeds affixed to the exhibits pointed up the moral, such as the poem beginning:

> Canst thou, Spectator, view this crimson'd Scene,
> And not reflect what these sad Portraits mean?
> Or can thy slaughter'd Brethren's guiltless Gore,
> Revenge, from Year to Year, in vain implore? [27]

The crowning event was a declamation by a well-known figure, who pulled out all the stops to do full justice to his theme. To quote one of the orators,

> . . . words can poorly paint the horrid scene—defenceless, prostrate bleeding countrymen—the piercing agonizing groans—the mingled moan of weeping relatives and friends—these best can speak, to rouse the luke-warm into noble zeal; to fire the zealous into manly rage, against the foul oppression of quartering troops, in populous cities, in times of peace.[28]

[25] For an exhaustive account of these patriotic libations, see R. J. Hooker, "The American Revolution Seen through a Wine Glass," *William and Mary Quar.*, ser. 3, XI (1954), 51–77.

[26] "Mentor" (Quincy) in the *Boston Evening-Post*, Feb. 11, 1771.

[27] *Boston Gazette*, March 8, 1773.

[28] Dr. Benjamin Church in 1773, Hezekiah Niles, ed., *Principles and Acts of the American Revolution* (rev. ed., N. Y., 1876), 37, in which work, 17–79, appear the texts of all the discourses. In 1774 Samuel Adams composed nearly all the

These addresses, besides harrowing those within earshot, reached a much greater public in pamphlet form and, as John Adams tells us, "were read, I had almost said by every-body that can read, and scarcely ever with dry eyes." [29] The yearly exercises continued—though necessarily away from Boston after the war began and the British held it—until the town authorities in 1783 substituted the celebration of the Fourth of July. Salem, Newburyport and perhaps other nearby communities also commemorated the Massacre, but apparently the sister colonies passed it over as having only a local Massachusetts significance. [30]

In line with the policy of anointing patriotism with godliness the New Englanders also appropriated the fast days and thanksgiving days which they had observed since Pilgrim times. Now, Hutchinson fumed, they used these occasions for "making a shew of religion, to promote the designs of political party," or, in General Gage's words, as "an opportunity for Sedition to flow from the Pulpits." [31] The Stamp Act begot the first partisan fasts—Connecticut taking the initiative—just as its repeal touched off the first partisan thanksgivings. In 1768 many Massachusetts towns likewise held fasts to sanctify the duty of obeying the nonimportation agreement against the Townshend Acts. The Intolerable Acts extended the practice for the first time beyond New England. In Virginia, for example, Jefferson, Patrick Henry and a few cronies straightway "cooked up" a resolution for a fast day, rushing it through the House of Burgesses before the Governor could kill it with a dissolution.[32] Then the Second Continental Congress, shocked by the outbreak of war at Lexington, gave the plan universal application, directing all the colonies to set aside July 20, 1775, for the solemn observance. The avowed purpose was to solicit God to speed a just reconciliation, but none could doubt the propaganda value of a whole people simultaneously meditating upon their wrongs. In the

---

oration, but the voice was the voice of John Hancock. W. V. Wells, *The Life and Public Services of Samuel Adams* (Boston, 1865), II, 138–140.

[29] Letter to Jedidiah Morse, Jan. 5, 1816, Adams, *Works*, X, 203.

[30] Hutchinson, *Massachusetts Bay*, III, 335–336; *Essex Journal*, March 8, 1775.

[31] Hutchinson, *Massachusetts Bay*, III, 307; Gage to Lord Dartmouth, May 30, 1774, Gage, *Correspondence*, I, 356.

[32] W. DeL. Love, *The Fast and Thanksgiving Days of New England* (Boston, 1895), 328–333; letter of Andrew Eliot, Sept. 27, 1768, Mass. Hist. Soc., *Colls.*, ser. 4, IV (1858), 429; Jefferson, *Papers* (J. P. Boyd, ed.), I (Princeton, 1950), 105–107; *Va. Gazette* (Purdie and Dixon), May 26, 1774.

New-York Packet's opinion, "nothing has so much contributed to the success of the continental councils." For good measure the Presbyterian Synod of New York and Pennsylvania backed up the call with a rousing pastoral letter to its congregations. The only articulate holdouts were Church of England divines, although those in Philadelphia, where the Congress sat, felt obliged to comply in order, as one of them privately admitted, to preserve their "religious usefulness." [33] As for their less amenable brethren elsewhere, patriot committees retaliated in a number of cases with harsh penalties.[34] By contrast the second Continental Fast Day, on May 17, 1776, passed without noteworthy incident, but by then many of the Anglican clergy had been forced to flee.[35]

"In America, as in the Grand Rebellion in England," wrote a British partisan, "much execution was done by sermons," [36] but no less fiery harangues marked legislative sessions and every concourse of the disaffected. According to one jaundiced observer,

> The orator mounts the rostrum, and in some preconceived speech, heightened no doubt, with all the aggravations which the fertility of his genius can suggest, exerts all the powers of elocution, to heat his audience with that blaze of patriotism with which he conceives himself inspired, . . . the threats of tyranny, and the terror of slavery, are artfully set before them; a measure need only be proposed to be resolved on: and I am well convinced many an American has given his assent to such a measure, from which a *little* reflection would have made him retract in horror.[37]

These speakers, as Emerson was to say of Daniel Webster, were indeed "cannon loaded to the lips." Some of them like Patrick

[33] *Va. Gazette* (Dixon and Hunter), Sept. 9, 1775 (for the pastoral letter); "A Friend of Liberty and Religion" in the *N.-Y. Packet*, Feb. 22, 1776; E. L. Pennington, "The Anglican Clergy of Pennsylvania in the American Revolution," *Pa. Mag. of History and Biography*, LXIII (1939), 413–415.

[34] The New Bern, N. C., committee forced the ousting of the delinquent; the Culpeper County, Va., committee ordered the culprit to flee; the Wallingford, Conn., unit placed the pastor under heavy bond not to misbehave again. W. L. Saunders, comp., *Colonial Records of North Carolina* (Raleigh, 1886–90), X, 115–116, 237–238; *Va. Gazette* (Dixon and Hunter), Jan. 20, 1776; G. M. Curtis, "Meriden and Wallingford in Colonial and Revolutionary Days," New Haven Colony Hist. Soc., *Papers*, VII (1908), 313–315.

[35] The Philadelphia committee, however, in order not to bias the Quaker inhabitants against other measures of the Congress, counseled the citizens to condone the noncompliance of those who acted "from a regard to their religious professions." *Pa. Evening Post*, May 16, 1776.

[36] Jonathan Boucher, *Reminiscences of an American Loyalist* (Jonathan Bouchier, ed., Boston, 1925), 118.

[37] "A Freeman" in the *N.-Y. Gazetteer*, July 28, 1774.

Henry and Richard Henry Lee won intercolonial renown. The youthful Alexander Hamilton first strode into history as an assailant of the Intolerable Acts in the "Fields" of New York City. Equally torrid discourses emanated from the bench, notably in the case of Chief Justice William Henry Drayton of South Carolina, who, as the final breach drew near, categorically instructed a grand jury, "The Almighty created America to be independent of Britain." [38] All in all, the country had never known such an outpouring of eloquence and has never known its equal since.

The political pot also simmered and seethed in the taverns. Among the favorite Whig resorts were the Green Dragon in Boston, adjoining the *Boston Gazette* office; Fraunces Tavern in New York; the London Coffee House in Philadelphia, which William Bradford owned together with the *Pennsylvania Journal*; the Raleigh Tavern in Williamsburg; and the Sign of the Bacchus in Charleston. At such centers congenial spirits gathered to eat, drink, read the latest newssheets and fortify one another's prejudices. "If the American Revolution was 'cradled' in any place," a recent student of the times goes so far as to suggest, "it was in the urban public houses." [39]

III

Though the masses had little grasp of constitutional subtleties, they eagerly took up catch phrases that gave an appearance of understanding. These slogans, as a Briton noted, "by being short could be most easily circulated and retained, at the same time that, by being extremely expressive, they carried with them the weight of a great many arguments." [40] "No taxation without representation," "Join or die" and the pejorative "Trial without jury" (evoked by the new powers of the vice-admiralty courts) galvanized resistance to the Stamp Act. The first of these, however, then tended to fall into disuse because it could be understood as a desire for colonial representation in Parliament, whereas, as the Stamp Act Congress made clear, the Americans demanded to be taxed solely by their legislatures. With equal avidity they seized on the designation "Sons of

[38] Niles, *Principles and Acts*, 334.
[39] Bridenbaugh, *Cities in Revolt*, 358–359.
[40] *Annual Register for 1765* (London, 1766), 50–51.

Liberty" after Isaac Barré "with Eyes darting Fire" so apostrophized the Stamp Act opponents in a speech in Parliament; and by the same token they attached to colonial parties the labels "Whig" and "Tory" since, in Hutchinson's words, "the common people, as far as they had been acquainted with the parties in England, all supposed the whigs to have been in the right, and the tories in the wrong." [41]

The semantics of patriotism contained other expressions that, to quote Judge Learned Hand in a different connection, "were not only the keys of persuasion, but the triggers of action." The stigmatizing of British policy as "tyranny," "oppression" and "slavery" had little or no objective reality, at least prior to the Intolerable Acts, but ceaseless repetition of the charge kept emotions at fever pitch. Even the coupling of vows of loyalty to the King with denunciations of the Ministry and Parliament helped to reconcile the timid to acts of opposition which might otherwise have alienated them. On the other hand, soul-stirring words like "liberty," "freedom" and "independence," though at first they connoted nothing more than the status the colonies had enjoyed before 1763, came in time to pack a revolutionary meaning.[42] Correspondingly, the magic term "American," implying a nationality and allegiance apart from the mother country, gradually replaced the older separatist designations of "New Yorker," "Virginian" and so on. Even tradesmen began to sell "AMERICAN PORTER" and "new-fashioned buttons" inscribed "UNION AND LIBERTY IN ALL AMERICA." [43]

To woo further support the Whigs identified the cause with admired public men of their own and earlier times, for they developed a hagiolatry as well as a demonology. In the final stage of the dispute this led parents to christen their children John Hancock, George Washington, Joseph Warren and the like; [44] and, throughout, the propagandists capitalized upon the fame of the seventeenth-century English paladins of freedom. Newspaper writers affected names like Locke, Clarendon, Algernon Sidney, Marchmont Nedham, John Hampden and Andrew Marvell, while orators and pamphleteers freely quoted the originals. Classical figures such as Callisthe-

---

[41] *Boston Gazette*, Aug. 12, 1765; Hutchinson, *Massachusetts Bay*, III, 103.
[42] John Adams elucidates the changing signification of the critical word "independence" in a letter to G. A. Otis, Feb. 9, 1821, Adams, *Works*, X, 394–395.
[43] *Pa. Evening Post*, Dec. 5, 1775; *Mass. Spy*, Feb. 16, 1775.
[44] A. M. Schlesinger, "Patriotism Names the Baby," *New England Quar.*, XIV (1941), 611–618.

nes, Aristides, Scævola and Cassandra provided other compelling pseudonyms. Thus the patriots grandiosely assumed the role of crusaders in an agelong struggle against tyranny.

With equal shrewdness they linked the movement with contemporary libertarians abroad. None filled the bill so well as the spectacular Englishman John Wilkes who after 1763 suffered ministerial persecution—libel suits, outlawry, imprisonment, annulment of his elections to Parliament—for defaming the King in No. 45 of his publication, the *North Britain*. To Americans, Wilkes despite his unsavory private life was a martyr to freedom of the press and to the subject's right to resist oppression. Their newspapers endlessly detailed his activities; printers advertised an "elegant copper" engraving of the man "fit for framing" as well as editions of his works; patriot diners toasted "his noble Struggles in the Cause of Liberty"; and parents accorded their tribute at the baptismal font.[45] In Boston the Sons of Liberty carried on a voluminous correspondence with the hero, and Wilkes's Society of the Supporters of the Bill of Rights in London elected Samuel and John Adams to membership.[46] The South Carolina Assembly even voted his Society £1500 sterling, while Virginia and Maryland admirers sent him consignments of tobacco in lieu of cash.[47] Until his political eclipse in the early 1770's, Wilkes was almost as great a popular darling in America as in Britain.

The patriots similarly embraced other comrades in what they deemed the common cause. Accordingly, Dedham, Mass., New York City and Charleston, S. C., honored America's friend, William Pitt, with statues; [48] Pennsylvanians, rendering double homage, called a hopeful new settlement Wilkes-Barre; and a Massachusetts town repentantly changed its name from Hutchinson to Barre. Going farther afield, Whig gatherings drank toasts to "The free and in-

---

[45] References to Wilkes in the several *Virginia Gazettes*, for example, fill ten columns of the *Virginia Gazette Index* (L. H. Cappon and Stella F. Duff, comps., Williamsburg, 1950) during the period 1766–1776.

[46] "John Wilkes and Boston," W. C. Ford, ed., Mass. Hist. Soc., *Procs.*, XLVII (1913–14), 190–214; "John Wilkes and William Palfrey," G. M. Elsey, ed., Colonial Soc. of Mass., *Pubs.*, XXXIV (1937–42), 411–428; Wells, *Samuel Adams*, II, 63–64.

[47] Edward McCrady, *The History of South Carolina under the Royal Government* (N. Y., 1899), 662–664, 683–692; *Va. Gazette* (Rind), Jan. 11, 1770.

[48] Charles Warren, *Jacobin and Junto* (Cambridge, 1931), 33–34; *N.-Y. Journal*, Sept. 13, 1770; McCrady, *South Carolina under the Royal Government*, 677–678.

dependent Cantons of Switzerland," "Dr. Lucas and the Patriots of Ireland," "The distressed Poles," "The brave Dantzickers, who declare they will be free in the face of the greatest monarch in Europe," "Added Vigour to the Spark of Liberty Kindling in Spain," and "Paschal Paoli and his brave Corsicans." Ebenezer Mackintosh, "Captain General of Liberty Tree" in Boston, named a son for the Corsican leader, and John Hancock called one of his vessels *Paoli*.[49]

No. 45 of the *North Britain*, the spark that set off the Wilkes conflagration at home, also supplied the Americans with a fiery numerical slogan. They lost no opportunity to drum the figure 45 into people's heads until, as a contemporary remarked, it was "repeated and echoed . . . through every part of the country and by many who could not tell what was signified by the term." [50] To the Whigs, however, it sufficed that the numeral should engender bitterness toward the Ministry, and to this end they displayed boundless ingenuity. The Bostonians, for example, strung 45 lanterns on Liberty Tree when celebrating the repeal of the Stamp Act; two years later, in 1768, a group at Norwich, Conn., eating from plates marked "No. 45," downed 45 patriotic toasts, while a nearby Liberty Tree flew a flag inscribed, "No. 45, WILKES & LIBERTY"; and a gathering of 45 New Yorkers on the 45th day of the year 1770 consumed 45 pounds of beefsteak cut from a bullock 45 months old.[51]

The vote of 92 to 17 by which the Bay Colony legislators in 1768 defiantly stood by their Circular Letter added two stirring emblems of native origin. In Hutchinson's words, "The number 92 was auspicious, and 17 of ill omen, for many months after, not only in Massachusetts Bay, but in most of the colonies on the continent." Doubtless he had in mind such an incident as that at nearby Petersham, where the Sons of Liberty, preparatory to dedicating their Liberty Tree, pruned its branches so that at the exercises 92 would remain after lopping off 17. In like fashion the figure 26 became a watch-

[49] Charles Lucas, the "Wilkes of Ireland," was crusading for larger rights for the Irish Parliament. The Poles were facing partition of their country at the hands of Russia and Prussia. The Danzigers were resisting aggression by Frederick the Great. The Corsicans were waging a losing fight to cast off the French yoke. The entries under "Paoli" and "Corsica" in the *Virginia Gazette Index* occupy more than seven columns. G. P. Anderson discusses "Pascal Paoli, an Inspiration to the Sons of Liberty," in Colonial Soc. of Mass., *Pubs.*, XXVI (1924–26), 180–210.

[50] John Witherspoon, *"An* ADDRESS *to the* NATIVES *of* SCOTLAND *residing in* AMERICA," *Essex Journal*, Aug. 23, 1776.

[51] *Boston Gazette*, May 26, 1766; *New-London Gazette*, June 17, 1768; *Mass. Gazette and Boston News-Letter*, March 1, 1770 (for New York).

word of the South Carolina patriots when 26 members of the Assembly flouted the Governor and the Ministry by adopting resolves in support of the Circular Letter.[52]

Often, to magnify the effect, the Whigs combined the symbols. 92 patriots would erect a Liberty Pole 45 feet high, or 92 enthusiasts quaff 45 toasts. A ball might have 92 jigs and 45 minuets, or the women of the community quilt 92 calico patches of one color and 45 of another. By the same sign the Boston Sons of Liberty shipped Wilkes a pair of turtles, one weighing 45 pounds and the two together 92, and the silversmith Paul Revere inserted "No. 45" on a commemorative bowl to the "glorious Ninety-Two Members." The Charlestonians, for their part, included their own special numeral with the others. Upon the arrival of the Pitt statue from England in 1770, for example, members Nos. 26 and 92 of Club No. 45 placed it on its pedestal in the presence of the 26 courageous legislators while 26 cannon boomed and a flag 45 feet high flaunted the words "Pitt and Liberty." [53] By thus infusing politics with arithmetic the Whig calculators strove to multiply their friends and divide their enemies.

IV

Efforts to further the cause with songs proved less successful, though not from want of trying. Every crisis produced its crop of patriotic ballads set to familiar tunes, with the known lyricists including such notables as John Dickinson, Joseph Warren, Thomas Paine and Benjamin Franklin. Dickinson's "Liberty Song," written in 1768 (with some lines by Arthur Lee) to the rousing melody of David Garrick's "Hearts of Oak," won the greatest acclaim, thanks

[52] Hutchinson, *Massachusetts Bay*, III, 197; *Boston Gazette*, Sept. 26, 1768; McCrady, *South Carolina under the Royal Government*, 607–609. For Whig toasts to the "Glorious Ninety-two" (variously worded) in different provinces, see the *Boston Gazette*, July 11, 1768; *Providence Gazette*, July 9, 1768; *N.–Y. Gazette and Weekly Mercury*, March 20, 1769; *Pa. Chronicle*, July 14, 1768; *Pa. Journal*, March 23, April 10, 1769.

[53] Richard Frothingham, *The Rise of the Republic of the United States* (Boston, 1872), 229; Mass. Hist. Soc., *Procs.*, XIII (1873–75), 199–200, XLVII (1913–14), 206; Charleston item in the *Boston Gazette*, Aug. 7, 1770. This newspaper indeed asserted on Feb. 7 that the numerals 92 and 45 had been mated ever since "Fourteen hundred 92" when the San Salvador Indians visited Columbus in canoeloads of 45 each.

probably to Dickinson's renown as the author of the recently published *Letters from a Farmer in Pennsylvania* denouncing the Townshend Acts. In sending the text to James Otis, Dickinson justified his unlawyerlike venture on the ground that "Cardinal de Retz inforced his political operations by songs," and John Adams, after helping sing the words at a Whig rally in Dorchester, agreed it was an excellent way of "cultivating the sensations of freedom." [54] Apart from this lone instance, however, musical propaganda had scant effect; even Dickinson's performance fell sadly short of a "Marseillaise." Nevertheless, the lyrics, broadcast in handbills, newspapers and almanacs, greatly swelled the output of patriotic verse and in this form undoubtedly forwarded the cause.

The slight esthetic merit of the bulk of this verse made little difference to an uncritical audience. Most of the effusions reached the public through the newspapers; some were posted on Liberty Trees and Poles or circulated in broadsides. The authors, usually nameless, invariably struck a belligerent note. When Governor Bernard of Massachusetts described an early specimen as "remarkable for its insolence to the King," he was in essence describing all of them.[55] The one entitled *Oppression*, for example, pictured the resistance to the Stamp Act—"That horrid day" when the scheme was "laid, T'oppress AMERICA, and cramp her trade"—as but the latest chapter in the glorious age-old Anglo-Saxon struggle for liberty. Another contributor, saying his say in a single quatrain, exhorted his countrymen after the bloodshed at Lexington and Concord:

> Let *Britons,* now sunk into tyrants and *slaves!*
> Submit to be govern'd by *fools* and by *knaves;*
> Not so will their kindred on this side the sea:
> *American Britons* will ever be FREE.

And on the same occasion "A Virginian," speaking still more plainly, started off his ten stanzas:

[54] Dickinson, *Writings* (P. L. Ford, ed.; Hist. Soc. of Pa., *Memoirs*, XIV, 1895), I, 421; Adams, *Works*, II, 218. For the whole subject, see A. M. Schlesinger, "A Note on Songs as Patriot Propaganda, 1765–1776," *William and Mary Quar.*, ser. 3, XI (1954), 78–88.

[55] Francis Bernard to Richard Jackson, Nov. 8, 1765, Bernard Papers (Sparks MSS., IV, Harvard College Library), V, 29. For partial collections of this verse, see Frank Moore, ed., *Songs and Ballads of the American Revolution* (N. Y., 1855), and F. C. Prescott and J. H. Nelson, eds., *Prose and Poetry of the Revolution* (N. Y., 1925).

> Americans! awake! awake!
> Your Liberty, your all's at stake:
> Behold your foes, huge angry swarms,
> Proclaim loud war, to arms! to arms! [56]

Nor did the poetasters as the final break approached neglect the opportunity to indoctrinate the rising generation. Thus "An Alphabet for Little Masters and Misses" taught:

> A stands for Americans—who scorn to be slaves;
> B for Boston—where fortitude their freedom saves;
> C stands for Congress—which, tho' loyal, will be free;
> D stands for defence—against force and tyranny.

And so on to:

> Z stands for Zero—but means the Tory minions,
> Who threaten us with fire and sword, to bias our opinions.[57]

Of the known versifiers only Philip Freneau and John Trumbull have won a permanent niche in American letters. Both were untypical, however, in choosing satire as their principal weapon. Freneau began gibing at British partisans while still a student at Princeton, but the Intolerable Acts three years after his graduation thrust him into the thick of the fray with his targets becoming legion. He not only impaled the faceless demolishers of New York's fourth Liberty Pole, but he let fly at such high dignitaries as General Gage, Admiral Thomas Graves (whose ships were bottling up Boston) and Lord North. Trumbull started by inditing a bitter "Elegy on the Times" against the Boston Port Act while a student in John Adams's law office; then later, "at the instigation of some leading members of the first Congress," he composed the opening portion of *M'Fingal*, published early in 1776. This rollicking poem—to which he appended a sequel at the war's close—lampooned the misfortunes of a rabid Tory as an object lesson to the whole "dastard" tribe. Unfortunately for the cause, however, it appeared too late to wield much influence.[58]

[56] "Oppression. A Poem. By an American," serialized in the *Pa. Packet*, Aug. 19–Sept. 23, 1775, after first publication as a pamphlet in 1765, according to the Library of Congress, *Quar. Jour.*, VI (1948–49), no. 3, p. 69; quatrain in the *Va. Gazette* (Dixon and Hunter), May 27, 1775; "A Virginian" in the *Pa. Packet*, May 13, 1776.

[57] *Constitutional Gazette* (N. Y.), Oct. 14, 1775, also Moore, *Songs and Ballads*, 88–89.

[58] Lewis Leary, *That Rascal Freneau* (New Brunswick, 1941), 31–36, 53–64; Alexander Cowie, *John Trumbull, Connecticut Wit* (Chapel Hill, 1936), chaps. vi–vii; Lennox Grey, "John Adams and John Trumbull in the 'Boston Cycle,'"

The theater necessarily held a lesser place in the Whig proceedings. Not only were playhouses few and the actors all transients from Britain, but a deep-seated religious prejudice discouraged attendance. The First Continental Congress, for instance, classed "shews" with gambling and cockfighting as a "species of extravagance and dissipation" unbecoming true lovers of their country. Nonetheless a Charlestonian, incensed by the Intolerable Acts, insisted that "every possible method should be adopted to establish the growing virtue of patriotism" and in particular urged his fellow townsmen to patronize an amateur production of "Busiris, King of Egypt," written by the early eighteenth-century English dramatist Edward Young. The piece, he pointed out, vividly depicted in another age and clime "an injured gallant people struggling against oppression," and the proceeds moreover would go to the victims of the Boston Port Act.[59] This venture, however, was the exception. American authors when they entered the lists designed their dramas for fireside reading rather than for stage presentation. In any case the endless dialogues, soliloquies and exhortations would have submerged the action. James Otis's sister, Mrs. Mercy Warren, the most diligent playwright, composed *The Adulateur* (1773), which pilloried Hutchinson and his intimates, and *The Group* (1775), built about the abrogation of the Massachusetts charter. She may also have helped with the anti-British farce, *The Blockheads: or, The Affrighted Officers* (1776). These and several similar offerings, mostly in the final year of the dispute, reached a limited public through newspapers and pamphlets.[60]

New England Quar., IV (1931), 509–514. Cowie, the leading authority on *M'Fingal*, believes that, apart from the lateness of its appearance, certain academic aspects of the poem, though enhancing its artistic value, militated against its value as Whig propaganda (p. 155).

[59] Continental Congress, *Journals* (W. C. Ford and others, eds., Wash., 1904–37), I, 78; "Ingenuus" in the *S.–C. Gazette*, July 2, 1774.

[60] W. C. Ford, "Mrs. Warren's 'The Group,' " Mass. Hist. Soc., *Procs.*, LXII (1928–29), 15–22, identifies the characters in *The Group* and *The Blockheads* and gives further facts concerning her plays. Other dramas in 1776 were *The Fall of British Tyranny, or American Liberty Triumphant*, attributed to John Leacock of Philadelphia; the *Battle of Bunker's-Hill*, written by Hugh H. Brackenridge for a Maryland school where he was teaching; and *The Patriots*, by Robert Munford of Mecklenburg, Va. M. J. Moses, ed., *Representative American Plays, 1765–1819* (N. Y., 1918), 209–350, reprints the texts of the first two, as well as of *The Group*; and Courtlandt Canby has edited *The Patriots* in the *William and Mary Quar.*, ser. 3, VI (1949), 437–503. For an account of an unpublished patriot play of 1775 or 1776, see S. F. Damon, "Varnum's 'Ministerial Oppression,' a Revolutionary Drama," Am. Antiquarian Soc., *Procs.*, n.s., LV (1947), 287–298.

Magazines counted for still less as propaganda. Besides the fact that there were very few, they considered it their function to emphasize purely literary material, and in any event none lasted long. Lewis Nicola's *American Magazine*, at Philadelphia in 1769, expired after only nine numbers. The *Royal American Magazine*, established at Boston by Isaiah Thomas in January, 1774, struggled on until the clash at Lexington. The *Pennsylvania Magazine*, founded at Philadelphia in January, 1775, by Robert Aitken with Tom Paine as a contributing editor, managed to survive till the Declaration of Independence. But, even if these monthlies had been politically designed, they could have exerted little influence because of their small circulations.[61]

V

By contrast, "almanacks," selling for a few pennies, found their way into practically every household, even, as one of the compilers boasted, the "solitary dwellings of the poor and illiterate, where the studied ingenuity of the Learned Writer never comes." [62] Ames's almanac, originating in Boston, had in 1764 sixty thousand subscribers with uncounted additional readers.[63] These publications, though appearing but annually, furnished edifying pabulum throughout the year. Besides meteorological data, they contained aphorisms, anecdotes, recipes, poetry, passages from history, political commentary and timely public documents; and as the tension with the mother country increased, so also did their strictures against British misrule.

"The sole end of government is the happiness of the people," asserted Nathaniel Ames, Jr., in his 1766 issue, and followed this up the next year with the admonition that, since "Ignorance among the

[61] F. L. Mott, *A History of American Magazines, 1741–1850* (N. Y., 1930), 26–27, 83–91; L. N. Richardson, *A History of Early American Magazines* (N. Y., 1931), 149–196.

[62] Cited from Daniel George's almanac for 1776 in C. N. Greenough, "New England Almanacs, 1766–1775, and the American Revolution," Am. Antiquarian Soc., *Procs.*, n.s., XLV (1935), 289. The later quotations are from this article or from the almanacs themselves. See also N. W. Lovely, "Notes on New England Almanacs," *New England Quar.*, VIII (1935), 264–277.

[63] Sam. Briggs, comp., *The Essays, Humor, and Poems of Nathaniel Ames, Father and Son* (Cleveland, 1891), 20 n. By way of comparison, Paine bragged of increasing the circulation of the *Pennsylvania Magazine* from 600 to 1500. *Complete Writings* (P. S. Foner, ed., N. Y., 1945), I, p. xi.

common people is the very basis and foundation of tyranny and oppression," all must now "become politicians" and "examine every
thing" for themselves. In this conviction the *American Calendar of
1767* in Philadelphia graphically recounted the opposition to the
Stamp Act, and in 1770 the annual gotten out by Edes and Gill of
the *Boston Gazette* summed up the then popular discontent in the
lines:

> Plagues, Taxes, lawless Rage and ranc'rous Foes
> Distract our Cities, and forbid Repose . . . .

Following the Intolerable Acts, Benjamin West's *New-England Almanack* at Providence pleaded:

> Americans! for Freedom firmly join,
> Unite your Councils, and your Force combine. . . .

And, more pointedly, Ames's 1775 edition after darkly observing that the decapitation of Charles I "established a *Memento for
Tyrants*" supplied practical directions for making gunpowder. Ames
did not exaggerate in saying that "Patriotism and *America for
Americans* beams from every syllable in this year's production."
Undoubtedly these well-thumbed manuals implanted a keener love
of liberty in both old and young.

Some of the compilers, moreover, reinforced their words with
emotion-charged illustrated covers. These ranged all the way from
allegorical engravings of British "tyranny" to drawings of alleged
examples and cuts of popular idols like Wilkes and Dickinson. Pictures also appeared in the few magazines and sometimes even in the
newspapers despite the greater mechanical difficulties caused by
their more frequent issue. The most notable journalistic achievement
perhaps was the image of a serpent divided into parts representing
the colonies, with the caption "JOIN or DIE." This conceit stemmed
from the folk belief that the glass snake (*Ophisaurus ventralis*)
broke into fragments when attacked and afterward recombined to
survive. Editors in the leading cities had first used the device in 1754
during the Seven Years' War just before the Albany Congress, but it
suited even better the Anglo-American emergency.[64] How it was
put to account at critical junctures will appear later.

[64] Albert Matthews, "The Snake Devices, 1754–1776, and the Constitutional
Courant, 1765," Colonial Soc. of Mass., *Pubs.*, XI (1906–07), 409–452; "Speculator" in the *N.–Y. Journal*, Sept. 1, 1774; Joseph Johnson, *Traditions and Reminiscences, Chiefly of the American Revolution in the South* (Charleston, 1851), 25.

The pictorial warfare scored most heavily, however, by means of broadsides, at which the Boston Son of Liberty, Paul Revere, excelled. Typical of his efforts were "A View of the Year 1765," which portrayed the colonies challenging the dragon "Stamp Act"; "A Warm Place—Hell" (1768), foretelling the awful fate awaiting the seventeen legislators who voted to rescind the Circular Letter; and "America in Distress" (1775), a seated female figure attended by wicked ministerial physicians. His "Bloody Massacre" (1770), hand-colored for greater vividness, proved especially inflammatory, for, besides depicting, as he said in the accompanying poem, the redcoats' "murd'rous Rancour," it touched the public on the raw by showing one of the muskets being discharged from the adjoining customhouse ("Butcher's Hall"). In the circumstances Josiah Quincy, Jr., at the soldiers' trial sternly warned the jurors against being biased by prints adding "wings to fancy." [65]

Revere evidenced like ability in fashioning oilpaper transparencies which, displayed on a frame in front of candles, lent color and drama to nocturnal Whig affairs. These exhibits typically juxtaposed pictures (often symbolical) of British malignity and American innocence. Revere's handiwork at the first anniversary of the Boston Massacre was particularly grisly, including among the assorted horrors the ghost of one of the slain with his finger "in the wound, endeavoring to stop the blood issuing therefrom." "The spectators were struck with solemn silence," the *Boston Gazette* reported, "and their countenances were covered with a melancholy gloom." [66] These lurid spectacles, along with the printed caricatures, confirmed the patriot stereotype of the British as heartless oppressors.

[65] Gordon, *Rise, Progress, and Establishment of the United States*, 292. Revere's version, to be sure, accorded with the official *Narrative* of the event prepared by the town of Boston from hastily gathered evidence. To Hutchinson, "It was incredible, that two persons, out of many hundreds, should see guns fired from the custom-house, and all the rest not observe them." *Massachusetts Bay*, III, 279–280. At the trial only one witness so testified, and a jury later convicted him of perjury. *Mass. Spy*, Dec. 13, 1770. The most recent student of the subject, however, holds that the evidence "seems beyond question." O. M. Dickerson, "The Commissioners of the Customs and the 'Boston Massacre,'" *New England Quar.*, XXVII (1954), 314–321. This and others of Revere's productions are discussed and reproduced in C. S. Brigham, *Paul Revere's Engravings* (Worcester, 1954), 18–92. Revere and the cartoonists in other colonies often plagiarized English originals. William Murrell, *A History of American Graphic Humor* (N. Y., 1933–38), I, 22, 25, 27–28. In a variation of this practice, Revere took the Massacre picture without acknowledgment from a drawing by Henry Pelham, a fellow townsman and half-brother of John Singleton Copley.

[66] E. H. Goss, *The Life of Colonel Paul Revere* (Boston, 1891), I, 27–29.

Broadsides, besides channeling cartoons to the public, also carried verbal propaganda. Timed to the particular occasion, attuned to the immediate popular reaction, they possessed the further advantage of affording anonymity to both writer and printer and so abetting the use of unbridled language. These handbills, clandestinely distributed, alerted the citizens at every emergency, inciting reprisals against stampmasters and East India Company agents, gibbeting foes of nonimportation, publicizing Whig doings and resolutions. The Crown officials railed against the "insolent" fliers, but aside from the difficulty of detecting the perpetrators, an attempt to punish them could not undo the damage already done. Indeed, in the notorious McDougall affair at New York in 1769 the effort, as we shall see, backfired, enabling the culprit to posture vaingloriously as the "Wilkes of America" and in the end to escape a court sentence. Happily for the patriots, this episode probably deterred other provincial administrations from creating like martyrs to freedom of the press. At any rate the gale of broadsides reached hurricane proportions in the final years of the dispute.[67]

Pamphlets, on the other hand, presented rounded statements of the colonial case. Their function above all else was to unify the thinking of the leaders, but they also sought to persuade the educated classes generally and to supply grist for America's supporters in Britain. The writers usually expounded the basic tenets of the home-rule position, striving to establish canons for testing the unconstitutionality or inexpediency of ministerial measures and adroitly tailoring their arguments to changing conditions. The authors, mostly lawyers, ransacked the provincial charters as well as English and classical history for precedents.[68] In addition to avowed political treatises, many politically slanted sermons reached a wide audience in this form, while colonial reprints of pro-American tracts

[67] For partial lists of these handbills, see "New York Broadsides, 1762–1779," N. Y. Public Library, *Bull.*, III (1899), 23–33, and W. C. Ford, comp., *Broadsides, Ballads, &c. Printed in Massachusetts, 1639–1800* (Mass. Hist. Soc., *Colls.*, LXXV, 1922).

[68] Virtually every history of the Revolution touches on the major pamphlets and pamphleteers. More particular discussions include H. L. Calkin, "Pamphlets and Public Opinion during the American Revolution," *Pa. Mag. of History and Biography*, LXIV (1940), 22–42, William MacDonald, "American Political Writing, 1760–1789," in W. P. Trent and others, *The Cambridge History of American Literature* (N. Y., 1917–21), I, 124–149, and, most recently, Clinton Rossiter, *Seedtime of the Republic* (N. Y., 1953), chaps. xii–xiv.

by Joseph Priestley, Richard Price and other British publicists provided further potent ammunition.

Though most of the pamphleteers wrote with high seriousness, a few assumed a lighter tone, doubtless on Franklin's principle that "odd ways of presenting Matters to the publick View sometimes occasion them to be more read, talk'd of, and more attended to." [69] The supreme example was *The First Book of the American Chronicles of the Times* (1775), which in antique scriptural language parodied the train of events from Boston's drowning of the tea to the assembling of the First Continental Congress. To a people steeped in the Bible nothing could have been more titillating. The nameless author blamed the colonists' woes on "the Lord the King" for ordering the "Americanites" to worship that heathen idol, the Tea Chest, "whose length was three cubits, and the breadth thereof one cubit and a half." Among the principal characters were "Mordecai, the Benjamite" (Franklin), "Thomas, the Gageite," and "Jeremiah, to-wit, Samuel Adams," who sat from morn till night on top of Liberty Tree. First published in Philadelphia, where "upwards of 3,000 copies were sold in a few days," the skit proved so popular that it was reprinted in whole or part in Salem, Providence, Norwich and New Bern.[70]

Although Tory pamphleteers also entered the arena, they struck their doughtiest blows in the tense aftermath of the Intolerable Acts, at a time when few printers would take their work because of the certainty of mob reprisals. Sometimes the authors themselves had to decamp. But at this stage the efforts to turn back the tide of opinion were in any event too late.

Of these many ways of kneading men's minds none, however,

[69] Benjamin Franklin to Thomas Cushing, Sept. 29, 1773, Franklin, *Writings* (A. H. Smyth, ed., N. Y., 1907), VI, 137.

[70] Philadelphia item in the *N.–C. Gazette*, March 24, 1775; J. R. Bowman, ed., "A Bibliography of *The First Book of the American Chronicles of the Times*," *American Literature*, I (1929), 69–74. M. C. Tyler, *The Literary History of the American Revolution* (N. Y., 1897), I, 259–266, reprints excerpts. The first performance of this type was "The Book of America" in the London *Gazetteer* early in 1766, approvingly recounting the Stamp Act resistance, and republished in several Boston papers in whole or part. Albert Matthews, ed., "The Book of America," Mass. Hist. Soc., *Procs.*, LXII (1928–29), 171–197. In this genre also were *Some Chapters of the Book of Chronicles of Isaac the Scribe, Written on His Passage from the Land of the Amerikites to the Island of the Albionites* (N. Y., n.d.), which satirized Governor Sir Henry Moore's regime in New York, and Francis Hopkinson's *A Prophecy* (Phila., 1776), an argument for Independence.

equaled the newspapers. Published from New Hampshire to Georgia, increasing in number with the rise of American opposition, issued with clocklike regularity and reaching every segment of society, they influenced events both by reporting and abetting local patriot transactions and by broadcasting kindred proceedings in other places. The press, that is to say, instigated, catalyzed and synthesized the many other forms of propaganda and action. It trumpeted the doings of Whig committees, publicized rallies and mobbings, promoted partisan fast days and anniversaries, blazoned patriotic speeches and toasts, popularized anti-British slogans, gave wide currency to ballads and broadsides, furthered the persecution of Tories, reprinted London news of the government's intentions concerning America and, in general, created an atmosphere of distrust and enmity that made reconciliation increasingly difficult. Besides, the newspapers dispensed a greater volume of political and constitutional argument than all the other media combined. Sometimes the editors serialized lengthy treatises which, if they excited sufficient attention, the authors then republished in pamphlet form. Dickinson's *Farmer's Letters* and John Adams's *Novanglus* essays are outstanding examples. Sometimes, as with Tom Paine's *Common Sense*, newspapers reversed the process by printing in whole or part tracts that had already appeared. More typically, however, they resorted to short, hard-hitting screeds which sought to quicken the emotional rather than the mental processes.

As Benjamin Franklin pointed out, the press could present the "same truths" repeatedly in "different lights" and hence not only "strike while the iron is hot" but "heat it continually by striking." And a Massachusetts Tory, wryly concurring, cried, "It is enough to make a wise man mad to see how tamely the common people suffer themselves to be fooled . . . . Tell them thro' the channel of a seditious news-paper the most improbable tale about grievances, and they believe it more firmly than they will those many parts of Holy Writ which enjoin submission to rulers, as a Christian duty." [71] Perhaps most important of all, the press bore the principal brunt of

---

[71] Franklin to Richard Price, June 13, 1782, Franklin, *Writings*, VIII, 457; Jonathan Sewall ("Sir Roger de Coverly"), *A Cure for the Spleen* (Boston, 1775), *Mag. of History*, extra no. 79 (Tarrytown, 1922), 38. In *Benjamin Franklin's Letters to the Press, 1758–1775* (Chapel Hill, 1950), Verner Crane identifies and reprints many of that veteran journalist's political contributions to British newspapers when in London as a colonial agent.

the struggle for liberty of expression and so emboldened patriots everywhere to speak their minds.

Because of these protean but scarce remembered services it is fitting to explore at some length the newspaper's place in colonial life and particularly its role in fueling the discontents that flamed into Independence.

PART II

"The Role of the Newspaper"

Chapter III

Journalistic Beginnings

IT WAS ONLY sixty years before the initial difficulties with the mother country that the first real newspaper appeared in America. As early as 1638, however, the colonies had presses for job printing, with Massachusetts taking the lead. The provincial authorities required means of publishing laws and other official documents, and they lured journeymen from England with the promise of a regular salary or a monopoly of the work. As time wore on, the larger towns acquired in this manner the mechanical equipment for broader community needs, as well as suitable craftsmen who in turn apprenticed natives to the trade. But until the eighteenth century the struggling settlements were too small to aspire to news organs, and when the first one came into being, it was largely by chance.

I

This was the *Boston News-Letter,* founded in 1704 by John Campbell in what was then America's largest city, with a population of around 7000. Campbell, a transplanted Scot, had become postmaster two years before, and being in a key position to learn the latest tidings, he soon supplemented his duties by occasionally writing out the more important items and franking them through the mails to leading men of the region. To improve and commercialize this service he then decided to put out his newsletter as a regular weekly bulletin. Printed on both sides of a single sheet 6¼ by 10½ inches, it proved too great a novelty to elicit immediate favor, and in the early years the legislature had to aid it financially.[1] In time,

[1] C. A. Duniway, *The Development of Freedom of the Press in Massachusetts* (Cambridge, Mass., 1906), 78–79 *n.* For accounts of colonial journalism and material dealing with the business operations of particular printers, see the Bibliographical Note at the end of the present volume.

however, the rising merchant class turned to it increasingly for maritime intelligence as well as to advertise their wares, and others also came to value it. With this mounting support the *News-Letter* presently won a firm footing. It was in fact destined to be the longest-lived of all colonial papers, with Campbell retaining charge for nineteen years.

Other towns somewhat timidly followed Boston's example. By 1725 New York and Philadelphia each had a weekly, by which time the Yankee metropolis possessed three. In another quarter-century the number of journals rose to thirteen, including additions in New York and Philadelphia as well as the first three in the South—at the provincial capitals, Annapolis, Williamsburg and Charleston—and a German-language biweekly at Germantown, Pa. In short, newspapers were beginning to become a normal appurtenance of urban life. Before the end of 1764, the year of the Sugar Act, the total reached twenty-three, including a German weekly in Philadelphia. They were by then also being published in Portsmouth, N. H., Newport and Providence, R. I., New London, New Haven and Hartford, Conn., New Bern and Wilmington, N. C., and Savannah, Ga. Only two colonies had none, but these—New Jersey and Delaware—did not notice the lack because of the ones circulating out of nearby New York or Philadelphia.[2] In fact they went without any till a year or more after the Declaration of Independence.

Despite this steady increase, newspapering was a hazardous occupation. Many sheets were bravely launched only to founder. Even the successful ones had difficulty in extracting pay from subscribers. James Parker of the *New-York Gazette or Weekly Post-Boy* declared that "in the best of my Times" at least a quarter failed to remit. His colleague on the *New-York Weekly Journal* complained that some of his subscribers were in arrears for "upwards of seven years." "The Publishers of this Paper," fumed the *New-Hampshire Gazette*, "have many Times call'd upon their Customers to remind them, that it is not possible to print News Papers without a Stock of Paper, Ink, Hands, and in Winters a good Fire." According to the owners of the *Connecticut Journal*, "they have not for this year past received from all the customers for this journal so much money as they have expended for the blank paper on which it is

---

[2] A newspaper attempted in Wilmington, Del., in 1762 succumbed in about six months.

printed." In lieu of cash editors had oftentimes to accept wheat, maize, rye, oats, firewood and other commodities.[3]

To make ends meet, the publishers relied in part on receipts from advertisements, generally short notices which totaled a quarter or more of their pages; and they supplemented this source when possible with work for the government. Indeed, the designation *Gazette* so commonly used arose from the widespread legal requirement that official announcements be inserted in "the gazette." Some newspapermen derived further income from printing statutes, legislative proceedings etc. in separate form. In fact, Benjamin Franklin of the *Pennsylvania Gazette* served at various times as public printer for New Jersey, Delaware and Maryland in addition to his own province. But "Poor Richard" was the most enterprising of all the journalists, as witness the fact that in 1748, at the age of forty-two, he was able to transfer his interests in the business to his foreman David Hall, cannily retaining a share of the earnings for the next eighteen years, however, as silent partner.[4]

Whenever they could, publishers also doubled as postmasters. Indeed, beginning with Campbell, every Boston postmaster until mid-century was an editor, though not every editor was a postmaster. Apparently, moreover, the position carried an advantage beyond the welcome remuneration, for Franklin while acting in that capacity at Philadelphia in 1740 barred a competitor for a time from the mail, alleging as his reason the latter's arrears in accounts with the Postmaster General.[5] Franklin's elevation to the office of Deputy Postmaster General in 1753 gave him and his fellow incumbent, William Hunter of the *Virginia Gazette*, as we have seen, oversight of the entire American service; and Franklin's peremptory dismissal from this station twenty-one years later was to furnish the colonists with a fresh grievance against the Ministry. Among others to draw postal salaries in the closing years were James Parker of the *New-York Gazette or Weekly Post-Boy*, John Holt during his editorship of the *Connecticut Gazette* and Peter Timothy of the

[3] Beverly McAnear, "James Parker versus New York Province," *N. Y. History*, XXII (1941), 7, quoting Parker in 1759; *N.-Y. Weekly Journal*, March 18, 1751; triple notice in the *N.-H. Gazette*, Jan. 15, 22, 29, 1768, accompanied with threats of court prosecution; *Conn. Journal*, April 2, 1773; *Conn. Courant* (Hartford), Dec. 12, 1768, Nov. 6, 1769.

[4] In this role Franklin realized an average of £467 annually. Carl Van Doren, *Benjamin Franklin* (Garden City, 1941), 123.

[5] *Pa. Gazette*, Dec. 11, 1740.

South-Carolina Gazette. In view of this traditional nexus of journalism and the mails it naturally followed that upon Franklin's discharge another newspaperman—William Goddard of the *Pennsylvania Chronicle* and the *Maryland Journal*—should head the movement to supplant the imperial system with a "constitutional" patriot one.

Editors also hit on other expedients. William Bradford of the *Pennsylvania Journal* was alone in conducting a coffeehouse on the side; but some, as has been seen, put out their own almanacs, and virtually all vended stationery and legal and business blanks, besides doing miscellaneous job printing and carrying a bewildering array of merchandise for sale. Bradford's uncle, Andrew Bradford of the Philadelphia *American Weekly Mercury*, for example, purveyed at various times spices, tea, rum, patent medicines, books, quadrants, spectacles, mirrors, stockings, whalebone and beaver hats. In brief, the printers in their quest for solvency strove to be all things to all men, incidentally providing the townsfolk with some of their best-stocked bookshops and general stores.

Happily, these efforts generally paid off, and the increase of newspapers, moreover, was attended by larger circulations. The *Boston News-Letter* in Campbell's day never mustered more than 300 subscribers; but by the 1750's editors, despite the greater competition, could hope for 500 or 600, and later the quarrel with the mother country boosted the figures in the larger towns to from 1500 to 3600.[6] At every stage, it need hardly be said, the actual number of readers greatly exceeded those on the books, for copies passed freely from hand to hand and were always available at the taverns.

Out-of-town patrons accounted for part of the rise in circulation. Franklin and Hunter's original postal reforms speeded the transmission of printed as well as written matter, and then five years later, in 1758, the two gave newspapers special assistance. They not only put distribution costs for the first time on a businesslike basis, but also sought to better publishers' receipts. Prior to this time a postmaster could exclude papers at will or, if he himself conducted one, undercut competitors by franking his own; and, to make matters worse, postriders often alienated customers by charging steep carriage fees. The new regulations established fair and uniform rates for all, with only exchange copies between editors going free; and

[6] See Appendix A for detailed data.

they also allowed a postmaster a one-fifth commission for collecting money from subscribers and held him financially responsible for any orders he himself sent in. It was doubtless no coincidence that the *New-York Mercury*, for example, could boast four years later that outside its own colony it entered "every Town and Country Village" in Connecticut, Rhode Island and New Jersey as well as all the provincial capitals from Nova Scotia to Georgia, not to mention such remoter places as the West Indies, the British Isles and Holland.[7] This wider reach of the press greatly enhanced its influence in the coming war of words with Britain.

II

Another factor also contributed notably to the newspaper's effectiveness in the controversy. The typographical fraternity constituted a foot-loose element, its members drifting freely from colony to colony, a circumstance as typical of the British-born as of the native breed. The elder William Bradford, for example, after learning his trade in London, performed job printing and government work for some years in Pennsylvania and New York and then in 1725 set up the *New-York Gazette*, Manhattan's first newspaper. And William Parks, another English pressman, successively fathered the original *Gazettes* in Maryland (at Annapolis) and Virginia (at Williamsburg) in 1727 and 1736. To consider an early publisher of American stock, teen-age Benjamin Franklin, fleeing Boston and an onerous apprenticeship to his brother James, tried vainly for a berth with Bradford in New York and then went on to Philadelphia, where in 1729 after several false starts he acquired the dying *Pennsylvania Gazette* while still only twenty-three. This, as we have seen, the youth succeeded in converting into a great success.

Three others of the clan, all later comers, call for particular notice because of their prominence in the contest with Britain. John Holt, a native of Williamsburg, began in 1755 as junior partner of James Parker on the New Haven *Connecticut Gazette*, the pioneer paper in that colony, next joined him in 1760 for two years on the *New-York Gazette or Weekly Post-Boy*, then, after conducting it

[7] Ruth L. Butler, *Doctor Franklin, Postmaster General* (Garden City, 1928), 56–58; *N.-Y. Mercury*, March 15, 1762.

alone till 1766, launched the *New-York Journal*, which he published until after the Revolutionary War. Isaiah Thomas, indentured to a Boston pressman in 1756 at the tender age of seven, ran off to Nova Scotia in 1765, where as editor of the *Halifax Gazette* he assailed the Stamp Act with such vigor that the authorities forced him to depart. The next few years saw him briefly in newspaper work at Portsmouth, N. H., and then—after a futile attempt to establish a sheet of his own at Wilmington, N. C.—in Charleston on the *South-Carolina and American General Gazette*. Eventually, in 1770, he returned to Boston and founded the *Massachusetts Spy*, only to branch out in 1773 to start the Newburyport *Essex Journal*. In the same tradition William Goddard, of New Haven birth, established the *Providence Gazette* in 1762, was employed for a time by Holt and Parker in New York, moved to Philadelphia in 1767 to set up the *Pennsylvania Chronicle*, and in 1773 commenced the *Maryland Journal* in Baltimore as a second string to his bow.

Benjamin Franklin, after he once settled down in Philadelphia, turned this itinerant proclivity of printers to his business advantage and thus further augmented the intercolonial movement of journeymen and the planting of papers. Training a succession of young hands in his shop, he saw with his characteristic blend of idealism and practicality how he could at the same time promote popular enlightenment and benefit his pocketbook. Hence from time to time he sent a promising graduate to some other community and agreed to pay a third of the neophyte's expenses over a six-year period in return for a third of the profits. By this or like means he brought about the *South-Carolina Gazette* at Charleston in 1732 and a short-lived bilingual sheet for the Pennsylvania Germans. In addition, he started James Parker on his New York journalistic career, and he enabled his brother James's son, James, Jr., to undertake the *Newport Mercury* in 1758 as well as his sister's son, Benjamin Mecom, to revive the New Haven *Connecticut Gazette* in 1765. In fact, his operations extended as far as Antigua, Jamaica and Dominica in the West Indies.[8]

Kinship ties, even in the absence of timely financial assistance, accounted for other wide-strewn newspapers. The custom of whole families working in the printing office often resulted in some of the

[8] J. C. Oswald, *Benjamin Franklin, Printer* (N. Y., 1917), chap. xiii; Van Doren, *Franklin*, 116–123.

members later striking out for themselves. Thus the New York editor William Bradford's son Andrew in 1719 sired Philadelphia's first organ, the *American Weekly Mercury*, and William's grandson and namesake in 1742 launched the *Pennsylvania Journal*, taking on his own son Thomas as partner in 1766. Similarly, William Goddard's mother and sister respectively ran the *Providence Gazette* and the *Maryland Journal* for a period of years; and in 1775 John Holt's nephew, John Hunter Holt, for a time published the *Virginia Gazette or Norfolk Intelligencer* until a British raiding party forced him to quit.[9]

But the outstanding case was the Green dynasty, stemming from Samuel Green who operated a printing press in Cambridge, Mass., as early as 1649. His descendants in the eighteenth century took naturally to the rising newspaper business, Bartholomew setting the example by printing the *Boston News-Letter* for John Campbell till 1723 when he became its owner. Timothy Green, Jr., and a partner followed suit in 1727 with the *New-England Weekly Journal* at Boston; and some years later, in 1745, Jonas established a new *Maryland Gazette* at Annapolis (where Parks's had long since lapsed) and was succeeded in 1767 by his widow, who shortly took her son in with her. Meanwhile Timothy, Jr., and other Greens, acting alone or with partners, started the *Boston Post-Boy* in 1757, the *New-London Summary* in 1758, the *New-London Gazette* in 1763, the *Connecticut Courant* at Hartford in 1764 and the *Connecticut Journal* at New Haven in 1767.[10]

Although no other family connection equaled this record, the Greens merely high-lighted a network of journalistic links which stood the patriots in good stead in the quarrel with Britain. To an unusual degree newspapermen possessed a continent-wide view of

[9] Victor H. Paltsits and other students identify John Hunter Holt as John Holt's son, but the elder Holt himself sets the matter straight in the *N.-Y. Journal*, Oct. 26, 1775. For the three generations of Sowers (Saurs), German printers in Pennsylvania, see J. C. Oswald, *Printing in the Americas* (N. Y., 1937), chap. xvi, and E. W. Hocker, *The Sower Printing House of Colonial Times* (Norristown, Pa., 1948).

[10] Some of these papers disappeared or changed their names before the troubles arose with the mother country. For this remarkable clan, see W. C. Kiessel, "The Green Family, a Dynasty of Printers," *New England Hist. and Genealogical Register*, CIV (1950), 81–93, and D. C. McMurtrie, "The Green Family of Printers," *Americana*, XXVI (1932), 364–375. John Green of the *Mass. Gazette and Boston Post-Boy*, great grandson of the original Samuel, was the only one to take the Tory side during the difficulties with Britain.

affairs, partly from having lived in different colonies, partly because of kinship ties, and partly from a knowledge of happenings elsewhere which they learned from exchange copies sent them by fellow editors. Insensibly they came to think of America as a single country rather than as thirteen disparate societies. Since few of them, moreover, had ever resided in England, they had no comparable familiarity with the homeland and could hardly be expected to regard sympathetically any radical departure from traditional imperial policy. It is noteworthy that Benjamin Franklin, who began a protracted stay in London as colonial agent in 1757 and retained his financial interest in the *Pennsylvania Gazette* through most of the Stamp Act era, kept that paper to a fairly moderate opposition. It is equally revealing that the most militant of the handful of Tory editors were all of British birth.

III

The typical newspaper after the early years consisted of four compactly printed pages roughly 10 by 15 inches, in size somewhat smaller than a modern tabloid. To accommodate an unusual volume of news or advertisements, the publisher might add a page or so as a "Supplement" or "Postscript" or "Extraordinary" (from which arose the modern term "extra"). The presses, made of wood, differed little from Gutenberg's two and a half centuries before, and until nearly the end of the colonial period they all came from England. Only a single page—one side of a sheet—could be struck off at a time. The master printer and his assistants, after hand-setting the text letter by letter from trays and locking the completed page in a frame, transferred the form to the press, where they inked the type with leather balls, placed over it a rough ragpaper sheet and, to finish the job, lowered the platen against the sheet by means of a large metal screw. It was a laborious process entailing a dozen separate manual operations.[11] With this clumsy apparatus it was possible to turn out only some 200 pages an hour.

The final product, as in England of the time, possessed little or no visual appeal. The type, closely set and jammed into the three

[11] For a detailed description, see August Klapper, *The Printer in Eighteenth-Century Williamsburg* (Parke Rowse and M. W. Thomas, eds.; *Williamsburg Craft Series*, no. 1, 1955), 15–21.

or four columns of the page, was so minute as to strain the modern eye. Headlines, if any at all, were one-line labels of column-width and usually gave simply the place and date of the item. Nor did editorials relieve the monotony, for these too had not yet appeared. As for pictures, the printers seldom went further than to adorn their name plates with emblematic designs, perhaps a postrider sounding his horn or an allegorical figure of Britannia. Beyond this, the advertisements occasionally contained miniature British-made stock cuts of an escaped slave, a house for sale, a departing ship and the like.

Within these limits, however, the publishers commonly affected a typographical style that was extremely expressive to the unsophisticated eighteenth-century reader. This was to use upper case for the first letter of each key word or to set in capital letters or italics entire words and sometimes whole passages. To quote a contemporary, the papers employed "*Italics*, SMALL CAPITALS, and CAPITALS without number, that they might make the greater impression." [12] Accordingly, the public was led to place the emphasis where the author or the editor intended, and inert print acquired something of the animation and impact of oral discourse. In the conflict with Britain the Whigs were to turn these practices to telling account.

Inasmuch as the subscriber had a full week to master the contents with little or no other reading matter to distract him, he did not need his paper to be sauced with headlines and illustrations. Moreover, he partook of what he considered a varied and nutritious fare, a veritable "Epitome of Modern History," which, as one contemporary put it,

> Brings Men of Merit into public View; promotes a spirit of Enquiry; is favourable to Civil and Religious Liberty; a cheap vehicle of Knowledge and Instruction to the Indigent; and attended with

[12] "A Countryman" in the *Pa. Chronicle*, Aug. 1, 1768. The success of these devices probably delayed the development of the modern headline. Later in the eighteenth century, when printers had settled upon a uniform style like that of today, Benjamin Franklin, then long out of the business, deplored the disuse of initial capitals and of italicization, remarking that the latter had been useful for denoting "Words on which an Emphasis should be put in Reading." He saw the new practices as "Improvements backward." Letter to Noah Webster, Dec. 26, 1789, Franklin, *Writings* (A. H. Smyth, ed., N. Y., 1907), X, 79. Actually, Franklin when in the trade had employed upper-case type more sparingly than most editors. Though not always consistently, he capitalized the first letter of every noun but usually not of pronouns or adjectives except, of course, at the beginning of sentences.

numberless commercial Advantages.—The perusal requires but a short Recess from Business; and the annual Expence is so inconsiderable, that few can be deprived of enjoying it, through Apprehension of trespassing, either upon their Time or their Pockets.[13]

This testimonial hardly overstated the case. Among many other attractions the reader was given a broad outlook on world affairs. Not until our own day, indeed, has the American newspaper covered the international scene so comprehensively. Reports from the London press brought the colonist regular tidings of the mother country, oftentimes of a derogatory character, and offered intelligence as well of Paris, Lisbon, Amsterdam, Rome, Vienna, St. Petersburg and other strange places. Nor did the delay of six or eight weeks in transmission dampen his interest, since the news was still the very latest available. The editors, assuming that the townsfolk already knew what their neighbors were doing, generally chronicled only such events as natural disasters, the executions of criminals, elections, deaths etc. for the sake of their distant subscribers; and by the same token they copied items from other colonial papers that might possess local interest. In addition, they carried an abundance of purely literary matter—the verse usually in "The Poet's Corner"—thus satisfying a taste that might have nourished the struggling magazines. The essays, some original, some clipped, treated subjects all the way from husbandry and politics to manners, morals and religion.

The printer, as he usually termed himself rather than publisher or editor, in reality performed all three functions along with most others pertaining to the business. Having no reporters, he and his journeymen wrote the local items; and with scissors and paste he culled news and miscellany from British and American contemporaries, sometimes obtaining additional tidbits from skippers in port and from private letters to himself or members of the community. This informal source could not be counted upon, however; hence the oft-repeated plea: "We should be much obliged to Captains of Ships, or any Ladies and Gentlemen in Country or Town, who will communicate to us Articles of well-authenticated Intelligence." [14] Only a rare newspaperman like Benjamin Franklin found the time or possessed the ability to pen essays and squibs of his own. Be-

---

[13] *Albany Gazette*, Dec. 2, 1771.
[14] *Pa. Chronicle*, Nov. 14, 1768; similarly, *S.–C. Gazette*, Feb. 2, 1734, *Md. Journal*, Aug. 20, 1773, and countless other papers.

sides, the printer had to supervise the circulation and also secure the advertising that could spell the difference between success and failure. In fact, he did practically everything but deliver the papers from door to door, a job he thankfully left to his apprentices.

IV

Not until the rise of the troubles with Britain did the editor come to think of himself as a maker of opinion as well as a transmitter of news and literary offerings. Yet he unwittingly did something, however little, in that direction by the very act of deciding what to put in or leave out of his paper, and once in a great while he offered a terse comment of his own. Indeed, he might even inspire others to prepare congenial political articles, which he then usually ran pseudonymously. This device not only concealed the author's identity, but enabled the contributor by varying his signature to create the impression of being a number of different persons. In the contest with the Ministry, Samuel Adams was to show himself a virtuoso in this respect.

Unless the editor kept within certain bounds, however, he faced official reprisals. Even before any newspapers existed, the provincial authorities, following English practice, forestalled objectionable publications by licensing pressmen. Hence when a proposed monthly news periodical *Publick Occurrences* appeared in Boston in 1690 without a legal permit, the Governor and Council suppressed it after a single number. The editor, Benjamin Harris, had compounded his offense by printing what they considered "Reflections of a very high nature," notably allegations of atrocities committed by Britain's Indian allies upon French captives.[15] This system, however, gradually died out after Parliament in 1695 abolished it at home, though the governors at the Ministry's behest strove for some years more to keep it going.[16]

The discontinuance of prior restraint marked a milestone in the

[15] V. H. Paltsits, "New Light on 'Publick Occurrences,'" Am. Antiquarian Soc., *Procs.*, LIX (1949), 75–88; W. C. Ford, "Benjamin Harris, Printer and Bookseller," Mass. Hist. Soc., *Procs.*, LVII (1923–24), 34–68.

[16] L. W. Labaree, ed., *Royal Instructions to British Governors* (N. Y., 1935), II, 495–496; Duniway, *Freedom of the Press in Massachusetts*, 78–79 n., 89 n., 102–103. For the English side of the story, see F. S. Siebert, *Freedom of the Press in England, 1476–1776* (Urbana, 1952).

Anglo-American struggle for journalistic independence, but it still did not leave an editor free to publish at will. In its stead the authorities drew a distinction, to be applied after the fact, between the liberty and the license of the press. Should an editor allegedly indulge in license, the legislature might on its own punish the printer or author of the article for breach of legislative privilege or for otherwise bringing its dignity into contempt. Alternatively, or in addition, the legislative or the executive branch might prosecute the offender in court for seditious libel (that is, derogatory reflections on the government or its representatives). In this instance the English common law prescribed that the accused be adjudged guilty irrespective of the truth of his allegations: the jury needed only to find that he was the responsible party; the bench handed down the sentence. And, finally, the ruling group possessed an effective financial leash on newspaper proprietors insofar as they executed or desired to execute government printing.[17]

Any of these devices acted as a powerful deterrent, yet occasional editors disregarded them, though never for long.[18] One of the boldest was James Franklin of the Boston *New-England Courant*, who reveled in needling bigwigs both civil and ecclesiastical. In 1722 the legislature jailed him for a month for complaining of the government's laxness in suppressing piracy. The following year, upon further provocation, it forbade him to continue to publish except

[17] This financial restraint also extended to local regimes. Thus, when the Boston selectmen in 1757 commissioned Edes and Gill of the *Boston Gazette* to print the votes of the town, they warned them that if they continued to publish attacks on the people's "religious principles" they "must Expect no more favours from Us." Duniway, *Freedom of the Press in Massachusetts*, 121 *n*. Apparently the British postal service never disciplined editors by dismissal from postmasterships. When Franklin was fired as Deputy Postmaster General in 1774, he had ceased being a newspaper publisher, and the reason was his obnoxious activity as Massachusetts colonial agent in London.

[18] The instances that follow may be found in L. R. Schuyler, *The Liberty of the Press in the American Colonies before the Revolutionary War* (N. Y., 1905), and Duniway, *Freedom of the Press in Massachusetts*. For further details of Bradford's difficulties, see Anna J. DeArmond, *Andrew Bradford* (Newark, Del., 1949), 21–30; and, for more on the Smith episode, A. F. Gegenheimer, *William Smith, Educator and Churchman* (Phila., 1943), 139–148, and W. R. Riddell, "Libel on the Assembly," *Pa. Mag. of History and Biography*, LII (1928), 176–192, 249–279, 342–360. The fullest accounts of the most celebrated incident are Livingston Rutherfurd, *John Peter Zenger* (N. Y., 1904), and Vincent Buranelli, *The Trial of Peter Zenger* (N. Y., 1957); a shorter treatment is R. B. Morris, *Fair Trial* (N. Y., 1952), chap. iii; and F. L. Mott reprints and edits *Zenger's Own Story* (*Oldtime Comments on Journalism*, II, Columbia, Mo., 1954) in convenient separate form.

under official supervision, whereupon he circumvented the order by bringing out the paper in the name of his brother Benjamin, then still in his employ, who thus commenced his notable career on the shady side of the law. Though an attempt to induce a grand jury to indict James for this dodge failed, he nevertheless left Boston several years later for the freer atmosphere of Rhode Island.

Andrew Bradford of the *American Weekly Mercury* in Philadelphia felt it safe enough to condemn the distant "Oppressors and Bigots" who had hounded James Franklin,[19] but when in 1722 he was confronted with a similar situation himself for publishing a mild criticism of the state of Pennsylvania finances, he humbly confessed his error to his own Provincial Council. In 1729 he again found himself in difficulties, this time for a didactic essay on the dangers to liberty of centralized power; but the Council, after precipitately arresting him, felt too unsure of its case or of a jury's reaction to pursue him in court for the "wicked & seditious Libell."

In 1742, with the scene once more back in the Bay Colony, Thomas Fleet of the *Boston Evening-Post* came to grief by reporting in good faith that Sir Robert Walpole, the British Prime Minister, would soon be taken into custody for mismanaging the war with Spain. The Governor's Council, after roundly berating the editor for the "scandalous and libellous Reflection," directed that he be prosecuted, but then, distrusting what a jury of Fleet's fellow townsmen might do, it followed the Pennsylvania example and quietly let the matter drop.

The ensuing years beheld the major clashes in New York, with that colony's legislature playing a somewhat contradictory role. When Governor George Clinton in 1747 instructed James Parker as public printer to omit certain objectionable material from the Assembly's proceedings, that body in high dudgeon pronounced the "arbitrary and illegal" order fatal to the "Liberty of the Press," whereupon Parker not only defied the Governor but also inserted the forbidden matter in his *New-York Gazette or Weekly Post-Boy*. A few years later, however, in 1753, the Assembly, now less mindful of the rights of the press, took Hugh Gaine to task for publishing some of its transactions without leave in his *New-York Mercury* and exacted an apology before letting him off with a warning and costs. In 1756 Parker found himself in hot water a second time, for

[19] *American Weekly Mercury*, Feb. 26, 1723.

an article that reflected on the way certain legislators had been elected. The Assembly, breathing fire, decreed that he, his partner William Weyman and the author, one Hezekiah Watkins, had all committed "a high Misdemeanor and a Contempt of the Authority of this House" and forthwith wrung from them pledges of future rectitude.

When, however, the Pennsylvania Assembly two years later proceeded similarly against William Smith for inserting in the *Philadelphische Zeitung* a "virulent and seditious libel" against some of its doings, that gentleman, a respected churchman and Provost of the College of Philadelphia, stoutly declined to make any amends and in the altercation that followed was thrice thrown into jail. Still intractable, he appealed to the Privy Council in London, which exonerated him on the technical ground that, as he had committed the offense after the Assembly's adjournment, no subsequent Assembly could punish him. Behind this exculpation doubtless lay the fact that Smith stood in high favor in England because of his ardent Anglicanism.

But the most famous case, and the only one to be carried to a petit jury, involved the German-born John Peter Zenger whose *New-York Weekly Journal* in 1734 had unleashed a series of attacks on the unprincipled and unfit royal executive, William Cosby. That enraged official vainly tried to get the grand jury to indict Zenger for seditious libel and failed again when the Assembly refused to take any action. Thereupon the Governor and the Council themselves charged the editor with "tending to raise Factions and Tumults among the People," directed that the "scurrilous" copies be publicly burned and, by-passing the grand jury, initiated his prosecution for seditious libel by the short-cut legal process known as an information. Unable to post the excessive bail, the printer lingered in jail for ten months until his trial in August, 1735, meanwhile getting out the paper with the help of his wife and political supporters.

Under the common law Zenger's guilt was undoubted: he had actually published the pieces, and the question of their veracity or falsity lay beyond the jury's competence. But his principal counsel, Andrew Hamilton of Philadelphia, flouting judicial precedent, contended that the one and only matter at issue was "the Liberty—both of exposing and opposing arbitrary Power (in these Parts of the

World, at least) by speaking and writing Truth"; and the jury, overriding the court's instructions, jubilantly acquitted the prisoner. A happy outcome for Zenger himself, it nevertheless left unchanged the legal status of other editors or even of himself on some future occasion. The decision, however, reverberated through America and Britain, one Englishman exclaiming, *"If it is not Law it is better than Law, it Ought to be Law, and Will Always be Law whereever Justice prevails."* [20] In the exciting events preceding the War for Independence the patriots time and again cited the verdict as justifying their own assaults on overweening authority.

Such practitioners of freedom of discussion, few and scattered though they were, stand out the more conspicuously because they could count on little or no support from fellow editors. These understandably timorous souls shrank from the stern penalties involved if they themselves should offend the authorities, and they accordingly faltered at rallying behind their more reckless brethren. Even Zenger, though eventually vindicated, had had to endure a galling confinement. The time had not yet arrived when the printers would act unitedly in behalf of their right to criticize public affairs.

Unlike the British press, however, colonial newspapers went untaxed until the Seven Years' War. Then Massachusetts in 1755 and New York in 1757 put into effect a stamp duty of a halfpenny a copy, in the one case for two years, in the other for three. Fortunately the good times enabled the publishers to soften the blow by temporarily raising their subscription rates; but, even so, Parker inveighed against the acts as discriminatory and ruinous, hysterically alleging that the Massachusetts levy "broke up one Printer," had "obliged another to remove to New-Hampshire" and caused still others to lose Connecticut orders at a heavy indirect cost to the province as a whole. The *Boston Gazette*, for its part, publicized English denunciations of the stamp tax in that country to imply that a similar threat to the "liberty of the press" was menacing America. In fact, however, the *Gazette*'s complaint, like Parker's, lacked validity, for the sole purpose of the duties was to meet emergency wartime needs.[21]

[20] "Z" in the *Pa. Gazette*, May 18, 1738.

[21] As to Parker's allegations, the *Boston Post-Boy*, to whom he obviously referred, suspended publication before the law took effect and for reasons unrelated to the tax, and the printer Daniel Fowle departed for Portsmouth because he was being prosecuted by the Massachusetts Assembly for a pamphlet he had issued. On

Although these protests failed to arouse the public at large, the laws were nevertheless allowed to die at their terminal dates, and the memory of them still rankled in the typographical trade when Parliament a few years later adopted its far more sweeping Stamp Act. Then the exactions alarmed the printers everywhere, not only in two provinces; and since the provisions also affected other segments of the community and in addition posed the issue of taxation without representation, the press instead of speaking for itself alone could voice a general indignation. Thanks to the new ministerial program, the tender shoots of journalistic independence thus came at last to full flower.

---

these two acts and their effects, see Beverly McAnear, "James Parker versus New York Province," *New York History*, XXII (1941), 321–330, and Duniway, *Freedom of the Press in Massachusetts*, 119–120; and, for the stamp duties in Britain, Siebert, *Freedom of the Press in England*, 306–322.

Chapter IV

Stamps Evoke the Power of the Press

Eᴠᴇɴ ʙᴇꜰᴏʀᴇ Pᴀʀʟɪᴀᴍᴇɴᴛ on April 5, 1764, adopted the Sugar Act, the Americans had entered the trough of depression that followed the Seven Years' War. This legislation, enacted with indifference to the hard times, deepened the distress by prescribing new import duties and tightening the clamps on smuggling, a major practice of colonial businessmen. The newspapers, especially in New England and the Middle provinces, bristled with accounts of protest meetings and of resolutions to retrench personal expenses and encourage domestic manufactures. "To send you all the incendiary papers which are published upon this Occasion would be endless," Governor Francis Bernard of Massachusetts wrote to the Ministry.[1]

[1] Bernard to John Pownall, July 11, 1764, Bernard Papers (Sparks MSS., Harvard College Library), III, 239–240. For a summary of the press reaction, see A. M. Schlesinger, *The Colonial Merchants and the American Revolution* (N. Y., 1918), 60–65. At the time of the passage of the Sugar Act the newspapers numbered 21, as follows: 9 in New England: the *New-Hampshire Gazette* (Portsmouth), the *Boston Evening-Post*, the *Boston Gazette*, the *Massachusetts Gazette and Boston News-Letter*, the *Boston Post-Boy*, the *Newport Mercury*, the *Providence Gazette*, the *New-London Gazette*, and the *Connecticut Gazette* (New Haven), which, however, suspended on April 14 for lack of support; 7 in the Middle colonies: the *New-York Gazette*, the *New-York Gazette or Weekly Post-Boy*, the *New-York Mercury*, the *Pennsylvania Gazette* (Philadelphia), the *Pennsylvania Journal* (Philadelphia), *Der Wöchentliche Philadelphische Staatsbote*, and *Die Germantowner Zeitung*; and 5 in the Southern colonies: the *Maryland Gazette* (Annapolis), the *Virginia Gazette* (Williamsburg), the *South-Carolina Gazette* (Charleston), which, however, issued but one number in the interval from March 31 to October 1, 1764, the *South-Carolina and American General Gazette* (Charleston), and the *Georgia Gazette* (Savannah). Three more papers were established later in 1764: the *North-Carolina Magazine* (New Bern, June 8), the *North-Carolina Gazette* (Wilmington, probably in September), and the *Connecticut Courant* (Hartford, Oct. 29).

The chorus grew shriller as London reports in the press made it evident that the worst was yet to come: that the Stamp Act, tentatively announced in March, 1764, would be passed by Parliament the next year. No measure could have occasioned wider resentment. It proposed a host of unprecedented and—in the American view—unconstitutional internal taxes; and, as though deliberately to provoke resistance, it saddled them largely on the printers, lawyers and merchants who, along with the clergy, formed the most literate and vocal elements of the population. But, despite the stormy reception in the colonies, the "fatal *Black-Act*," as James Parker termed it, became law on March 22, 1765, to go into effect the following November 1.[2]

I

On the printers the Stamp Act imposed hardships affecting every branch of their trade. It assessed a halfpenny on each copy of a newspaper printed on what was called "half a sheet" and a penny on the next larger size. It then added 2s. for each advertisement, an amount which by any standard was excessive, since the publisher himself received only from 3 to 5s. and still less for repeated insertions.[3] It further handicapped job printing with a halfpenny tax or more on single copies of pamphlets, 2d. and upward on every almanac, and from 3d. to £6 on a long list of legal and business forms. Any presswork in other than English must, moreover, pay double the regular rates, a veritable decree of bankruptcy for the Pennsylvania German typographers. Penalties for violations ranged according to the degree of gravity from 40s. to £10 and, if the publication in question were anonymous and unstamped, to £20, with the proviso that these should all be enforceable without jury trial in an admiralty court. Finally, the statute struck at the training school of the craft by levying a toll of 2½ to 5 per cent on apprenticeship indentures.

But, though the effects were economically disastrous, politically,

[2] 5 George III, c. 12; Parker to Benjamin Franklin, June 14, 1765, Mass. Hist. Soc., *Procs.*, ser. 2, XVI (1902), 198.

[3] For example, the *Newport Mercury* charged 3s. 9d. for three insertions not exceeding 12 lines each and 1s. thereafter; the *Maryland Gazette*, 5s. for an ad of "moderate length" and 1s. thereafter; the *Virginia Gazette*, 3s. the first time and 2s. thereafter.

as a contemporary pointed out, they proved "fortunate for the liberties of America," because, to continue in his words,

> Printers, when uninfluenced by government, have generally arranged themselves on the side of liberty, nor are they less remarkable for attention to the profits of their profession. A stamp duty, which openly invaded the first, and threatened a great diminution of the last, provoked their united zealous opposition.[4]

Their first reaction, though, was one of daze and indecision. While the bill was still before Parliament, Franklin, who had lobbied indefatigably to prevent its passage, warned his partner David Hall of the *Pennsylvania Gazette* in Philadelphia, "I think it will affect the Printers more than anybody, as a Sterling Halfpenny Stamp on every Half Sheet of a Newspaper, and Two Shillings Sterling on every Advertisement, will go near to knock up one Half of both." His sole thought, however, was to comply with the law as painlessly as possible; hence he ordered a hundred reams of oversized half-sheets for the *Gazette*—the kind used by the London *Chronicle*—in the vain expectation of evading the full penny tax.[5] About the same time Parker, who a few years before had rented his print shop and the *New-York Gazette or Weekly Post-Boy* to John Holt and was now planning on a paper in Burlington, N. J., mourned to Franklin that "the News of the Killing Stamp, has struck a deadly Blow to all my Hopes on that Head." [6]

Indeed, at this stage the pressmen generally hesitated openly to flout the enactment, having no rooted tradition of law defiance and being uncertain as yet of support from their fellow citizens. Resolved, however, to cushion the shock, they strove strenuously to collect "the Cash due to them for Sundries in their Way of Trade as Printers, Booksellers and Stationers." To this end the *New-Hampshire Gazette*, for example, bordering its announcement of the law's passage with thick black rules, declared that the act would "oblige the Printers on this Continent to Raise more Money every Year, than was ever raised at the year's end, and perhaps be obliged to

---

[4] David Ramsay, *The History of the American Revolution* (Phila., 1789), I, 61–62.

[5] Letter to David Hall of Feb. 14, 1765, Franklin, *Writings* (A. H. Smyth, ed., N. Y., 1905–07), IV, 363–364. For the failure of his tax-dodging scheme, see *ibid.*, IV, 364–365, V, 159–160.

[6] Letter of April 25, 1765, in William Nelson, "Some New Jersey Printers and Printing in the Eighteenth Century," Am. Antiquarian Soc., *Procs.*, n.s., XXI (1911), 25.

pay the Stamp Duty weekly." And the *Boston Evening-Post*, hoping to jog its own delinquent patrons, warned them that in Philadelphia the printers

> have peremptorily demanded their Dues, which if not immediately complied with, they shall "take such Measures as cannot be agreeable to either Party." Those at Virginia have actually put their Threats in Execution "as their Circumstances more particularly required it, in order to square with those they were obligated to." New York, New Hampshire, Rhode Island, Connecticut &c have, or are about doing the same.

The Maryland and Georgia *Gazettes* served notice that to make ends meet they would in addition have to raise their subscription rates.[7]

II

From the outset, however, the bolder spirits entertained hopes of nullifying the Stamp Act. As November 1, the date of its execution, drew on, indications multiplied that the printers, far from standing alone, had stout allies in other disaffected groups of the community. Their pages detailed the mounting opposition and spread before the public furious denunciations of the injustice and illegality of the exactions. The merchants and the legal profession, both subject to taxes on essential documents, joined in the attack, and many persons doubtless came to share John Adams's view in the *Boston Gazette* that the Ministry purposed "to strip us in a great measure of the means of knowledge, by loading the press, the colleges, and even an almanack and a newspaper, with restraints and duties." The town of Worcester accordingly instructed its representatives in the Massachusetts Assembly to "take special care of the LIBERTY OF THE PRESS." "The press," the *Connecticut Gazette* enjoined its readers, "is the test of truth, the bulwark of public safety, the guardian of freedom, and the people ought not to sacrifice it." "The liberty of free inquiry," concurred "A Freeman of the Colony of Connecticut" in the *New-London Gazette*, "is one

7 *N.–H. Gazette*, May 17, 1765; *Boston Evening-Post*, Sept. 30; P. H. Giddens, "Maryland and the Stamp Act Controversy," *Md. Hist. Mag.*, XXVII (1932), 83; L. T. Griffith and J. E. Talmadge, *Georgia Journalism, 1763–1950* (Athens, 1951), 5.

of the first and most fundamental of a free people." [8] It has little bearing on the genuineness of these alarms that the historian finds no evidence in the deliberations of Parliament that the law was intended to shackle the colonial mind or that it was anything more than what it purported to be: a simple fiscal measure.

A curious case of misreporting meanwhile lent unexpected impetus to the agitation. On May 30, 1765, the young Virginia hotspur, Patrick Henry, had induced a thinly attended House of Burgesses to adopt a series of resolutions which, after asserting the colonists' historic rights as Englishmen, arrogated to the legislature the "sole exclusive Right and Power" of taxation and stigmatized any opposer of this view as an "Enemy to this his Majesty's Colony." The next day, Henry having left Williamsburg, a fuller House in cooler mood expunged the more extreme utterances, but already someone had hurried copies of the original set northward. This misleading account, appearing first in the *Newport Mercury* on June 24 and then elsewhere, had an electrifying effect on the public, for Virginia was both the oldest and most populous of the colonies. "Two or three months ago," Governor Bernard of Massachusetts advised his English superiors on August 15, "I thought that this people would submit to the Stamp Act without actual opposition. . . . But the publishing of the Virginia Resolves proved an alarm bell to the disaffected," or, as General Thomas Gage in New York put it, "the signal for a general outcry over the Continent." [9]

At the forefront of the clamor in the Bay Colony stood Benjamin Edes and John Gill of the *Boston Gazette* and the Fleet brothers, Thomas and John, of the *Boston Evening-Post*. Edes worked hand in glove with the local Whig leaders, being himself one of the "Loyall Nine" who secretly manipulated the Sons of Liberty.[10] The

---

[8] Adams, "A Dissertation on the Canon and Feudal Law," *Boston Gazette*, Aug. 26, 1765, also Adams, *Works* (C. F. Adams, ed., Boston, 1850–56), III, 464; J. T. Buckingham, ed., *Specimens of Newspaper Literature* (Boston, 1850), I, 31 (for the Worcester instructions); *Conn. Gazette*, Nov. 1, 1765; the Rev. Stephen Johnson of Lyme in the *New-London Gazette*, Nov. 1.

[9] E. S. and Helen M. Morgan, *The Stamp Act Crisis* (Chapel Hill, 1953), 89–98; letters of Bernard and Gage, British Papers Relating to the American Revolution (Sparks MSS., Harvard College Library), I, 43, III, 85. See also Thomas Hutchinson, *The History of the Province of Massachusetts Bay*, III (London, 1828), 119.

[10] Adams, *Works*, II, 178–179; Henry Bass to S. P. Savage, Dec. 19, 1765, Mass. Hist. Soc., *Procs.*, XLIV (1910–11), 688; G. P. Anderson, "A Note on Ebenezer Mackintosh," Colonial Soc. of Mass., *Pubs.*, XXVI (1924–26), 356, 358.

Gazette's most venomous screeds, the Governor learned, came from the "violent and desperate" James Otis, "perhaps as wicked a man as lives," and at one point he considered asking the legislature to take action against this "most factious paper in America." Upon second thought, however, he refrained, doubtless fearing that the members would only back up the editors.[11] John Adams, another of the anonymous writers, urged the proprietors to still greater exertions:

> The stale, impudent insinuations of slander and sedition, with which the gormandizers of power have endeavored to discredit your paper, are so much the more to your honor. . . . Be not intimidated, therefore, by any terrors, from publishing with the utmost freedom, whatever can be warranted by the laws of your country . . . . I must and will repeat it, your paper deserves the patronage of every friend to his country.[12]

One barbed item in the *Boston Evening-Post* read: "Saturday last was executed Henry Halbert . . . for the murder of the son of Jacob Woolman.—*He will never pay any of the taxes unjustly laid on these once happy lands.*" [13]

In New York, John Holt, Parker's successor on the *New-York Gazette or Weekly Post-Boy,* set the pace, garnering such favor with the Sons of Liberty that they aided him financially from time to time. Once, to keep him out of jail, they defrayed a business debt of £440. Jonathan Watts, a member of the Governor's Council, wrote an English friend, "You will think the printers all mad, Holt particularly," and Lieutenant Governor Cadwallader Colden, then in charge of the province, raged that the newspapers employed

> every falshood that malice could invent to serve their purpose of exciting the People to disobedience of the Laws & to Sedition. At first they only denied the authority of Parliament to lay internal Taxes in the Colonies, but at last they have denied the Legislative authority of the Parliament in the Colonies . . . .

He imputed these subversive pieces to "some of the most popular lawyers," who were "Countenanced by some of the Judges & others

11 Bernard Papers, IV, 7–9, 275–276, V, 4, 46, 89, 100. Otis, however, actually blew hot and blew cold on the subject of parliamentary taxation. See Ellen E. Brennan, "James Otis: Recreant and Patriot, " *New England Quar.,* XII (1939), 691–725.

12 "A Dissertation on the Canon and Feudal Law," Adams, *Works,* III, 457–458.

13 *Boston Evening-Post,* Nov. 4, 1765, cited in *Acts of the Privy Council* (Colonial Ser., W. L. Grant and James Munro, eds.), VI (Hereford, 1912), 416.

in the highest trust in Government." General Gage, at Colden's elbow, pressed him to sue the culprits for seditious libel; but when the Lieutenant Governor and the Council on September 9, 1765, deliberated the matter, they, like the Bay Colony executive, judged that, "considering the present temper of the People, this is not a proper time to prosecute the Printers & Publishers." The Attorney General, trembling for his personal safety, eagerly concurred.[14]

News of the incident evidently leaked out, for the editors were more cautious during the next few weeks, and the propaganda temporarily assumed a different form. On September 21 a fake new journal, the *Constitutional Courant*, appeared on the streets, allegedly "Printed by ANDREW MARVEL, at the Sign of *the Bribe refused*, on *Constitutional Hill, North-America*," and "containing Matters interesting to LIBERTY, and no wise repugnant to LOY—ALTY." Actually, William Goddard, then in Holt's employ, had secretly struck off the sheet at Parker's shop in Woodbridge, N. J., on a press which, appropriately enough, seems to have once belonged to Zenger. The cartoon of the divided snake, earlier used at the time of the Albany Congress, headed the first page with the injunction: "JOIN or DIE." The unsigned articles dilated on "the chains of abject slavery just ready to be riveted about our necks," rejected the contention that to protest was treason, and excused the mass violence as "most justly chargeable to the authors and abettors of the Stamp Act." Indeed, stormed one writer, "We might as well belong to France, or any other power; none could offer a greater injury to our rights and liberties than is offered by the Stamp Act." [15]

Colden and the Council, though discovering where the publication had originated, again concluded that any punitive action would only "be the occasion for raising the Mob," so Colden compromised by glumly reporting his impotence to London. Away from New

[14] Beverly McAnear, "James Parker versus John Holt," N. J. Hist. Soc., *Procs.*, LIX (1941), 89; Watts to Lionel Monckton, Sept. 24, 1765, Mass. Hist., Soc., *Colls.*, ser. 4, X (1871), 576; Colden to H. S. Conway, Colden, *Letter Books* (N.-Y. Hist. Soc., *Colls.*, IX–X, 1876–77), II, 33–34, 36, 37, and *Letters and Papers* (*idem, Colls.*, LVI, 1923), VII, 58, 62.

[15] Albert Matthews, "The Snake Devices, 1754–1776, and the Constitutional Courant, 1765," Colonial Soc. of Mass., *Pubs.*, XI (1906–07), 421–446; Beverly McAnear, "James Parker versus William Weyman," N. J. Hist. Soc., *Procs.*, LIX (1941), 5–6. Andrew Marvell (1621–78) was a poet and M. P. who had opposed Charles II and advocated a republic.

York, the *Constitutional Courant* had no less effect. Presses in Boston and (presumably) in Philadelphia surreptitiously reprinted it, the *Boston Evening-Post* reproduced the snake design in one of its issues, and the *Newport Mercury* publicized some of the text. Like the New York executive, Governor Bernard rushed a copy of the "seditious" production to London, terming it "an infamous libell against the Government of Great Britain." He felt certain that Edes and Gill had perpetrated the local edition.[16] As no further numbers came out, Goddard and his confederates evidently felt they had sufficiently aroused the public.

Meanwhile, in Philadelphia, William Bradford of the *Pennsylvania Journal* headed the assault, with his two fellow editors not far behind. Like Edes and Holt, Bradford was a high Son of Liberty, serving on the committee of seven which forced John Hughes, the stamp agent, to resign. We catch another glimpse of him when he and Hall of the *Pennsylvania Gazette* provided a drum to call out one of the Stamp Act mobs. Joseph Galloway complained to Franklin that the newspapers of the town had "combined" to "print every thing inflammatory and nothing that is rational and cool"; but he overstated the case, for as "Americanus" he himself succeeded in publishing in Bradford's columns his own argument that the law, though unwise, was not unconstitutional—probably a concession by the printer to Galloway's importance in the community. Naturally Henry (Henrich) Miller, proprietor of the *Philadelphische Staatsbote*, the city's other sheet, stressed his special cause for grievance, though he reached only German readers. Along with argumentative material translated from Anglo-American contemporaries he displayed in large type the double tax on non-English publications and in righteous indignation assailed the "Stämpfel-Acte" as *"das unlandsverfassungsmässigste Gesetz so diese Colonie sich je hätten vorstellen können"*—the most unconstitutional law the colonies had ever known. He caustically reminded his readers that All Saints' Day, when the law was to go into force, was also the date of the dreadful Lisbon earthquake.[17]

---

16 Colden, *Letter Books*, II, 38–39, 45; Matthews, "Snake Devices," 435; Bernard correspondence in British Papers, IV, 30, and Bernard Papers, IV, 167–168, V, 34.
17 J. W. Wallace, *An Old Philadelphian, Colonial William Bradford* (Phila., 1884), 98–101, 365–366; Morgans, *Stamp Act Crisis*, 251, 254; Galloway to Franklin, Jan. 13, 1766, J. C. Miller, *Origins of the American Revolution* (Boston,

Though the newspapers in the smaller Northern towns wielded less influence, they too fed the conflagration. For example, Jared Ingersoll, who had been appointed the Connecticut stampman, anticipated Galloway in asserting that the press of his province seldom published "any thing that serves to inform the mind of such matters as tend to abate the peoples prejudices." As in Galloway's case, however, he managed to get his very protest printed. Even in New Jersey, which lacked any papers of its own, the royal governor testified that "the many Seditious inflammatory Writings" emanating from New York and Philadelphia had set the populace afire.[18]

Elsewhere, whenever the patriots felt it desirable, they founded new organs. On January 21, 1765, while the Stamp Act was yet in the offing, the Portsmouth Whigs, unduly apprehensive of the stand of the *New-Hampshire Gazette*, set up the *Portsmouth Mercury* to defend "the People, whose Liberties are dearer to them than their lives." And on July 5 Benjamin Mecom, though acknowledging that "Perhaps there was never a more unpromising Time for the Encouragement of another News-paper," resuscitated the New Haven *Connecticut Gazette* which had not appeared for more than a year, proclaiming his creed in a continuing, page-wide streamer: "Those who would give up *Essential Liberty*, to purchase a little *Temporary Safety*, deserve neither *Liberty* nor *Safety*." [19] But a similar effort by Goddard, who returned briefly from New York to reestablish the *Providence Gazette*, which had suspended in May for want of subscribers, did not at this time get beyond a single number: *A Providence Gazette Extraordinary*. Appearing on August 24, it hopefully displayed the motto: "VOX POPULI, VOX DEI," along with the biblical text: *"Where the Spirit of the Lord is, there is Liberty."*

Although the Southern editors exhibited less initiative than their Northern brethren, they played up all local evidences of indignation

---

1943), 289; "Americanus" in the *Pa. Journal*, Jan. 9, 1766; C. F. Dapp, "The Evolution of an American Patriot," Pa.-German Soc., *Procs.*, XXXII, pt. xxxii (1924), 19, 25–26, citing the *Staatsbote*, April 9, Oct. 27, 1765.

[18] Ingersoll in the *Conn. Gazette*, Sept. 13, 1765, cited in New Haven Hist. Soc., *Papers*, IX (1918), 333–334; William Franklin to the Board of Trade, Nov. 13, 1765, British Papers, IV, 52.

[19] Isaiah Thomas, *The History of Printing in America* (rev. ed., Am. Antiquarian Soc., *Trans. and Colls.*, V–VI, Albany, 1874), II, 86, 95. Mecom's motto probably originated with his uncle, Benjamin Franklin, who had used it in his *Historical Review of the Constitution and Government of Pennsylvania* (London, 1759).

and added descriptions of the Northern excitements as well as controversial articles from that section. John Hughes in accounting for his own ousting as Pennsylvania stamp agent blamed South and North alike for the gale of opinion that blew the collectors into limbo. "As a prelude to the destruction and disorder made by those mobs," he declared, "the printers in each Colony, almost without exception, stuffed their papers weekly for some time before with the *most inflammatory pieces* they could procure, and *excluded every thing that tended to cool the minds of the people.*" [20]

III

Even though no stamp officers were on hand when the fateful November 1 arrived, the heavy penalties for disobedience prescribed by the statute nevertheless remained in effect. Law was law despite the breakdown of the machinery of enforcement. Hence the editors had to determine what course to pursue. None meant to pay the tax, but this did not settle the question of whether or how to continue their papers.

As early as October 10 the *Maryland Gazette* began affixing to its title *Expiring: In uncertain Hopes of a Resurrection to Life again.* On the 28th the *New-York Mercury* announced it too would stop (providently adding, however: "May be had of the Printer hereof, *The Oppressive* STAMP–ACT, *Price 1s.*"), while concurrently the *Philadelphische Staatsbote* revealed its decision by donning black borders with a death's-head as its idea of the stamp. And then just before the appointed day the *Maryland Gazette* along with five other papers on the 31st—the *New-Hampshire Gazette*, the *New-York Gazette or Weekly Post-Boy*, the *Pennsylvania Journal*, the *Pennsylvania Gazette* and the *South-Carolina Gazette*—assumed similar mourning with piteous editorial farewells to their readers. The New-Hampshire sheet, moaning that the law was "as fatal to almost all that is dear to us, as the *Ides* of *March* were, to the Life of *Cæsar*," gasped, "*I must die*, or submit to that which *is worse* than Death, *be Stamp'd*, and lose my Freedom." The *Pennsylvania Journal*, topping all others in lugubrious display, made up its front page to

[20] John Hughes to the Commissioners of Stamps in London, Oct. 12, 1765, *Pa. Journal*, Sept. 4, 1766.

resemble a tombstone with funeral urns and skulls and crossbones. Under his title Bradford placed the legend: "EXPIRING: In Hopes of a Resurrection to LIFE again" and, along the margin, "Adieu, Adieu to the LIBERTY of the PRESS," with a coffin on the last page betokening the paper's demise "Of a STAMP in her Vitals."

If, as seems evident, the editors were merely testing public sentiment, they had every reason to rejoice at the results. "John Hampden," for example, threatened Holt in his own pages that, "should you at this critical Time, shut up the Press, and basely desert us, your House, Person, and Effects, will be in imminent Danger," and in Boston the printers were similarly warned of retaliation by "the enraged people." [21] Heartened by such signs of popular support—which the newspapermen themselves may have inspired—some chose to defy the law openly, others by subterfuge. Only a minority decided, for the time at least, to quit altogether.

The *New-London Gazette* and the *Connecticut Gazette*, both issued on November 1, set the pattern of brazenly continuing without stamps. The *Boston Gazette* on the 4th and the *New-York Gazette or Weekly Post-Boy* on the 7th followed their example, with Holt flaunting the motto: "The United Voice of all His Majesty's *free* and *loyal* subjects in America—LIBERTY, PROPERTY and *no* STAMPS," a fashion which the *New-Hampshire Gazette*, the *Boston Evening-Post* and the *Boston Post-Boy* under different circumstances imitated. Most surprising of all, William Weyman, who had halted regular publication of the *New-York Gazette* six months earlier because of business reverses, resumed full blast on November 25 also without stamps. On the other hand, Goddard's best attempts to "keep alive a Spirit of Liberty" by reviving his old journal in Rhode Island produced but a single further number, *A Providence Gazette Extraordinary*, which he brought out stampless on March 12, 1766.

A second group of journals also ignored the odious stamps but in a manner they hoped would circumvent the attendant penalties. Though retaining their regular titles they appeared anonymously. The *Newport Mercury* did this for two numbers before resuming undisguised, the *Boston Post-Boy* until March 17, 1766, and the *New-Hampshire Gazette*, the *Boston Evening-Post* and the *Massa-*

[21] *N.-Y. Gazette or Weekly Post-Boy*, Nov. 7, 1765; Boston report in the *N.-Y. Mercury*, Nov. 4.

chusetts *Gazette and Boston News-Letter* (the last dropping the second half of its name for further concealment) until news of the repeal reached America in May, 1766. Had the owners read the act carefully, however, they would have realized that the lack of an imprint actually exposed them to the extreme rigors of the law.[22] Three other organs—the *Pennsylvania Journal,* the *Pennsylvania Gazette* and the *New-York Mercury*—started on a similar path of evasion, using captions like *No Stamped Paper to be had*; but after a few weeks they restored their regular titles and later, with growing confidence, even the publishers' identities, though the *Gazette* did not do the latter until Franklin dropped his connection with it on January 30, 1766.[23]

The remaining journals, mostly in the South, met the crisis by suspending.[24] Only the *Georgia Gazette* ventured to continue openly and unstamped, the editor explaining, "No Stamp-Officer having yet arrived . . . this paper will be carried on as usual till he arrives, and begins to issue his stamps"; but then, under pressure of the royal governor and even before the stampman showed up, it too quit on November 21.[25] The *Maryland Gazette,* however, thanks probably to its proximity to the Northern centers of contagion, reversed the process. On December 10 appeared a lone number without stamps called *An Apparition of the late Maryland Gazette, which is not Dead but only Sleepeth*; on January 30, 1766, more hopefully, *The Maryland Gazette, Reviving*; and finally, on February 20, *The Maryland Gazette, Revived.*

Other Southern printers as time went on also resumed, though not always willingly. At Wilmington a mob compelled Andrew

[22] Such printers also usually omitted their papers' serial numbering, doubtless with the hope of putting their publications in the class of handbills, which apparently did not require stamps; but this scheme, even if held allowable by the courts, would not have saved them from the two-shilling tax on every advertisement "in any gazette, news paper, or other paper."

[23] The *Mercury* dropped its regular title for three issues, the *Journal* for one, and the *Gazette* for two (its second designation being *Remarkable Occurrences*); the publishers' names reappeared respectively on Dec. 2 and 19, 1765, and Feb. 6, 1766.

[24] According to Dapp, "Evolution of an American Patriot," 8, the *Philadelphische Staatsbote* also suspended and then, after skipping two numbers, started up again on unstamped paper, apparently without change of title or omission of imprint. The course of the biweekly *Germantowner Zeitung* cannot be determined, because no issues in 1765 and before Aug. 7, 1766, have survived.

[25] *Ga. Gazette,* Oct. 31, Nov. 14, 21, 1765. The stamp master, an Englishman, did not arrive until Jan. 3, 1766.

Steuart of the *North-Carolina Gazette* to do so on November 20, 1765, "at the Hazard of Life, being maimed, or have his Printing-Office destroy'd." His first number, containing no imprint, displayed a death's-head instead of a stamp. Unhappily, however, he faced the necessity of serving two masters. He presently found himself threatened with a horsewhipping for an article critical of the patriots, and then the Governor and Council suspended him as public printer for publishing "inflammatory Expressions" on the popular side. Steuart's last known issue was on February 26, 1766. In Charleston, where neither paper could be induced to resume, the Whigs persuaded Charles Crouch, a onetime apprentice of Peter Timothy's on the *South-Carolina Gazette*, to commence a third publication, the *South-Carolina Gazette and Country Journal*, on December 17, 1765.[26]

At Williamsburg, on the other hand, Alexander Purdie, announcing he was "Tired with an involuntary recess from business," started the *Virginia Gazette* again on March 7, 1766, unstamped and over his own imprint, with assurances that it would "be as free as any Gentleman can wish, or desire." Despite these fair words Purdie did not enjoy the Whigs' complete confidence; hence "some of the hot Burgesses"—to use Governor Francis Fauquier's phrase—got William Rind, lately of the *Maryland Gazette*, to undertake a rival *Virginia Gazette* in Williamsburg on May 16 with the promise of the legislative printing.[27] Though the newcomer took as his slogan "Open to ALL PARTIES, but Influenced by NONE," these words, as everyone understood, did not signify a free forum of discussion but, rather, that the contents would not have "an Imprimatur from a private Quarter" (the Governor), as was suspected of Purdie.[28] Whether or not Purdie lacked the required devotion at this period, he as well as Rind was to champion the cause zealously in the years ahead.

[26] W. L. Saunders and others, eds., *Colonial and State Records of North Carolina* (Raleigh, 1886–1906), VII, 124–125, 187–188; Thomas, *History of Printing*, II, 173; Peter Timothy to Benjamin Franklin, Sept. 3, 1768, *S. C. Hist. Mag.*, LV (1954), 162.

[27] Governor Francis Fauquier to the Board of Trade, April 7, 1766, British Papers, IV, 82; J. C. Oswald, *Benjamin Franklin, Printer* (Garden City, 1917), 147; Thomas, *History of Printing*, I, 335–336.

[28] Unsigned article in the *Va. Gazette* (Rind), May 30, 1766. As "A Constant Customer" put it, in the *Va. Gazette* (Purdie and Dixon), April 20, 1769, the motto afforded "an easy screen" behind which Rind "can, at any time, want room to do what he has not a mind to do."

IV

Thus throughout the colonies the printers in one manner or another defied the Stamp Act. Nearly all of them, moreover, continued to publish without interruption or else presently resumed, and the outburst of popular resentment was such as to beget four new sheets, two in New England and two in the South. Never again in like circumstances would the press present so united a front.

With the November day of reckoning once behind them, the editors only redoubled their propaganda, indicting British "tyranny," whipping up sentiment for transacting legal and other business without stamps, and abetting the boycott of British imports. As the Virginia Governor reported to the Ministry, "the Colonies reciprocally inflame each other, and where the fury will stop I know not." When stamped copies of Barbados and Nova Scotia papers reached Philadelphia, mobs promptly consigned them to the flames.[29]

In Massachusetts the "flagitious writings," so Governor Bernard notified London, rendered it hopeless for him to obtain the Assembly's co-operation in executing the Stamp Act. When he persisted in trying, however, a contributor in the *Boston Gazette*, January 6, 1766, bade him to "Retreat or you are ruined"—a thinly veiled warning which caused one of his supporters (and doubtless more than one) to burst out that Edes and Gill "ought to be committed for that single stroke." [30] A better opportunity offered itself, however, when Otis, writing as "Freeborn Armstrong," charged Lieutenant Governor Hutchinson with secretly proposing measures of enforcement in the Council. This time the nettled Bernard asked the upper chamber to take action against the printers for a "breach of priviledge tending to over throw all Government," but the Council, believing that they would only "be rescued by the Mob," contented itself with a bald denial.[31]

From the Crown officials in New York arose similar anguished cries. Indeed, in Bernard's view, the Manhattan editors even sur-

[29] Fauquier to H. S. Conway, Dec. 11, 1765, British Papers, II, 47; *Pa. Journal*, Dec. 12, 19.

[30] Bernard to H. S. Conway, Nov. 25, 1765, and to John Pownall, Jan. 11, 1766, Bernard Papers, IV, 170, V, 71; John Adams, *Works*, II, 181.

[31] Bernard to the Board of Trade, March 10, 1766, Bernard Papers, IV, 210–211; Hutchinson, *Massachusetts Bay*, III, 145–146; *Boston Gazette*, Jan. 27, Feb. 3, 1766.

passed the Boston newspapermen in "declarations of Intention to resist" and other "acts of Mischief." As earlier, however, the authorities, like those in the Bay Colony, were afraid to move against the offenders. When the Sons of Liberty heard that an officer on a visiting British warship had said that "Holt, was he in England would be hanged for the licentiousness of his Paper," they vainly demanded a retraction and then assembled a mob to board the craft and seize the culprit. Only formidable preparations by several naval vessels in the harbor saved his skin.[32]

In two other colonies the still unslaked wrath against the former stamp agents led the press to deal them a final blow. Late in November, 1765, the Connecticut Sons of Liberty frightened Ingersoll into surrendering his letters concerning the Stamp Act, and early in January the *New-London Gazette* published garbled passages from them. "It is a time," Ingersoll frothed privately, "when mankind Seem to think they have a right not only to Shoot at me with the Arrow that flyeth by Day, but to Assassinate me in the dark . . . ." The disclosures so incensed the populace that the unlucky man had to promise to write nothing further to England without prior inspection by the Whig leaders.[33]

At Philadelphia, Hughes found himself in a similar plight when the *Pennsylvania Journal* on September 4, 1766, divulged two letters he had written the Stamp Commissioners in England. These, which Bradford said he had obtained from a Londoner "of character and integrity," advocated condign suppression of the defiers of the law and particularly the printers, whose "violent and inflammatory pieces . . . exceed the North Britain, No. 45." Hughes, denying that he had been fairly quoted, immediately filed a libel suit for £1200 against Bradford, but then as quickly withdrew it, doubtless realizing that a jury would almost certainly find against him. The editor, however, attributed Hughes's change of heart to

[32] Bernard to H. S. Conway, Jan. 23, 1766, Bernard Papers, IV, 195; John and James Montresor, *Journals* (G. D. Scull, ed.; N.-Y. Hist. Soc., *Colls.*, XIV, 1881), 353–354. For General Gage's explosive views of the New York press, see his *Correspondence with the Secretaries of State* (C. E. Carter, ed., New Haven, 1931–33), I, 78, 82, II, 317.

[33] Ingersoll to W. S. Johnson, Dec. 2, 1765, New Haven Colony Hist. Soc., *Papers*, IX (1918), 361; Ingersoll's "Advertisement," *ibid.*, 369–371, taken from the *Conn. Gazette*, Jan. 10, 1766; L. H. Gipson, *Jared Ingersoll* (New Haven, 1920), 200–202. In self-justification he published the correct text of the letters in pamphlet form in June.

"consciousness of his guilt" and flayed him for seeking to "demolish the Liberty of the Press, that invaluable privilege of a free people." [34] Hughes had wrecked whatever chance he still had of reestablishing himself in public esteem.

V

The *Boston Gazette* gleefully commented that, *"If any of* Hughes's *Brother* Stampmerchants . . . *have transmitted similar Letters, . . . 'tis hoped proper Diligence will be used to detect and expose them to the Contempt and Infamy they deserve."* [35] But the time was past for harassing any more of the tribe. In May official word had arrived of the repeal of the Stamp Act on March 18, and hosannas replaced the former dirges in the newspapers. No element of the population, indeed, could view the outcome with such profound satisfaction as the pressmen. Though Parliament granted only partial relief to the merchant class and in the Declaratory Act affirmed the unqualified right to tax America, it made a clean sweep of the special burdens on the printer-editors and did this without imposing any punishment on them. In fact, it absolved all violators of the act on the curious ground that no stamped paper had been available.[36]

Little wonder that the newspapers emerged from the contest with an exhilarated sense of their role in the community. No longer mere purveyors of intelligence, they had become engines of opinion. By braving with impunity constituted authority and asserting their right to criticize they had demonstrated the power of the press and earned the lasting regard of their countrymen. "Had it not been for the continual informations from the Press," wrote one commentator, "a junction of all the people . . . would have been scarcely conceivable." "The argumentative pieces, letters and addresses in the newspapers have had a singular use in the great and good cause," asserted another, who considered that "The press hath never done greater service since its first invention." "However little some may think of common News-Papers," added a third, "to a wise man they

---

[34] *Pa. Journal*, Sept. 4, 11, 18, 1766. The interest elsewhere in the Hughes incident is shown by the fact that the *N.–Y. Mercury*, Sept. 11, and the *Boston Gazette*, Sept. 22, reprinted the letters.

[35] *Ibid.*, Sept. 15, 1766.

[36] *Parliamentary Debates* (T. C. Hansard, comp.), XVI (London, 1813), 161.

appear the Ark of God, for the Safety of the People. Their fullness of general entertainment, small Bulk and Price, recommend them to everyone, and . . . awaken the Minds of many to a solid inquiry of interests they would otherwise not dream of." [37]

In future political struggles the editors would hold fast the ground they had so hardily won. Though no such emergency loomed at the moment, they nevertheless strengthened their ranks when Goddard, obtaining at last his desired guarantee of 800 subscribers, re-established the *Providence Gazette* on a permanent basis on August 9, 1766. In New York, however, it looked for a time as if the Whigs would lose their most fiery tribune. Holt, bogged down in debt for the lease of Parker's printery several years before, had no choice but to return it to its owner with the *New-York Gazette or Weekly Post-Boy*. The Sons of Liberty, however, solved the difficulty by helping Holt obtain a press and equipment of his own. Accordingly, when Parker resumed his paper on October 16, Holt on the same day started a new one which, significantly enough, revived the name of Zenger's famous *New-York Journal*. Declaring that he had never "deserted the Cause of Liberty and his Country, when it was most dangerous to assert them," Holt asked that "his former Services will not be forgotten" with tranquillity now restored.[38] He was not disappointed in this hope.

The successful defiance of the imperial enactment, however, did not leave the press free to discuss local affairs undisturbed. In October, 1766, the editors of the two *Virginia Gazettes* found themselves facing trial for an identical article allegedly libeling the highest provincial court for granting bail improperly in a murder case, but the grand jury quickly released them. The next month the New York Assembly reprimanded Weyman for carelessness in publishing in the *New-York Gazette* a grossly inaccurate text of a legislative

[37] "A Countryman" in *A Providence Gazette Extraordinary*, March 12, 1766; "A Son of Liberty" in *ibid.*, also in the *Boston Post-Boy*, March 24, and the *N.–H. Gazette*, April 11; "Providus" in the *Providence Gazette*, Dec. 12, 1767, also in the *N.–H. Gazette*, Dec. 24, the *Pa. Gazette*, Jan. 7, 1768, and the *Va. Gazette* (Purdie and Dixon), Jan. 7. See further *"An* ODE *Occasioned by the Repeal of the* STAMP–ACT, *and the present* FREEDOM *of the* PRESS," in *ibid.*, Aug. 15, 1766.

[38] Parker's letters to Benjamin Franklin, Mass. Hist. Soc., *Procs.*, ser. 2, XVI (1902), 210–217; and New Haven Colony Hist. Soc., *Papers*, IX (1918), 400–402. According to Frederic Hudson, *Journalism in the United States, from 1690 to 1872* (N. Y., 1873), 121, George Clinton and Philip Schuyler were the prime movers in Holt's new venture. The quotation is from a trial number of the *Journal* on May 29, 1766.

document.[39] But these attempts at restraint could hardly reassure the Crown officials and their followers, who knew that they could not count on newspaper support if a conflict between the colonies and the mother country were involved. Their best hope lay in fighting fire with fire with a Tory-oriented press. That was the lesson they learned from the Stamp Act troubles and the strategy they sought to employ when the next crisis arose.

[39] *Va. Gazette* (Purdie and Dixon), June 20, July 11, 18, 25, Aug. 22, 29, Sept. 12, 19, Oct. 10, 17, 1766; anon., "Old Virginia Editors," *William and Mary College Quar.*, VII (1899), 15; and, for Weyman, Thomas, *History of Printing*, II, 111–112.

Chapter V

Boston: Foundry of Propaganda

THE POLITICAL BREATHING SPELL came to an end when Parliament in June, 1767, inaugurated a new plan of imperial control. This legislation, fathered by Charles Townshend, Chancellor of the Exchequer, assessed duties on American imports of glass, lead, paper, painters' colors and tea, stiffened further the regulations against smuggling, and set up a Board of Customs Commissioners in Boston to administer the provisions. Since the program was not to take effect until November 20, the colonists had several months to ponder the situation. From a constitutional standpoint they occupied a somewhat weaker position than during the Stamp Act. Then they had stressed the unlawfulness of internal or excise taxes but had not always made it clear that they felt equally strongly about external or tariff duties. Hence to many minds, both British and American, their argument left the gate ajar for unlimited port levies, and indeed Townshend had based his scheme on just that distinction. Parliament in the same session violated the high Whig conception of colonial home rule in still another way by suspending the New York legislature until it should fully carry out an act of 1765 for quartering British troops.[1]

[1] George III, cc. 41, 46, 56, 59; C. R. Ritcheson, *British Politics and the American Revolution* (Norman, 1954), 99–100. The measure respecting New York proved to have only an academic importance, for, unbeknownst to the Ministry, the legislature had made the concession a few days in advance of the passage of the act. C. H. Van Tyne, *The Causes of the War of Independence* (Boston, 1922), 276–278.

85

I

There were at this time twenty-six newspapers in America, distributed geographically very much as before.[2] The editors, flushed by their victory over the Stamp Act, would doubtless in most cases have opposed the Townshend Acts without a special incentive to do so, but, as before, the legislation provided one. Parliament, taking advantage of the fact that the colonial production of paper was so small that most of it had to be brought from England, had placed taxes on sixty-seven grades of the imported article. The pressmen thus faced higher costs not only as journalists but also as job printers, book publishers and stationers. And, considering the persisting hard times, they could not, if they had wished, pass on these added expenses to their customers.

A newspaper writer hardly needed to point out that "in *substance* and *right*" no difference existed between paying "the rates mentioned in the *Stamp-Act*, on the *use* of paper," and "these duties, on the *importation* of it. It is nothing but the edition of a former book, with a new title page." Moreover, he warned, "If the parliament have a right to lay a duty of Four Shillings and Eight-pence on a hundred weight of glass, or a ream of paper, they have a right to lay a duty of any other sum on either." [3] In the long run the printers might hope for partial relief from an increased output of the untaxed domestic paper, and they did what they could to bring this about,[4] but meanwhile they joined the general outcry against the Townshend system as a whole.

"The proceedings in the newspapers are precisely the same as those preceding the former disturbances," reported Governor Bernard two months after Parliament passed the acts, and Lieutenant Governor Colden similarly wrote shortly after the levies took effect, "Every suggestion that could tend to lessen the attachment to the mother Country, and to raise an Odium against her, have been re-

---

[2] This figure does not include the *Portsmouth Mercury* and the *North-Carolina Gazette*, which appear to have ceased before 1767, or a new sheet, the *Wahre und Wahrscheinliche Begebenheiten* (Germantown), which lasted for only a few numbers during 1766.

[3] "The Pennsylvania Farmer" (John Dickinson) in the *Pa. Chronicle*, Dec. 9, 1767, Jan. 11, 1768, also Dickinson, *Writings* (P. L. Ford, ed.; Hist. Soc. of Pa., *Memoirs*, XIV, 1895), I, 317, 356.

[4] See later, Appendix B, for the efforts to promote colonial papermaking.

peatedly published. The People are familiarised to read Seditious if not treasonable Papers." [5] In reality, however, the press even in Boston and New York was still blindly groping for a clear-cut theoretical argument against the impositions, while in the other colonies the protests avoided the constitutional question almost entirely. The *Boston Gazette*, August 17, 1767, seeking a way out of the impasse, spread on its first page the English Petition of Right of 1628, that "beautiful and strong Pillar of the English Constitution, whose Foundation is laid in the natural Rights of Men," and followed it the next week with copious extracts from Magna Charta. But these historic documents shed very inconclusive light on the constitutional issues currently at stake.

Trying then a different approach, the *Gazette* opened its columns to attacks on Parliament's coercion of New York. "If our legislative authority can be suspended whenever we refuse obedience to laws we never consented to," wrote "A. F." on August 31, "we may as well . . . acknowledge ourselves slaves." "Sui Imperator" in the same number averred that "my blood is chill'd, and creeps cold through my stiffened veins" because of the "shocking" encroachment on colonial rights. Agreeing with "A. F." that this restraint on one province threatened all the others as well, he recalled the lines of the "celebrated Poet":

> When Flames your Neighbour Dwellings seize
> With instant Rage your own shall blaze,
> Then haste to stop the spreading Fire,
> Which if neglected rises higher.

But these exhortations also brought little response. Indeed, in Bernard's opinion, "a general Abhorrence of the inflammatory Papers" was "expressed thro' the Town." [6]

In the circumstances the newspapers at this stage strove mainly to play up the harmful effects of the commercial and revenue restrictions on an economy mired in depression. Parliament's heartless action, they cried, called for retaliation in kind. As "M. Y." put it in

[5] Bernard to Lord Shelburne, Aug. 24, 1767, British Papers Relating to the American Revolution (Sparks MSS., Harvard College Library), I, 74; Colden to Shelburne, Nov. 23, *Letter Books* (N.-Y. Hist. Soc., *Colls.*, IX–X, 1876–77), II, 135.

[6] Letter to Richard Jackson, Sept. 14, 1767, Bernard Papers (Sparks MSS., Harvard College Library), VI, 47. For the reaction in Parliament, see later, Appendix C.

the *Boston Gazette*, September 14, 1767, "the free-born sons of those truly brave ancestors, who traversed a boisterous ocean, and settled a howling wilderness," must import and use as little British merchandise as possible. The press throughout the Northern colonies soon rang with the slogan: *"Save your Money, and save your Country!"* [7] Other scribes urged domestic manufacturing as the handmaid of nonimportation, the *Boston Gazette* and the *Newport Mercury* going so far as to offer free advertising to local weavers.[8]

II

Something more was needed, however, to evoke the united front of Stamp Act times. Appeals to material self-interest could excite only a limited reaction. Even in the North, where the Townshend Acts had their chief economic impact, an unmistakable constitutional issue would further energize the forces of opposition; in the South, where the economic objections had less bearing, it was essential. Such a reinforcement would also cement the support of America's well-wishers in Britain.

At this critical moment the *Pennsylvania Chronicle* published the "Letters from a Farmer in Pennsylvania to the Inhabitants of the British Colonies" in twelve successive installments from December 2, 1767, to February 15, 1768. So masterly was this demonstration of the unconstitutionality of the duties that the press almost universally reprinted the essays, affording them a speedy continent-wide circulation.[9] They also came out in pamphlet form several weeks after the *Chronicle* brought them to a close. The endless speculation provoked by the mystery of the "Farmer's" identity further whetted popular interest. Governor Bernard, scouting the report that Daniel Dulany of Maryland was the author, thought at first that the series had originated in New York, then afterward came to believe that parts of it at least carried an unmistakable Boston stamp.

---

[7] *Boston Gazette*, Nov. 2, 1767; *Pa. Chronicle*, Nov. 11; *Boston Evening-Post*, Nov. 16; *Boston Post-Boy*, Nov. 16; *Pa. Journal*, Nov. 26; *Pa. Gazette*, Nov. 26; *N.–H. Gazette*, Nov. 27; *Newport Mercury*, Nov. 30.

[8] *Boston Gazette*, Nov. 2, 1767; *Newport Mercury*, Dec. 7.

[9] According to P. L. Ford, the editor of Dickinson's *Writings*, I, 283, every newspaper "with but four known exceptions" carried the series. They were even reprinted locally in the *Pennsylvania Gazette* and the *Pennsylvania Journal*.

As late as a month after the "Letters" concluded, a Philadelphian heard variously that they had emanated from New England or been written by John Dickinson or Joseph Galloway.[10] No one, apparently, took seriously the fiction that an actual farmer was responsible.

The unknown, it presently transpired, was indeed Dickinson, a prominent lawyer-politician in Pennsylvania, who had earlier indited an influential pamphlet against the Stamp Act. Explicitly rejecting the distinction between internal and external taxes, Dickinson propounded one between taxation as incidental to the regulation of imperial trade and taxation primarily for purposes of revenue. Only Parliament could impose the first; only the provincial legislatures the second. He likened the Townshend exactions to "a bird sent out over the waters, to discover, whether the waves, that lately agitated this part of the world, are yet subsided," and laid down as maxims *"that we cannot be* HAPPY, *without being* FREE —that we cannot be free, *without being secure in our property—* that *we* cannot be secure in our property, *if, without our consent, others may, as by right, take it away."*

The "Pennsylvania Farmer" wrote calmly, almost with an air of Olympian detachment. He strongly counseled against "hot, rash, disorderly proceedings," declaring that the way to redress lay in petitions supported by abstention from British manufactures and the cultivation of industry and thrift.[11] Though the advice against violence made little impression, his constitutional formula supplied what the Whigs in every colony had been avidly waiting for. Even Bernard realized that Dickinson had articulated "a Bill of Rights in the Opinion of the Americans," and foresaw rightly that "Parliament may enact declaratory Acts as many as they please; but they must not expect any real obedience." While the newspapers proceeded to step up their attack, town assemblages and grand juries voted thanks to the "celebrated Farmer," patriot diners toasted the "ingenious Author," and writers in the press extolled his virtues in

[10] Bernard to John Pownall, Jan. 9, 16, Feb. 8, 1768, Bernard Papers, VI, 59–60, 62–63, 89; John Macpherson, Jr., to William Patterson, March 11, 1768, *Pa. Mag. of History and Biography*, XXIII (1899–1900), 53–54. In England, Lord Hillsborough suspected Franklin of being the author. V. W. Crane, ed., *Benjamin Franklin's Letters to the Press* (Durham, 1950), 121.

[11] Dickinson, *Writings*, I, 324–325, 327–328, 396, 400.

both prose and poetry. Samuel Adams could conceive of no greater compliment to the Philadelphian than to say after meeting him, "He is a true Bostonian." [12]

The journalistic warfare touched off by the "Farmer's Letters" raged most fiercely in New England and the Middle provinces, whence it spread to the South, thanks to what a Tory called "the dirty trade of copying." [13] For additional effect the editors in every section regularly clipped pro-American items from the London prints and documented these with extracts from letters of English sympathizers to colonial friends.[14] A welter of local incidents—legislative wrangles with governors, collisions between mobs and customs officers, the dispatch of British forces to Boston in 1768, conflicts between civilians and soldiers in both New York and Boston two years later—sowed other dragon's teeth. And in these circumstances the issue of liberty of the press once more came to the fore.

Meanwhile the movement to boycott British imports, starting in the autumn of 1767, coursed through the Northern provinces during 1768 and then swept over the South. The newspapers ardently furthered the crusade, and when growing opposition to the restraints threatened to undermine the agreements, the printers publicized the decrees of the enforcement committees stigmatizing violators as "Enemies to their Country." [15] They thus played an essential role in proscribing fellow citizens for doing what the law of the land gave them every right to do.

[12] Bernard to Richard Jackson, Feb. 20, 1768, Bernard Papers, VI, 93; Adams to Joseph Warren, Sept. 25, 1774, W. V. Wells, *The Life and Public Services of Samuel Adams* (Boston, 1865), II, 236. Among other numerous marks of esteem a Charleston waxworks displayed Dickinson's image "as large as the Life." *S.–C. Gazette*, Jan. 31, 1771.

[13] Jonathan Watts of New York to Lionel Monckton, Jan. 23, 1768, Mass. Hist. Soc. *Colls.*, ser. 4, X (1871), 600.

[14] British colonial officials took particular umbrage at these English letters. In the words of Governor Sir Henry Moore of New York, they "could serve no other purpose but that of widening the breach between the Mother Country and the Colonies." Letter to Lord Hillsborough, June 3, 1769, E. B. Callaghan and Berthold Fernow, comps., *Documents Relative to the Colonial History of the State of New York* (Albany, 1856–87), VIII, 171. See also Thomas Gage, *Correspondence with the Secretaries of State* (C. E. Carter, ed., New Haven, 1931–33), I, 197, II, 522.

[15] The New York merchants' agreement of Aug. 27, 1768, appears to have first adopted the practice and to have employed this precise phrase. The Philadelphia merchants preferred the expression "an Enemy to the Liberties of America"; the Bostonians, "an Enemy to the Constitution of his Country"; and the Savannah nonimporters, "no Friend to his Country." *N.Y. Journal*, Sept. 8, 1768; *Pa. Gazette*, Aug. 3, 1769; *Boston Gazette*, Aug. 14, 1769; *Ga. Gazette*, Sept. 20, 1769.

In these divers ways the press built boldly upon the foundations laid during the Stamp Act crisis.

III

The Boston editors set the pattern for New England and in considerable degree for the other colonies as well. In the Yankee metropolis were found the shrewdest Whig politicians in all America, past masters at the game of flouting authority; and there too now was the Customs Board, the imperial agency charged with executing the Townshend program. Provincial issues, adroitly exploited in the newspapers, had kept the popular leaders squabbling with Governor Bernard ever since the repeal of the Stamp Act, for the patriots had a humorless way of construing his every move to thwart their plans as an infraction of their constitutional rights. "As the Business of the faction is to conduct the Proceedings of the Genl Court to the purpose of inflamg the People," Bernard complained, "they print everything." [16]

Until the publication of the "Farmer's Letters," however, this propaganda had failed to arouse the public to the much greater peril of the new ministerial measures. Dickinson, far off in Philadelphia, took regretful note of this. Sending an advance text of his essays to James Otis, he observed that, "whenever the Cause of American Freedom is to be vindicated, I look towards the Province of Massachusetts Bay. She must, as she has hitherto done, first kindle the Sacred Flame . . . ." [17] With the ammunition Dickinson himself so opportunely provided, the Bostonians made a new start. As the Customs Commissioners noted, the very "moderation" and "parade of learning" of Dickinson's treatise had a "most mischievous tendency." [18] Moreover, coming from a distant colony, the "Letters" elevated the local partisan bickerings to the plane of a continental struggle for basic liberties.

The dingy office on Queen Street, where Edes and Gill each Mon-

[16] Letter to Richard Jackson, Feb. 18, 1767, Bernard Papers, VI, 14.

[17] Letter of Dec. 5, 1767, John Adams and others, *Warren-Adams Letters* (W. C. Ford, ed.; Mass. Hist. Soc., *Colls.*, LXXII–LXXIII, 1917–25), I, 3. Bernard deduced the existence of this advance copy from the fact that the "Printers of the Faction" published some of the installments sooner than had the Philadelphia newspapers. Letter to John Pownall, Jan. 16, 1768, Bernard Papers, VI, 62–63.

[18] Letter to the Lords of the Treasury, Feb. 12, 1768, Mass. Hist. Soc., *Procs.*, LV (1921–22), 265.

day put out the *Boston Gazette,* buzzed with activity. There Otis, Samuel Adams, Joseph Warren, Josiah Quincy, Jr., Benjamin Church and their cronies consorted to draft jeremiads against the Townshend Acts and local Crown officials. Similar sessions at other times and places occurred at least weekly, according to Lieutenant Governor Hutchinson. John Adams, for example, tells of spending a Sunday evening with Otis, Samuel Adams, William Davis and the printer John Gill "preparing for the next day's newspaper,—a curious employment, cooking up paragraphs, articles, occurrences, &c., working the political engine!" With good reason Bernard deemed Otis and Samuel Adams "the principal Managers of the Boston Gazette." Little wonder that Edes and Gill won the Tory opprobrium of "foul-mouthed Trumpeters of Sedition." [19]

Adams, if less brilliantly endowed than Otis, possessed the steadier purpose as well as a talent which Hutchinson acidly described as that of "artfully and fallaciously insinuating into the minds of his readers a prejudice against the characters of all whom he attacked." [20] This grim, tireless patriot wrote for the *Gazette* under twelve or more pseudonyms during the Townshend years, besides overseeing the work of fellow contributors; as "Vindex" alone he furnished five articles.[21] "The temper of the people may be surely learnt from that infamous paper;" attested a leading Tory, ". . . for if they are not in the temper of the writer at the time of the publication, yet it is looked upon as the ORACLE, and they soon bring their temper to it." [22] No doubt this jaundiced soul relished the story of the Negro who, upon hearing from one of the editors that news

[19] Edes in the *Boston Gazette,* Jan. 1, 1797, and Sept. 17, 1798, reprinted in Frederic Hudson, *Journalism in the United States* (N. Y., 1872), 165–167; Thomas Hutchinson to John Cushing, Aug. 5, 1768, Mass. Hist. Soc., *Procs.,* ser. 2, XX (1906–07), 536; Thomas Hutchinson, *The History of the Province of Massachusetts Bay,* III (London, 1828), 167; John Adams's diary, Sept. 3, 1769, in his *Works* (C. F. Adams, ed., Boston, 1850–56), II, 219; Bernard to Lord Shelburne, March 5, 1768, Bernard Papers, VI, 273; "Tacitus" in the *Boston Gazette,* Dec. 21, 1767.

[20] Hutchinson, *Massachusetts Bay,* III, 295.

[21] H. A. Cushing, the editor of *The Writings of Samuel Adams* (N. Y., 1904–08), supplies these identifications. See also Wells, *Samuel Adams,* I, 445 *n.* Evidence of his supervision of other writings is indicated by the fact that some of the articles of Josiah Quincy, Jr. (who used the pen names "Hyperion" and "An Independant"), bore the direction to the editors: "Let Samuel Adams Esq. correct the press." Josiah Quincy, *Memoir of the Life of Josiah Quincy Jun.* (Boston, 1825), 11–13, 18–29.

[22] Letter of Andrew Oliver, May 11, 1768, Thomas Hutchinson and Andrew Oliver, *Letters* (London, 1774), 27. See also *ibid.,* 30–31.

was scarce, replied, "Well, if you've nothing new, massa Edes, I s'pose you print the same dam old lie over again." [23]

The *Boston Evening-Post* provided still another outlet. Dr. Thomas Young, a fiery partisan, wrote for it under nine different pen names during 1768–69,[24] and among other contributors the indefatigable Adams, dividing his energies, managed to do six pieces for it as "Candidus." The Fleet brothers, however, opened their vehicle to British supporters as well. As one Tory put it, the "Dirtcasters" of the patriot party filled "all the Pages and Columns" of the *Gazette* and only "the Holes and Corners and other private Purlieus" of the *Evening-Post*.[25] Bernard, for his part, saw no difference between the two, reporting to the Ministry that both *"teemed with Publications of the most daring nature, denying the Authority of the Supreme Legislature and tending to excite the people to an Opposition to its Laws."* [26] It probably did not escape him that the Fleets along with Edes and Gill attended the Sons of Liberty banquet at Dorchester in 1769 to celebrate the original rioting against the Stamp Act.[27] Undoubtedly the Governor applauded, if in fact he did not inspire, the Vice-Admiralty Court's withdrawal that year of its advertising from the two papers.[28]

The press, moreover, practiced the art of concealment as well as of disclosure. Thus, when Bernard could find no mention of a futile mob demonstration against a customs inspector, he learned that "the Sons of Liberty had forbid all the Printers publishing any Thing of it." To the home authorities he directed the not unnatural query: "If *the King's Government* should assume such a Power, what would they say?" To add to his unhappiness came word of the establishment in Salem of the *Essex Gazette* on August 2, 1768, the first Massachusetts journal outside Boston. Its founder Samuel Hall, lately of the *Newport Mercury*, promptly announced he would "assiduously endeavor" to promote "a due sense of the Rights and Lib-

---

[23] William Tudor, *The Life of James Otis* (Boston, 1823), 450 *n*.

[24] Harbottle Dorr, a Boston Son of Liberty, provided these and other identifications in marginal notations on a collection of newspapers now in the Massachusetts Historical Society.

[25] "Tacitus" quotes this comment in the *Boston Gazette*, Dec. 21, 1767.

[26] *The Barrington-Bernard Correspondence* (Edward Channing and A. C. Coolidge, eds., Cambridge, 1912), 266.

[27] Mass. Hist. Soc., *Procs.*, XI (1869–70), 140–142.

[28] "Journal of the Times," April 14, 1769, in the *Boston Evening-Post*, June 12, 1769.

erties of our Country." The new paper brought timely support to the patriot press at the capital.[29]

Boston's two other sheets leaned to the British side, but neither possessed the grit for militant advocacy. Richard Draper of the *Massachusetts Gazette and Boston News-Letter* was also the official printer for the Governor and Council. Mild-mannered and sickly, he undoubtedly quailed at the *Boston Gazette*'s warning: "Thy Paper will never gain the better Circulation if too frequently thou art made a Cat's paw to Individuals, or a Party in judging thy Superiors." [30] At any rate Draper emulated the Whig editors in publishing the "Farmer's Letters" and from time to time carried other patriot propaganda. John Green and Joseph Russell, who conducted the *Boston Post-Boy*, were also, in John Adams's opinion, "harmless, dovelike, inoffensive." Perhaps to keep them in this subdued state, the Whig-controlled branch of the legislature had given them its business. Nevertheless the Customs Board, assured by Bernard that the pair were privately "well affected to Government," awarded them its own printing, the largest contract of the kind in all America, from which the partners eventually derived nearly £1931 down to 1775. On the Board's confidential advice they declined to publish the "Farmer's Letters," and this fact, coupled with the stigma of running a subsidized press, soon lost them the bulk of their subscribers, as well as the work of the House of Representatives with considerable other trade. In their own words, "almost their whole dependance" was thereafter on their pay from the Crown, though as editors they continued to show little spirit.[31]

Disappointed with this feeble journalistic support, the Governor's Council on April 11, 1768, provided for a new organ, the *Massa-*

[29] Bernard to Lord Hillsborough, July 18–19, 1768, Francis Bernard and others, *Letters to the Ministry* (Boston, 1769), 44–46; Harriet S. Tapley, ed., *Salem Imprints* (Salem, 1927), 8–10; J. D. Phillips, *Salem in the Eighteenth Century* (Boston, 1937), 299.

[30] "Anonymous" in the *Boston Gazette*, Oct. 5, 1767. Isaiah Thomas characterizes Draper in *The History of Printing in America* (rev. ed., Am. Antiquarian Soc., *Trans. and Colls.*, V–VI, 1874), I, 145–147. Draper received government pay for all official insertions (except the Governor's speeches, which he treated as news) at the rate of one dollar for three column-inches and four dollars for a whole column. Robert Thompson to Richard Bulkeley, March 23, 1768, Andrew Oliver, Letter Book (Gay Transcripts, Mass. Hist. Soc.), I, 9–10.

[31] John Adams, Notes, 1770 (MS. in Mass. Hist. Soc.); O. M. Dickerson, "British Control of American Newspapers on the Eve of the Revolution," *New England Quar.*, XXIV (1951), 455–459, 466–467, and *The Navigation Acts and the American Revolution* (Phila., 1951), 263.

chusetts Gazette, in umbilical connection with these two sheets. Beginning on May 23, this supplement, frankly labeled "Published by Authority," appeared on Monday with the *Boston Post-Boy* and on Thursday with Draper's paper, which accordingly shortened its name to the *Boston News-Letter*. The strange publication won a derisive reception from the townsfolk as the "Court Gazette" and the "Adam and Eve paper" and, in fact, proved too official in tone to accomplish its intended purpose. Hence after sixteen months, on September 25, 1769, this open attempt to manipulate opinion came to an end, with Draper resuming his longer title and Green and Russell enlarging theirs to the *Massachusetts Gazette and Boston Post-Boy*.[32] By that time, however, as we shall see, the British cause had acquired a bellicose champion in an unexpected quarter.

IV

While seeking to meet propaganda with propaganda, the government also employed legal weapons against the opposition. It moved first against Joseph Hawley, a Northampton attorney and member of the House of Representatives, who had belabored the Superior Court in the *Evening-Post*, July 6 and 13, 1767, for holding one of his clients guilty of complicity in a Stamp Act riot. In high dudgeon Hutchinson as Chief Justice told the grand jury at its August session that "it is very dangerous to meddle with, or strike at this Court." Though "Liberty of the Press is doubtless a very great Blessing," he conceded, it "means no more than a Freedom for every Thing to pass from the Press without a Licence," not "a Liberty of reviling and calumniating all Ranks and Degrees of Men with Impunity, all Authority with Ignominy." Nevertheless he did not venture to request an indictment, contenting himself with disbarring Hawley from further practice before the tribunal.[33]

[32] Albert Matthews, "Bibliographical Notes on Boston Newspapers, 1704–1780," Colonial Soc. of Mass., *Pubs.*, IX (1907), 430–432, 470–471, 484–493.

[33] Later regretting this action in the belief that it had driven Hawley into the arms of the extremists, Hutchinson after two years secured his reinstatement without, however, changing Hawley's political course. On this whole episode, see Josiah Quincy, Jr., *Reports of Cases Argued and Adjudged in the Superior Court of Judicature of the Province of Massachusetts Bay between 1761 and 1772* (S. M. Quincy, ed., Boston, 1865), 244–250; E. F. Brown, *Joseph Hawley, Colonial Radical* (N. Y., 1931), 63–68, 118, 121; *Boston Gazette*, Sept. 28, 1767.

The incident, as Hutchinson might have foreseen, produced just the opposite of the desired effect. "Freedom of Speech," shrieked the *Boston Gazette*, "is the great Bulwark of Liberty; they prosper and die together: *And it is the Terror of Traytors and Oppressors, and a Barrier against them*." [34] As other contributors joined in, Hawley himself returned to the fray in the *Evening-Post*, January 18, 1768. Declaring that a lawyer when admitted to the bar did not thereby relinquish the "common rights and liberties of his fellow subjects" to criticize public acts, he compared the Court's conduct to "the secrecy and darkness of a Romish inquisition."

For the moment the government party took no further step. "The Time is not yet come," Bernard informed London, "when the House is to be moved against Popular Printers however profligate and flagitious." [35] But within a few weeks an article in the *Boston Gazette* stung him beyond self-control. Joseph Warren, writing as "A True Patriot" on February 29, 1768, lashed the unnamed but clearly indicated Governor for his *"obstinate Perseverance in the Path of Malice,"* particularly his "insolence" in vilifying Whig politicians to the Ministry, and he wound up with the savage taunt:

> *Men totally abondoned to Wickedness, can never merit our Regard, be their Stations ever so high.*
> > "If such Men are by God appointed,
> > "The Devil may be the Lord's anointed." [36]

The philippic offended even many patriots, though doubtless most shared Andrew Eliot's view that, nonetheless, "the liberty of the press must be preserved sacred, or all is over!" The chief executive himself, however, had no such reservations. With the Council's unanimous support Bernard the next day referred the "libellous and seditious publication" to the legislature as something which, "if unnoticed, must endanger the very being of government." On March 3 the Council, acting now as the upper chamber, duly recorded its "utmost Abhorrence" of the "libel," but the popular branch, arguing legalistically that the article had not specifically mentioned Ber-

---

[34] *Boston Gazette*, Nov. 9, 1767, quoting (without attribution) from [John Trenchard and Thomas Gordon], *Cato's Letters* (6th ed., London, 1755), I, 100, a favorite textbook of the patriots.

[35] Letter to Lord Shelburne, Jan. 30, 1768, Bernard Papers, VI, 263.

[36] The couplet, except for the substitution of "Men" for "Kings," was taken from "The History of Insipids" (1676) by John Wilmot, Earl of Rochester. See his *Poems* (V. DeS. Pinto, ed., Cambridge, Mass., 1953), 113.

nard, declined to go along. Instead, it read the Governor a lecture on the freedom of the press, that "great Bulwark of the Liberty of the People" which the people's chosen guardians must always uphold.[37]

Bernard then asked the Council on its own account to join him in prosecuting Edes and Gill for seditious libel. He hoped thus to force the printers to divulge the identity of the "True Patriot" as well as of other "treasonable" contributors. But his official family had lost heart for further proceedings.[38] In the Chief Justice, however, he found a fervent ally. Hutchinson, still licking his wounds from his brush with Hawley, informed the grand jury on March 8, "There are People who make it their Business to furnish the Press with the most scandalous and defamatory Pieces" such as not the freest government in Europe would tolerate. Citing numerous precedents to show that writings might be libelous even without naming anyone, he instructed the jurors that they would violate their oaths by withholding an indictment. Under the spell of his eloquence they requested the Attorney General to draw up a bill against Edes and Gill; but overnight "Otis and creatures"—so it later reached Hutchinson's ears—got busy and won over a narrow majority to rescind the action.[39]

The *Boston Gazette* hailed the outcome as another victory for popular rights. The "True Patriot," who had meanwhile on March 7 compounded his original offense by berating the "odious doctrines" of passive obedience and the divine right of wicked rulers, assured the public in the next number, after the grand jury's defiance of Hutchinson, that he would continue to "strip the serpents of their stings, & consign to disgrace, all those guileful betrayers of their country." And in a neighboring column Samuel Adams as "Populus" added, "There is nothing so *fretting* and *vexatious,* nothing so justly TERRIBLE to tyrants, and their tools and abettors, as

[37] Eliot to Thomas Hollis, April 18, 1768, Mass. Hist. Soc., *Colls.*, ser. 4, IV (1858), 425; Quincy, *Reports*, 270–275; Alden Bradford, comp., *Speeches of Governors of Massachusetts, 1765–1775* (Boston, 1818), 118–119; *Boston Gazette*, March 7, 1768; Bernard and others, *Letters to Ministry*, 8–10; Hutchinson, *Massachusetts Bay*, III, 186–187.

[38] Letter to Lord Hillsborough, Jan. 25, 1769, Bernard Papers, VII, 126–127; Bernard and others, *Letters to Ministry*, 9–10.

[39] Quincy, *Reports*, 263–270; Hutchinson and Oliver, *Letters*, 9; Bernard's letters to John Pownall, Richard Jackson and Lord Shelburne, March 12 and 14, 1768, Bernard Papers, VI, 102, 103, 278–280.

a FREE PRESS." Four days later a civic group honoring the re-
peal of the Stamp Act jubilantly drank toasts to *"The Boston-
Gazette, and the worthy Members of the House who vindicated the
Freedom of the PRESS,"* and to *"The worthy and independent
Grand Jurors."* [40]

Hutchinson, his head bloody but unbowed, still hoped to repair
the damage; but upon discovering at the August term of the Superior Court that "Abettors of the Boston Mobs" had infiltrated the
grand jury, he let the occasion pass with a curt and indefinite con-
demnation of "inflammatory, seditious Libels." By the March sit-
ting in 1769 he finally admitted that the law was powerless to avert
"this atrocious Crime"; he could only trust that the libels had become "so common, so scandalous, so entirely false and incredible,"
as no longer to be accepted.[41] Actually both he and Bernard had
come to believe that the only remedy lay in direct intervention by
the home government. In this hope, however, they as well as the
Crown officials elsewhere in America were doomed, both then and
later, to disappointment.[42]

Undeterred either by the efforts at counterpropaganda or by the
menaces of the law, the Whig batteries kept up their bombardment,
skillfully picking their targets with an eye to local resentments. But,
as Governor Bernard rightly perceived, "Men and Measures are
only nominal Defendants, the Authority of the King, the Supremacy
of Parliament, the Superiority of Government, are the real Objects
of the Attack . . . ." [43] The autumn of 1768 afforded fresh evidence as rumors began flying that the incessant rioting excited by
popular resentment was about to bring British troops down on the
town. "READER, ATTEND!" cried a nameless writer in the *Boston
Gazette*, September 5, who, after arraigning the King's representatives for conspiring against the people's welfare, maintained that
such acts in principle destroyed the compact with the mother country, dissolving the ancient connection. Bernard tried to keep dark his
proposals to the Council for quartering the soldiers, but though he
enjoined the strictest secrecy, the members, increasingly radical in

[40] *Boston Gazette*, March 7, 14, 21, 1768.
[41] Quincy, *Reports*, 305, 309; Bernard and others, *Letters to Ministry*, 51.
[42] Bernard to Lord Hillsborough, Jan. 25, 1769, Bernard Papers, VII, 127.
For the British government's attitude toward journalistic excesses in the colonies,
see later, Appendix C.
[43] Bernard and others, *Letters to Ministry*, 11–12.

their sympathies, voted 7 to 3 during the Governor's absence to insert the transactions in the press, where the public learned of them on October 10. James Bowdoin, the Council chairman and one of the refractory majority, justified the betrayal on the ground that the citizens "in their present Temper" would not tolerate concealment. The outraged executive properly retorted that no "civilized Government upon Earth" could function effectively when its intimate deliberations were "canvassed by Tavern Politicians, and censured by News Paper Libellers." [44]

Bernard's days of usefulness were plainly running out. The patriot printers, conniving with the party heads, helped to deal the final blow. On April 3, 1769, the *Boston Gazette* and the *Evening-Post* startled the town with the news that the Ministry had laid before the House of Commons Bernard's confidential correspondence about conditions in Massachusetts; and shortly afterward, upon receiving the initial batch of the letters, Edes and Gill, at the instance of the Council, published them in pamphlet form.[45] Although they contained few political sentiments the Governor had not openly expressed, his uninhibited language and harsh reflections on individuals provoked bitter recriminations in the *Gazette*, with Samuel Adams anonymously leading the pack; and the Council forthwith demanded Bernard's recall. The Ministry acceding, he sailed on August 1 to the accompaniment of a "Flag hoisted on Liberty Tree —the Bells Ringing—Great Joy to the People." For nine years past, declared the *Boston Gazette* by way of adieu, he "has been a Scourge to this Province, a Curse to North-America, and a Plague to the whole Empire." Far off in Williamsburg, Rind's *Virginia Gazette* echoed: *"May he never more cross the atlantic, but meet the reward justly due to him, in his native country!"* [46]

When the remainder of the Bernard letters reached Boston, they were found to include some written by the Customs Commissioners, so the press next turned its guns on those hated officials. From foreknowledge of the contents Otis anticipated the actual publication in the two liberal journals with a signed piece in the *Boston Gazette*, September 4, 1769, denouncing the Commissioners for defaming

---

[44] *Ibid.*, 72–75; Bernard Papers, VII, 56–62.

[45] Bernard to John Pownall, April 12, 1769, *ibid.*, VII, 280–282; Hutchinson, *Massachusetts Bay*, III, 226–230.

[46] John Rowe, *Letters and Diary* (Anne R. Cunningham, ed., Boston, 1903), 190; *Boston Gazette*, Aug. 7, 1769; *Va. Gazette* (Rind), Aug. 24.

him and his associates as rebels and traitors. In retaliation John Robinson, one of the Board, brutally assaulted him the next evening at the British Coffee House with the help of friends, leaving him wounded and bleeding. Though the affair had obviously occurred spontaneously, the *Gazette* dressed it up as an "intended and nearly executed Assassination," and Samuel Adams, parading as "An Impartialist," likewise contended that it was a "preconcerted plan to assassinate Mr. Otis." [47] Even so, the Whigs did not accomplish the object of ridding Boston of the Commissioners, and they suffered a still graver setback from the fact that the attack impaired Otis's mental faculties, disqualifying him for further leadership.

V

Meanwhile the Whig captains unleashed a journalistic offensive against the newly arrived redcoats. Seizing the opportunity to enlist the support of their brethren in other colonies, they established an undercover news service to spread far and wide an intensely partisan account of the intruders. This constituted the most ambitious venture in systematic and sustained propaganda by the press that the patriots ever attempted anywhere; and unlike Dickinson's "Farmer's Letters," the dispatches struck at the emotions rather than the minds of the public. An inner group concocted a day-by-day record of alleged happenings, seasoned with editorial comments usually italicized, and then sent each week's installment to Holt of the *New-York Journal*, who published it about a fortnight later under a Boston date line as the "JOURNAL of OCCUR–RENCES" or "JOURNAL of the TIMES" or "JOURNAL of Transactions." From this source editors all the way from Salem, Mass., to Savannah, Ga., reprinted the contents in whole or part.[48]

The diary started with September 28, 1768, the date of the troops' arrival, and concluded on August 1, 1769, when the harassed Bernard took off for England. Week after week readers ev-

---

[47] Tudor, *Otis*, 360–366; *Boston Gazette*, Sept. 11, 25, 1769.

[48] For a list of these papers and a discussion of the probable authorship of the "Journal," see later, Appendix D. The complete "Journal" has been published by O. M. Dickerson in *Boston under Military Rule (1768–1769) as Revealed in a Journal of the Times* (Boston, 1936), using the text in the *New-York Journal* as his principal source.

erywhere shuddered at the effrontery of the military, the hazards to the fair sex of seduction and rape and the continuing tyranny of the Crown officials. The jottings for a single day will illustrate their sensational nature and the not uncharacteristic indefiniteness as to names:

> *Dec.* 12, 1768. A Married Lady of this town was the other evening, when passing from one house to another, taken hold of by a soldier; who other-ways behaved to her with great rudeness; a woman near Long Lane was stopped by several soldiers, one of whom cried out seize and carry her off; she was much surprised, but luckily got shelter in a house near by; another woman was pursued by a soldier into a house near the north end, who dared to enter the same, and behave with great insolence: Several inhabitants while quietly passing the streets in the evening, have been knocked down by soldiers: One of the principal physicians of the town, was the last friday, about 12 o'clock at night, hailed by an officer, who was passing the street, but not of a patrolling party; the Doctor refused to answer, and resented this treatment; whereupon the officer seized him by the collar, asserting that he was on the King's duty, and swearing that he would have an answer; this so provoked the Doctor that he gave him a blow, which bro't the officer to the ground; he then seized him, but a soldier or two coming up at that instant, he tho't proper to let him go. *These are some further specimens of what we are to expect from our new conservators of the peace: The inhabitants however still preserve their temper and a proper decorum; in this they have doubtless disappointed and vexed their enemies: Under all the insults and injuries received, we are patiently waiting the result of our petitions and remonstrances, for a redress of grievances, and an alteration of measures: We cannot but flatter ourselves that administration must soon be convinced of the propriety and necessity of putting affairs upon the old footing, which experience now demonstrates to be the best for both countries.*[49]

As to the truth of these reports one can only say that none of the local newspapers contained any of them at the time the incidents were stated to have occurred.

The *Boston Evening-Post* usually waited about two months after the purported incidents to reprint the installments, by which time, as Hutchinson noted, only a dim recollection remained, making credi-

[49] *Boston Evening-Post*, Feb. 6, 1769. For allegations of seduction and attempted rape, see the "Journal" for April 30, May 16 and 17, June 14 and July 4, 1769, in *ibid.*, June 26, July 17, 31, and Aug. 14, 1769.

ble "glosses, exaggerations, and additional circumstances." Indeed, he averred, "some pretended facts of an enormous nature were published of which so much as the rumour could not be remembered." He considered nine tenths of the contents "either absolutely false or grossly misrepresented." Other Tory worthies reacted with equal bile, Bernard raging that "To set about answering these Falsities would be a work like that of cleansing Augeas's Stable . . . ." Only James Murray, a minor member of the regime, essayed the task. He had drawn the "Journal's" fire for allowing troops to be quartered in his sugar refinery. Declaring in the press that he had been traduced as "a *jacobite,* a *rebel,* and a *drunkard,*" he challenged his anonymous accuser to repeat the charges over his own name or else "stand convicted of being an infamous liar." "John M'Quirck," replying in pretended alarm in the *Boston Gazette,* warned "that *Rascal* of a Journalist" to save his hide by keeping out of Murray's way; and in the *Boston Evening-Post,* "Scrutator"—presumably the rascal himself—jeered:

> Rail on, while my revenge shall be
> To speak the very truth of thee!

Murray wisely did not pursue the matter further, even though the "Journal" in due course repeated the aspersions.[50]

On December 18, 1769, the *Boston Evening-Post,* trailing the *New-York Journal* of November 30, printed the last of the series. Why the authors desisted after ten months is not clear. If they intended to drive the redcoats from the town, they had not succeeded. They had, however, accomplished a wider purpose: their woeful portrayal of Boston's plight helped galvanize the patriot cause throughout America. As the "Journal of Occurrences" emphasized, "if the spirit of liberty was once thoroughly quelled *in this capital,* it must not only be *extinguished* through the *province,* but in all the colonies." In Boston itself the articles had inspired many other "nameless scandal-mongers"—Murray's phrase—to lift their voices and had stirred the caldron of popular emotion until the

---

[50] Hutchinson, *Massachusetts Bay,* III, 225; Hutchinson to Israel Williams, Jan. 26, 1769, Williams Papers (Mass. Hist. Soc.); Bernard to Lord Hillsborough, Feb. 25, 1769, Bernard Papers, VII, 148–150; Murray in the *Boston Gazette,* the *Boston Evening-Post* and the *Boston Chronicle,* all on May 29; "M'Quirck" in the *Boston Gazette,* June 5; "Scrutator" in the *Evening-Post,* June 5; "Journal" entry in *ibid.,* July 31, 1769.

hot liquid coursed through the veins of nearly everyone.[51] Clashes between the townsfolk and the "Bloody-Backs" multiplied, culminating on March 5, 1770, in the killing of some civilians by Captain Thomas Preston's men.

Though the mob had been the aggressor and the rattled soldiers had fired in the belief that Preston had ordered them to, the *Boston Gazette* and the *Evening-Post*, following the official Whig line, magnified the incident into a "bloody Massacre" and strongly intimated that some of the shots had come from a customhouse window. This accorded with the design to unite the people's loathing of the military with their hatred of the Customs Board. To harrow their readers further, Edes and Gill bordered their account with heavy black rules and displayed an engraving by Paul Revere of four coffins inscribed with death's-heads and the victims' initials. (When a fifth rioter died a few days later, they devoted a special cut to him in their next issue.) As a final touch the *Gazette* predicted disclosures that would, among other dire things, explain "the Assassination of Mr. Otis some Time past" and "open up such a Scene of Villainy acted by a dirty Banditti, as must astonish the Public." [52] By contrast, Draper's *Massachusetts Gazette and Boston News-Letter*, published four days earlier, dealt with the affair gingerly on the ground that the precise facts were yet to be discovered. Had not the troops been removed to a fort in the harbor, more collisions would almost certainly have ensued. Ahead, however, lay the opportunity for additional propaganda when Preston and his men should stand trial. Samuel Adams and his coadjutors were determined to make the Boston Massacre an enduring symbol of British "tyranny."

VI

While the "Journal of Occurrences" was still going the rounds and the Bostonians seemed definitely to be winning the battle of ink, they encountered a formidable antagonist who seriously endangered

[51] *Ibid.*, April 10, July 31, 1769; James Murray, *Letters* (Nina M. Tiffany, ed., Boston, 1901), 162.

[52] *Boston Gazette* and *Boston Evening-Post*, March 12, 1770; E. H. Goss, *The Life of Colonel Paul Revere* (Boston, 1891), II, 75–77. For some unknown reason, the *Gazette* brought out two different editions on March 12, though the alterations affected only the advertisements. See H. W. Cunningham in Mass. Hist. Soc., *Procs.*, LIX (1925–26), 253–259.

their hard-won gains. This godsend to the Tory cause was John Mein; his paper, the *Boston Chronicle*; and his grudge, a personal more than a political one. The pugnacious Scotsman had shown up in Boston in 1764 to become a bookseller and book publisher and the founder of its first circulating library. As he expanded his activities he teamed up with John Fleeming, a fellow countryman, and on December 21, 1767, a month after the Townshend duties went into effect, they began publication of the *Chronicle*.[53] Typographically it was the finest newspaper in America, and the partners at the beginning of 1769 showed further enterprise by turning it into a semiweekly, the only venture of the kind in any of the colonies save for that short-lived hybrid, the *Massachusetts Gazette*.

Interested in profits rather than politics, Mein announced that, "Whenever any dispute claims general attention, the arguments on both sides shall be laid before the public with the utmost impartiality"; [54] and this at first he honestly did. On the one hand, he published the "Farmer's Letters," and he even printed the *Chronicle* on undutied paper made in nearby Milton; on the other, he opened his pages to pro-British articles, usually clippings from the London press. But, in Whig eyes, to be above the battle was to be suspect. Hence "Americus" (whom Mein believed to be Otis, then still in his prime) blasted him in the *Boston Gazette*, January 18, 1768, for reprinting an English attack on the patriots' idol, William Pitt. When the *Gazette* editors refused to divulge the writer's identity, the peppery Scot brutally clubbed Gill on the street a few nights later. In the *Gazette*, February 1, Samuel Adams under the pseudonym of "Populus" termed the affair in no sense a private one but a "Spaniard-like Attempt" on the freedom of the press, and so at Mein's trial did Otis as Gill's counsel. Mein was fined £130, and though on appeal he got the amount cut to £75, he still suffered a severe penalty.[55]

[53] Accounts of Mein may be found in J. E. Alden, "John Mein: Scourge of Patriots," Colonial Soc. of Mass., *Pubs.*, XXXIV (1937–42), 571–599; C. M. Andrews, "The Boston Merchants and the Non-importation Movement," *ibid.*, XIX (1916–17), 227–230; C. K. Bolton, "Circulating Libraries in Boston," *ibid.*, XI (1906–07), 196–200; O. M. Dickerson, "British Control of American Newspapers on the Eve of the Revolution," *New England Quar.*, XXIV (1951), 461–466; and A. M. Schlesinger, *The Colonial Merchants and the American Revolution* (N. Y., 1918), 159–178.
[54] Mein, *Proposals for Printing a New Weekly, called The Boston Chronicle* (Oct. 22, 1767).
[55] Alden, "John Mein," 581–586.

The Customs Board, seeing an opening to enlist a fearless adherent, now put him on its payroll as a supplier of stationery; and a year and a half later, when he was flailing the patriots right and left, it made him the sole supplier. This business brought the partners (including the payments to Fleeming after Mein fled Boston) a total of more than £819 down to April, 1775. The Board, however, it is to be observed, did less to create a situation than to exploit one. What turned Mein into an all-out foe of the Whigs was an innate aversion to having the "Heads of the Faction" bully him into signing the nonimportation agreement against the Townshend Acts. He had resisted similar pressure during the Stamp Act, and though threatened that "the Crisis was now arrived, in which Neutrality was criminal," he bluntly asserted his right to run his affairs as he pleased.[56]

Toward the end of May, 1769, the Committee of Merchants, headed by John Hancock, called upon the citizens to boycott some nonimportation violators. Though they did not include Mein, he abused the Committee in the *Chronicle*, June 1, for seeking "in the most unjust, cruel manner possible, to affect them in their business." He also accused the Committee of shielding friends who were equal offenders, and from data secretly furnished by the Customs Board he gave a summary of the imports entered at Boston in past months, including large quantities in the proscribed category; as yet, however, he did not name any of the guilty. A meeting of the nonimporting merchants on August 11 struck back by posting the Scotsman himself for boycott and on the same occasion adopted resolutions contrasting the virtues of the "Well Disposed" with the iniquities of the "Enemies to the Constitution of their Country." [57]

In the *Chronicle* six days later Mein gleefully seized upon the self-vaunting phrase "Well Disposed," applying it thenceforward with deadly satire to the Merchants' Committee. To support his charges of hypocrisy and double-dealing he serialized cargo lists of importations, identifying the recipients. Then, on September 21, he intensified his attack with a continuing "Catechism of the 'Well Disposed' "; and on October 26 he offered "Outlines of the characters of some who are thought to be 'Well Disposed,' " blackening the

[56] Dickerson, "British Control of American Newspapers," 461, 463, 465; Andrews, "Boston Merchants," 228 *n.*
[57] *Boston Gazette*, Aug. 14, 1769.

various individuals with such epithets as "Johnny Dupe, Esq." (Hancock) and "Muddlehead" (Otis).[58] Mein took particular delight in needling the Committee's egotistical chairman. When he did not deride Hancock as a *"Milch-Cow . . .* surrounded with a croud of people, some of whom are stroaking his ears, others tickling his nose with straws, while the rest are employed in riffling his pockets," he called him a furtive infringer of the very regulations he was professing to administer.[59]

Mein did not forge all these verbal shafts himself. Behind the scenes he had help from William Burch of the Customs Board as well as from Samuel Waterhouse, a subordinate revenue officer whom John Adams considered "the most notorious scribbler, satirist, and libeller, in the service of the conspirators against the liberties of America." He also had assistance from the merchant Joseph Green, a nonsigner of the agreement and local wit. Green indeed may have penned the malicious suggestion that the patriots should buttress their nonimportation pact with a pledge of nonmarriage, since the Ministry would be "more shockingly mortified" by "our fixed determination to depopulate the country" than by the mere withholding of trade. In such case, however, he insisted that he himself be named chairman of the committee to segregate the females.[60]

Mein's enraged victims crammed the press with anguished rebuttals ranging all the way from flat disclaimers to abuse of their tormentor as a "conceited empty Noddle of a most profound Blockhead." The accuracy of his allegations is less important in the present context than their effect on public opinion. It is nevertheless evident that the protesters were not always the sacrificial souls they tried to make themselves out to be, for some indulged in practices that we would call chiseling. More, however, offended through sheer

[58] Though readers at the time required no "Key to the Characters," Mein privately prepared one that is useful for posterity. See Papers Relating to New England (Sparks MSS., Harvard College Library), III, 45–47.

[59] The most damaging charge can be quickly disposed of. Hancock had violated the spirit but not the letter of the agreement by allowing some of his ships to carry prohibited goods as freight, a practice not expressly proscribed until later on July 26, 1769. On Sept. 6 he accordingly sent appropriate instructions to his London correspondents. *Mass. Gazette,* July 31, 1769; John Hancock, *John Hancock His Book* (A. E. Brown, ed., Boston, 1898), 166. The passage quoted is from the *Boston Chronicle,* Oct. 26, 1769. For Mein's chief articles against Hancock, see *ibid.,* Aug. 21, 28, Sept. 4, 18, Oct. 9, 1769.

[60] *Boston Gazette,* Sept. 11, 1769; Hudson, *Journalism in the United States,* 128; Adams, *Works,* II, 182 n.; *Boston Chronicle,* Jan. 18, 1770.

inadvertence. But Samuel Adams, who jealously eyed the proceedings from first to last, judged that "The Merchants in general have punctually abode by their Agreement, to their very great private loss." [61]

Part of Mein's design was to disillusion the rest of America as to the good faith of the Bostonians and thus drive a wedge between them and the sister colonies. Since not many persons outside Massachusetts read the *Chronicle*, he and his partner struck off 500 pamphlets containing his strictures with 4000 sheets cataloguing the principal importations, and these the customs employees helped distribute throughout the continent. [62] Soon even the patriotic *Newport Mercury* was remarking that Hancock "would perhaps shine more conspicuously" if he were not so busy "getting rich, by receiving freight on goods made contraband by the Colonies," and in Philadelphia the *Pennsylvania Chronicle* felt it necessary to caution the public that the pamphlets were intended solely "to set the good people of the other colonies by the ears." [63] Still more important, the Merchants' Committees in New York and Philadelphia betrayed increasing distrust of their Boston brethren. [64] Mein's revelations, even when not wholly believed, supplied an excellent pretext for those who elsewhere were tiring of the nonimportation regulations. To his aggressive journalism must in some degree be ascribed the eventual defection of New York and Philadelphia and, thus indirectly, the abandonment of the agreements in other colonies.

Meanwhile Mein's presence in Boston was goading the Whigs beyond endurance. The Free American Fire Company expelled him from membership; customers deserted his newspaper and bookstore by droves; unseen hands broke his windows and daubed his business signs with filth. Alarmed by threats to his personal safety, he began to go about armed. On October 28, 1769, two days after the *Chronicle* travestied the "characters of some who are thought to be 'Well

[61] *Boston News-Letter*, Sept. 21, 1769; Samuel Adams to Peter Timothy, Nov. 21, 1771, Adams, *Writings*, II, 65. For a critical examination of Mein's contentions, see Schlesinger, *Colonial Merchants*, 166–170.

[62] Andrews, "Boston Merchants," 228. The original pamphlet covered the period from Jan. 1 to Aug. 17, 1769, and later editions (issued by Fleeming after Mein forsook Boston) extended the tabulation successively to Jan. 1, 1770, and to June 19, 1770.

[63] "American Spy" in *Newport Mercury*, Sept. 4, 1769; *Pa. Chronicle*, June 28, 1770. "Civis" in the *N.–H. Gazette*, July 6, 13, 1770, also expressed shock at Hancock's alleged conduct.

[64] Andrews, "Boston Merchants," 229, 250–252.

Disposed,' " a mob attacked him and Fleeming on the street, and in the ensuing confusion Mein wounded a soldier bystander with a pistol shot. Some of the crowd thereupon swore out a warrant against him "for having put innocent people in bodily fear," and Mein in terror of his life fled to a ship in the harbor and thence to England, where a grateful monarch duly rewarded him with a gift of £200.[65]

Mein's flight, however, did not afford the relief the popular chieftains had expected. Undaunted by the purging of his partner, Fleeming and the *Chronicle* corps of contributors manfully kept up the barrage. Each number now blandly asked in large type: "*Is not the detection of the* 'WELL DISPOSED' *owing to the Glorious* LIB– ERTY *of the* PRESS?" But liberty for the opposition was not the patriots' ideal. Fortunately for them, Mein had incurred heavy business losses during his Boston sojourn; and on March 1, 1770, Hancock, acting for Mein's London creditors, placed an attachment on the newspaper and bookshop. Though Murray and other friends "set the press a going again" by standing provisional surety, this merely postponed the inevitable.[66] On June 25 the *Chronicle* announced that "in the present state of affairs" it could no longer continue. So passed from the scene the most brilliant journalistic champion the government party was, with a single possible exception, anywhere to possess, and the Boston Whigs rid themselves of a deadly adversary.

VII

Elsewhere in New England the press generally took its cue from the radical newspapers of the metropolis. Governor Bernard in complaining to the Ministry of a "treasonable" piece in the *Providence Gazette* of March 18, 1769, called it a "common Trick" of the Boston troublemakers to plant political articles in other papers so as to

---

[65] *Boston Evening-Post*, Oct. 30, 1769; "Veritas" (Mein?) in the *Gazetteer and New Daily Advertiser* (London), Jan. 16, 1770; Alden, "John Mein," 586–589; George III, *Correspondence* (Sir John Fortescue, ed., London, 1927–28), V, 468.

[66] Murray, *Letters*, 169–174; Alden, "John Mein," 590–592. Fleeming apparently remained in Boston as a printer until after the outbreak of hostilities. On Aug. 8, 1770, he married the sister of Dr. Benjamin Church, and in 1775 acted as an intermediary in Church's treasonable correspondence with the British authorities. Carl Van Doren, *Secret History of the American Revolution* (N. Y., 1941), 19–23.

give them greater effect when copied locally.[67] In any event, the Rhode Island and Connecticut editors joined wholeheartedly in flaying the Townshend measures and urging the disuse of British wares, and luckily they had no Bernard or Hutchinson to threaten reprisals. Moreover, a new Whig organ, the *Connecticut Journal*, made its bow on October 23, 1767, at New Haven, where Benjamin Mecom was already conducting the *Connecticut Gazette*. The community, however, was too small to support two papers, and Mecom stopped his on February 19, 1768, preliminary to setting up anew in Philadelphia some months later.

Only Daniel and Robert Fowle of the *New-Hampshire Gazette* sought to take a moderate if not neutral position, thanks to Portsmouth's strong loyalist sympathies. The Boston Massacre in March, 1770, revealed the editors' true sentiments, however. Headlining their first notice of the affair *"Bloody Work in Boston,"* they followed it in the next issue with the *Boston Gazette*'s bitterly partisan version, including the black borders and the cuts of the four coffins.[68] The next week "Consideration" hopefully compared the past apathy of the citizens to "Subterranean Fires which burn long conceal'd," but now, he went on, "The Streets of BOSTON have already been bathed with the BLOOD of innocent Americans! Shed by the execrable Hands of the diabolical Tools of Tyrants!—O AMERI–CANS! this BLOOD calls aloud for VENGEANCE!" But local pressures soon came into play again, and the sudden blaze subsided almost as quickly as it had flared up. Understandably the printers, unsupported by public opinion, lacked the boldness of their fellow New Englanders.

[67] Letters of March 25, 27 and April 8, 1769, to John Pownall and Lord Hillsborough, Bernard Papers, VII, 155–156, 273–274, 276–277.

[68] *N.-H. Gazette*, March 9, 16, 1770. On March 23 the publishers, again imitating the *Boston Gazette*, displayed the fifth coffin. This number also contained the article by "Consideration."

Chapter VI

The Campaign Outside New England

OUTSIDE NEW ENGLAND the major newspaper centers were New York and Philadelphia. New York, as we have seen, first published the Boston-inspired "Journal of Occurrences," and Philadelphia on its own motion launched the influential "Farmer's Letters." For the most part, however, the editors in these cities pursued a course dictated by local circumstances, and, like their Massachusetts colleagues, they soon ran into threats to the liberty of the press, though in each case of a different kind. In the South, thanks to the lack of sizable towns and the difficulties of communication, partisan journalism played a smaller role, but even there certain printers contributed significantly to the agitation.

I

New Yorkers read four newspapers when the Townshend Acts were passed in June, 1767, though Weyman's *New-York Gazette*, for reasons unconnected with politics, did not outlast the year.[1]

[1] Weyman in his valedictory number, Dec. 28, 1767, blamed the *Gazette's* demise on his competitor and former partner James Parker who, as comptroller of the postal service, had forbidden postriders to distribute it because Weyman would not or perhaps could not comply with the requirement of providing special saddlebags to separate the damp pages from the rest of the mail. Isaiah Thomas, *The History of Printing in America* (rev. ed., Am. Antiquarian Soc., *Trans.*, V–VI, 1874), II, 112–115.

Holt, who conducted the *New-York Journal,* and Parker of the *New-York Gazette or Weekly Post-Boy* were both devoted patriots, while Gaine of the *New-York Mercury* usually supported the Crown. As an Anglican vestryman Gaine doubtless mirrored the views of the royal officials and provincial bigwigs who controlled that sect; and he had further incentive when the Assembly on January 15, 1768, made him its printer, since the dominant element in that body also wished to avoid trouble with the mother country.[2] In recognition of this remunerative tie Gaine on February 1 altered the name of his paper to the *New-York Gazette and Weekly Mercury.*

During the early months of the revived controversy the Manhattan editors confined themselves largely to political news and propaganda lifted from the Massachusetts press. Governor Bernard believed this to be a deliberate scheme whereby "all Publications shall originate at Boston, whilst it appears to be neglected at New York"; and Sir Henry Moore, the New York executive, agreed that the Bay Colonists were "taking the lead again" in "spreading seditious principles among the neighbouring Provinces." It was not till the publication of the "Farmer's Letters" a few weeks later that Sir Henry discovered that another source of infection lay to the south.[3]

When the New Yorkers entered the lists on their own account, they directed their first volleys not against the Townshend regulations, but against the supposed design of the Ministry to foist an Anglican episcopate on America. For many years the Church of England communicants and the Presbyterians had been vying for control of the province, and in the scheme for colonial bishops the Presbyterians saw an assertion of imperial power that menaced the people's political as well as religious freedom. William Livingston, assisted apparently by two fellow Presbyterian lawyers John Morin

---

[2] A writer in the *Boston Gazette,* Jan. 22, 1770, ascribed the differing attitudes of the Massachusetts and New York Assemblies to the fact that in the Bay Colony the members were chosen annually by written ballot; in New York, for seven-year terms by *viva voce* vote. For the Assembly's payments to Gaine, see his *Journals* (P. L. Ford, ed., N. Y., 1892), I, 47–49. He also was official printer for the city of New York.

[3] Bernard to Richard Jackson, Sept. 14, 1767, Bernard Papers (Sparks MSS., Harvard College Library), VI, 47–48; Moore to Lord Shelburne, Oct. 5, 1767, British Papers Relating to the American Revolution (Sparks MSS.), I, 240; Moore to Lord Hillsborough, May 12, 1768, E. B. O'Callaghan and Berthold Fernow, eds., *Documents Relative to the Colonial History of the State of New York* (Albany, 1853–87), VIII, 68.

Scott and William Smith, led the attack.[4] Beginning in Parker's *Gazette*, March 14, 1768, Livingston as "The American Whig" penned hard-hitting screeds that went on for more than a year. He pictured "ecclesiastical bondage" as the natural concomitant of Britain's ruinous encroachments on America's economic well-being. "Is this a time," he stormed, "to think of episcopal palaces, of pontifical revenues, of spiritual courts, and all the pomp, grandeur, luxury, and regalia of an American Lambeth?" The proposed episcopate, he said, was, if anything, a greater evil than the Townshend measures, for they at least "affect not the right of conscience." [5]

Livingston's onslaught brought into the arena "Timothy Tickle, Esq.," who, commencing on April 4 in Gaine's *Gazette,* contributed a series on the other side of the question entitled "A Whip for the American Whig." This performance, also of joint authorship, engaged the pens of Samuel Seabury, Charles Inglis, John Vardill and Myles Cooper, all Church of England divines, who insisted that the bishops would not exercise any secular power; hence the project was of no possible concern to non-Anglicans.[6] Their writings in turn evoked "A Kick for the Whipper" by "Sir Isaac Foot" in Parker's pages. In the heat of the exchanges both sides dealt in distortion and hyperbole, hurling invectives that probably did no more than confirm the prior convictions of their respective adherents. Before the tempest spent itself in July, 1769, Livingston and his group had, however, effectively harnessed religious fervor to political bias in the fight against Britain.

Meanwhile the Whigs gained a new spokesman through the establishment of the *New-York Chronicle* on May 8, 1769. Oddly enough, James Robertson, who joined his brother Alexander in this undertaking, had formerly been a journeyman on Mein's *Boston Chronicle*, a fact which may have suggested the paper's name. The

---

[4] Dorothy R. Dillon, *The New York Triumvirate* (N. Y., 1949), chap. ii. A. L. Cross, *The Anglican Episcopate and the American Colonies* (N. Y., 1902), 196–203, summarizes the New York controversy of 1768–69. In Massachusetts, where the question also occasioned debate, the exchanges took the form mainly of pamphlets, though Samuel Adams as "A Puritan" sought to equate Anglicanism with "Popery" in three articles in the *Boston Gazette*, April 4–18, 1768. Andrew Eliot wrote Thomas Hollis, Jan. 29, 1769, "The Episcopal controversy makes but little noise in our Province . . . . At New York it is otherwise." Mass. Hist. Soc., *Colls.*, ser. 4, IV (1858), 436.

[5] *N.–Y. Gazette or Weekly Post-Boy*, March 14, May 16, 1768.

[6] *Dictionary of American Biography* (Allen Johnson and Dumas Malone, eds., N. Y., 1928–36), IV, 409, XVI, 529, XIX, 222.

Robertsons were native Scotsmen who eventually were to side with the Tories. At this juncture, however, perhaps because they resented the drive for an Anglican episcopate, they promoted the patriot cause. Like Parker's and Holt's contributors, "Peter Twist," "Nauticus" and others in the *Chronicle* denounced British oppression, with "Cethegus" chiming in to urge the boycott of imported wares.[7] On November 23 the Robertsons changed their paper to a semiweekly; but despite this show of enterprise they were poor businessmen— "Paper Spoilers" and "ignorant Blockheads," according to Parker —and their venture barely survived the year.

The journalistic propaganda increasingly alarmed the Crown officials. Lieutenant Governor Colden informed the Ministry early in 1768, "Papers at this time are continually published, denying the legislative authority of the Parliament," without "the least enquiry into the Authors or Publishers of them, by any of the Courts of Justice or by the Council or Assembly." But the home government, distant from the scene, serenely counseled that "the flagitious & inflammatory Publications" be treated "with the contempt they deserve, which will conduce the most effectually to the Disappointment of the Authors." To this Governor Moore ruefully replied that the silent treatment had had the opposite result of leading "all Ranks and conditions of People" to embrace the pernicious doctrines.[8]

Doubtless the Whig leaders got wind of these complaints, for the Sons of Liberty on March 18, 1769, when commemorating the repeal of the Stamp Act drank to "The Liberty of the Press, and Disappointment to those who endeavour to subvert it," with a special potation to John Wilkes, the English champion of a free press; and the Robertsons' *Chronicle* added its own praise of the Briton's fortitude in both prose and verse. It was idle for Gaine's paper to remonstrate that the reckless denunciations of Parliament were only hardening the members against rescinding the Townshend Acts. "Speaking and writing without restraint, are the great privi-

---

[7] *N.-Y. Chronicle*, May 8, 29, June 8, 22, 29, 1769. For biographical data on the Robertsons, see Thomas, *History of Printing*, I, 192–193, 313; and for Parker's characterization, his letter to Benjamin Franklin, Feb. 2, 1770, Mass. Hist. Soc., *Procs.*, ser. 2, XIV (1902), 221.

[8] Colden to Lord Halifax, Jan. 29, 1768, *Letter Books* (N.-Y. Hist. Soc., *Colls.*, IX–X, 1876–77), II, 164; Lord Hillsborough to Moore, Feb. 25, 1768, and Moore's reply, May 12, O'Callaghan and Fernow, *Documents*, VIII, 11, 68. For the English government's self-restraint regarding colonial freedom of the press, see later, Appendix C.

leges of a free people," retorted Parker's *Gazette*. *"The liberty of the Press . . . .* ought to be defended with our lives and fortunes, for neither will be worth enjoying, when freedom is destroyed by arbitrary measures." And the ever-watchful Sons of Liberty, recurring to the theme at a dinner on November 1, imbibed toasts to "The Liberty of the Press, and Confusion to all Imprimaturs," and, by way of reminder, to "The Printers who nobly disregarded the detestable Stamp-Act, preferring of the public Good to their private Interest, in 1765." [9]

II

The overt attack on untrammeled discussion, when it occurred, did not come, however, from the Crown authorities but from the Assembly. Ever since British forces had been stationed in New York following the Seven Years' War, friction had existed between them and the townsfolk. Holt in scooping the American press with the "Journal of Occurrences" undoubtedly hoped that the lurid recital would also sharpen resentment against the local redcoats. On December 15, 1769, a few weeks after the series concluded, the Assembly, having earlier made its regular annual appropriation for the troops, substantially increased the amount. This action touched off a blaze.

The next day a broadside by "A Son of Liberty" addressed to "THE BETRAYED INHABITANTS OF THE CITY AND COL-ONY OF NEW YORK" appeared on the streets, followed a few days later by a companion piece signed "Legion." The Assembly promptly pronounced them "infamous" and "seditious" and directed Colden, who had become Acting Governor upon Moore's death in September, to post rewards for the author's discovery. A journeyman in James Parker's shop then blabbed that his employer had been the printer; and the ailing Parker, threatened with the possible loss of his comptrollership of the post office, implicated as the author Alexander McDougall, a merchant and flaming patriot. McDougall himself, however, declined either to admit guilt or give bail, and on

<hr>

[9] *N.–Y. Gazette and Weekly Mercury,* March 20, April 4, Nov. 2, 1769; "Nauticus" and others on Wilkes in the *N.–Y. Chronicle,* June 8; *N.–Y. Gazette or Weekly Post-Boy,* July 11.

February 8, 1770, defiantly went off to jail to await action by the grand jury.[10]

The immediate issue involved fugitive publications, but its import for the regular press was too plain to be ignored. Hence the Whigs with an eye on the forthcoming session of the grand jury aired the question fully in the newspapers, while Parker, eager to atone for his indiscretion, made his sheet their principal vehicle, besides contributing pieces of his own. The Zenger case of some thirty years before supplied potent ammunition, and the contemporaneous persecution of Wilkes in England afforded an added spice of drama.

Parker, having only recently defended the freedom of the press in a different connection, hotly reaffirmed that it was "one of the greatest Bulwarks of the British Constitution." "The Body Politic is often sick," he went on, "and a free Discussion is certainly the best means of pointing out the Disease, that so a suitable Remedy may be applied." Though he had lost subscribers by this stand, he vowed he would sooner sacrifice his paper than his principles "during the Remainder of his short Span of Life." To refute the common-law doctrine of seditious libel that truth was no defense, he filled a column and a half with extracts from Andrew Hamilton's argument in the Zenger trial. He further lectured the Assembly that "Attempts to prevent the *Liberty of the Press* in this Province, will be in Vain, while there is a free Press on the Continent," since "all Causes gain Ground by Persecution. . . . French, Spaniards or Turks, may bear the Yoke; but true Englishmen will never yield." [11]

Meanwhile McDougall, savoring his role as "the Wilkes of America," was in such demand by callers that he had to appoint visiting hours, and he informed Parker's readers that his martyrdom was "converting Chains into Laurels, and transforming a Gaol into a Paradise." Writing sometimes as himself and sometimes as "A Son of Liberty," he too inveighed against "the infamous Star Chamber Doctrine of Libels," that "Consummation of all Nonsense," which "Liberty herself, in the Form of ZENGER," had demolished. If "this *Star-Chamber Trumpery*" were now to be revived, he exhorted "all the American Assemblies to bring in Bills for the Banishment of

[10] E. B. O'Callaghan, comp., *Documentary History of the State of New York* (Albany, 1849–51), III, 528–536; *N.-Y. Gazette and Weekly Mercury*, Dec. 25, 1769; *N.-Y. Gazette or Weekly Post-Boy*, Feb. 12, 1770.

[11] *Ibid.*, Jan. 29, Feb. 19, March 19, 1770.

such tyrannical Tenets" and to vote no appropriations until the bills were approved. "Brutus" and other scribes proved no less vehement, and the Sons of Liberty at their celebration of the repeal of the Stamp Act on March 19, 1770, drank feelingly to "The Memory of Andrew Hamilton, Esq.," to "Zenger's Jury, who regardless of the Directions of the Court, refused to bring in a special Verdict, and acquitted the Prisoner," and to "A total Abolition of the Star-Chamber Doctrine of Libels." [12]

Gaine's *Gazette*, as was to be expected, zealously upheld the Assembly. Its principal effort comprised twelve weekly articles entitled "The Dougliad." Their unnamed author at times bedeviled McDougall for his "VAIN, IDLE, FORWARD, MALEVOLENT, CONTENTIOUS, MEDDLING, IMPERTINENT, TURBULENT, FACTIOUS, SEDITIOUS TEMPER," and at others soberly defended the common-law view of seditious libel as well as the Assembly's boosting of the military appropriations. [13] In the end the friends of government won out, for the grand jury on April 27, 1770, obeying Chief Justice Daniel Horsemanden's instructions, brought in an indictment. [14]

The rage of the Whigs knew no bounds. McDougall, writing as "A Son of Liberty," bluntly accused the sheriff of packing the jury. Taking the members one by one, he charged that each possessed business, social or blood ties with the leaders of the Assembly. Parker, for his part, shuddered that fellow Americans should "abridge the Liberty of the Press, suppress the Spirit and Freedom of Enquiry, or damp the Ardour of the People." The printer then unintentionally saved the situation by opportunely dying on June 2, 1770. With this removal of the principal witness against McDougall, the case never reached the petit jury for final determination. The exasperated Assemblymen nevertheless had the last say. Irked at seeing McDougall out on bail after his indictment, they summoned him before them on December 13, and when he still refused to incriminate himself, they peremptorily committed him to jail for "high contempt," where he lingered until March 4, 1771. [15]

---

12 *Ibid.*, Feb. 12, March 19, 26, April 9, 1770.
13 *N.–Y. Gazette and Weekly Mercury*, April 9–June 25, 1770. "New-York Satyrist" and "Hoadly" on McDougall's behalf responded with equal scurrility in the *N.–Y. Journal*, April 19, and the *N.–Y. Gazette or Weekly Post-Boy*, May 7, 14.
14 *Ibid.*, May 7, 1770.
15 *Ibid.*, May 7, 1770; *N.–Y. Gazette and Weekly Mercury*, April 30, 1770;

Despite the outspokenness of the press in defense of McDougall the government's unrelenting course had meanwhile had in other respects a chastening effect on the editors. Though the townsfolk's ill will toward the military had steadily mounted, little evidence of it appeared in print. Even when the so-called Battle of Golden Hill on the night of January 18, 1770, inflicted injuries on several soldiers and civilians, both Holt and Parker ignored its inviting propagandist possibilities. Parker, for example, four days later did not so much as mention the affair, and even the next week he again passed it over with the excuse that "a real true Account is difficult to come at, because whatever Side relates a Story, generally does it with a Bias." Not till February 5, when popular feeling had considerably cooled, did he give "the most impartial Account" he had been able to obtain, to the extent of four columns.

The newspapers treated the bloodier collision in Boston on March 5 with like caution. The *New-York Journal* ten days afterward published a concise factual report avoiding the word "Massacre." Elsewhere in the paper Holt even said that, "as a Printer, he is of no Party, but equally at the Service of all." On the 19th both Parker and Gaine printed a restrained version—again without the provocative term "Massacre"—taken from the pro-British *Massachusetts Gazette and Boston News-Letter*. Neither then nor later did the press present the patriot view of the incident or seek to use it to besmirch the local soldiery.

The Whig cohorts took a bolder line, however, when Parliament on April 12, 1770, removed all the Townshend duties save the one on tea and the Merchants' Committee began agitating to confine the nonimportation agreement to that article alone. But this new quarrel involved divisions within the same political camp, not a direct set-to with the government. Holt's and Parker's contributors flayed the proposal, insisting that the basic principle of unconstitutionality remained unaffected and that the "Mercantile Dons" sought only their selfish private gain. Gaine's *Gazette*, true to form, backed up the Committee, and the latter by a poll of the city (which the patriots scored as grossly unrepresentative) reported a majority for its side. Two days later, on July 11, a vessel departed for England with

---

O'Callaghan, ed., *Documentary History*, III, 536; Thomas, *History of Printing*, II, 262–263. The best over-all account of McDougall's difficulties is Dillon, *New York Triumvirate*, chap. vi.

orders reopening trade in everything but tea. The journalistic fire-works, however, continued unabated for many weeks. The *New-York Gazette or Weekly Post-Boy,* now conducted by James Park-er's son Samuel, joined Holt in condemning this base betrayal of the continental cause, and both published blistering items from other colonies to the same effect. Gaine's writers retorted with slurs on the good faith of the merchants elsewhere, particularly of "the *high* TOWN, the *mighty* TOWN, the *wise* TOWN, the *wonderful* TOWN of BOSTON." [16] The damage was in any case done beyond repair. The desertion of so important a mercantile center dealt a body blow to the whole intercolonial system which it could not long survive.

III

In Philadelphia meanwhile the *Pennsylvania Gazette* and the *Pennsylvania Journal* ardently supported the patriot cause, while the *Pennsylvania Chronicle,* thanks to internal rifts over editorial pol-icy, pursued an ambivalent course.[17] The *Chronicle,* a newcomer, had been founded on January 26, 1767, by Joseph Galloway and the wealthy Quaker merchant, Thomas Wharton, in the interests of weakening the Proprietor's authority over provincial legislation and, if possible, substituting a regime directly under the King. The particular grievance was the privileged tax status of the extensive lands of the Penn family. This had long been a political issue in Pennsylvania, with John Dickinson the principal spokesman of those who preferred to bear the ills they had rather than fly to oth-ers they knew not of. Religiously the question tended to array the well-to-do Quakers, who believed that the change would mean lower taxes for them, against the Presbyterians, who for secular as well as sectarian reasons opposed a closer connection with Crown.

Galloway and Wharton, unwilling to appear openly in their jour-nalistic venture, induced the 26-year-old William Goddard to re-move to Philadelphia to conduct the *Chronicle.* They agreed to sup-

[16] Quoted from "Ichabod Snuffle" in the *N.–Y. Gazette and Weekly Mercury,* Sept. 3, 1770. On this whole episode, see A. M. Schlesinger, *The Colonial Mer-chants and the American Revolution* (N. Y., 1918), 222–229.

[17] This account is in large part condensed from A. M. Schlesinger, "Politics, Propaganda, and the Philadelphia Press, 1767–1770," *Pa. Mag. of History and Biography,* LX (1936), 309–322.

ply half the capital in return for half the profits, and Galloway as Speaker of the Pennsylvania Assembly further guaranteed him the legislative printing. Since the political skies with England were then unclouded, the silent partners overlooked Goddard's militant course at the time of the Stamp Act in favor of his practical newspaper experience in Providence and New York. Moreover, the secret agreement obliged the printer to consult with them "in every material step, or transaction, relating to the said business." Despite this restriction Goddard believed he had adequately preserved his liberty of action by the stipulation, upon which he had insisted, that he be allowed to "keep a free press." [18] Before long both sides were to rue their bargain.

From the outset Goddard flaunted the motto: "RARA TEM-PORUM FELICITAS, UBI SENTIRE QUAE VELIS, ET QUAE SENTIAS DICERE LICET," which, without undue violence to Tacitus, may be rendered, "Happy the age in which one can think what he pleases and say what he thinks." For a time things went smoothly. Goddard obediently ran a series of articles to refute the *Pennsylvania Journal*'s charges that Benjamin Franklin as colonial agent had only lukewarmly opposed the Stamp Act.[19] This furthered his associates' purpose of rehabilitating the reputation of the most distinguished figure in the antiproprietary party. The editor in like fashion excluded from his columns a bitter attack on Galloway and his political cronies. When the *Journal* then printed the rejected piece, he could only bluster that the freedom of the press did not require his "publishing all the Trash" of "every rancorous, illiberal, anonymous Scribbler." [20]

These and similar actions dictated from behind the scenes soon aroused public resentment. Less than three months after the start of the paper Goddard angrily reported that "some *few* Persons" were demanding that "he should be *roughly handled,* for the Freedom of his Publications"; and shortly after, on April 4, a company at the British Coffee House threw him bodily out of doors, with William Bradford of the *Pennsylvania Journal* pulling at his hair. The par-

---

[18] William Goddard, *The Partnership: or the History of the Rise and Progress of the Pennsylvania Chronicle &c.* (Phila., 1770), 6–10; William Franklin to Benjamin Franklin, Nov. 13, 1766, Benjamin Franklin, *Complete Works* (John Bigelow, ed., N. Y., 1887–88), IV, 276–278.

[19] "A Lover of Justice" in the *Pa. Chronicle*, Feb. 9, 16, 23, March 9, 23, 1767.

[20] *Pa. Journal*, March 12, 1767; *Pa. Chronicle*, March 16.

ticular reason was that Goddard had refused space to William
Hicks, a prominent proprietarian, to deny charges made in the
Chronicle that he had anonymously written certain anti-Galloway
screeds. Following the Coffee House incident Hicks printed his disclaimer in both the *Journal* and the *Gazette* with the contemptuous
remark that poor Goddard had only followed "superior Direction."
Goddard answered with a three-column justification. Especially interesting, in view of his later admissions, was the avowal: "I am under no other *direction* but my own judgment, which has never been
bias'd, in the least degree, to the injury of the Public, or the poorest
individual." [21]

In reality the printer despite his bold front was beginning to find
his situation intolerable.[22] Instead of running a free and impartial
sheet, as he had expected, he must dance to his secret associates'
piping. True, he had agreed only to seek their advice, not follow it,
but their power to withhold funds gave them the whip hand. This
went particularly hard with a journalist to whom the independence
of the press was the very breath of life. It was made still harder by
letters from his aged mother Sarah Goddard, now in charge of his
old paper, the *Providence Gazette*, who with "aching heart and
trembling hand" implored him to extricate himself from his "unhappy uncomfortable position."

The passage of the Townshend Acts steeled him to action. During
the late summer and autumn of 1767 the Philadelphia newspapers
closely followed the brewing opposition in Massachusetts but with
little comment of their own. How Goddard knew of Dickinson's
well-kept plans to enter the controversy is impossible to say; but he
not only published the "Farmer's Letters" ahead of the city's other
editors as well as of anyone else in America, he also inaugurated the
series on December 2 in a special issue. Few things could have af-
fronted his partners more, for Dickinson's views of the limited powers of Parliament flatly contradicted those which Galloway as
"Americanus" had expressed at the time of the Stamp Act. Added to
this, they readily identified the "Farmer" as none other than their
most feared proprietarian adversary.

The editor, called on the carpet, justified what he had done as
both a circulation builder and a vital service to the patriot cause; but

---

21 *Ibid.*, March 9, 16, April 6, 13, 1767; *Pa. Journal* and *Pa. Gazette*, April 9.
22 Goddard, *The Partnership*, 8–19, relates his tribulations.

Galloway, so Goddard tells us, "ridiculed my notions about liberty and the rights of mankind," shouting that the Pennsylvanians, unlike the Rhode Islanders and Bostonians, were "none of *your* damned republican breed." Goddard, however, stood his ground, even to the point of inserting other strictures against the Townshend Acts and rejecting a series in answer to the "Farmer's Letters." In words Goddard himself might have used, "A.L." demanded in his pages on May 30, 1768, "Where will be the difference between being slaves under a Proprietary or Royal Government?" Goddard also reprinted portions of Dickinson's earlier pamphlet against the Stamp Act, which had accused Franklin and the other colonial agents of hoping to rivet the "fatal fetters" on their native land in order to secure "part of the horrid plunder in *oppressive offices* for THEMSELVES and THEIR CREATURES." [23] The *Chronicle* was, moreover, the first Philadelphia newspaper to carry the sensational Boston "Journal of Occurrences." [24] Goddard's partners nevertheless stopped him from issuing the "Farmer's Letters" as a pamphlet, and he had no choice but to allow them to loose a "host of angry scribblers" in the *Chronicle* to combat Dickinson's rising political fame.[25] This scurrilous campaign probably helped defeat the "Farmer" for the Pennsylvania Assembly in October, 1768, at the very time the colonists elsewhere were perfuming him with praise.

Behind doors the "unnatural alliance" waxed increasingly explosive. If Goddard's associates found him "imperious and obstinate," he found them "arrogant and supercilious." Disputes over finances further poisoned relations. Finally, in May, 1769, Galloway and Wharton withdrew from the business after forcing Goddard to accept his journeyman, Benjamin Towne, as partner by threatening to start a rival paper. By lending Towne £526 for the purpose they had effectively secured his loyalty. But this proved no better solution, for the new yokemates also wrangled endlessly, with the result that in the following February Towne abandoned the premises and later the partnership.[26] Goddard, however, did not forget his more

[23] *Pa. Chronicle*, July 4, 1768.
[24] The *Chronicle* inaugurated the series on Oct. 17, 1768. The *Gazette* did not pick it up till Nov. 17, and the *Journal* not till Dec. 8.
[25] For this onslaught, see "Frank Meanwell," "A Barbadian," "Country Farmer," "Machiavel," "Little John" and others in the *Pa. Chronicle*, July 25–Aug. 29, 1768.
[26] Goddard in *The Partnership*, 22–63, and in the *Pa. Gazette*, Aug. 2, 1770;

powerful antagonist. To defeat Galloway for the Assembly in October, 1770, he published a pamphlet on *The Partnership: or the History of the Rise and Progress of the Pennsylvania Chronicle* to expose the candidate's surreptitious role in the paper's management. The maneuver might well have succeeded if Galloway had not decided to run from his country seat in Bucks County.[27]

IV

Though Goddard had to fight for editorial independence against financial control, neither he nor his fellow publishers encountered official menaces to their freedom as did their brethren in Massachusetts and New York. Perhaps the Pennsylvania authorities were influenced by the futility of the efforts at suppression in these other colonies. The newspapers nevertheless kept the public alive to the issue of liberty of the press by recounting in detail Wilkes's troubles with the British government and by devoting many columns to McDougall's difficulties in New York. When the Sons of St. Patrick forgathered on March 17, 1769, they drank as a matter of course to "Mr. Wilkes," adding the sentiments: "May the liberty of the Press remain free from ministerial restraint," and, more jovially, "May all authors who by their writings support the cause of liberty be introduced into Heaven by St. Patrick." [28] For a while it appeared that the Whigs would gain additional support from a new organ, the *Penny Post*, which Benjamin Mecom ambitiously established as a triweekly on January 9, 1769. But the feckless printer, having failed at newspapering in New Haven and elsewhere, did even worse in his new location. His undertaking did not outlast the month.

The press campaign against the Townshend Acts aimed first at building a public sentiment that would prod the slow-moving merchants into following the examples of Boston and New York in ap-

Towne in the *Pa. Journal*, Aug. 16. There followed an acrimonious aftermath of words between the two men, with each buying space in the *Journal* and the *Gazette* to blacken the character of the other. See, for example, the *Pa. Journal*, July 19, 26, Aug. 9, 16, 30, Sept. 6, 1770.

[27] E. H. Baldwin, "Joseph Galloway, the Loyalist Politician," *Pa. Mag. of History and Biography*, XXVI (1902), 301. For later attacks by Goddard on Galloway and Wharton, see the *Pa. Chronicle*, Sept. 23, 1771, Feb. 24, April 27, May 11, 25, July 13, 1772.

[28] *Pa. Journal*, March 23, 1769.

plying economic pressure on Britain. And so, week after week, "A Freeborn American," "Cato," "Agricola," "Monitor" and their like bade the citizens cast off the "chains of slavery" by shunning British wares and thereby coercing the mercantile community into a nonimportation agreement. Galloway as "A Chester County Farmer" defended the recalcitrants against the charges of deficient patriotism, declaring that the Bostonians had launched the movement because their business was bad anyway, but "C." caustically returned, "No Thief ever voluntarily subscribed the penal laws against Felony. . . . The good of the whole community is the supreme law." [29] At long last the merchants on February 6, 1769, took the desired step.

Philadelphia also had a counterpart of the New York controversy over an Anglican episcopate, though it proved less acrimonious. Dickinson, both as leader of the proprietary party and as the constitutionalist of the "Farmer's Letters," took exception to this proposal of a closer tie with Britain. With his collaboration and perhaps that of others, the Reverend Francis Alison, the Presbyterian Vice-Provost of the College of Philadelphia, beginning on March 24, 1768, contributed twenty-one consecutive articles on the subject to the *Pennsylvania Journal*, under the name of "The Centinel." Like their prototypes in New York, the "Centinel" group condemned the plan as "an open acknowledgement of the Claims which the Enemies of America have lately set up, and which are totally subversive of our Rights and Liberties." [30] In an opposing series of almost equal length Dr. William Smith, the Anglican head of the College, replying as "The Anatomist," entered the same denials of the political implications of the move as his Manhattan confreres were making.[31] In the end, however, he patriotically gave up the debate, explaining to the "Centinel" in the *Gazette* and the *Journal*, January 12, 1769, "But, in truth, from the gloomy prospect that seems gathering against us on the other side of the *Atlantic*, it might be better

---

[29] Galloway also wrote against a nonimportation as "A.B." His articles and the replies by "Martinus Scribblerus" and "C." are in the *Pa. Chronicle*, June 16 and July 25, 1768, and the *Pa. Gazette*, July 21 and Aug. 4.

[30] *Pa. Journal*, May 12, 1768.

[31] "The Anatomist's" nineteen articles began in the *Gazette* and the *Journal*, Sept. 8, 1768, and in the *Chronicle*, Sept. 19. For fuller treatments of the dispute, see Cross, *Anglican Episcopate*, 203–210; R. J. Hooker, ed., "John Dickinson on Church and State," *American Literature*, XVI (1944), 82–98; and A. F. Gegenheimer, *William Smith, Educator and Churchman* (Phila., 1943), 189–191.

for you, and for me, to cultivate *domestic harmony* for the present, and suspend the settlement of our remaining differences to a more convenient season . . . ."

The newspapers regularly chronicled the defiant doings of the Massachusetts Whigs; and after the Boston fashion they even reported the encounter between the populace and the soldiers on King Street as the "bloody Massacre." [32] Parliament's abrogation of all the Townshend duties except that on tea only spurred them to new exertions. If the merchants on so slight a pretext should now abandon nonimportation, raged a *Chronicle* writer on May 7, 1770, they would ignobly betray the American cause. Others met a further argument against continuing the agreement by defending the Boston nonimporters against charges of hypocrisy.[33] Even when the news of New York's defection arrived, the press kept up the battle. "A True Son of Liberty" expressed his sense of shock in verses beginning:

> Amaz'd!—Astonished!—what *New-Yorkers* flee!
> Those *once boasted Sons* of sweet *Liberty!*
> Surely it can't be so!—I dream!—I stand!
> What!—*Yorkers* join with curs'd *oppression's-band!* [34]

"A Jersey Man," "Amor Patriae," "Nestor" and a host of others with similar intent employed the artillery of prose.

But dissenting voices now began to be heard in increasing number.[35] On September 20, the day set by the merchants for deciding the issue, the *Pennsylvania Gazette* at the urging of "Civis" repeated from Gaine's New York paper the table of Boston's importations earlier in the year. This timely—or untimely—disclosure no doubt made it easier for the merchants to follow New York in restricting the agreement to tea alone. The journalistic agitation had postponed, it could not avert, the inevitable.

---

[32] *Pa. Gazette*, March 22, 1770; *Pa. Chronicle*, March 26, July 30.

[33] Especially "A House Carpenter" in *ibid.*, June 18, 1770, and "Justice" in the *Pa. Gazette*, June 21.

[34] *Pa. Journal*, July 26, 1770.

[35] Note particularly "Philo-Veritas," *Pa. Gazette*, July 19, Aug. 2, 1770, and "A Philadelphian," Aug. 16.

V

In the provinces to the south, where newspapers were few and far between, the press in most places did little more than disseminate political news and reprint controversial articles from Northern and English journals. Even in far-off Georgia, Governor James Wright complained of "the inflammatory publications from the Northward," noting particularly that "Mr. Farmer" had "most plentifully sown his seeds of faction and Sedition to say no worse." In Maryland the lack of initiative probably reflected absorption in exciting local issues. Though Adam Boyd's establishment of the *Cape-Fear Mercury* at Wilmington on October 13, 1769, gave North Carolina a second organ, neither it nor the older *North-Carolina Gazette* exhibited any independent zeal in the patriot movement. Boyd undoubtedly disclosed the reason in refusing Isaiah Thomas's application for a job. "The Times are very critical," he wrote, "and at all Times the Director of a printing Office is liable to Censure and when this would happen You would like as little to bear Censure for Me as I would for you." [36]

The newspapers in the two remaining Southern colonies, however, took a stronger lead. In the Old Dominion, Arthur Lee wrote "The Monitor's Letters" in ten fiery installments in Rind's *Virginia Gazette*, February 25–April 28, 1768, to aid the "Farmer's Letters" in "alarming and informing" the public. When Rind combined Lee's essays with Dickinson's in a pamphlet, he could not print copies fast enough to meet the demand. [37] Both *Virginia Gazettes*, moreover, assiduously followed Wilkes's trials and tribulations. [38] As interest developed in a nonimportation agreement, George

[36] Wright to Lord Hillsborough, May 23, 30, Nov. 18, 1768, British Papers Relating to the American Revolution (Sparks MSS., Harvard College Library), II, 271, 272, 278; C. A. Barker, *The Background of the Revolution in Maryland* (New Haven, 1940), 316–317; Boyd to Thomas, Dec. 2, 1769, Isaiah Thomas Papers (Am. Antiquarian Soc.), I. The other newspaper in North Carolina, the *North-Carolina Gazette*, begun by James Davis at New Bern on May 27, 1768, appears to have been in effect a continuation of his *North-Carolina Magazine*, in existence since 1764.

[37] *Va. Gazette* (Rind), July 27, 1769; R. H. Lee, *Letters* (J. D. Ballagh, ed., N. Y., 1911), I, 42; R. H. Lee, *Life of Arthur Lee* (Boston, 1829), I, 220, 244.

[38] According to Stella Duff, "The Case against the King: The *Virginia Gazettes* Indict George III," *William and Mary Quar.*, ser. 3, VI (1949), 390, Wilkes "was discussed and quoted in the *Virginia Gazettes* more than any other single man."

Mason stressed in a letter to George Washington on April 5, 1769, the importance of having "something preparatory to it in our Gazettes," and accordingly, as "Atticus," he himself set forth America's grievances in the two papers, May 4, and then the next week pointed out that "no ministerial mandates nor circular letters, no instructions to Governors, nor orders to Generals, can oblige us to buy goods which we do not choose to buy." On May 18 the contemplated action was taken. A year later, after the partial repeal of the hated duties, Mason proposed to Richard Henry Lee that the agreement be amended to provide for publishing the names of violators in the press; and again he prevailed.[39] But in Virginia, as elsewhere, it was then too late to save the situation.

Charleston as the South's only real urban center and the fourth largest city on the continent displayed even greater activity. True, the *South-Carolina and American General Gazette*, published by Robert Wells, avoided political disputation as much as possible, but the other two papers—Charles Crouch's *South-Carolina Gazette and Country Journal* and particularly Peter Timothy's *South-Carolina Gazette*—entered wholeheartedly into the fight. Timothy, in fact, was the only Southern editor to enclose his report of the Boston Massacre in heavy black rules.[40] Early in 1769 writers in the Charleston press began to urge economic reprisals against England. "You cannot expect the merchants will begin this matter themselves," stated "A Planter" in the *South-Carolina Gazette*, June 1, ". . . Oblige them to it, by declaring you will deal with none that do import extra articles." Three weeks later the Whig chieftain, Christopher Gadsden, addressing the "Planters, Mechanicks and Freeholders" under the pen name of "Pro Grege et Rege," assailed the "numberless *weak* and *groundless reasons*" against a nonimportation, and on June 29 the *Gazette* submitted an agreement for the purpose with the warning that those failing to sign within a month would be boycotted. Though the merchants managed to publish a few articles on their side, they had no choice but to accept regulations substantially like those proposed.[41] Little wonder that Lieu-

[39] Mason to Washington, George Washington, *Writings* (J. C. Fitzpatrick, ed., Wash., 1931–44), II, 504 *n.*; Mason to Lee, June 7, 1770, Kate M. Rowland, *The Life of George Mason* (N. Y., 1892), II, 144–145.

[40] *S.–C. Gazette*, April 5, 1770.

[41] For defenses of the merchants, see "The Merchants of Charles-Town," *S.–C. and American General Gazette*, July 10, 1769, and "Pro Libertate et Lege," *S.–C. Gazette*, July 13.

tenant Governor William Bull bitterly called Timothy one of the "subalterns" in this movement.[42]

Though the Whig leaders had won their object, they unexpectedly encountered a newspaper adversary who threatened to cheat them of the fruits of victory. William Henry Drayton, an English-educated planter and wealthy kinsman of the Lieutenant Governor, was later to become a flaming patriot, but at this stage of his career he had not yet outgrown his natural conservatism. Very much like John Mein in Boston, he abhorred the clause in the agreement for black-listing nonsigners and violators; and Timothy, perhaps out of deference to so important a personage, made it possible for him to explode in print.[43]

Opening his campaign in the *South-Carolina Gazette*, August 3, 1769, Drayton as "Freeman" compared the penalty of public exposure to the "Popish method" of gaining converts "by fire and faggot" and declared that only the provincial legislature could lawfully stigmatize anyone "with the infamous name of *an enemy to his country*." As for Christopher Gadsden (whom he identified without naming), he was not only a *"vain demagogue,"* but a "traitor or madman" who should be forcibly confined, "at least during the ensuing change and full of the moon." "C.G." clawed back in the next *Gazette* with equal abuse, to which "Freeman" responded in kind the following week. When Drayton in September found himself on the proscribed list, he returned to the charge, anathematizing "illegal Restraints upon the free Wills of free Men," and voicing utter contempt for the *"profanum vulgus,"* whom he only reluctantly accepted as *"humani generis."* [44] The mechanics on the enforcement committee acidly rejoined that "Every man is not so lucky as to have a fortune ready provided to his hand, either by his own or his wife's parents." [45] Gadsden, for his part, combated Drayton's contention that the nonimportation agreement was a "confederacy" to injure others and hence unlawful. On the contrary, Gadsden insisted, as had "Atticus" in Virginia, that no law forbade free men to combine

[42] Leila Sellers, *Charleston Business on the Eve of the American Revolution* (Chapel Hill, 1934), 210.

[43] Whether Drayton knew of Mein's activities is uncertain, but Mein reprinted some of Drayton's most effective strictures in the *Boston Chronicle*, Oct. 30, 1769, and Jan. 11, 1770.

[44] *S.–C. Gazette*, Sept. 21, 1769.

[45] *Ibid.*, Oct. 5, 1769.

to trade with whomever they pleased.[46] When Drayton reiterated his stand, Gadsden, shifting to loftier ground, maintained that the people had merely exercised those *"inherent* rights of SOCIETY, which *no climate, no time, no constitution, no contract,* can ever destroy." [47]

Drayton found life growing constantly more difficult. Even the crops he raised on his plantation became a drug on the market.[48] When the legislature in December curtly rejected his petition for redress, he gave up the unequal fight and on January 3, 1770, sailed for England. The next day Timothy listed among the unacceptable goods returning on the ship "WILLIAM HENRY DRAYTON, ESQ., *Author of several late Political Pieces signed* FREEMAN." The one-man crusade had failed, but in the end Drayton's objective was attained without his help when South Carolina in December followed the Northern ports in limiting the nonimportation agreement to tea.

[46] *Ibid.,* Sept. 28, 1769.

[47] Drayton in *ibid.,* Oct. 12, 26, 1769, and "A Member of the General Committee" (Gadsden), Oct. 19. For fuller accounts of this controversy, which included lesser figures as well as Drayton and Gadsden, see Edward McCrady, *The History of South Carolina under the Royal Government* (N. Y., 1899), 651–662, and Schlesinger, *Colonial Merchants,* 202–206.

[48] Drayton's petition to the legislature, *S.–C. Gazette,* Dec. 14, 1769.

Chapter VII

Dead Center

T HE NEWSPAPERS had waged a spirited fight against the Townshend regulations and in doing so had asserted both by precept and example their freedom to criticize public men and measures. Along with other agencies of opposition, moreover, they had actually brought about a removal of nearly all the duties, including the burdensome ones on paper. This very success, however, was to sap their crusading zeal during the next few years. The colonists as a whole rejoiced at Parliament's concessions, regarding the remaining tax on tea as largely a face-saving gesture, and through most of the continent the editors concurred.

The return of good times after the long postwar depression further quieted men's nerves. Hugging the prospect of steady employment and better mercantile profits, the bulk of the people now frowned upon "officious Patriots," who "have nothing to lose, but when public rule and order are broken in upon and all things are thrown into confusion, they may be the gainers." [1] General Gage thankfully reported home, "I have nothing New to tell your Lordship but that harmony subsists throughout this Country, even at Boston . . . ." And in that difficult city Hutchinson, who had been acting as Governor since Bernard's ignominious departure in 1769, gleefully added that the gentleman who had greatly assisted the troublemakers "by his money, and by the reputation which his fortune gives him" was now shunning his quondam associates. Disillusioned, John Hancock undoubtedly was, for, among other things, his business affairs had gone awry while he played the politician.

---

[1] "Chronus" in the *Mass. Gazette and Boston News-Letter*, Jan. 2, 1772. Hutchinson was suspected by the Whigs of being the writer (*Mass. Spy*, Jan. 9, 16, 30, 1772), who was actually Dr. Henry Caner, rector of King's Chapel. See Thomas Hutchinson, "Additions to 'History of Massachusetts Bay,'" Catherine B. Mayo, ed., Am. Antiquarian Soc., *Procs.*, LIX (1949), 42.

John Adams shared his disenchantment. "I have stood by the people much longer than they would stand by themselves," he complained in his diary. "But I have learned wisdom by experience; I shall certainly become more retired and cautious; I shall certainly mind my own farm and my own office." In every colony but New York and Pennsylvania the inhabitants obediently paid the duty on tea despite the patriot agreements against doing so, and the apparent rectitude of these lone exceptions stemmed rather from the greater availability of the cheaper smuggled variety than from any devotion to principle.[2]

I

This tranquillity, welcome as it was to men like Thomas Hutchinson and Joseph Galloway, distressed Samuel Adams and the other Boston extremists, who believed that America was being lulled into a false sense of security. "If the People are at present hushd into Silence, is it not a sort of sullen Silence," Adams hopefully queried an intimate, but in the very next breath he admitted that "Too many are affraid to appear for the publick Liberty, and would fain flatter themselves that their Pusilanimity is true Prudence." The great danger, as he saw it, was that the colonists would think there was none. Lacking issues of obvious import as in the Stamp Act and Townshend crises, Adams and his "group of gloomy mortals" faced a situation that sorely tried their mettle.[3]

Fortunately they could bank on the unflagging support of Edes and Gill, who ran the *Boston Gazette*; and if Hutchinson was right, "seven eighths of the people read none but this infamous paper." Adams continued to write voluminously for it, using such signatures as "Candidus," "Vindex," "Valerius Poplicola" and "Cotton

[2] Gage to Lord Barrington, March 8, 1771, Gage, *Correspondence with the Secretaries of State* (C. E. Carter, ed., New Haven, 1931–33), II, 570–571; letter of Hutchinson, Jan. 31, 1772, British Papers Relating to the American Revolution (Sparks MSS., Harvard College Library), I, 137; John Adams's diary, May 2, 1771, in his *Works* (C. F. Adams, ed., Boston, 1850–56), II, 260; A. M. Schlesinger, *The Colonial Merchants and the American Revolution* (N. Y., 1918), 244–251, as to the consumption of tea.

[3] Samuel Adams to James Warren, March 25, 1771, John Adams and others, *Warren-Adams Letters* (W. C. Ford, ed.; Mass. Hist. Soc., Colls., LXXII–LXXIII, 1917–25), I, 9; "Chronus," *Mass. Gazette and Boston News-Letter*, Jan. 2, regarding the Adams group.

Mather," but this multiplicity of disguises probably fooled no one, least of all Hutchinson, who warned the Ministry that the stiff-necked partisan "would push the continent into a rebellion tomorrow, if it was in his power." [4] Among other outstanding contributors was Josiah Quincy, Jr.—known in Tory circles as "Wilkes Quincy"—who masqueraded variously as "Mentor," "Callisthenes," "Tertius in Nubibus" and the like. Perhaps to pursue this avocation more handily, he removed his law office in July, 1771, from King Street to a room under Edes and Gill's print shop on Queen Street.[5]

The irreconcilables also had access to the *Boston Evening-Post*, for the Fleets continued to conduct it as an open forum. Far more important, however, they acquired an outspoken new organ in the *Massachusetts Spy* which Isaiah Thomas, after trying his luck as a journeyman in several other colonies, set up in Boston on July 17, 1770, with the help of a temporary partner. Intended primarily for mechanics, the *Spy* got off to a poor start, changing from a triweekly to a semiweekly to a weekly, all within seven months, but then it won a secure footing.[6] Thomas many years later stated that at the outset he welcomed contributors regardless of party, but the files hardly bear him out. Within three months, indeed, he was openly soliciting articles from authors "supporting the LIBERTY for which our Fathers suffered in transferring it to us," and avowing it his ambition to be "as great a *Friend to True Liberty* as any of his profession in the four quarters of the Globe." Naturally the *Spy* office

---

[4] Hutchinson to Francis Bernard, Aug. 20, 1770, W. V. Wells, *The Life and Public Services of Samuel Adams* (Boston, 1865), I, 244, and to Lord Hillsborough, Oct. 17, 1771, Richard Frothingham, *Life and Times of Joseph Warren* (Boston, 1865), 162. Twenty-nine articles with the four pen names listed above are reprinted from the *Boston Gazette* in Samuel Adams, *Writings* (H. A. Cushing, ed., N. Y., 1904–08), II–III, which also cites others. "A. Z." in the *Mass. Gazette and Boston News-Letter*, Feb. 6, 1772, further perceived the "cloven Foot of the chief Director" in pieces by "An Elector" and "B. Y.," and Hutchinson informed Lord Dartmouth on Sept. 1, 1773, that those by "A." published during July and August probably had the same authorship. British Papers, I, 173. Undoubtedly many pseudonyms remain undetected.

[5] Josiah Quincy, *Memoir of the Life of Josiah Quincy, Junior* (rev. ed., Eliza S. Quincy, ed., Boston, 1874), 51–52; Frothingham, *Joseph Warren*, 157; *Mass. Spy*, July 18, 1771.

[6] Zechariah Fowle, to whom Thomas had once been apprenticed, was his partner until Oct., 1770, when Thomas bought him out with the help of friends. It was currently believed, however, that for a while in 1771–72 Joseph Greenleaf, a fellow Whig, was concerned in the business, and a letter of Thomas, March 30, 1772, to an unnamed correspondent (apparently Greenleaf) lends color to this surmise. Thomas Papers (Am. Antiquarian Soc.).

came to rival the *Boston Gazette* rooms as a Whig rendezvous. In fact, the youthful printer attracted the "more violent class of politicians." [7]

About his contributors Thomas in his autobiographical account is singularly reticent. One of the more thoughtful, "Centinel," published forty consecutive essays covering every conceivable grievance against the mother country.[8] Three others proved less successful in cloaking their identity, and these did most to give the paper its ultrasensational tone. Joseph Greenleaf ("Mucius Scævola"), a recent arrival from Abington, was perhaps the most audacious. Thomas himself also appeared occasionally, usually without concealment, though he rendered his greatest service by blending editorial opinion with the news, an art in which he surpassed all his contemporaries. Dr. Thomas Young, pungent writer of Townshend days in the *Evening-Post*, scored his hits most frequently as "Leonidas" and "Speculator, Jun." [9] "What a wretched Triumvirate!" sneered a Tory commentator, "a poor shiftless erratic Knight from Abington, a dunghill-bred Journeyman Typographer, and a stupid phrensical Mountebank." [10] Possibly, too, as Hutchinson believed, James Bowdoin supplied some of the "virulent pieces." [11]

Hutchinson, though ascribing the truculence of the press to "half a dozen disappointed men in distressed circumstances," nevertheless did not underestimate their capacity for mischief despite the prevailing political calm. Reluctant to seek legal recourse in view of past frustrations, he also found it difficult to secure the firm backing he desired from the two progovernment organs, Draper's *Massachusetts Gazette and Boston News-Letter* and Green and Russell's *Massachusetts Gazette and Boston Post-Boy*. Thus, when he had his

[7] Isaiah Thomas, *The History of Printing in America* (rev. ed., Am. Antiquarian Soc., *Trans. and Colls.*, V–VI, Albany, 1874), II, 63; *Mass. Spy*, Dec. 10, 1770; "A. Z." (Dr. John Eliot), "A Narrative of Newspapers Printed in New-England," Mass. Hist. Soc., *Colls.*, ser. 1, VI (1799), 73.

[8] *Mass. Spy*, May 2, 1771–March 26, 1772. Hutchinson attributed the series to John Adams who in turn stated in his diary that he believed he knew the writer, though unfortunately he did not name him. Adams, *Works*, II, 289, 293. The *Spy* itself kept mum, while the *Boston Gazette* without adding much illumination "confidently asserted" on Jan. 6, 1772, that the author was "a private Gentleman of a neighbouring Town, who has many Years been a close Student in the Law." This was probably another reference to John Adams.

[9] "Americanus" in the *Mass. Gazette and Boston News-Letter*, Aug. 15, 1771, and Richard Draper in *ibid.*, April 16, 1773.

[10] *Ibid.*, Aug. 8, 1771.

[11] Letter to Francis Bernard, May 29, 1772, Wells, *Samuel Adams*, I, 474.

friend Israel Williams of Hatfield indite an anonymous criticism of the agitators, Draper begged off publishing it "for fear of offending the Town and losing his customers." Not until four months later did the article appear, and then in the nonpartisan *Evening-Post*.[12]

One can only guess at the means Hutchinson employed to stiffen Draper's backbone, but he admitted engaging "two or three" writers for the paper.[13] The editor may also have plucked up courage because the *Evening-Post* was running some trenchant progovernment propaganda by "Philanthrop" (Attorney General Jonathan Sewall) with no visible damage to its circulation.[14] In any event the results quickly became apparent. "Americanus," "A Layman," "Æquitas," "Lelius" and other pseudonymous British sympathizers now crowded Draper's pages. One was undoubtedly Lieutenant Governor Andrew Oliver, whose son was detected by a *Boston Gazette* correspondent delivering copy to the Tory printer.[15] Another was Dr. Benjamin Church, a professed patriot;[16] and still another, the clergyman Dr. Henry Caner ("Chronus"). Even Draper himself, emboldened by the high-toned company he was keeping, sometimes inveighed against his and their foes.

The *Massachusetts Gazette and Boston Post-Boy*, however, proved a harder nut to crack. The editors, content with retailing a bare chronicle of events, sedulously avoided political contentions. Hutchinson and his advisers, after experimenting briefly with a new journal as we shall see, finally decided to replace Green and Russell with two younger men, Nathaniel Mills and John Hicks, the latter a one-time employee of John Mein. This did not occur, however, till April 26, 1773, and even then the paper at first displayed little more vigor.[17]

[12] Hutchinson to "Mr. Cheeseborough," Feb. 11, 1771, *Boston Gazette*, Jan. 15, 1776; correspondence of Hutchinson, Williams and Draper, Dec. 10, 1770–April 1, 1771, Israel Williams Papers (Mass. Hist. Soc.), II, 165–167; *Boston Evening-Post*, June 3, 1771.

[13] Letter to Francis Bernard, Dec. 3, 1771, *Boston Gazette*, Nov. 6, 1775.

[14] Draper nevertheless felt that the public would hold him to blame when it would not the Fleets, since they "print for both Sides." Letter to Israel Williams, Feb. 25, 1771, Williams Papers, II, 165. Hutchinson disclosed Sewall's identity in a letter to Williams, Jan. 10, 1771. *Ibid.*, II, 166. John Adams regarded the able Attorney General—his one-time friend—as a past master of disseminating "lies and slanders against his country." *Works*, II, 251.

[15] "Scarron" in the *Boston Gazette*, Dec. 7, 1772.

[16] Hutchinson to Francis Bernard, Jan. 29, 1771, Mass. Archives (State House, Boston), XXVII, 103.

[17] Thomas, *History of Printing*, I, 171–174.

In a more desperate move to improve conditions the Hutchinson group sought to coerce the *Massachusetts Spy* into becoming a Tory mouthpiece. This was not so wild an idea as might be supposed, for Thomas on taking over his partner's interest had assumed a mortgage on the press and types, and its holder, a royal official, now gave him the choice of either toeing the government line or straightway discharging the debt. The editor, however, foiled the scheme by borrowing the money from a patriot friend, whereupon his Tory subscribers melted away, and the Customs Board for a time denied him the vital news of ship arrivals and clearances in the hope of alienating still other readers.[18] Thomas exposed the meanness of these "petty lords" on May 23, 1771, and no doubt derived more than ordinary satisfaction when the Harvard Seniors shortly afterward commissioned him in Draper's stead to print their commencement theses.

The loss of this college account enraged Draper, who vented his wrath at considerable length in his *Gazette*, while a poetaster chided the erring class in halting grammar:

> How can ye patronize a Press,
> The Engine of all Ill,
> The God of Discord who caress,
> The World with Slander fill?

The *Spy* retorted by rebuking Draper's "foul-mouthed impertinence" and charging that his patron Hutchinson had surreptitiously tried to keep the job from Thomas. The *"low attempts of this great man"* to help *"a tool of his,"* commented the editor, *"needs but be told, to make it appear that he is a* TYRANT *in the* ABSTRACT." He even reported Hutchinson as snarling, *"Long ago would I have stopped the press, could I but have persuaded a majority of the ------- [Council] to have joined with me."* [19] Clearly the administration's attempt to suborn Thomas had had the effect of only making a bad situation worse.

---

[18] *Ibid.*, I, 165–166. His new creditor was apparently Joseph Greenleaf. See Thomas's letter of March 30, 1772 (Thomas Papers), cited earlier.

[19] The principal newspaper articles concerning this episode are in W. C. Lane, "The Printer of the Harvard Theses of 1771," Colonial Soc. of Mass., *Pubs.*, XXVI (1924–26), 1–15.

II

In the *Boston Gazette*, the *Spy* and the *Evening-Post* the Massachusetts incendiaries possessed an effective bellows, but to kindle a lasting flame they needed proper fuel as well. Where was this to be found in an era of good feelings? This difficulty, far from proving a deterrent, merely spurred them to greater endeavors. Lacking grievances of intercolonial scope as in Stamp Act and Townshend times, they grasped at a succession of local irritations, with the frustrating result, as we shall see, that the fires they set quickly burned to ashes. When late in 1773 success finally crowned their efforts, it was due less to their perseverance than to ministerial folly in providing an issue which involved not Massachusetts alone but all the colonies.

They first strove to make political capital out of the verdicts awarded the redcoats charged with the Boston Massacre. Although this ill-starred affair had occurred on March 5, 1770, the government postponed the trials till late in the autumn in order, as General Gage said, to allow the people's "Rage and Fury to Subside," and the jury then acquitted all the defendants but two, who escaped with being branded in the hand. Even though John Adams and Josiah Quincy, Jr., had represented the accused, the other Adams had no thought of forgoing so compelling an issue. "S. A--ms under the name of Vindex is trying the Soldiers over again," Hutchinson fumed to an intimate on January 11, 1771. Throughout that month "Vindex" argued stormily in the *Boston Gazette* that there had been a miscarriage of justice, while "Philanthrop" (Attorney General Sewall) countered his points one by one in the *Evening-Post*. Other Whig writers joined in, professing horror at the sight of British regulars still on the streets and execrating armies and "Military Tyranny" on principle. "Is this a Time," cried "Sidney," "for us to set up *gay Assemblies*, and show Tokens of Mirth, by *Dancing in our Chains*?" [20] On the first anniversary of the Massacre the *Boston Gazette* and the *Spy*, following the lead of Salem's *Essex Gazette*, appeared with emphatic type, black column borders and bloodcur-

[20] Thomas Gage to Lord Barrington, Nov. 12, 1770, Gage, *Correspondence*, II, 563; Hutchinson to Israel Williams, Williams Papers, II, 166; "Sidney" in the *Boston Gazette*, Jan. 14, 1771, and "Philo Patriae," Feb. 11.

dling rhetoric,[21] and the first two repeated the performance the next year.

The *Spy* in particular kept insisting that, if the troops were not recalled, what had happened once was bound to happen again. A contributor on May 2, 1771, portrayed the soldiers' continuing insolence, while another, citing the civil strife then raging in North Carolina, insinuated that Governor William Tryon's gory exploits against the Regulators foreshadowed Boston's own fate. On a still more intimate plane "A Bachelor" told in rhyme why local swains now shied at marriage:

> Of late the *red coat stranger,* silver'd round,
> The *gold tipt hilt,* the *black cockade* abound . . . .
> Still one more question! doleful as the first
> Remains!—'tis this! this answer!—is it worse
> To marry red coats leavings, or a - - - - - ! ! ! ?
> Read this, and trouble bachelors no more.

Later on, the *Spy* along with the *Boston Gazette* and the *Evening-Post* reported an attempted assault by a sailor off a warship upon two seamstresses on King Street, and the items severally concluded: "We should be much obliged to the Author of the late Journal of Occurrences for the resumption of his Pen on these occasions, which for some months past have been but too frequent among us." [22] The author (or authors), however, ignored the hint.

So meager was the effect of this propaganda that the malcontents next turned eagerly to a different and more promising issue. Nobody was surprised when Hutchinson on March 8, 1771, received a commission to be Governor in his own right, with Oliver as Lieutenant Governor; but the ministerial provision for defraying their salaries out of the imperial revenue was an innovation which freed those officials from future financial dependence on the Whig-controlled legislature. The *Massachusetts Spy*, announcing the new arrange-

---

[21] *Essex Gazette,* March 5, 1771; *Mass. Spy,* March 7; *Boston Gazette,* March 11. As a rule, however, the Salem publication followed rather than led the Boston press, copying most of its articles and, despite its Whig convictions, including also Tory pieces. The most effective local writer against the government was "Johannes in Eremo" (the Rev. John Cleaveland of Ipswich), whose articles began appearing on Jan. 8, 1771. Alice M. Baldwin, *The New England Clergy and the American Revolution* (Durham, 1928), 114–115.

[22] "Mucius Scævola" (Joseph Greenleaf) in the *Mass. Spy,* June 27, Sept. 5, 1771; "A Bachelor" in *ibid.,* March 14; *Boston Gazette* and *Boston Evening-Post,* Nov. 11, 1771; *Mass. Spy,* Nov. 14.

ment on the 14th under the scare heading "INTELLIGENCE EX–TRAORDINARY," grimly commented, "God save the free-born people of America!"

The news, long rumored in the newspapers, set off a train of protest and recrimination that lasted for months. Fearful of what might befall the liberty of the press under British-paid executive heads, Thomas began to pound away at the necessity of unalterably preserving that right. These disquisitions, if adding little to former ones on the subject, aimed to alert somnolent citizens to the danger. Employing a common dodge of Whig editors, he now paraded the motto "Open to ALL Parties, but influenced by NONE," and in the same number "Eleutherius" maintained that security of property and freedom of discussion ever went hand in hand. "In those wretched countries where a man cannot call his tongue his own," he affirmed, "he can scarce call any thing else his own." [23] A subsequent correspondent inserted two powerful essays on the theme from *Cato's Letters*. According to this British-penned bible of the patriots,

> What are usually called libels, undoubtedly keep great men in awe, and are some check upon their behaviour . . . . It is certainly of less consequence to mankind, that an innocent man should be now and then aspersed, than that all men should be enslaved. . . . The best way to prevent libels, is not to deserve them . . . . Guilty men alone fear them, whose actions will not bear examination, and therefore must not be examined.[24]

"W-----m S-----w" (the Reverend Charles Chauncy) gave a practical twist to the argument in the *Boston Gazette* by urging voters in the coming election for the Assembly to reject candidates "who are enemies to FREEDOM with the PEN" and "long for constituted *inspectors of the press*." [25]

Meanwhile the journalistic foray against the revamped regime gathered momentum. The *Spy* on March 21, 1771, printed a sheaf of fake congratulatory addresses to the Governor acidly parodying

---

[23] *Ibid.*, March 7, 1771.

[24] *Ibid.*, April 19, 1771. The essays, which appeared on March 28 and April 19 and 25, were *"Of FREEDOM of SPEECH; That the same is inseperable from public LIBERTY,"* and *"DISCOURSE upon LIBELS."* The joint authors of this work, as was noted in a previous chapter, were Thomas Gordon and John Trenchard.

[25] *Boston Gazette*, May 6, 1771. For the identification, see Harbottle Dorr's file of newspapers in the Massachusetts Historical Society.

those he had really received. The next week "Ultor" dilated on the danger of rulers immune to popular restraint: "This, political writers stile a *power* without a *check*, i.e. a *tyranny*." "Leonidas" (Dr. Young), "Candidus" (Samuel Adams) and others in the *Spy* and the *Boston Gazette* stepped up the barrage. In "Centinel's" opinion, the Assembly's loss of the power of the purse changed Massachusetts "from a free state to a petty monarchy." "Leonidas" labeled Hutchinson "a traiterous usurper, a most ungrateful, subtle, cruel, and ambitious tyrant." [26] And all agreed that the ministerial grant of salaries infringed the provincial charter.

The progovernment writers concentrated on destroying the critics rather than the criticisms. "Impavidus" derided "the delusions of a few Firebrands against Order," while "Publius" emitted such epithets as "braying Brethren," "Pseudo-Patriots," "vindictive Rage," "villainous Attempts" and "frothy Ebullitions of a disordered Imagination." "Lelius," predicting that the "impious efforts of a few desperate Incendiaries" could only breed "hostility and bloodshed," conjured up "the horrors of a civil War" with "the various barriers of private felicity broken down,—Father against Son, Son against Father, every endearing tie dissolved." [27]

The Whig spokesmen at first affected to scoff at the frenzied rebuttal, "Leonidas" gibing that the "Court Scribblers" plainly upheld "a desperate Cause" since "neither the National Treasury nor the American Revenue Chest can produce more plausible defenders." [28] But, as the barbs sank deeper, "Musacolis" rebuked Draper in the *Spy*, August 8, for "midwifeing into day-light such detestable trash," and pointedly remarked, "are you, after the example of your friend Mein, contriving to multiply enemies, and resolving to exasperate them to that degree, that some of them, may be tempted to usher you into public notice, by breaking your bones?"

Though the patriot journalists considered Hutchinson their chief quarry, they did not neglect the Lieutenant Governor. Oliver was suspect not only as an ex-stampmaster, but because his appointment converted the Massachusetts government into something of a family compact. As the *Boston Gazette*, April 22, 1771, correctly

---

[26] "Centinel" in the *Mass. Spy*, May 16, 1771, and "Leonidas," May 2.

[27] "Impavidus" in the *Mass. Gazette and Boston Post-Boy*, May 6, 1771; "Publius" in the *Mass. Gazette and Boston News-Letter*, May 23, 30; "Lelius" in *ibid.*, June 6.

[28] *Boston Gazette*, May 27, 1771.

noted, Hutchinson and Oliver were brothers-in-law, Oliver's daughter was the spouse of one of Hutchinson's sons, each of the parents had a brother on the Superior Court, and each too had children married to other members of that tribunal.

Fresh ammunition for the onslaught came from the pen of Arthur Lee, since 1768 in England, where he was a crony of John Wilkes and a correspondent of Samuel Adams. Taking advantage of the current popularity of a more famous "Junius," the Virginian as "Junius Americanus" was occupying himself in flaying Britain's colonial policy in the London press. One article charged that Oliver when secretary of the Governor's Council had been censured by the members as a "perjured traitor" for misrepresenting to the Ministry their discussions following the Boston Massacre. When the *Spy* on October 17, 1771, and the *Boston Gazette* four days later reprinted the screed, Governor Hutchinson, anxious to spike the story, had the Council on October 24 pronounce the allegation "false, groundless, and malicious." [29] The *Boston Gazette*, however, took away much of the effect by disclosing that only eight of the twenty-six Councilors had been on hand when the vote was taken.[30] The net result was to cause the patriot writers to insist more vehemently than ever upon the original version.

If Oliver had followed his personal inclinations, he would have prosecuted the editors, but the almost certain prospect of a hostile jury made him support the milder course adopted by the Council.[31] Nevertheless the fires were building up for the more drastic action, with Hutchinson awaiting the most propitious moment. For some months the "Court Scribblers" had been preparing the public for this step. Thus "Lelius" queried rhetorically in Draper's *Gazette*, June 6, 1771, "whether the liberty of the subject, the welfare of the community, would be more in danger from the authority of an established *Imprimatur*, than from the turbulent lucubrations of a few conceited, sanguinary Demagogues," and "Benevolus" on Au-

---

[29] *Mass. Gazette and Boston News-Letter*, Oct. 24, 1771. Lee's article appeared in the *London Gazetteer*, June 27, 1771, and *Bingley's Journal*, June 29. For the identity of "Junius Americanus," which was widely suspected at the time, see R. H. Lee, *Life of Arthur Lee* (Boston, 1829), I, 24, 199–200. Draper's *Gazette*, Nov. 14, published a three-page vindication of Oliver.

[30] *Boston Gazette*, Oct. 28, 1771. Hutchinson, *Massachusetts Bay*, III, 320, confirms this.

[31] Letters to Francis Bernard, Nov. 1, 1771, May 29, 1772, Andrew Oliver, Letter Book (Gay Transcripts, Mass. Hist. Soc.), II, 54, 85.

gust 8 assured the chief executive that by curbing the licentiousness of the press he would in fact be protecting the true liberty of the press.

A philippic by "Mucius Scævola" in Thomas's *Spy*, November 14, 1771, presented the Governor with the hoped-for occasion. The unnamed author, Joseph Greenleaf, foaming with rage, branded Hutchinson "a usurper" whose signature on a legislative act could have no legal binding effect. "A ruler, independent on the people," he went on, "is a monster in government," and "the council, according to the charter, should take upon itself the government of this province." The *Evening-Post* called the article probably the "most daring production ever published in America." [32]

On November 16 the Council summoned Thomas for questioning and, when he declined to attend, unanimously voted to sue him for seditious libel.[33] Their instructions to the Attorney General, however, left it unclear whether the usual resort would be had to a grand jury or the case be taken directly to court by an "information." The Whig zealots, seizing on the ambiguity, charged the authorities with not only menacing liberty of the press but also with furthering the pernicious doctrine of the end justifying the means. "Hyperion" (Quincy) declared that the government desired to by-pass the grand jurors because of their known aversion to "the star chamber law of libels," while "A.B." argued, "The Freedom of a people must be very far gone indeed, when they are subjected to answer to INFORMATIONS for no crime, unless it be a crime to enquire whether Mr. Hutchinson is in fact a Constitutional, Charter Governor . . . ." [34]

Regardless of which method the government might choose, the *Spy*, November 28, invoked the "venerable, great and good" Andrew Hamilton's argument in the Zenger trial that truth was always a defense in cases of seditious libel, and it added a long passage from an essay by William Bollan, the Council's own agent in London, the gist of which was that "The more *injurious* the *designs* of men, the greater their *solicitude* will ever be to *prevent* the FREE

---

[32] *Boston Evening-Post*, Nov. 18, 1771.

[33] *Mass. Spy*, Nov. 22, 1771; Thomas, *History of Printing*, I, 166–168, II, 255–256.

[34] "Hyperion" in the *Boston Gazette*, Nov. 25, 1771; "A. B." in the *Mass. Spy*, Nov. 22. The identification of "Hyperion" is from Harbottle Dorr's file of newspapers in the Massachusetts Historical Society.

EXAMINATION of them." In a protracted series of articles "Centinel" traced the history of the iniquitous Star Chamber in England and cited numerous legal opinions to prove a jury's right to decide the truth. He maintained that "crushing *Mucius*" would in effect be "crushing the *Press* itself." [35]

How, indeed, "Ambidexter" blandly inquired in the *Boston Gazette*, November 18, had "Mucius Scævola" borne false witness: "Is not a ruler independent on the people a *monster* in government?" "Cotton Mather" (Samuel Adams) heartily agreed in the next number that "Scævola" had uttered only "words of *truth* and *soberness*," and so did "Centinel" in two learned essays in the *Spy*, November 22 and 28. "Mucius Scævola," now resuming his pen, marveled that anyone could think it "unlawful, *barely* to *ask*, . . . Whether the person in the Chair is a lawful and constitutional Governor." [36] In this spate of ink the writers conspicuously omitted the titles of respect due the chief magistrate. "Hyperion" (Quincy) explicitly addressed his diatribe in the *Boston Gazette*, November 25, *"To the Man whom Conscience forbids to stile my Governor."*

The Council, unshaken by this clamor, acted first against Greenleaf, "generally reputed to be concerned with Isaiah Thomas" in publishing the *Spy*. On December 10, 1771, it declared him guilty of contempt for refusing to show up for examination and then dismissed him as Justice of the Peace in Plymouth County.[37] "O MON–STRUM HORRENDUM!" screamed the *Spy* on the 12th. "Massachusettensis" in the same number denied the Council's right to exercise the powers of a court without express authority of the charter or of provincial law. A versified comment,[38] after reciting the decree

> That the said G-------f be no more,
> A justice as he was before!

continued,

> This is a new fashion law and right!
> This is a tyrant's boyish spite!

[35] *Ibid.*, Dec. 5, 12, 19, 26, 1771, Jan. 2, 1772. The quotation is from the final installment.

[36] *Ibid.*, Nov. 28, 1771.

[37] *Ibid.*, Dec. 19, 1771, Jan. 9, 1772; Greenleaf in the *Boston Gazette*, Jan. 13, 1772.

[38] "A MODERN TALE" in the *Mass. Spy*, Feb. 27, 1772.

and closed with the defiance:

> However lordly fools would be! ! !
> FOREVER shall the PRESS be FREE! ! !

At the Boston session of the Superior Court in February, 1772, the government struck at the greater offender. In view of the outcry against an information it had decided upon the less exceptionable alternative.[39] Crowds jammed the courtroom. After the Chief Justice harangued the grand jury on the unlawfulness of subversive publications, the Attorney General presented a bill of libel against Thomas, but the jurors refused to indict. The authorities, convinced that the jury had been packed, then directed the Attorney General to file an information against the printer.[40] On sober second thought, however, they chose to drop the matter. "No writer needs now to stand in fear of you," "Leonidas" (Dr. Young) taunted Hutchinson in the *Spy*, July 30, "for if prosecutions by information be given up, we are under no dreadful apprehensions from the court doctrine of the most undeniable truths being found the most offensive and punishable libels."

Hutchinson might not have yielded so readily if the malcontents had proved more successful in alarming the public. The surface waters had indeed been ruffled, but the depths remained placid. After all, the Ministry's assumption of the top administrative salaries relieved the provincial budget of a heavy annual charge—£1500 in the Governor's case alone—and this could not deeply offend a people chronically averse to being taxed. Moreover, "Chronus" and his able colleagues on Draper's *Gazette* preached through thick and thin the gospel of contentment and good times while roundly scoring the hypocrisy of a "few pretended Patriots." In this spirit "Philanthrop, junior," took as his theme:

> Behold yon Patriot bellowing loud
> For Liberty—that darling Theme.
> Pull off the Mask—'tis private Grudge
> Or Party Rage that forms the Scheme.[41]

---

[39] Hutchinson, "Additions," 46–47.

[40] *Mass. Spy*, Feb. 27, 1772; Thomas, *History of Printing*, I, 168; *Censor*, March 7, 1772; "Philanthrop, junior," in *Mass. Gazette and Boston News-Letter*, April 9.

[41] *Ibid.*, April 9, 1772.

A Tory correspondent in the *Evening-Post,* April 27, 1772, described the country folk as "so far from approving our scandalous News-Papers, that I question whether one in ten of the common people, that take them, so much as give them a reading."

Still, Hutchinson did not allow himself to become overconfident. On November 23, 1771, nine days after "Mucius Scævola's" jeremiad, he helped to establish a new government organ, the *Censor,* conducted by Ezekiel Russell, a brother of the spineless Joseph Russell of the *Massachusetts Gazette and Boston Post-Boy.* This latest ally, Hutchinson assured Bernard in England, "says he will not be frightened, and I hope for some good effect." The first number assailed "Scævola," "Candidus," "Leonidas" and other *"state-desperadoes"* so savagely that, as the printer informed his readers the following week, *"a certain sett of partizans"* denied him *"the use of the press which had hitherto been open to him,"* and only *"the bounty of his benevolent Friends"* had enabled him to continue. Avowedly a journal of opinion, the *Censor* rarely bothered to print news and never reported local happenings. Typical of its temper was the *"Recipe* to make a *modern* PATRIOT for the *colonies,* especially for the *Massachusetts"*:

> Take of impudence, virulence, and groundless abuse, *quantum sufficit;* of flowing periods, *half a drachm;* conscience a *quarter* of a *scruple;* atheism, deism, and libertinism, *ad libitum;* false reports well adapted, and plausible lies, with groundless alarms, *one hundred wt. avoirdupois;* a malignant abuse of Magistracy, a pusillanimous and diabolical contempt of divine revelation and all its abettors *an equal quantity;* honour and integrity not quite an *atom;* fraud, imposition, and hypocrisy, any *proportion* that may seem expedient; infuse these in the credulity of the people, *one thousand gallons* as a *menstrum,* stir in the *phrenzy* of the *times,* and at the end of a year or two, this judicious composition will probably bring forth a Y----, an A----, an O---, and a M-------.[42]

Probably the *Censor's* most eminent contributor was Lieutenant Governor Oliver who as "Freeman" turned out a series of six cogently reasoned articles in defense of Hutchinson's policies.[43] Ini-

[42] Hutchinson to Francis Bernard, Dec. 3, 1771, *Boston Gazette,* Nov. 6, 1775; "Recipe" of "T. N." in the *Censor,* Feb. 8, 1772. The initials stood for Thomas Young, Samuel Adams, James Otis and William Molineux, the last a fomenter of riots.

[43] *Ibid.,* Dec. 14, 1771–Jan. 18, 1772. Hutchinson identified "Freeman" in a letter to Francis Bernard, March 23, 1772, *Boston Gazette,* Nov. 6, 1775. The

tially the sheet attracted subscribers, and its chief patron reported to the Ministry on January 31, 1772, "The plain dispassionate pieces in favour of Government which are now published with freedom in our Newspapers, and dispersed through the Province have done great service." [44] But the public soon tired of a newspaper without news; and its "benevolent Friends," either from unwillingness to continue financial help or because they felt the *Censor* had already accomplished its mission, let it die on May 2, 1772.

III

The government's success in wooing the populace dismayed nobody more than Samuel Adams. Writing as "Candidus," he sternly warned the citizens against the "Court Scribblers." "They are daily administering the opiate with multiplied arts and delusions;" he said, "and I am sorry to observe, that the gilded pill is so alluring to some who call themselves the *friends of Liberty*." [45] Thomas, brooding over his assorted woes, began to wonder whether the game was worth the candle and even made tentative inquiries about becoming a printer in Bermuda.[46] Actually, however, the popular apathy stimulated both men to redoubled efforts. Perhaps they felt they had erred in the past only by being too restrained. At any rate the *Boston Gazette* in particular now scaled dizzy heights of political speculation and prediction that strangely anticipated the great newspaper debate early in 1776 over Independence.

"Monitor," one of the *Spy* group, cited the "Farmer's Letters" as his authority for affirming that "no legislative body on earth has a greater right to meddle with the internal policy of our government, than we have with that of Great-Britain or Morocco," [47] but some

---

Boston Gazette, May 11, 1772, repeated the rumor that "the Commissioners, their understrappers and others of their stamp" wrote for the *Censor*. For a more detailed account of this paper, see L. N. Richardson, *A History of Early American Magazines* (N. Y., 1931), 158–162.

[44] *Censor*, Dec. 21, 1771; Hutchinson to Lord Hillsborough, British Papers, I, 137.

[45] *Boston Gazette*, Oct. 14, 1771. "Crispin" in the *Mass. Spy*, Jan. 16, 1772, and "Philo Veritatis," Jan. 23, expressed like sentiments.

[46] Letter of March 18, 1772, to an unnamed Bermudian, Isaiah Thomas Papers, I.

[47] *Mass. Spy*, Dec. 5, 1771.

of his fellows on the *Boston Gazette* far outdistanced him. "An American," for example, declaimed on January 6, 1772,

> The Americans well know their weight and importance in the political scale; that their alliance, and the privilege of a free trade with them, will be courted by all the powers in Europe . . . . Their situation is such, their natural advantages so great, and so immense will be their sources of wealth and power, that . . . they may soon become the arbiters among nations, and set bounds to kingdoms . . . .

If the mother country did not mend her ways, he continued, the course the colonists "probably will take, is, to form a government of their own, similar to that of the United Provinces in Holland, and offer a free trade to all nations in Europe." "America Solon," agreeing in the *Gazette* of the 27th, calculated that in twenty years the colonies would have as many people as all England, and in fifty years twice as many. "By one stroke of policy," he cried, "they can form an independent state," and "this they can do immediately if they please," but he deemed it an acceptable alternative "to let the several parliaments in Britain and America be (as they naturally are) free and independent of each other," with the King as the only "centre of union." This proposal in effect denied to the parent country even the right to regulate colonial trade.

Other writers delivered a similar ultimatum, "Fervidus" on March 16th threatening that, "If public measures be not speedily and diametrically changed, the people, quite weary of oppression and insult, will unite their force, like a torrent or hurricane, and drive their oppressors, from the face of the American world . . . ."[48] In a later screed (May 18) this journalist called Hutchinson and his crew "the greatest of criminals—more worthy to be 'delivered into the hands of the executioner' than private robbers, assassins or murderers." Enjoining his countrymen to cultivate the military art, he went on, "we should all, as one man, be in utmost *readiness* to resist, *even unto blood*, the cruel enemies of our

---

[48] The *Boston Gazette*, Feb. 17, 1772, reprinted a piece of this tenor, signed "Verax," from the *N.–H. Gazette*, Jan. 10, which otherwise followed a conservative line through these years. "Foresight" in the *Essex Gazette*, Feb. 25, declared, with better luck than most political seers, that the independence of the colonies was "very near—'tis not probable that it is at a distance of fifteen years." For other quotations from such writers, see Richard Frothingham, *The Rise of the Republic of the United States* (Boston, 1872), 291 *n.*

liberty. . . . If they attack us there must be a most horrible scene of slaughter and *garments rolled in blood . . . .*"

How accurately these utterances revealed the deeper purposes of the extremists it would be hard to determine. The student must be on guard, for a knowledge of later events often distorts the shape of earlier ones. The defiances may have been pure bombast; they may merely have exemplified the Yankee's trick of overstatement in order to drive a better bargain; or they may have been intended as so many straws to test the wind. Whatever the object, the writers did not speak for the rank and file of patriots, who undoubtedly felt with Thomas Cushing that a redress of grievances would come more readily "if these high points about the supreme authority of Parliament were to fall asleep." [49]

Hutchinson himself believed that the agitators hoped to stampede him into another libel prosecution in order to "raise fresh riots and other disorders." Probably for this reason his supporters said little in return. "A.Z.," however, in a well-considered discourse in Draper's *Gazette* combated the contention that the empire was, or should be, a mosaic of self-sufficient commonwealths. And "Philanthrop, junior," maintained that an independent America, far from securing foreign protection in exchange for its trade, would find itself "in the same wretched State" as a great part of Flanders during the last century and more—"the object of War between the Powers of Europe." [50]

At this juncture reports of the Ministry's plan to confer financial security on the Superior Court shunted the patriot attack in a new direction. Newspaper protests against the similar provision for the Governor and Lieutenant Governor had never ceased, thus giving the propagandists the benefit of an advance build-up of sentiment. This latest move, they maintained, proved beyond doubt the purpose of *"setting up an absolute tyranny* over us." [51] "Now is the time when the sacred fire should enkindle and catch from breast to breast," screamed "Americus" in the *Boston Gazette*, August 31, 1772. "Is it possible," demanded "Callisthenes" (Josiah Quincy,

[49] Letter to Arthur Lee, Sept. 30, 1773, Mass. Hist. Soc., *Colls.*, ser. 4, IV (1858), 360.

[50] Hutchinson to Lord Hillsborough, Oct. 1, 1772, British Papers, I, 149; "A.Z." and "Philanthrop, junior," in the *Mass. Gazette and Boston News-Letter*, March 5, April 9, 1772.

[51] *Boston Gazette*, June 15, 1772, and *Mass. Spy*, June 25. See, similarly, "Simon Zelotes" in the *Spy*, Aug. 27.

Jr.) in the same pages, September 28, that this last aggression "should not move us and drive us, not to desperation, but to our duty?" "Mary Truth," with an "Amazonian glow" warming her breast, implored in the *Spy*, October 1, "Arise, my countrymen! consult what is to be done, and the Lord will be with you." "America Solon" pointed out that the new ministerial policy infringed not only the provincial charter but also the colonists' natural rights.[52]

Although Hutchinson had remained proof against the talk of American independence, this fresh offensive momentarily threw him off balance. The precipitating cause was a piece by "Akolax" in Thomas's *Spy*, September 10, 1772, boldly addressed "*To the KING.*" The unidentified author berated George III for corrupting the home government with "sinecures for every dirty booby who was thought a convenient tool" and, beyond this, for enforcing "with charged bayonets" laws which did not have the colonists' consent. He threatened that American resistance to the salary grant would not be the play-acting of Stamp Act days: "Every one knows what they have done, what they ought to have done, and what they now ought to do."

Could anything be more subversive of imperial authority? The irate Governor resolved to proceed against the printer by an information, but the Council, remembering the earlier uproar, persuaded him to present the matter to the grand jury. News of the proposed step brought James Otis hurrying to the *Spy* office, his darkened mind still capable of flashes of legal acuteness. Scrutinizing the offending piece paragraph by paragraph, he declared at the end of each, "There is no treason in that," until he reached the most reckless passage when, after repeated reading, he exclaimed, "Touch and go, by God." Pronouncing the article as a whole within the law, the veteran patriot volunteered to act as Thomas's counsel.[53]

The weakness of the government's position lay in the fact that similar calumnies in the English press currently went unpunished. To drive this point home, Thomas copied into the *Spy*, October 8, an intemperate address to George III from the *Middlesex Journal*, remarking that *"No notice was taken of it, either by the King, his privy council, Lord Mansfield, or the Attorney General."* Indeed,

---

[52] *Boston Gazette*, Oct. 12, 1772.
[53] Hutchinson to Lord Hillsborough, Oct. 1, 1772, British Papers, I, 149; Thomas, *History of Printing*, II, 258.

the Ministry itself advised Hutchinson that, "in the present temper of the times, prosecutions will be of no effect," and that the citizens could without prompting be trusted to despise reflections on "the person of their Sovereign." Hutchinson on cooler thought therefore called off the proceedings, and the next spring Chief Justice Peter Oliver of the Superior Court, following the ministerial bidding, lamely instructed the grand jury that newspaper libelers had made themselves so "nauseous to the public" that they themselves had become ashamed of their "criminal" actions.[54] Meanwhile, however, the incident had opened new sluice gates of rhetoric over the freedom of the press. Should this be once destroyed, warned Thomas, *We may next expect padlocks on our lips, fetters on our legs, and only our hands left at liberty to slave for our* worse than Egyptian task masters, *or—or*—FIGHT OUR WAY TO CONSTI–TUTIONAL FREEDOM!" [55] Naturally enough, the Whig protagonists linked this issue with the hated grant of judicial salaries, which, they insisted, would "ever incline dependent Judges" to "punish all who speak or write in opposition to tyranny." [56]

Samuel Adams and his lieutenants now decided that the Ministry's move in regard to the justices warranted action by the Boston town meeting. Speaking as "Valerius Poplicola" in the *Boston Gazette*, October 5, 1772, he prepared the ground by reminding the citizens that their past docility had resulted only in *"Pensioners* multiplying like the Locusts in Egypt." "Let every Town assemble," he enjoined. "Let Associations & Combinations be every where set up, to consult and recover our just Rights." Behind doors the patriot higher-ups perfected the scheme. A revealing glimpse can be caught from the diary of Samuel's well-known kinsman. Drawn back into politics despite his earlier qualms, John Adams tells of finding Paul Revere in Edes and Gill's office one morning in late October listening to Otis, "his eyes fishy and fiery," descant on ways and means of opposing the new salary decree. The day before, Otis, Samuel Adams and Thomas Cushing had participated in a similar conference. On November 2 the town meeting, after a spirited colloquy with

54 Lord Dartmouth to Hutchinson, Dec. 9, 1772, State Papers (Gay Transcripts, Mass. Hist. Soc.), XIII, 60–62; "Speculator, Jun." (Dr. Young) in the *Mass. Spy*, April 8, 1773. For British tenderness toward colonial liberty of the press, see later, Appendix C.

55 *Mass. Spy*, Oct. 8, 1772.

56 "America Solon" in the *Boston Gazette*, Oct. 12, 1772. "Oliver Cromwell" argued similarly on Oct. 19, as did "Middlesex" on Dec. 21.

Governor Hutchinson over the judges' stipends, appointed a standing committee of correspondence on American rights and requested other Massachusetts communities to do likewise. Otis was the first chairman, but, retiring soon to the madhouse, he was succeeded by the "Grand Incendiary of the Province," as Hutchinson termed Samuel Adams. In addition, the membership of twenty-one included Josiah Quincy, Jr., Joseph Greenleaf, Thomas Young and Joseph Warren, all adepts at newspaper propaganda. Hutchinson doubtless had some of these as well as the chairmen in mind when he told the Ministry that at least three or four of the group were "as black-hearted fellows as any upon the globe." [57]

The committee-of-correspondence plan was designed both to supplement and intensify the journalistic agitation. As Samuel Adams wrote a political intimate, "where there is a Spark of patriotick fire, *we* will enkindle it." As town after town accepted Boston's call, usually under the pressure of aggressive minorities, the newspapers of the metropolis spread the votes and resolutions before the public. In due course the responses grew so numerous that they had to be divided up for publication. Nevertheless, the system of cross-fertilization, though amounting to more than the "foolish scheme" Hutchinson at first privately considered it, was at this stage still far from being the "most venomous serpent ever issued from the eggs of sedition," as another Tory was later to call it. Before that came about, a much more formidable grievance—and one of continental rather than merely of provincial proportions—would arise to galvanize the committees. [58]

The journalistic marksmen, however, did the best they could with the ammunition at hand. John Adams, once more active in the fray, employed his legal learning in a somewhat ponderous debate with William Brattle of the Governor's Council over the question of judicial salaries, [59] while other writers renewed the earlier threats of

[57] Adams, *Works*, II, 299–301; Records Commissioners of the City of Boston, *Reports* (Boston, 1876–1908), XVIII, 92–93; Hutchinson, *Massachusetts Bay*, III, 361–368; Hutchinson to Thomas Gage, March 7, 1773, Wells, *Samuel Adams*, I, 488, and to Lord Hillsborough, Nov. 10, 1772, Mass. Hist. Soc., *Procs.*, ser. 1, XIX (1882), 140.

[58] Samuel Adams to James Warren in Plymouth, Dec. 9, 1772, *Warren-Adams Letters*, I, 14; *Mass. Spy*, Oct. 7, 1773; Hutchinson to unknown, Nov. 10, 1772, Mass. Hist. Soc., *Procs.*, ser. 1, XIX, 140; "Massachusettensis" (Daniel Leonard) in the *Mass. Gazette and Boston Post-Boy*, Jan. 2, 1775.

[59] Brattle in the *Mass. Gazette and Boston News-Letter*, Dec. 31, 1772, Jan. 7, 1773, the *Mass. Gazette and Boston Post-Boy*, Jan. 4, and the *Boston Gazette*, Jan.

disunion. Unless Parliament recognized that "no people on earth have a right to make laws for the Americans but themselves," declared a *Boston Gazette* contributor, "we shall become a separate state," for, with the country constantly attracting new settlers "of all trades, arts and sciences," it followed that "in a short time the Americans will be too strong for any nation in the world." [60]

But such discussions and manifestoes failed as before to elicit any genuine popular response, so the propagandists, pitching their argument at the level of personal abuse, reverted thankfully to the man whom they deemed the real author of their woes. For this the victim himself was unintentionally responsible. Over many years Hutchinson had been piling up hatreds. Now he compounded his offenses by condemning the committees of correspondence in a message to the legislature on January 6, 1773. From that moment, the evidence indicates, the Whig strategists determined to drive him from office. Individuals like "Mucius Scævola" had earlier broached the idea; it now became the concerted purpose. In the weeks that followed the Governor's blast the press reported at length the crossfire of communications between the executive and the legislature over the salary matter and the related issue of parliamentary supremacy.[61] According to "E. Ludlow," addressing "Mr." Hutchinson in the *Boston Gazette*, March 1, the real question was "whether you ought not, of right, to be forthwith renounced and discarded by this people, as an illegal, unconstitutional, and dangerous person" to rule them.

Then a fortuitous occurrence seemed to deliver him into his enemies' power. "For several days past," the *Massachusetts Spy* noted on June 3, 1773, "some extraordinary discoveries have been talked of, which were expected to amaze the whole province. Hints have been thrown out, that the characters of some men in power would appear infamous in the highest degree . . . ." The members of the Assembly, the paper continued, had already considered the disclosures in secret session, and "very important matters will soon transpire, which will bring many *dark* things to *light*—gain many proselytes to the cause of freedom—make tyrannical rulers trem-

25; Adams in the *Boston Gazette* from Jan. 11 to Feb. 22. Adams, *Works*, III, 516–574, reprints both sets of articles with some omissions and errors as to dates of publication.

[60] "Age and Experience" in the *Boston Gazette*, Jan. 11, 1773.

[61] Hutchinson, *Massachusetts Bay*, III, 370–390.

ble." In this cryptic manner the public first learned of a batch of letters written to England by Hutchinson, Andrew Oliver and other Tories, which had fallen into the Whigs' hands. As Hutchinson remarked, the advance publicity "was a necessary part of the plan, that the people might be impressed with an opinion of something very bad, in order to render them more susceptible of the construction which was to be put upon the letters, when they should be produced." [62]

The treasure-trove had come from Benjamin Franklin, the Assembly's agent in London, who had obtained the correspondence surreptitiously. Though he had enjoined that no copies be transcribed, the patriot leaders, remembering their coup in ousting Hutchinson's predecessor by a similar dodge, went ahead anyway. The letters, far from bearing an official character, were personal ones addressed to an antiministerial member of Parliament in 1767–69, several years before Hutchinson and Oliver had attained their present posts. Moreover, only six of the seventeen were from Hutchinson. But none of this deterred his assailants, not even the fact that the correspondence, as in the earlier instance of Governor Bernard, revealed nothing the public did not already know. Hutchinson had always frankly avowed that, while Britain as a wise mother ought ever to exercise self-restraint, she was nevertheless omnipotent and that the colonists, beyond petitioning against unjust legislation, had no choice but to obey her behests. In one of his letters, however, he had carelessly observed that "there must be an abridgment of what are called English liberties." [63] The Whigs, wrenching this remark out of context and coupling it with the harsher expressions of some of his fellow correspondents, represented him as plotting to enslave America.

The legislature passed resolutions denouncing the Governor and Lieutenant Governor and petitioning the Crown to "remove them forever from power in the province." [64] Naturally the newspapers kept up the din. For nearly three months the purloined correspond-

[62] *Ibid.*, III, 395.

[63] Hutchinson actually meant nothing more than that in the matter of representation in Parliament it was impracticable for the distant colonists to enjoy the same rights as the Englishmen at home. "If I had supposed they [the letters] would be printed, I should have expressed myself more carefully," he wrote to a friend on Oct. 16, 1773. J. K. Hosmer, *The Life of Thomas Hutchinson* (Boston, 1896), 293.

[64] *Boston Gazette*, June 28, 1773; Hosmer, *Hutchinson*, 269–270.

ence ran serially in the *Spy*, the *Boston Gazette*, the *Evening-Post* and Salem's *Essex Gazette*, besides being published by Edes and and Gill as a pamphlet. "Honestus" in the *Spy*, June 24, 1773, likened the letters to "foot-steps *stained with blood*" that betrayed the "execrable source" of the "burdens we have been groaning under." Another contributor on July 29 aspersed the senders as "vipers whose poison has already destroyed the health of your province and spilt the blood of your people," while others displayed equal passion.

As on earlier occasions, however, the popular furor did not last. Hutchinson himself attributed this largely to a series in his defense by "Philalethes" (Attorney General Sewall) in Draper's *Gazette*,[65] but the deeper reason lay in the continuing good times and the absence of a really compelling political grievance. Hutchinson in fact remained at the helm for nearly a year longer, until his mishandling of the tea crisis impaired his further usefulness to the Crown. Indeed, the only tangible outcome of the episode of the letters—an unhappy one for the patriots—was the Ministry's dismissal of Benjamin Franklin as Deputy Postmaster for North America for his part in the affair.

The truth is that in the interval since the partial repeal of the Townshend duties Samuel Adams and his redoubtable journalistic allies had never been able except for brief periods to revive the old spirit of popular discontent and opposition. Their greatest achievement—and it was no mean one in the circumstances—was to keep open the channels of press discussion. This would yield them rich returns in the critical times ahead.

IV

What the Boston extremists could not achieve on their own ground they were in no position to accomplish elsewhere. Yet Samuel Adams and his confederates never ceased trying, for, as "Verus" surmised in Draper's *Gazette*, they could not "bear the tranquil state" of the rest of America. Adams in his role of "Candidus" insisted that the Ministry was concentrating its venom on a single

[65] *Mass. Gazette and Boston News-Letter*, June 26–July 22, 1773; Hutchinson, *Massachusetts Bay*, III, 412.

province simply to delude the others as to their safety, though a Tory writer perhaps came closer to the mark in observing, "While every neighbour colony behaves with respect and decency to the parent state, the British government will find less difficulty in correcting one froward child." [66]

Unfortunately for the froward child, the Ministry's assumption of executive salaries excited little interest away from Massachusetts, since that plan already prevailed in New York, Virginia and one or two other places.[67] The parallel grant to the Superior Court justices seemed, however, a more auspicious issue. With it Adams hoped to "arouse the continent" to indignation. He asked his brother-in-law, a recent settler in Georgia, to persuade the *Georgia Gazette* to insert articles from the Boston press on the subject. He also urged the "Pennsylvania Farmer" to publish his views on the constitutional implications; but Dickinson, while deploring his province's "political lethargy," politely begged off with the excuse that the cause was already in such "excellent hands." [68] At Thomas Cushing's instance, however, Richard Henry Lee placed in Purdie and Dixon's *Virginia Gazette* a flaming declaration of colonial grievances by the town of Boston, though with no supporting comment of his own.[69] So indifferent were the New Jersey and New York Whigs to the danger of a British-paid bench that those colonies in 1772 and 1773 allowed their Chief Justices to go on that basis without protest.[70] Peter Timothy of the *South-Carolina Gazette* was probably not the only printer in the "tranquil" climes of America to feel that past opposition to imperial policy had involved undue financial losses for himself and his family.[71]

The Rhode Island press alone showed any disposition to relive the earlier excitements, but the reasons there were strictly local.

[66] *Mass. Gazette and Boston News-Letter*, May 16, 1771; *Boston Gazette*, Sept. 11; "Freeman" (Andrew Oliver) in the *Censor*, Jan. 4, 1772.

[67] L. W. Labaree, ed., *Royal Instructions to British Colonial Governors* (N. Y., 1936), I, 316, 332–333, 340.

[68] Correspondence with A. E. Wells, Oct. 21, 1772, and with John Dickinson, March 27, April 10, 1773, Wells, *Samuel Adams*, I, 493, II, 59–61.

[69] Lee to Cushing, Feb. 13, 1773, Frothingham, *Rise of the Republic*, 276 n.; *Va. Gazette* (Purdie and Dixon), Feb. 25, 1773.

[70] *N.–H. Gazette*, Sept. 4, 1772; *Boston Gazette*, May 3, 1773. In South Carolina the Chief Justice had been paid out of the colony's quitrents under royal warrant since 1735. W. R. Smith, *South Carolina as a Royal Province* (N. Y., 1903), 299.

[71] Letter to Benjamin Franklin, Aug. 24, 1772, *S. C. Hist. and Genealogical Mag.*, XXXV (1934), 127.

The intensified diligence of British naval craft during 1772 in policing illicit trade bred a deep indignation which the newspapermen did their utmost to exploit. Solomon Southwick, editor of the *Newport Mercury* since 1768, set the pace. Regarding one of the patrols he exploded on February 24, "Some say this p-r-t-c-l schooner belongs to K. G----- the Th--d; but we should think it a little below his Br-t--n-c Majesty to keep men of war employed in robbing some of the poorest subjects," and he entreated, "America take CARE of your PROPERTIES!" (In retrospect a Rhode Island Tory termed this outburst "the prelude to the diabolical" burning of the *Gaspee* some three months later.) Other *Mercury* gibes were no less provocative. One writer, for example, after relating that a brig had foundered in a storm as a result of being detained by a revenue cruiser, concluded, "Poor New-England! The Spaniards taking your Whale-Men in the West-Indies, and your (*pretended*) Friends taking and harrassing your Trade on your own Coasts, and even in your Harbours and little Coves and Creeks! ! !" [72]

Southwick had already reported the arrival of the *Gaspee* off Providence, "but for what intent," he jeered, "we cannot learn, unless it be to meet, and manfully attack, those enemies who have treated with contempt the whole English nation." [73] The schooner's destruction by a mob at midnight on June 9, 1772, had only bare factual coverage in the press; but when the *Providence Gazette*, December 19, revealed on the basis of a confidential letter from Lord Dartmouth to Governor Joseph Wanton that the Crown had appointed a commission to investigate the "high treason" with power to convey the perpetrators to England for trial by armed force, resentment began to mount again. [74] John Carter, who had

---

[72] Charles Dudley to unknown, July 22, 1772, J. R. Bartlett, *A History of the Destruction of His Britannic Majesty's Schooner Gaspee* (Providence, 1861), 40 *n.*; *Newport Mercury*, June 1, 1772. A scathing article on July 13 explained the Ministry's neglect of the Spanish depredations on the score that such a move would not pay off in "Fortunes for numerous dependants," while "A Committee of Observation" in the same number hoped that impending events abroad would free America from "the curse of being tyrannized over by a parcel of dependant tools of arbitrary power, sent hither to enrich themselves and their MASTERS."

[73] *Ibid.*, Feb. 24, 1772.

[74] Dartmouth when he heard of this harmful publicity upbraided Wanton for communicating the letter to the press, but the Governor denied divulging the contents to anyone but "Officers of Government." Evidently some of these felt no obligation to observe secrecy, for Deputy Governor Darius Sessions and Chief Justice Stephen Hopkins on Dec. 25, 1772, joined with Assemblyman John Cole and the merchant Moses Brown in sending the significant passages to Samuel

taken over the *Gazette* in 1768, was carrying on in the best tradition of its founder William Goddard.

In announcing the intelligence the *Providence Gazette* condemned the scheme of transporting suspects 3000 miles "at the points of bayonets" as "repugnant to every dictate of reason, liberty and justice" and one "in which, Americans and freemen ought never to acquiesce." "Americanus" in the *Newport Mercury* two days later branded "this new-fangled court" as more "horrid" in its "exorbitant and unconstitutional power" than any in Spain or Portugal, and he urged the people in "a truly Roman spirit" to "prevent the fastening of the infernal chains . . . or nobly perish in the attempt!" As might be expected, the Massachusetts agitators, warming their hands before the blaze, did what they could to feed it. This outrageous business, Samuel Adams counseled a Rhode Island correspondent, "should awaken the American Colonies, which have been too long dozing upon the Brink of Ruin." One Bostonian informed the *Newport Mercury* that Admiral John Montagu "swore by God (some time ago), that he would burn the town of Providence to ashes." Another, no less comforting, wrote in the *Providence Gazette* that regiments from Massachusetts and New York were about to converge on Rhode Island, where "the same tragedy may be acted in Newport and Providence, which makes the 5th of March so memorable at Boston." [75]

The commission of inquiry carried on its work during the first half of 1773 with the newspapers keeping sleepless watch. When John Cole, a member of the Assembly's newly appointed committee of correspondence, testified before the tribunal—which he did unwillingly and unhelpfully—the *Providence Gazette* castigated him for betraying "the faith and confidence reposed in him by his country." The wrathful victim took legal action against the printer for

---

Adams. Bartlett, *History of the Destruction*, 134; Wanton to Lord Dartmouth, July 1, 1773, British Papers, III, 51; Wells, *Samuel Adams*, II, 14. The excerpts appeared in the *Mass. Spy*, Dec. 31, 1772, and the *Boston Gazette*, Jan. 4, 1773.

[75] Adams to Darius Sessions, Dec. 28, 1772, Adams, *Writings*, III, 391–392; *Newport Mercury*, Dec. 21, 1772; *Providence Gazette*, Dec. 26. For other samplings of the Rhode Island press, see W. R. Leslie, "The Gaspee Affair: a Study of Its Constitutional Significance," *Miss. Valley Hist. Rev.*, XXXIX (1952–53), 233–256. By the time the rumor of the advancing regiments reached Williamsburg it had swollen into the report of an engagement four miles from Newport, "in which eighteen of the Rhode Island People were wounded and about six of them killed, and . . . some of the Regulars were slain likewise. The Troops, however, entered Newport that Evening." *Va. Gazette* (Purdie and Dixon), Jan. 28, 1773.

the "false, scandalous, and malicious libel," but the grand jury at the Inferior Court of Common Pleas of Providence County refused to indict. *"This very extraordinary attempt to destroy the liberty of the press,"* declared Carter in announcing his vindication, *". . . did not fail to alarm the friends of freedom . . . ."* [76] Meanwhile the commissioners found no one to arrest, and with a simultaneous relaxation of the navy's activity against smuggling, quiet returned to the colony.

V

Despite this temporary flurry in neighboring Rhode Island, Samuel Adams was plainly tilting at windmills when he proposed in the *Boston Gazette* in September, 1773, over the signature of "Observation," that "a congress of American states" be called to "draw up a BILL OF RIGHTS" and "choose an Ambassador to reside at the British court, to act for the united colonies." The will for co-ordinated action simply did not exist, though the *Newport Mercury*, the *Connecticut Courant* and Purdie and Dixon's *Virginia Gazette* ventured to reprint the plea without comment.[77] Hutchinson was not far wrong in stating that the Yankee swashbucklers were "despised by their former brethren in New York and Pennsylvania; and it must be something very extraordinary ever to reconcile them," though he little dreamed that he himself was destined to be the agent. Accordingly, the Massachusetts dissensions occasioned little concern in the public prints elsewhere, and theoretical discussions of imperial relations virtually stopped. As William Samuel Johnson of Connecticut warned during the *Gaspee* affair, such questions "serve to whet the Wits of Men," but "they more surely sharpen their Tempers." [78] By the same token, resounding essays on liberty of the press ceased outside the Bay Colony, even though the issue itself continued to arise in connection with provincial politics.

[76] *Providence Gazette*, July 3, 1773; Bartlett, *History of the Destruction*, 105–106, 118; *Newport Mercury*, Aug. 2.

[77] *Boston Gazette*, Sept. 27, 1773; *Newport Mercury*, Oct. 4; *Conn. Courant*, Oct. 12; *Va. Gazette* (Purdie and Dixon), Nov. 11. "Time and Judgment" and "Z." (Samuel Adams) made like suggestions in the *Boston Gazette*, Aug. 2 and Oct. 11, as also did "Steel" in the *Mass. Spy*, Sept. 9. For the Adams identifications, see Wells, *Samuel Adams*, I, 445 n.

[78] Hutchinson to unknown, June 22, 1772, Frothingham, *Joseph Warren*, 188; Johnson, as quoted in Oscar Zeichner, *Connnecticut's Years of Controversy* (Chapel Hill, 1949), 138.

In New Hampshire and North Carolina, hostility to the Massachusetts brand of journalism reached the boiling point. When the *Boston Gazette* on November 2, 1772, reported from England that Peter Livius, a bitter foe of New Hampshire's Tory Governor John Wentworth, had been named Chief Justice of that province, the *New-Hampshire Gazette* cautioned its readers that the item had doubtless been *"fabricated"* by *"Geniuses who can upon any occasion set in their own Chimney-Corners and Write a Letter from London."* In a subsequent exchange of amenities the paper declared that "Edes and Gill, or some of their Hireling Writers," had "become so accustomed to Libel and Defamation, that they never take up the Pen without charging it with Poison of Scandal and Detraction." In fact, however, the Boston Whig organ was in this instance more sinned against than sinning, for the Ministry had actually issued a warrant for the appointment and afterward withdrawn it.[79]

In North Carolina the animosity was a by-product of the intermittent civil war which the mortgage-ridden farmers of the back country—known as Regulators—had been waging since 1768 against the harsh administration of justice. The *North-Carolina Gazette* at New Bern sided with the rebels, at least to the extent of an article, December 14, 1770, which lashed at Judge Maurice Moore of the Superior Court for persecuting debtors and further accused a "confederacy of extortionate officers" of having jailed Hermon Husband early in the troubles to "cow him from bringing their extortions to light." Husband (or Husbands), a well-to-do farmer, was at the time of the publication a member of the Assembly. Though he denied any hand in the piece, that body forthwith expelled him for "gross prevarication," for fathering a "seditious Libel" and for seeking to "intimidate the Members from a due discharge of their duty." The Chief Justice thereupon committed him to jail, where he remained until the grand jury released him in February, 1771.[80]

[79] *N.–H. Gazette*, Nov. 6, 20, 1772; *Boston Gazette*, Nov. 16; L. S. Mayo, "Peter Livius, the Trouble-maker," Colonial Soc. of Mass., *Pubs.*, XXV (1922–24), 127.
[80] *Va. Gazette* (Rind), Jan. 10, 1771; *N.–C. Gazette*, Dec. 21, 1770, as reprinted in the *Mass. Gazette and Boston Post-Boy*, March 4, 1771; M. DeL. Haywood, *Governor William Tryon and His Administration in the Province of North Carolina* (Raleigh, 1902), 108–109. In the absence of files of the North Carolina press for these years, it is necessary here and later to use clippings appearing in other newspapers.

News of the North Carolina disorders appeared in the papers of other colonies from time to time, but it was not until Governor Tryon's forces crushed the Regulators at the Battle of Alamance on May 16, 1771, that the disturbances received more than passing notice. The *North-Carolina Gazette*, doubtless eager now to atone for its earlier affront to the government, acclaimed the outcome as a "glorious and signal Victory" over "lawless Desperadoes" and termed Husband (who was not at the fight) a "Cataline" who had conspired to massacre Tryon's troops and divide the provincial offices among the insurgents.[81] But the Boston patriots, especially the *Massachusetts Spy* crew, regarded the defeated Carolinians as martyrs in a common cause, even though Husband himself after fleeing North Carolina stated his belief that the Governor had not acted "under ministerial influence." [82] "Leonidas" (Thomas Young) in an open letter to Tyron demanded that he explain his "avarice, ambition, injustice, perjury, perfidy and murder," since "the presses in North-Carolina . . . confess it is dangerous to reason in reach of your artillery." To that end he submitted six questions and besought honest answers. What "Leonidas" neglected by way of vilification "Mucius Scævola" (Joseph Greenleaf) supplied in a companion screed.[83]

When this number of the *Spy* reached New Bern, an indignation meeting on July 29 denounced the articles as "replete with the basest misrepresentations" and pronounced the allegation of a terrified press a "high insult." Liberty of the press, the gathering scolded Boston, consisted in a "discreet" publishing of "real facts and opinions," not in spewing forth "private scandal or public abuse." The company then humorlessly ordered its proceedings to be printed in the New Bern and Wilmington newspapers as "proof to the Massachusetts Spy, of the freedom of the press in North Carolina." Two days later a follow-up assemblage strung figures of Thomas and "his two co-partners in iniquity, Leonidas and Mucius Scævola,"

[81] *N.–C. Gazette*, May 24, 1771, as reprinted in the *Va. Gazette* (Purdie and Dixon), June 13; and *N.–C. Gazette*, June 19, as in the *Mass. Gazette and Boston News-Letter*, July 25.

[82] "A Fan for Fanning, and a Touch-Stone to Tryon" (1771), *Some Eighteenth Century Tracts Concerning North Carolina* (W. K. Boyd, ed., Raleigh, 1927), 344. This anonymous pamphlet is generally ascribed to Husband.

[83] *Mass. Spy*, June 27, 1771. "Humanus" in the *Spy*, July 25, and "Leonidas," Aug. 1, renewed the assault. W. L. Saunders, ed., *The Colonial Records of North Carolina* (Raleigh, 1886–1900), VIII, 635–648, reprints articles from the *Boston Gazette*, July 22, Aug. 12, Oct. 21, similar in object but less vitriolic.

on the gallows, while the sheriff read their imagined dying confession to the effect that, having been "seduced by the Devil," they did "wantonly and wickedly, utter, print and publish, the most audacious lies, bitter invectives, and scurrilous epithets, against a distinguished gentleman, of the most exalted character." Eager hands then flung the effigies into a fire.[84]

Upon receipt of these transactions in Boston the *Spy* frothed with indignation. "Centinel" prophesied that posterity would hardly believe that a crowd of North Carolinians had vented their spleen against "a poor Printer of a distant province, several hundred miles off, for suspecting the goodness of their governor." "Leonidas" opined that a satisfactory answer by Tryon to his six questions would have produced greater conviction "than the united resolves of all the lawyers and bums in North Carolina." Thomas, for his part, unctuously called himself "a meer Printer" of an "impartial" sheet, while "Mucius Scævola" derided the pretensions to freedom of discussion in a province whose newspapers had never dared speak the truth about Tryon. In similar strain the *Boston Gazette*, displaying a belated aversion to popular commotions, reviled the "worse than Indian rage and fury" of New Bern's inhabitants: "God! how depraved is human nature!" [85]

But the press in other provinces showed scant disposition to make common cause with either the Regulators or their self-appointed champions of the *Massachusetts Spy*. Purdie and Dixon's *Virginia Gazette* indeed ran three articles by "Phocion" in Tryon's defense, though it also published one by "Atticus" savagely arraigning him.[86] The *Pennsylvania Journal* contented itself with remarking that it could not "imagine any body of men" engaging in "so dangerous an opposition to government, unless they found themselves aggrieved, and had reason to despair of relief from any other quarter." [87] On the other hand, a writer in the *Connecticut Journal* hailed

[84] *N.–C. Gazette*, July 29, Aug. 2, 1771, as reprinted in the *Mass. Spy*, Aug. 29, Sept. 5.

[85] "Centinel" and Thomas in *ibid.*, Aug. 29, 1771, and "Leonidas" and "Mucius Scævola," Sept. 5; *Boston Gazette*, Sept. 9.

[86] "Phocion" in the issues of Sept. 17, Dec. 5, 13, 1771; "Atticus" on Nov. 7. F.–X. Martin, *The History of North Carolina* (New Orleans, 1829), I, lvii, identifies "Atticus" as Judge Maurice Moore, who suffered a change of heart after his earlier harshness toward the Regulators. On this shift of attitude, see also Haywood, *Tryon and His Administration*, 155–166.

[87] *Pa. Journal*, Aug. 8, 1771. *The Colonial Records of North Carolina*, VIII, 643–648, reprints an article of similar tenor from the *Journal*, Oct. 8.

Tryon's victory as nipping in the bud a horrid "Scheme of all the Sons of Faction" to destroy "Government in North America." [88] The transfer of the North Carolina executive to the New York governorship in July, 1771, offered an exceptional opportunity to discredit him in his new post, yet the Manhattan prints, too, let the occasion pass, with General Gage happily noting the absence of the "Billingsgate" of the Boston press.[89]

Perhaps an even better index of the New York editors' docile mood was the failure of any of them to join battle when the legislature in April, 1771, voted special additional funds for the local British garrison. The like appropriation less than a year and a half before had touched off the memorable McDougall explosion. Draper's beleaguered *Massachusetts Gazette* could wistfully report toward the end of 1771 that in New York "there has been scarce an instance of a calumniating defamatory Piece." To ensure a continuance of this blessed state, Myles Cooper in 1772 joined with three other Anglican clergymen for the purpose of "watching all that should be Published, whether in Pamphlets or News-Papers, and for suffering no thing to pass unanswered, that had a tendency to lessen the respect or affection that was due to the Mother Country." [90]

VI

Though the subject of current imperial relations was taboo in the press outside Massachusetts except transiently in Rhode Island, the editors in these other colonies did not eschew partisanship in local concerns. In Philadelphia, Goddard, still smarting from his rough handling by Galloway when the latter was his secret partner, continued to take pot shots at him in the *Pennsylvania Chronicle*. So telling was this sniping that his thin-skinned adversary twice sought public vindication. In the one instance "A Friend of Liberty," turning back the calendar to 1766, had charged Galloway with the

---

[88] *Conn. Journal*, Sept. 13, 1771.

[89] Letter to Lord Barrington, Aug. 6, 1771, Gage, *Correspondence*, II, 586–587. "I. S." in a quotation from Lord Lyttleton in the *N.-Y. Gazette or Weekly Post-Boy*, July 29, 1771, may, however, have been obliquely striking at Tryon for slaying fellow countrymen.

[90] *Ibid.*, April 25, 1771; *Mass. Gazette and Boston News-Letter*, Dec. 5; Cooper's memorial in the Public Record Office, C. H. Vance, "Myles Cooper," *Columbia Univ. Quar.*, XXII (1930), 274.

"blackest of all guilt" in having as "Americanus" upheld the consti-
tutionality of the Stamp Act. This, said his critic, convicted him of
"asserting the cause of slavery" and *"treacherously undermining the
capital pillars of the Constitution of his* NATIVE COUNTRY." The
next day the Assembly at Speaker Galloway's urging repudiated
the "scandalous & malicious" piece as "a daring Insult to, and a
Breach of the Privileges of this House," but the members, fearful
perhaps of the outside reaction, did not commit the printer for
contempt.[91]

Galloway's other counterthrust at Goddard had an even more in-
glorious outcome. Having received an anonymous letter early in
April, 1772, demanding a £ 50 loan with instructions to leave it behind a certain milestone outside the city, he concluded, after the
posting of rewards failed to bring results, that only Goddard could
have been the culprit, and he had him arrested for indictment by the
grand jury when the Mayor's Court should convene in July.[92] In the
interval the editor, out on bail, employed the *Chronicle* to smite his
enemy hip and thigh for the "cruel and wanton Attack," which,
Goddard said, resulted from his accuser's having been "intoxicated
with Liquor for several Days before." Other articles renewed the
charge that Galloway had "treacherously" tried to "establish" the
Stamp Act and asserted, moreover, that he was now scheming in
the Assembly to rook the people for unneeded roads and bridges.
Probably because Galloway had no actual proof of his suspicions, he
failed to appear at the time set for the hearing, and the case was perforce dismissed. "Mr. *Galloway's conscious Guilt*" of attempting a
"villainous Assassination of my Character" stands revealed to all,
Goddard chortled in his next paper.[93]

The virulence of this feud between printer and politician should
not obscure the fact that it concerned personalities rather than principles; the references to the Stamp Act dealt with a past evil, not
the present good. Besides, as Samuel Adams had discovered when
he tried to trigger John Dickinson into action, other Philadelphians
had no greater desire to emulate the reckless Bostonians. Josiah
Quincy, Jr., visiting the city in the spring of 1773, sighed in his di-

[91] "A Friend of Liberty" in the *Pa. Chronicle*, Sept. 23, 1771; *Pa. Gazette*,
Sept. 26, also Samuel Hazard and others, comps., *Pennsylvania Archives* (Phila.
and Harrisburg, 1852–1907), ser. 8, VIII, 6683–6684.
[92] *Pa. Gazette*, April 16, 1772; *Pa. Journal*, April 23.
[93] *Pa. Chronicle*, April 23, May 11, 25, June 29, July 13, 1772.

ary: "The political state of Pennsylvania is at this time the calmest of any on the continent." [94]

In Maryland about the same time the principal journalistic polemics revolved about the issue of whether the chief executive of the province or the legislature had the legal right to set officers' fees. During the first six months of 1773 Daniel Dulany as "Antilon" and Charles Carroll of Carrollton as "First Citizen" unmercifully mauled each other over the question in the *Maryland Gazette*, which impartially gave space to both.[95] Dulany, whom all America remembered for a hard-hitting pamphlet against the Stamp Act, this time took the side of prerogative, upholding Governor Robert Eden's assumption of the power, whereas Carroll insisted that, since official fees had the same force as taxes, only the people's elected representatives could fix them. The public seethed with excitement, crowding the *Gazette* office on Thursdays when the paper came out, while mobs in Annapolis and Frederick staged mock funerals over the corpse of the cherished right. In the end the Governor, unwilling to defy an aroused people, backed down. It is noteworthy, however, that throughout the long debate Carroll considered the dispute a purely family affair, not once alluding to "British tyranny" or seeking to rally the sister colonies to his side.

At Charleston a little later the *South-Carolina Gazette* became the focus of a heated controversy over a bill against counterfeiting which the Assembly had passed but the Council had killed. Thomas Powell, the editor during Timothy's temporary illness, on August 30, 1773, published a protest by two of the Councillors against their colleagues' action. William Henry Drayton, one of the twain, had given Powell a copy from the confidential minutes. The next day the Council declared the printer "guilty of a high breach of the privileges, and a contempt of the house," and, upon his refusing to apologize, jailed him. The issue now shifted from the intrinsic merits of the rejected measure to the larger one of the right of the press to

[94] Entry of May 9, 1773, Quincy, *Josiah Quincy, Junior*, 107.

[95] Each disputant contributed four articles in the period from Jan. 7 to July 1, 1773, which E. S. Riley has brought together in *Correspondence of "First Citizen" —Charles Carroll of Carrollton, and "Antilon"—Daniel Dulany, Jr.* (Balt., 1902). Kate M. Rowland, *The Life of Charles Carroll of Carrollton* (N. Y., 1898), I, 97–128, Ellen H. Smith, *Charles Carroll of Carrollton* (Cambridge, 1942), 99–114, N. D. Mereness, *Maryland as a Proprietary Province* (N. Y., 1901), 386–400, and Charles Barker, *The Background of the Revolution in Maryland* (New Haven, 1940), 347–358, give narrative accounts.

report legislative doings. The Assembly leaders, having their own ax to grind, sprang to Powell's defense. On September 2 Speaker Rawlins Lowndes and a fellow Assemblyman released him on a writ of habeas corpus in their capacity of Justices of the Peace. The prisoner, Lowndes held, had carried the piece at a Council member's behest and in so doing had acted "lawfully" and "only in the way of his profession." The same day the *Gazette*, with Drayton again its informant, printed another extract from the secret minutes bearing on the case, but the chastened Council this time ignored Powell while formally pronouncing the account itself "false, scandalous and malicious." Later, in an exchange of recriminations between the two chambers, the Assembly unanimously declared the printer's arrest to have been unconstitutional and oppressive; and there the matter rested.[96] Though this dispute too pertained only to provincial interests, it was to have wider consequences, for it marked the definite beginning of Drayton's attachment to the popular party.

In summary, then, the resolute efforts of the Massachusetts journalists to revive the continental line against England had foundered. With the best of will they had failed to solve the ancient dilemma of making bricks without straw; only Rhode Island had responded momentarily and then for its own special reasons. Nevertheless these other editors, while going their own way, had stubbornly resisted threats to freedom of the press in local affairs. Their preservation of this right would stand the American cause in good stead when a change of policy in London once more brought the printers to Boston's support.

[96] For more extensive treatments of this episode, see Thomas, *History of Printing*, I, 345–350; John Drayton, *Memoirs of the American Revolution* (Charleston, 1821), I, 101–103, 118–124; Edward McCrady, *The History of South Carolina under the Royal Government* (N. Y., 1899), 715–723; and Smith, *South Carolina as a Royal Province*, 389–393. The ever watchful *Mass. Spy*, Sept. 30, Oct. 7, 21, 1773, reprinted all the relevant documents.

Chapter VIII

The Crusade Against the East India Company

THE ERA OF PEACE and plenty of the early 1770's produced additional news vehicles as well as bulging wallets. Although New Jersey and Delaware continued to rely on their neighbors' journals (as they would go on doing until after the final break with Britain), newspapers sprang up in communities that had never possessed any, and new ones appeared in New York and Philadelphia. A Bay Colony editor in mid-October, 1773, listed a total of thirty-one from New Hampshire to Georgia exclusive of the two German-language publications in Pennsylvania—a gain of three in two years, not counting those that had been started but discontinued.[1] Boston was still the principal center with five papers, followed by Philadelphia with four in English and one in German, New York with four, and Charleston with three. Save for the short-lived *Censor* of the Massachusetts Tories, all the later ones were, as befitted the times, nonpolitical undertakings. Events were shaping up, however, which would soon cause them, like their older contemporaries, to take sides in a fresh conflict with the mother country.

I

The first of the new crop was the *Pennsylvania Packet* which John Dunlap, a Philadelphia book printer, established in that city

[1] *Mass. Gazette and Boston News-Letter*, Oct. 21, 1773.

on October 28, 1771. It was said of him that "he never inserted a paragraph which wounded the feelings of an individual," [2] but this imputation of timorousness did him an injustice. Though his taste in this politically stagnant period ran heavily to moralistic essays on themes like "Thoughts of Death" and "The Fatal Effects of Luxury and Idleness," he inadvertently revealed a different temper by occasionally lifting daring controversial pieces by "America Solon" and others from the *Boston Gazette*.

Dunlap's prickly fellow citizen William Goddard planted the pioneer newspaper in Baltimore, the *Maryland Journal*, on August 20, 1773. This he conducted with one hand while devoting the other to his earlier love, the *Pennsylvania Chronicle*. If he may be believed, he launched the venture with "a single solitary Guinea." [3] Hoping doubtless to supplement the precarious earnings of his Philadelphia organ, Goddard also took care not to export his reputation for reckless partisanship to his new scene of activity. While he would be pleased to publish articles *"in Favour of Liberty and the Rights of Mankind,"* he declared in the opening number, the language must be *"decent and compatible with good Government"*; the *Journal* would *"be FREE and of NO PARTY."*

Meanwhile Alexander and James Robertson, rebounding from their recent fiasco with the *New-York Chronicle*, started the *Albany Gazette* on November 25, 1771, with the help of Sir William Johnson, Superintendent of Indian Affairs, who advanced the money for the press and types. But the brothers, meeting no better luck at the little frontier outpost than they had earlier in the metropolis, abandoned the enterprise in August, 1772.[4] The next year, however, they tried again, this time at Norwich, Conn., in partnership with John Trumbull, an experienced printer, who is not to be confused with the poet or the painter of the same name. The *Norwich Packet*, making its bow on October 7, 1773, turned out successfully, though the Robertsons as time went on found themselves at political odds with their Yankee associate.

The most notable addition to the journalistic ranks, however, was

[2] Isaiah Thomas, *The History of Printing in America* (rev. ed., Am. Antiquarian Soc., *Trans. and Colls.*, V–VI, Albany, 1874), I, 259.

[3] *Md. Journal*, Aug. 20, 1773; L. C. Wroth, *A History of Printing in Colonial Maryland* (Balt., 1922), 127–129.

[4] Thomas, *History of Printing*, I, 313. Albany went without a second newspaper until the advent of the *N.–Y. Gazetteer* on June 3, 1782.

James Rivington who upon the renewal of difficulties with Britain would in due course emerge as a raging lion on the Tory side. The son of a well-to-do London bookseller and publisher, "Jemmy" had plied the parental trade in New York since his arrival in 1760. An advantageous marriage had enhanced his growing affluence as well as his social standing and enabled him to indulge his taste for luxurious living. Not till 1771 did he publicly display another side of his nature: his irascibility. Then he abruptly canceled his subscription to the *New-York Gazette or Weekly Post-Boy* as a sheet revolting to "a Good Citizen, and an Honest Man." Inslee and Car, the editors, obviously puzzled, could only expostulate that they invariably avoided "publishing one Line containing Insults against any respectable, public or private Character whatever." The next year Rivington erupted into type again when the paper printed the outburst of an imprisoned debtor who blamed his pitiful plight on the heartlessness of Rivington and his stepson. Rivington answered the "attrocious libel" with a self-vindication which indeed carries greater conviction than his assailant's retort that Rivington was a barefaced liar and *"turbulent animal."* [5] (Evidently the editors, though making partial amends by inserting Rivington's rejoinder, had slipped up on their rule against character assassination.)

Perhaps Rivington commenced to feel the need of a mouthpiece of his own. At any rate a newspaper was a logical extension of his book-publishing business, and in his new project, moreover, he was "honored with Encouragement from the first Personages in this Country." The *New-York Gazetteer*, after a trial flight on March 18, 1773, began regular publication on April 22. In the judgment of a well-qualified contemporary, "no newspaper in the colonies was better printed, or was more copiously furnished with foreign intelligence." Like Boston's John Mein a few years before, and somewhat like his fellow editor, Hugh Gaine of the *New-York Gazette and Weekly Mercury*, Rivington joined typographical excellence with a naturally conservative temperament. In tune with the times, how-

[5] V. H. Paltsits, "James Rivington," *Dictionary of American Biography* (Allen Johnson and Dumas Malone, eds., N. Y., 1928–37), XV, 637–638; Alexander Graydon, *Memoirs of His Own Time* (J. S. Littell, ed., Phila., 1846), 77–78; *N.-Y. Gazette or Weekly Post-Boy*, Aug. 19, 1771, July 13, 27, 1772. Samuel Inslee and Anthony Car, earlier in James Parker's employ, were now the printers, having leased the newspaper on Aug. 13, 1770, from Parker's son Samuel who had had charge since his father's death the preceding July 2.

ever, he announced he would strive to please readers of all *"Views and Inclinations"* and eschew *"personal Satire, and acrimonious Censures on any Society or Class of Men."* [6] Whether he so intended or not, the *Gazetteer*'s instant success with the public hastened the demise of the *Gazette or Weekly Post-Boy*, the weakest of his three competitors. Published since 1747, that paper, so long serviceable to the patriot cause, folded before the close of the year.[7]

II

On May 10, 1773, Parliament passed an act which, as its full implications dawned on the colonists, completely shattered the existing good will toward Britain and revived for a time the bonds of continental unity for which the Boston malcontents had been vainly striving. The law was designed to save the East India Company from bankruptcy by enabling it to market its huge overstock of tea directly by means of its own agents in America instead of, as hitherto, through independent dealers; the measure also provided a subsidy by remitting all the levies which the Company had been required to pay on the commodity in England.[8] These concessions, it was believed, would greatly boost sales through lowering the cost to the overseas consumer. The statute retained the old threepenny Townshend duty in the colonies, but the Ministry had no reason to anticipate trouble on that score, because the American protests against this survival of taxation without representation had long since subsided.

The news reached the colonial press in mid-July. "When the intelligence first came to Boston," Governor Hutchinson afterward

[6] Rivington's advance notice of his project in the *Mass. Gazette and Boston News-Letter*, April 1, 1773; Thomas, *History of Printing*, II, 123; *N.-Y. Gazetteer*, April 22, 1773.

[7] Because of the lack of extant numbers after July 12, 1773, the exact date of discontinuance is unknown, but contemporary references indicate the time as between Dec. 9, 1773, and Jan. 3, 1774. See *N.-Y. Gazetteer*, Dec. 9, 1773, and a letter of Governor William Tryon to Lord Dartmouth, Jan. 3, 1774, E. B. O'Callaghan and Berthold Fernow, comps., *Documents Relative to the Colonial History of the State of New York* (Albany, 1856–87), VIII, 400–401.

[8] 13 George III, c. 44; A. M. Schlesinger, *The Colonial Merchants and the American Revolution* (N. Y., 1918), 262–264; C. R. Ritcheson, *British Politics and the American Revolution* (Norman, 1954), 154–155.

testified, "it caused no alarm. . . . The body of the people were pleased with the prospect of drinking tea at less expense than ever." [9] A similar mood prevailed in New York, Philadelphia, Charleston and other places. In truth the act went without adverse newspaper comment for a full three months. This stemmed partly from the deep-rooted popular contentment, partly from the Ministry's delay in putting the provisions into effect. But more important was the fact that the patriot leaders did not at first grasp the far-reaching economic bearings of the law. Besides, for a time many people believed through a misreading of the act that Parliament had actually repealed the American tea tax.[10] John Dickinson, writing as "Y.Z." in the *Pennsylvania Journal*, November 3, however, cleared up this point "for any person of common understanding," [11] and meanwhile, in mid-October, the press terminated the chapter of waiting and inaction by breaking the news that the British government had licensed the East India Company to ship some 500,-000, pounds of the herb to Boston, New York, Philadelphia and Charleston.

The roar of protest that surged with such apparent spontaneity from the press of the three Northern ports suggests an advance exchange of views among the editors or at least among the politicians with whom they were allied. The newspaper writers ignored the fact that the people of nearly all the colonies had been cheerfully paying the "unconstitutional" tea duty, and though invoking once again the principle of taxation without representation, they bore down most heavily upon the dangers to the current prosperity. This tried their skill to the utmost. It was not hard to demonstrate that the plan would ruin the independent tea merchants, both the legitimate and smuggling traders, for the East India Company, now exempt from taxes in Britain and dealing through their own representatives in America, could undersell all competitors. But it was also necessary

[9] Hutchinson, *The History of the Province of Massachusetts Bay*, III (London, 1828), 422. To similar effect, see his letter to the Directors of the East India Company, Dec. 19, 1773, Mass. Archives (State House, Boston), XXVII, 597–598.

[10] Governor Tryon of New York to Lord Dartmouth, Nov. 3, 1773, *Documents Relative to the Colonial History of New York*, VIII, 400–401; "A Citizen" in the *N.-Y. Journal*, Nov. 4; Abraham Lott of New York to William Kelly, Nov. 5, F. S. Drake, ed., *Tea Leaves* (Boston, 1884), 269–270; "A Mechanic" in the *Pa. Chronicle*, Nov. 15; "Poplicola" (John Vardill) in the *N.-Y. Gazetteer*, Nov. 18, Dec. 2.

[11] Reprinted in John Dickinson, *Writings* (P. L. Ford, ed.; Hist. Soc. of Pa., *Memoirs*, XIV, 1895), I, 457–458.

to convince the commercial community as a whole that it somehow shared in the peril and at the same time persuade the common folk to resist their natural inclination to use the cheaper commodity. Few campaigns have ever scored a more brilliant success.

The Whig journalists usually bracketed the argument of unconstitutionality with a portrayal of the fatal economic consequences of the law. In this spirit "A Consistent Patriot" in the *Massachusetts Spy*, October 14, 1773, denounced the scheme as "not only destructive to trade" but "designed to promote and encrease a revenue extorted from us against our consent," and, more concisely, "Causidicus" on November 4 called it a case of "Taxation without consent and monopoly of trade establishing itself together," with many others taking the same line.[12] Governor Tryon, indeed, characterized the agitation in New York, where tea smugglers particularly abounded, as "calculated to sow sedition and to support and make popular the cause of those who are deepest concerned in the illicit Trade to foreign countries." [13]

The opposers further argued that, if the present limited monopoly went unchallenged, an unlimited one would inevitably follow, for they predicted that the East India Company would acquire like advantages for marketing its spices, drugs, chinaware, silks, calicoes and other fabrics. This was a telling point, since these additional imports of the Company into America seldom amounted to less than £600,000 annually. In Philadelphia alone they made up something like a third of all purchases from England.[14] "If you receive the portion [of tea] designed for this city," "Hampden" warned the readers of the *New-York Journal*, October 28, "you will in future have an India warehouse here; and the trade of all the commodities of that country will be lost to your merchants and be carried on by the company, which will be an immense loss to the colony." In similar vein "A Mechanic" in the *Pennsylvania Gazette*, December 8, forecast that

[12] For example, "Reclusus" in the *Boston Evening-Post*, Oct. 18, 1773; "Phileleutheros" in the *N.-Y. Journal*, Oct. 21; "Scævola" in the *Mass. Gazette and Boston Post-Boy*, Oct. 25; "A Merchant" in the *Mass. Spy*, Oct. 28; "Prædicus" in the *Boston Gazette*, Nov. 1; and "A Citizen" in the *N.-Y. Journal*, Nov. 4.

[13] Letter of Nov. 3, 1773, to Lord Dartmouth, *Documents Relative to the Colonial History of New York*, VIII, 400.

[14] "Some Thoughts upon the East India Company's Sending Out Teas to America," Drake, *Tea Leaves*, 218; Joseph Reed to Lord Dartmouth, Dec. 22, 1773, W. B. Reed, *Life and Correspondence of Joseph Reed* (Phila., 1847), I, 53.

they will send their own Factors and Creatures, establish Houses
amongst US, Ship US all other *East-India* Goods; and, in order to
full freight their Ships, take in other Kind of Goods at under
Freight, or (more probably) ship them on their own Accounts to
their own Factors, and undersell our Merchants, till they monopo-
lize the whole Trade. Thus our Merchants are ruined, Ship Building ceases. . . . Our Artificers will be unemployed, and every
Tradesman will groan under dire Oppression.[15]

"A Countryman" in the *Pennsylvania Packet*, October 18, grimly
reminded the people of the fate of the Trojans who innocently "drew
a horse into their city full of armed men, by whom they were presently destroyed." Nor was this the full extent of the nightmare, for,
as someone asked in the *Pennsylvania Chronicle*, November 15,
"would not the opening of an East-India House in America encourage all the great Companies in Great Britain to do the same? If so,
have we a single chance of being any Thing but *Hewers of Wood
and Drawers of Waters* to them?"

Moreover, these writers asserted, if the great trading corporation
once fastened its tentacles on America, how could the people hope
to escape the barbarities inflicted on the natives of India? Even
Dickinson lost his judicial calm in contemplating this dreadful prospect. The East India Company, he averred over the pen name of
"Rusticus," "has given ample Proof, how little they regard the Laws
of Nations, the Rights, Liberties, or Lives of Man. . . . Fifteen
hundred Thousand, it is said, perished by Famine in one Year, not
because the Earth denied its Fruits, but this Company and its Servants engrossed all the Necessaries of Life, and set them at so high a
Rate, that the Poor could not purchase them." And now, he went
on, they "cast their Eyes on *America,* as a new Theatre, whereon to
exercise their Talents of Rapine, Oppression and Cruelty." [16] Along
with others, "A Mechanic" in the *Pennsylvania Gazette*, December
8, added his warning that these ruthless men, "well versed in TYR–

[15] For further expressions of this view, see "Scaevola" (Thomas Mifflin) in the
Pa. Chronicle, Oct. 11, 1773; "Casca" in the *Pa. Packet*, Oct. 27; "A Citizen" in
the *N.–Y. Journal*, Nov. 4; and the *S.–C. Gazette*, Dec. 6. For the identity of
Mifflin, see letter of Benjamin Rush to William Gordon, Oct. 10, 1773, Rush,
Letters (L. H. Butterfield, ed., Princeton, 1951), I, 82.

[16] Dickinson's blast, dated Nov. 27, 1773, first appeared as a broadside in
Philadelphia and was then taken up by the press elsewhere: for example, the *Newport Mercury*, Jan. 10, 1774, and the *Mass. Spy*, Jan. 27, 1774. The full text is in
his *Writings*, I, 459–463. To similar effect, see "A.Z." in the *Pa. Journal*, Oct. 20,
1773, and "Hampden" in the *N.–Y. Journal*, Oct. 28.

ANNY, PLUNDER, OPPRESSION and BLOODSHED," would "leave no Stone unturned to become your Masters." As a correspondent in Rivington's newspaper summed up the Whig strategy, "To create an odium against the British company is the main point at which they have laboured." [17]

The propagandists directed the same alarmist tactics against the tea-loving masses. While crying up the evil of unconstitutional taxation, they cried down the expected boon of bargain prices. "Tho' the first Teas may be sold at a low Rate to make a popular Entry," declared "Reclusus" in the *Boston Evening-Post*, October 18, "yet when this mode of receiving Tea is well established, they, as all other Monopolists do, will meditate a greater profit on their Goods, and set them up at what Price they please." "Hampden" in the *New-York Journal*, October 28, and "Mucius" in the *Pennsylvania Packet*, November 1, reiterated that "Every purchaser must be at their mercy" and censured this shabby trick "to cajole the poor."

Finally, the opinionmongers strove to frighten tea drinkers by depicting the noxious effects of the habit. Though, as "A Woman" scoffed in the *Massachusetts Spy*, no one had heard of these "scarecrow stories" until the beverage had again become a party issue, Dr. Thomas Young cited eminent Old World medical authorities to prove that the introduction of the custom into Europe had caused "spasms, vapors, hypochondrias, apoplexies of the serous kind, palsies, dropsies, rheumatisms, consumptions, low nervous, miliary and petechial fevers." Indeed, cried "Philo-Alethias" in the *Pennsylvania Journal*, "the general State of Health has undergone a great Revolution by it, so that our Race is dwindled, and become puny, weak, and disordered," while a *Connecticut Courant* writer added that the herb bred fleas, that Chinese coolies trampled it with their "nasty feet" and that most English and French taverns had stopped serving the pernicious brew. Dr. Benjamin Rush in Philadelphia, posing as "Hamden" in the *Pennsylvania Journal*, confirmed that the "baneful chests" contained a physical as well as a political "slow poison." To make it easier for addicts to resist temptation, "Philo-Alethias" recommended seventeen substitutes that could be prepared from native plants.[18]

---

[17] *N.–Y. Gazetteer*, Nov. 18, 1773.
[18] *Mass. Spy*, Dec. 23, 1773; Young in the *Boston Evening-Post*, Oct. 25, and the *Mass. Spy*, Dec. 30; *Conn. Courant*, Nov. 30, Dec. 14; Rush in the *Pa. Journal*,

Considering the original reaction to the law the violence of the agitation caught the Tories by surprise. They did what they could, however, to refute the arguments. As a matter of course they derided the appeals to constitutional principle, unkindly reminding the public that the tax had been paid for several years uncomplainingly.[19] With the Custom Board's connivance they even published tables of the importations.[20] In the *Boston Evening-Post*, October 25, 1773, "Z" exposed another logical fallacy of the patriot protagonists by comparing the outcry against this trifling exaction with the continued acquiescence in the duties of 1764 and 1766 on sugar, molasses and wine "from which more than three quarter parts of the American Revenue has and always will arise" and which, moreover, he said, had been levied for precisely the same objects. Curtly dismissing the feverish talk about monopolies, "Poplicola" among others blamed the independent tea merchants and particularly the illicit dealers for fomenting the hullaballoo.[21]

As for the East India Company's ugly record in India, "A Farmer" pointed out in Rivington's *New-York Gazetteer*, December 2, that the Dutch traders who supplied the American tea smugglers had treated the natives with equal cruelty. And as regards the suddenly discovered unhealthfulness of the beverage, "L.H." in Purdie and Dixon's *Virginia Gazette* only hoped "the People of England will not reason so in the Matter of Tobacco" since that would cost his province "many Hundred Thousand Pounds a Year," and the *New-Hampshire Gazette*, hitting similarly at a staple Yankee product, reported a Hinsdale town meeting as affirming that rum had destroyed "the Lives and Liberties of Thousands, where Tea hath or ever will One." [22]

Notwithstanding this point-by-point rebuttal the pro-British spokesmen were neither so impassioned nor so numerous as their adversaries. They suffered further from the fact that most of the press was closed against them, thus fatally restricting the number of

---

Oct. 20, and "Philo-Alethias," Dec. 22. For Rush's pseudonym, see his letter to William Gordon, Oct. 10, 1773, Rush, *Letters*, I, 82.

[19] See, for example, the *Mass. Gazette and Boston News-Letter*, Oct. 28, 1773.

[20] *N.–Y. Gazetteer*, Nov. 11, 1773; "Q" in the *Mass. Gazette and Boston Post-Boy*, Nov. 15; letter of Richard Clark & Sons, Boston, to Abraham Dupuis, London, Drake, *Tea Leaves*, 290; "L.H." in the *Va. Gazette* (Purdie and Dixon), Jan. 20, 1774.

[21] "Poplicola" (John Vardill) in the *N.–Y. Gazetteer*, Nov. 18, 1773.

[22] *Va. Gazette* (Purdie and Dixon), Jan. 20, 1774; *N.–H. Gazette*, June 17.

minds they could reach. Perhaps most important of all, the public itself, at last awaking from its sleep, had become politically alert again and in no mood to listen to a reasoned presentation of the case.

III

As this agitation reveals, the most aggressive editors were those who had fed the spirit of disaffection in the 1760's. In Boston they merely reshaped their propaganda of the intervening years to exploit the more favorable situation now at hand, while in New York and Philadelphia they gladly threw off the wrappings of popular lethargy that had recently enveloped them.

The *Boston Gazette* and the *Massachusetts Spy*—those "scourges of TYRANTS," in Samuel Adams's admiring phrase—led the assault in the Bay Colony. Naturally they seized upon the damaging fact that two of Governor Hutchinson's sons as well as a nephew had been named East India Company agents. With this as a starter, "A Friend to the Community" in the *Boston Gazette*, December 13, 1773, accused the chief executive of being a secret partner in his sons' tea house. If the patriots had been surer of their ground, they could have made much more of this point, but it was not until nearly two years later that the proof came to light.[23]

The *Spy*, like the *Gazette*, pressed the stock arguments against the law, but occasionally it sounded a more defiant note. "Shall the island BRITAIN," demanded "Sydney," "enslave this great continent of AMERICA which is more than 99 times bigger, and is capable of supporting hundreds of millions of people? Be astonished all mankind, at her superlative folly!"[24] Thomas, following Goddard's example of a few months before, now extended his newspaper interests to a neighboring town, increasing the Whig phalanx of Massachusetts organs with one at Newburyport, the first in that thriving

[23] The quoted phrase is from "B.Y." (Samuel Adams) in the *Boston Gazette*, March 23, 1772. As appears later (see page 243), the Massachusetts Committee of Safety after the outbreak of the war in 1775 seized Hutchinson's manuscripts at his farm in Milton, and William Gordon, the patriot clergyman, inserted extracts of the correspondence in the Whig press. For Hutchinson's connection with his sons' tea business, see his letters published in the *Boston Gazette*, Dec. 4, 1775, and, for further evidence, Schlesinger, *Colonial Merchants*, 282 and footnote references.

[24] *Mass. Spy*, Nov. 11, 18, 1773, and similarly "Determination," Dec. 9.

community. He founded the *Essex Journal* on December 4 when the excitement over the tea controversy was nearing its peak, entrusting it to Henry-Walter Tinges, a journeyman from the *Spy* office, as his partner.[25] Though the paper in its first number professed it would print *"both* Sides" of every political question, actually its contents consisted largely of bellicose articles from the parent sheet.

The Boston Tories, for their part, were able to muster but a feeble press support. They could still gain access to the neutral *Evening-Post* and did so from time to time. Thus Richard Clarke, the nephew of Hutchinson's who was an East India Company appointee, inserted the piece by "Z" (earlier cited), which inquired how the patriots could rightly object to the tea duty while meekly paying the heavier ones on sugar and other imports. Even so, Clarke privately admitted that he had written only "with as much freedom as the temper of the times would bear" and that probably for this reason his effort did "not seem to have had its designed effect." [26]

Unfortunately for the pro-British advocates, the two *Massachusetts Gazettes* imitated the *Evening-Post* in opening their columns to both parties. Despite continuing financial favors from the government the editors shrank from braving the wrath of the repeated mass meetings which the crisis had evoked. As Hutchinson wrote of one of these occasions, "all the printers," not alone those of Whig convictions, were "enjoined" to publish the incendiary resolutions— a veiled threat which not even the unfriendly dared ignore. Although the Crown officials had been cured of seeking legal methods of repression, the "True Sons of Liberty" nevertheless posted placards about the town pledging their support to any pressmen using handouts from the Boston Committee of Correspondence. Draper probably surprised no one more than himself when he copied into his *Gazette* a handbill defending the East India Company plan in face of the action of a popular gathering censuring the flier as *"false, scandalous* and *base";* he even went so far as to query whether such public condemnations did not endanger the freedom of the press.[27]

[25] The paper at first failed to pay its way and Thomas pulled out nine months later, on Aug. 17, 1774, but Tinges continued it with various other partners. Thomas, *History of Printing*, I, 179–180; C. K. Shipton, *Isaiah Thomas* (Rochester, 1948), 29.
[26] Letter of mid-Nov., 1773, to Abraham Dupuis in London, Drake, *Tea Leaves*, 280–282.
[27] W. V. Wells, *The Life and Public Services of Samuel Adams* (Boston, 1865), II, 116, 117; *Mass. Gazette and Weekly News-Letter*, Nov. 11, 1773.

But such spurts of courage were too exceptional to comfort the Tory politicians, who must have rued the day they had discontinued the militant *Censor* a year and a half before.

In New York meanwhile Holt surpassed all his colleagues in stridency. His *New-York Journal*, for example, published the inflammatory series by "Hampden," appropriately styled "The Alarm," which had first appeared in leaflet form.[28] No other controversial pieces of the day were so widely reprinted through the rest of the continent. James Parker would assuredly have stood by Holt's side, but the veteran printer now lay in his grave, and his paper in less capable hands was also dying. Gaine of the *New-York Gazette and Weekly Mercury* prudently emulated the government press in Boston, admitting the arguments of both parties notwithstanding his personal British bias.

Only Rivington definitely threw his weight to the Tory side, though even he stopped short of provoking the mob. At a later stage he would show greater pluck, but at this juncture he compromised by giving the opposition only as much space as was needed to save his skin. Perhaps, too, he remembered his promise when founding the *Gazetteer* to represent all *"Views and Inclinations."* On one occasion he justified printing a Whig outburst by "Legion" by citing the author's admonition: "Let the inclosed be published in your next paper. In this fail not at your peril." And when the writer submitted a follow-up piece, the editor again made known that he had been bidden to *"Publish this in your next paper as you tender the resentment of* LEGION." [29] But "Jemmy" more than made up for such lapses with a multitude of Tory screeds, notably the slashing ones by "Poplicola," beginning on November 18, 1773. John Vardill, the unnamed contributor, had crusaded with Myles Cooper and other Anglican clerics for a colonial episcopate back in 1768–69, and Cooper in his turn helped Vardill on this new series.[30] The Whig disputants vainly challenged "Poplicola" to cast off his disguise, and "An Old Prophet," going over the author's head, threatened Rivington with the public's indignation if the "paltry, *puny,* and

[28] In announcing the series on Oct. 14, 1773, the *N.–Y. Journal* said that "friends to liberty in Great Britain and in the colonies" had initiated the undertaking. The identity of the writer or writers remains unknown.

[29] *N.–Y. Gazetteer*, Nov. 11, 18, 1773.

[30] Lewis Einstein, *Divided Loyalties* (Boston, 1933), 411; C. H. Vance, "Myles Cooper," *Columbia Univ. Quar.*, XXII (1930), 275.

POINTED scurrilities" continued.[31] The paper nevertheless continued them for another month and a half.

At Philadelphia the Tories had no press outlet at all. There William Bradford, unsatisfied with merely propagandizing against the ministerial plan in the *Pennsylvania Journal*, buttonholed people right and left until a sufficient number agreed upon a mass meeting to condemn those citizens who had been designated tea agents; and when the occasion arrived, he helped draft the resolutions. This gathering, on October 16, 1773, the earliest in any of the colonies, proved of more than ordinary importance, for it lighted the fuse that set off similar ones up and down the coast. Meanwhile, William Goddard, mingling personal animus with patriotism, raged in particular against Thomas Wharton, one of his former partners on the *Pennsylvania Chronicle*, for being an East India Company commissioner, assuring the public, however, that Wharton "generally officiated in the character of Devil." It was almost with chagrin that the *Chronicle* reported a week later that popular pressure had caused that "very great man" to renege, "so that he is now despised somewhat less than he used to be." As a final thrust Goddard voiced the faint hope that Wharton would "not for the sake of rendering this single virtuous act the more conspicuous let it stand alone." [32]

The *Pennsylvania Gazette* and the *Pennsylvania Packet* opposed the ministerial move with equal ardor, while the *Philadelphische Staatsbote* indoctrinated its readers largely with translations from the American press. Aroused by the gravity of the crisis, "Saville" in the *Packet*, November 8, implored the "Pennsylvania Farmer" to "step forth in behalf of the liberties of America," crying, "The genius of America once more kneels at your feet." But Dickinson, who had resisted Adams's plea at the time of the Massachusetts salary affair, now needed no urging. Unbeknownst to his fellow citizens he had as "Y.Z." already demonstrated in the *Journal* a few days before that the parliamentary act perpetuated the old port tax on tea, and soon as "Rusticus" he would blast the East India Company for its unmatched brutality toward those who fell in its clutches. With like intent the *Packet*, departing momentarily from sober political argument, parodied the advertisements of unhappy spouses, so often

[31] *N.–Y. Gazetteer*, Dec. 9, 1773. See also "Brutus" on Dec. 16.

[32] F. D. Stone, "How the Landing of Tea Was Opposed in Philadelphia by Colonel William Bradford and Others," *Pa. Mag. of History and Biography*, XV (1891–92), 385–387; *Pa. Chronicle*, Oct. 18, 25, 1773.

found in the press. One, for example, signed "American Liberty," read:

> WHEREAS my husband Loyalty hath, in a late advertisement, forwarned all persons from trusting me on his account; this is to inform the public, that he derived all his fortune from me; and that by our marriage articles, he has no right to proscribe me from the use of it.—My reason for leaving him was because he behaved in an arbitrary and cruel manner, and suffered his domestic servants, grooms, foxhunters, &c. to direct and insult me.[33]

The rapier of banter, however, was a rare weapon in the Whig armory.

From the three Northern centers the strictures and appeals as well as the remonstrances of mass meetings found their way into the lesser newspapers of that section and then into the journals of the Southern provinces. Even the *New-Hampshire Gazette* warmed up to the agitation, reporting the truculent resolutions of the Boston assemblages, and once going so far as to permit "Americanus," a local contributor, to denounce the East India Company project. The *Newport Mercury* also inserted occasional articles of its own; one writer, opening a rankling sore, exhorted the Rhode Islanders to send "to GASPEE" any of the odious shipments that might come their way.[34]

The "dirty business of copying," as a Tory had called it at the time of the Townshend Acts, never yielded better returns. In Charleston, Lieutenant Governor William Bull blamed the distempers very largely on the "great threats of violence" reverberating in the Northern press, and "Landon Honduras" in Purdie and Dixon's *Virginia Gazette* even more heatedly scored the "wrong headed and restless People at Boston, New York, and Philadelphia." The Williamsburg paper, though accessible to Tory pens, clarified its own stand, however, when "Thousands" lauded "the firm and virtuous Opposition" of the Northerners and blasted those "few Virginians" who would "exchange Liberty for Slavery, for the paltry Consideration of the Difference between ten Shillings and a Pistole in the Purchase of a Pound of Tea." [35]

[33] "S.T." in the *Pa. Packet*, Nov. 22, 1773.
[34] *N.–H. Gazette*, Nov. 26, 1773; "Legion" in the *Newport Mercury*, Dec. 13.
[35] Bull to Lord Dartmouth, Dec. 24, 1773, British Papers Relating to the American Revolution (Sparks MSS., Harvard College Library), I, 244; *Va. Gazette* (Purdie and Dixon), Nov. 25, Dec. 23.

IV

None of the Whig propagandists, not even the "wrong headed and restless" Bostonians, purposed, however, to destroy the East India Company consignments. The object, rather, was to nullify the parliamentary enactment by public opinion and to effect this without the mob violence of Stamp Act times. Those commotions had needlessly antagonized the law-abiding, and in any event the recent interlude of harmony with Britain suggested the advantages of orderly methods. Hence the strategy, threefold in character, was to revive the old agreements against dutied tea, prevail upon the Company's agents to resign, and get the shipmasters to return their cargoes unbroken.

This triple drive succeeded without a hitch in New York and Philadelphia, where the Crown officials proved amenable, but in the two other ports unforeseen snags developed. In neither, however, did the adoption of boycott resolutions pose any real difficulties, though Charleston, being distant from the major scenes of excitement, acted more slowly than Boston. The Carolinians, as the second step in the campaign, also induced the tea commissioners to quit, but the Bostonians despite their utmost endeavors could not budge those in their city, backed as these were by the stubborn and self-interested Hutchinson. Even this need not have proved fatal if the captains of the tea ships had been kept from landing the East India Company freight.

In both towns, however, the patriots condoned the removal of other merchandise aboard, and under the Acts of Trade this required the vessels to make entry at the customhouse. Once this happened, the tea became subject to seizure if the duty remained unpaid for twenty days. The Charleston Whigs solved the problem by inaction, allowing the customs authorities to confiscate and store the herb at the end of the period notwithstanding that this impliedly recognized the legality of the tax. In Boston, on the other hand, the irresistible force met the immovable body. The press kept the public's nerves on edge by harping on the intransigence of Hutchinson and the East India Company agents; and Edes and Gill recruited armed patrols who day and night attended the tea ships to balk any attempt at unloading, with Edes himself one of the guard. A newspaper notice by "The People" early in December—which Hutchinson later embedded in his history—served warning that any persons who abetted the landing would be "treated as wretches unworthy to live" and "made the first victims of our resentment." [36] Nevertheless Samuel Adams and his auxiliaries exhausted every peaceable expedient before resorting to force.

In secret conferences they settled upon their course of action should alternative means fail. Edes and Gill were privy to the machinations, and though Thomas's name appears in no surviving account, he doubtless was also; at any rate one of his intimates, Dr. Thomas Young, helped execute the plan. On the afternoon of December 16, 1773, the final day for the payment of the tax, a meeting at Edes's home perfected the arrangements while young Peter, his son, mixed punch for the conspirators in a nearby room. Adjourning after dark to the *Gazette* office, the party there donned their Indian regalia, and at a predetermined watchword spoken by Samuel Adams a few hours later before a great throng in the Old South Church, they rushed to the wharf and, joined by other bands along the way, staged the Boston Tea Party.[37]

V

"This was the boldest stroke which had yet been struck in America," Hutchinson affirmed in his history of these years.[38] Had the stroke in fact been overbold? The Whig high command doubtless pondered this question with growing concern in the sobering aftermath. They themselves had tried to avoid a violent outcome and hence had to face realistically how the unexpected turn of events would affect the sister provinces as well as the mother country. Only shortly before, they had hailed "the happy circumstance of their fellow colonists being embarked in the same cause," [39] but,

[36] Hutchinson, *Massachusetts Bay*, III, 430 n., 434–435, 436–437; William Bull to Lord Dartmouth, Dec. 24, 1773, and a letter of John Morris, the Charleston Comptroller of Customs, Dec. 22, Drake, *Tea Leaves*, 340–342, and (for Edes and Gill), pp. xlvi, xlix.

[37] *Ibid.*, pp. xlvi, lxvi, xciii; Peter Edes to B. C. Edes, Feb. 16, 1836, Mass. Hist. Soc., *Procs.*, ser. 1, XII (1871–73), 174–175.

[38] *Massachusetts Bay*, III, 439.

[39] *Mass. Gazette and Weekly Post-Boy*, Dec. 20, 1773, quoting a Boston letter of Nov. 25 to a Philadelphian.

now that a mob had demolished £ 15,000 worth of private property, was the harmony likely to endure? The patriots nowhere else had gone to this extreme and, moreover, had long distrusted the trigger-like reflexes of the Bostonians. As for the Tea Party's effect on the Ministry, would it be to wring concessions, as in the case of the Stamp Act, or rather to convince the government that at long last the time had come for a showdown?

Because of these uneasy afterthoughts the reports and comments in the Boston press uniformly minimized the lawlessness of the destruction, stressing the participants' singular high-mindedness, their gentlemanly demeanor, the absence of damage either to the vessels or to personal belongings; even the "Court Gazettes" did not venture to do otherwise.[40] Then, adopting another familiar propaganda trick, the Whigs blamed the entire affair on their opponents. In the words of "An Impartial Observer" in the *Boston Gazette* four days after the Tea Party, a patient citizenry had acted only after "finding all their efforts to preserve the property of the East India Company and return it to London, frustrated by the tea consignees, the collector of the customs and the governor"; and "E. Ludlow" in the *Massachusetts Spy*, December 23, singling out the patriots' favorite whipping boy, demanded, "How will you settle this account, Mr. Hutchinson?" "Marchmont Nedham" (Josiah Quincy, Jr.), recurring to the Governor's alleged betrayal of America's rights in his recently published correspondence, relentlessly embroidered that well-worn theme in "Nedham's Rememb'rancer," a *Boston Gazette* series which ran from December 20, 1773, to February 7, 1774. As "Simon Zelotes" wailed in the *Spy*, January 20, the people had got rid of the "villain" Bernard only to obtain the "viper" Hutchinson.

In a special plea to British friends of the colonies the journalists defended the Tea Party on the further ground that, besides asserting colonial principles, it would "rouse the dormant spirit of liberty in England, give a check to luxury and a spring to virtue." As another *Boston Evening-Post* correspondent phrased the argument, "It has long been evident, that Britain declines in virtue, liberty and political wisdom," but now "her Sons being roused by Americans, may shake off the infamous shackles of arbitrary power, and no longer

[40] Later, when Draper copied a skit by "Corporal Trim, Jr.," from Purdie and Dixon's *Va. Gazette* purporting to uphold the doctrine of parliamentary supremacy, he carefully added the note: *"Observe, The Publisher reprints the above only as a Piece of Humour." Mass. Gazette and Boston News-Letter*, Jan. 13, 1774.

have *masters* instead of *servants,* to rule the state." To America's foes at the seat of empire "A Friend to Britain" in the same pages, parroting an increasingly popular Yankee opinion, boasted that no power on earth could vanquish the colonists, who in truth could "subdue the armies of their enemies without shedding their blood by making every foreign officer and soldier a freeman of America (upon condition he joins the Colonies) and giving him lands to settle on, and other advantages." Though "A Patagonian" in the *Boston Gazette* took a different line, freely conceding Britain's superior strength, he too contended that "a *forced* compliance to *unjustifiable* measures" would cost the mother country dearly, for by alienating her American offspring she *"must then bleed at every vein, and* WILL SOON EXPIRE." [41]

In great elation Samuel Adams assured a political crony, "I think we have put our Enemies in the wrong; and they must in the Judgment of rational Men, be answerable for the Destruction of the Tea, which their own Obstinacy had rendered necessary." And with equal confidence John Hancock asserted, "No one circumstance could possibly have taken place more effectively to unite the Colonies than this manouvre of the Tea." [42]

These men could hardly have been more wrong, for in fact only the nearby press rallied to Boston's defense. In this spirit "An Old Prophet" and "Zeno" in the *New-Hampshire Gazette* justified the resort to force as indispensable for warding off a future "dreadful catalogue of grievous taxes" that would omit "Nothing we possess, whether Lands, Houses, Chattles, Money, or any Thing else." With like fervor "A Countryman" in the *Newport Mercury* bade his compatriots unite as one man behind the cause of "your dear native country, your own lives, your wives, your children, & all posterity," while "A Poor Man" warned, "We are now at the most critical of epochas. If we do not withstand the danger that threatens us, our reputation and liberty are at an end." [43]

But outside New England, even in New York and Pennsylvania,

[41] "A Friend to Britain" in the *Boston Evening-Post*, Feb. 7, 21, 1774, and anonymous on Feb. 14; "A Patagonian" in the *Boston Gazette*, Feb. 21.

[42] Samuel Adams to James Warren, Dec. 28, 1773, John Adams and others, *Warren-Adams Letters* (Mass. Hist. Soc., *Colls.,* LXXII–LXXIII, 1917–25), I, 20; John Hancock to his London agents, Dec. 31, A. E. Brown, *John Hancock His Book* (Boston, 1898), 178.

[43] *N.–H. Gazette,* Jan. 7, Feb. 18, 1774; *Newport Mercury,* Feb. 7, March 7.

the sentiment was chillingly reserved. The newspapers for the most part contented themselves with reprinting accounts of the Tea Party from the Boston press without comment. There were virtually no expressions of approval or support; rather, a stunned silence. In Philadelphia none other than Dickinson voiced his regret at the vandalism, and though less circumspect Whigs sought to change his attitude by pointing out that his own writings had helped spark the outbreak, he took the lead in persuading a public gathering to withhold resolutions of commendation.

As for the reaction in Britain, Franklin himself, then still abroad, deplored "carrying Matters to such Extremity, as, in a Dispute about Publick Rights, to destroy private Property." He branded it a "violent Injustice on our part," while America's long-time friend William Pitt, now the Earl of Chatham, went so far as to term it "certainly criminal." Quite understandably, the King, mulling over the troubles since the Stamp Act, blamed this culminating defiance upon "the fatal compliance in 1766." "The popular current," Edmund Burke informed the New York Assembly's Committee of Correspondence, "both within doors and without, at present sets sharply against America." [44] When Parliament resorted to punitive measures against Massachusetts, however, it accomplished what the Bostonians had been unable to achieve for themselves: a reforging of the continental front on a firm and lasting basis.

[44] Schlesinger, *Colonial Merchants*, 342–344; Franklin to the Mass. Assembly's Committee of Correspondence, Feb. 2, 1774, Franklin, *Writings* (A. H. Smyth, ed., N. Y., 1905–07), VI, 179; Ritcheson, *British Politics and the American Revolution*, 157–159.

Chapter IX

The Press Defies the Intolerable Acts

O̲N MARCH 31, 1774, Parliament laid down its initial terms for the Bay Colonists in the Boston Port Act. It closed the city to shipping from June 1 onward until the East India Company should be indemnified and people evince in other respects a dutiful attitude, the customhouse meanwhile to be shifted to Marblehead and the seat of government to Salem. Then in May and June followed three more "Intolerable Acts" which imposed not temporary but permanent restraints on all Massachusetts. One measure reconstituted the provincial government from top to bottom to make it less democratic. Another provided that trials for murder committed while suppressing disorders might be removed to a sister province or to England. The third greatly extended the Governor's power for quartering troops. According to "a late London paper" cited by the *Massachusetts Spy*, the legislation was designed to stamp out all "sources of sedition," leaving "the good people of Boston" only "to bluster at their own fire-sides, and to raise the admiration of their wives, children and negroes, over their punch and tobacco; and to print their scandal and scurrility in their own news-papers." [1]

Whigs up and down the coast who had thought Boston had gone too far were now convinced that London had gone too far: almost overnight mobbish Boston became martyred Boston. In patriot eyes

[1] 14 George III, cc. 19, 39, 45, 54, also *Boston Gazette*, May 16, June 6 and Aug. 15, 1774; *Mass. Spy*, Oct. 6.

Parliament by overriding the provincial charter and indicting a whole people for the guilt of a few had wielded an authority more ominous than taxation without representation or invidious trade regulations. Though Massachusetts was the one province directly involved, the Ministry had flung down a challenge which the other colonies could not ignore, since none knew when its own turn might come. As Lieutenant Governor John Penn of Pennsylvania informed the home government, "They look upon the chastisement of the people of *Boston* to be purposely rigorous, and held up by way of intimidation to all *America* . . . ." Franklin in London and Dickinson in Philadelphia, who shortly before had condemned the Tea Party, fully shared this change of attitude.[2]

The Americans, moreover, were not long in finding out that the Ministry had spurred the Commons to action by quoting from "the incendiary scribbling and printing in the different colonies."[3] True, Parliament withheld any punishment of the "dangerously inflammatory" writers, but this afforded little comfort, since the newspapers spread abroad a London report that the Ministry had sent a bribe to "some one Printer in each Colony" to defend its vengeful program. In the case of New York a handbill fixed the amount at £500.[4] Almost from the beginning therefore the Tory press fell under suspicion of venality in its support of the legislation.

I

The journalistic line-up was the same as it had at first been respecting the East India Company law. The Southern Whig editors, incensed to a degree they had not been earlier, now asserted them-

[2] Penn to Lord Dartmouth, July 5, 1774, Peter Force, comp., *American Archives* (ser. 4, Wash., 1837–46), I, 514; Benjamin Franklin to William Franklin, Sept. 7, *Writings* (A. H. Smyth, ed., N. Y., 1905–07), VI, 241; Dickinson to Arthur Lee, Aug. 20, R. H. Lee, *Life of Arthur Lee* (Boston, 1829), II, 305.

[3] *Mass. Spy*, May 5, 1774, citing the London *White Hall Evening Post* of March 15; "Patkul" in the *Pa. Journal*, April 27. For the British government's hands-off attitude toward the American press, see later, Appendix C.

[4] Letter from London, April 19, 1774, cited in the *Boston Gazette*, July 11, the *Mass. Spy*, July 15, the *Salem Gazette*, July 15, and the *N.–C. Gazette*, Sept. 2; a similar London letter, July 7, in the *Pa. Journal*, Sept. 9; handbill, dated July 25, quoted in C. R. Hildeburn, *Sketches of Printers and Printing in Colonial New York* (N. Y., 1895), 136.

selves on their own account. Nevertheless their brethren in the Northern ports continued to lead the agitation.

In New England the old faithfuls, Isaiah Thomas and Edes and Gill, stood at the van, followed closely by Solomon Southwick of the *Newport Mercury*. The Rhode Islander's forthrightness at first cost him subscribers, thanks, as he told his readers, to "the base endeavors of a few of the greatest enemies this country has," but being *"determined to* DIE or be FREE," he stuck to his guns and gained considerably more circulation than he had lost. At New London, Timothy Green of the *Connecticut Gazette* also met some opposition. Greatly exasperated on one occasion, he publicly exposed the "fruitless Attempt of Half a Dozen unreasonable Men, to sully his Reputation and destroy the Liberty of the Press." Proclaiming that his paper was "sacred to LIBERTY," he too vowed he would "DIE OR BE FREE." [5] Generally in New England, however, the patriot journalists had things pretty much their own way.

John Holt still conducted the only out-and-out Whig organ in Manhattan. From the editor's standpoint it was *"one of the most* FREE, and USEFUL *papers, printed in America,"* but, as the Tories saw it, the *New-York Journal* "industriously" prosecuted "the narrow views of a party" and was "a receptacle for every inflammatory piece" appearing throughout the continent as well as in Britain.[6] When Samuel and John Adams and their fellow delegates stopped off in the town late in August en route to the First Continental Congress at Philadelphia, they gratefully seized the opportunity to pay their respects to "friend Holt, the liberty printer." [7]

In the Quaker City, where the patriots monopolized the press, ministerial partisans, charging that the "sons of violence" had cowed the editors, resorted perforce to Rivington's and Gaine's sheets in New York to ventilate their views. "And is this LIBERTY!" they bitterly asked, "hear this, ye Americans! it is held CRIMINAL for

[5] *Newport Mercury*, July 18, 25, 1774; *Conn. Gazette* (until Dec. 17, 1773, the *New-London Gazette*), Aug. 19, 1774.

[6] "Mercator" in the *N.-Y. Gazetteer*, Aug. 11, 1774, also *Salem Gazette*, Aug. 26. The author, who shortly identified himself as Benjamin Booth, unjustly charged that "extreme poverty" had caused Holt "to sell himself and his paper to the highest bidder" and that the *Journal's* contributors were "generally of the lowest class." Holt scathingly answered this "abusive Piece of Scurrility" in the *N.-Y. Journal*, Aug. 18, Sept. 1.

[7] John Adams, *Works* (C. F. Adams, ed., Boston, 1850–56), II, 354.

a free British subject to declare his sentiments." [8] In some irritation William Bradford and his son Thomas finally let one of the group sound off in the *Pennsylvania Journal*, but only for the purpose of emphatically, if unconvincingly, rebutting the accusation.[9]

The militancy of the Southern press appeared at every turn. In Williamsburg, for example, Clementina Rind, who had taken over the younger of the two *Virginia Gazettes* upon her husband William's death in 1773, unhesitatingly branded *"with infamy"* Parliament's *"despotic proceedings,"* and the House of Burgesses just as unhesitatingly made her his successor as official printer, to an annual amount of £450.[10] A third *Virginia Gazette*, founded by William Duncan and Company at Norfolk on June 9, 1774, with the subtitle *Norfolk Intelligencer*, helped broaden the base of the agitation beyond the provincial capital. Though the new journal professed impartiality toward the "alarming Crisis" and did in fact carry articles on both sides, it betrayed its true attitude in its second number by placing under its name plate the slogan: "Do thou! Great Liberty! Inspire our Souls! Or may our Deaths be Glorified in thy Just Defence." [11]

The newspapers in the Carolinas were equally outspoken. Governor Josiah Martin of North Carolina indeed had been complaining of the *Cape-Fear Mercury*'s political heresies since the preceding January and hence could hardly have been surprised that it should flay the Intolerable Acts. So valuable was the Wilmington organ to the Whigs that when its editor Adam Boyd suspended pub-

[8] Benjamin Booth, a New York visitor in Philadelphia, in the *N.-Y. Gazetteer*, July 7, 1774; similarly "Veritas" on July 14, and "A Philadelphian" in the *N.-Y. Gazette and Weekly Mercury*, July 25.

[9] The protesting article was by "A Tradesman of Philadelphia" in the *Pa. Journal*, Aug. 17, 1774. Characteristically, the *N.-Y. Gazette and Weekly Mercury*, Aug. 22, and the *N.-Y. Gazetteer*, Aug. 25, reprinted the piece without the editorial disclaimer.

[10] Statement of editorial policy, *Va. Gazette* (Rind), May 19, 1774; Julia C. Spruill, *Women's Life and Work in the Southern Colonies* (Chapel Hill, 1938), 265–266. Mrs. Rind, who had taken charge with the issue of Aug. 26, 1773, died on Sept. 25, 1774, after which John Pinkney published the paper at first on behalf of her children and then from April 6, 1775, on his own account.

[11] One of the Tory pieces, by "An Englishman," provoked "Americanus" in Rind's *Va. Gazette*, July 21, 1774, to threaten the author with *"indelible marks"* of the public's disfavor should his identity become known. Because of a later pro-British article by the same writer, thirty subscribers in Alexandria canceled their subscriptions. *Va. Gazette* (Purdie and Dixon), Nov. 10. Duncan's motto was a somewhat garbled quotation from Joseph Addison's *Cato, a Tragedy*, Act III, Scene 6, which the editor corrected on June 23. The *Mass. Spy* had been using the accurate version since Nov. 22, 1771.

lication in the autumn, for reasons now obscure, the local Committee of Safety on January 30, 1775, voted to encourage him to resume, which he did after a lapse of several months. The province's other newspaper, the *North-Carolina Gazette* at New Bern, proclaimed its stand with the motto: "SEMPER PRO LIBERTATE, ET BONO PUBLICO." [12]

In Charleston the *South-Carolina Gazette* blazoned its sentiments by displaying the Boston Port Act in mourning borders and thereafter continuing to fan the flames of resentment. "The Stamp Act, with all its ruinous consequences, portended less evil to this Continent than the present gathering storm," it raged. ". . . Rise just indignation! Rise patriotism! to the aid of our much injured country." Peter Timothy, going beyond the call of editorial duty, also helped organize and direct various patriotic committees, writing to Samuel Adams with evident relish that the "Enemies to Liberty" deemed him as dangerous a foe as Christopher Gadsden. [13] And even the *Georgia Gazette*, though under close government surveillance, occasionally broke loose, one contributor contending that, if Parliament could put a tax on his tea, then "why not on my breath, why not on my daylight and smoak, why not on everything?" [14]

II

Never since the Stamp Act had the British adherents stood in such dire need of journalistic support. Indeed, it was alleged in the London press that "not a single news-paper" in America "would admit so much as a paragraph in favour of the Mother country." This, however, was an exaggeration, as Rivington properly pointed out by instancing his own and Gaine's papers in New York. [15]

[12] Martin to Lord Dartmouth, Jan. 13, 1774, and Committee vote, Jan. 30, 1775, W. L. Saunders, comp., *Colonial Records of North Carolina* (Raleigh, 1886–90), IX, 819, 1118–1119. Badly broken files make it impossible to ascertain the first appearance of the *Gazette* motto, but it was in use by Sept. 2, 1774.

[13] *S.–C. Gazette*, June 13, 1774, also 4 *American Archives*, I, 382–384; Timothy to Adams, June 9, 1774, Boston Committee of Correspondence Papers (N. Y. Public Library), II, 527. See also Timothy's letter to Benjamin Franklin, June 12, 1777, *S. C. Hist. and Genealogical Mag.*, XXXV (1934), 128.

[14] "The Case stated," *Ga. Gazette*, July 27, 1774; similarly, "A Georgian" in the same number.

[15] Rivington in the *N.–Y. Gazetteer*, Aug. 11, 1774, in reply to an article in Woodfall's *New Lloyd's Evening Post* (London), May 9. For another London piece of like tenor, see "Poor Old England" in the *Public Advertiser*, May 30.

In Boston, too, the Tory organs, though less aggressive than the *New-York Gazetteer*, evinced greater courage than had been usual in the past. General Gage, Hutchinson's successor as Governor under the Intolerable Acts, did much to "spirit up" the publishers, and luck also lent a hand when Richard Draper died on June 5, 1774, leaving the *Massachusetts Gazette and Boston News-Letter* to his widow Margaret. She, it quickly appeared, did not share that "Equanimity of Temper" which had always sustained her husband "through the Rage of the Times." Indeed, in the jaundiced eyes of the *Boston Gazette*, the "old Lady" perpetrated *"palpable falshoods"* and generally exhibited "a malignant Heart" toward her countrymen.[16] Similarly, Mills and Hicks of the *Massachusetts Gazette and Boston Post-Boy* became more combative, thanks to new contributors, some of them reputedly army officers.[17] At a little later stage they would provide "Massachusettensis" with a platform for belaboring the patriots and all their works for weeks on end.

Away from New York and Boston, however, the few pro-British editors definitely preferred discretion to valor, and, like James Johnston of the *Georgia Gazette*, admitted occasional pieces from Whig pens or, like Robert Wells of the *South-Carolina and American General Gazette*, shunned politics almost entirely. A new paper at Salem, the Massachusetts capital under the Port Act, seemed for the nonce to promise better results. Ezekiel Russell, former proprietor of the short-lived *Censor* in Boston, launched the *Salem Gazette* on June 24, 1774, with the slogan *"Influenced neither by* COURT *or* COUNTRY" and the assurance that he would uphold the true liberty of the press "which in times past has been shamefully denied to him in his *Native Place*." Under this banner Russell, while ever making believe to purvey *"the most impartial accounts of the transactions of the present times,"* gave the lion's share of his space to cuttings from the *New-York Gazetteer* and the *Massachu-*

---

[16] Thomas Gage to Lord Dartmouth, July 5, 1774, Gage, *Correspondence with the Secretaries of State* (C. E. Carter, ed., New Haven, 1931–33), I, 359. The characterization of Draper is from an obituary notice in the *Mass. Gazette and Boston Post-Boy*, June 6. On April 19 John Boyle, a patriot printer, had become Richard Draper's partner, but he withdrew on Aug. 4 because of a dispute with the widow over his contract. John Boyle, "Journal of Occurrences in Boston," *New England Hist. and Genealogical Register*, LXXXIV (1930), 374–375, 377. Boyle's brief tenure did not perceptibly affect the paper's political tone. For the criticism of Mrs. Draper, see the *Boston Gazette*, June 30, July 11, 1774.

[17] Isaiah Thomas, *The History of Printing in America* (rev. ed., Am. Antiquarian Soc., *Trans. and Colls.*, V–VI, Albany, 1874), I, 174.

setts Gazette and Boston Post-Boy.[18] He misjudged his audience, however, and was unable to keep going for so long as a year.

III

Although both sides from time to time invoked the principle of freedom of the press, in reality the issue had now emerged in a new form. So far as the patriot editors were concerned, they no longer had to fear attempts at legal repression—only the occasional loss of disgruntled subscribers and, as we shall see, hindrances from the postal authorities; accordingly, the ghost of John Peter Zenger quietly sank back into its grave. In the interests of consistency, however, they felt obliged to justify their suppression of opposition writings. But this presented scant difficulty to dedicated souls: they simply contended that liberty of speech belonged solely to those who spoke the speech of liberty. In Holt's words, "My paper is sacred to the cause of truth and justice, and I have preferred the pieces, that in my opinion, are the most necessary to the support of that cause" rather than to propagate "barefaced attempts to deceive and impose upon the ignorant." [19]

To the Tories such talk was unadulterated hypocrisy. "Can there be a grosser Attempt to impose upon Mankind than this?" stormed a *New-York Gazetteer* correspondent.[20] Being now the underdogs, they insisted that freedom of the press required editorial impartiality. Rivington, the most vocal on this theme, invariably claimed that he was conducting the *Gazetteer* not as a party mouthpiece but as a paper "equally open to the sons of freedom, and to those who have differed in sentiments from them." [21] To underline the point he began on May 5, 1774, to place under his name plate the legend: "PRINTED at his OPEN and UNINFLUENCED PRESS." But notwithstanding these fine professions he, too, con-

[18] *Salem Gazette,* June 24, Sept. 23, 1774; Harriet S. Tapley, *Salem Imprints, 1768–1825* (Salem, 1927), 36–39.

[19] *N.-Y. Journal,* Jan. 5, 1775, and, similarly, *Pa. Journal,* Aug. 17, 1774, and *Va. Gazette* (Rind), Aug. 18, 1774.

[20] "A Real Churchman" in the *N.-Y. Gazetteer,* Jan. 9, 1775.

[21] *Ibid.,* May 12, 1774; similarly, on Jan. 3, Feb. 10, July 7, Aug. 11, Sept. 2. For Rivington's private assurance to the same effect, see his letter to Henry Knox in Boston, April 20, Mass. Hist. Soc., *Procs.,* LXI (1927–28), 281–285, and another to Charles Thomson in Philadelphia, June 24, William Bradford Papers (Hist. Soc. of Pa.), II, 182.

fessed to rejecting articles which transgressed "the line of decorum" or what one of his followers termed "a decent discussion of a question," [22] and this afforded him ample leeway to give his sheet its violently partisan cast.

Ironically, the only known plea to the First Continental Congress to "enter into some noble and spirited resolves to fortify the freedom of the press" in the colonies came from a Tory, not a Whig, source, with the *New-York Gazetteer* again the vehicle. The key resolution proposed to the body ran, "That whoever, as an instrument of tyranny, or the leader or abetter of a mob, shall go about, either by threats, or any other methods to violate the liberty of the press, is an enemy to every thing for which a man of sense would think it worth his while to live, or would dare to die." [23] Despite the carefully balanced phrasing no *Gazetteer* reader could mistake which horn of the dilemma gave the writer and the editor their real concern. The Congress, however, content with things as they were, remained unmoved.

IV

A campaign arising from a quite different grievance anticipated the opposition to the Intolerable Acts and augmented its fury. In the early stages of this drive the Whig editors played the exclusive role.

As far back as the Stamp Act troubles some New York Sons of Liberty had pronounced the British postal establishment in America an egregious instance of taxation without representation. But that was not then the prevailing opinion, for, as Franklin testified before the House of Commons, the colonists as a whole regarded the service as a regulation and a convenience rather than as a tax. But indignation at his "infamous" removal as Deputy Postmaster General in January, 1774, altered this attitude, and the patriots, particularly after the passage of the Intolerable Acts, came to fear that an unfriendly administration of the mails would handicap their political activities. This was because postmasters possessed the authority under certain conditions to open letters and could by their own devices

[22] *N.–Y. Gazetteer*, Jan. 3, Sept. 2, 1774. For a specific instance of exclusion, see a protest in the *N.–Y. Journal*, Sept. 15.

[23] Unsigned article by a resident of New Jersey in the *N.–Y. Gazetteer*, Sept. 2, 1774.

hamper the delivery of what they deemed objectionable matter.[24] Besides, since the system did actually yield a revenue over costs, more and more people, however belatedly, questioned America's long submission to the "tribute"; one editor insisted that the *"parliamentary establishment, which levies a* TAX *in the very heart of the colonies,"* was even *"more* oppressive and arbitrary than the TEA DUTY."* Others, while not going so far, agreed that the imperial setup involved the "dangerous and unconstitutional Precedent of Taxation without consent." Indeed, particularized the *Massachusetts Spy*, it had supplied the *"precedent for a* Stamp-Act, *a* declaratory law for binding the colonies in all cases whatsoever, *a* Tea Duty, *and other attempts to extort our money from us, and infringe our rights and privileges."* [25]

The press took special fright because, as the *Boston Gazette* said, "our News-Papers, those necessary and important Alarms in Time of public Danger, may be rendered of little Consequence for want of Circulation. Whenever it shall be thought proper to restrain the Liberty of the Press, or injure an Individual, how easy may it be effected!" This consideration, Holt wrote Samuel Adams, was more serious even than official eavesdropping on private correspondence, since "the Carriage of News papers is of Importance to more than twenty Times as Many Persons as the Carriage of Letters, and there are very few persons but who are much more solicitous to receive their News papers, than Letters, by the Post." [26]

But how to combat the reprehensible system without doing greater harm to the colonies than to the home government? A simple boycott would not avail, as it had in the case of commercial grievances, for that would deprive a widely dispersed people of facilities vital for personal and business reasons and now, more than ever, for political ones as well. An open letter by "A Pennsylvanian" to Lord North in a London newspaper a few days after Franklin's dismissal

---

[24] James Parker to Franklin, July 16, 1766, Mass. Hist. Soc., *Procs.*, ser. 2, XVI (1902), 211; Franklin, *Writings*, IV, 430; William Goddard in the *Md. Journal*, July 16, 1774. Postmasters could open any mail with the approval of the British Secretary of State or of the Crown-appointed Secretary of the particular province. Benjamin Franklin to Thomas Cushing, Feb. 15, 1774, *Writings*, VI, 192.

[25] *Md. Journal*, July 2, 16, 1774; *Boston Gazette*, May 2; *Conn. Gazette*, April 1; *N.-Y. Journal*, June 1; *Md. Gazette*, July 28; *Mass. Spy*, March 24.

[26] *Boston Gazette*, May 2, 1774, also *Mass. Spy*, May 5, *Md. Journal*, July 2, and *Md. Gazette*, July 28; Holt to Adams, Jan. 29, 1776, J. C. Oswald, *Printing in the Americas* (N. Y., 1937), 253.

from his deputyship forecast the solution. The Americans, the writer said, being no longer constrained by their "unbounded affection for the person that held that office," would institute their own carrier service and "entirely starve your Post." [27]

This idea had already occurred to William Goddard. Nothing could have appealed more strongly to that political knight-errant always avid for new adventures. Both as a printer and a patriot he responded to the challenge and straightway set about organizing a "Constitutional" mail establishment. The plan involved a voluntary network of local offices financed by subscribers and extending upward to a postmaster general in New York who should be chosen by the various provincial postal committees, the whole system to operate at cost. [28]

Announcing the project in his *Maryland Journal*, February 2, 1774, and in his *Pennsylvania Chronicle* on the 8th, Goddard then discontinued the latter and, after putting the *Journal* in charge of his sister Mary K. Goddard, sallied forth on a tour of New York and New England and later of Virginia to enlist support. Along the way the Whig editors provided effective publicity, the *Massachusetts Spy* recommending the promoter as one who had "long been noted as the Proprietor and Employer of a very FREE PRESS." [29] The *Spy* indeed reported that the imperial agency was already "obstructing intelligence from colony to colony, by subjecting the news-papers to an ENORMOUS POSTAGE," which "nothing can prevent but establishing posts of our own." Soon the *Newport Mercury* was accusing the hated service of declining to distribute the *New-York Journal* and the *Pennsylvania Journal* while carrying Gaine's "virulent trash"; and Holt in New York and Purdie and Dixon in Williamsburg made like charges. [30]

---

[27] *Public Advertiser* (London), Feb. 5, 1774, reprinted in the *Mass. Spy*, April 22, also 4 *American Archives*, I, 500 *n*. Franklin, who entertained the same hope, may have inspired the piece. See a letter from London to James Bowdoin, Feb. 20, 1774, Mass. Hist. Soc., *Procs.*, ser. 1, VIII (1864–65), 85. As a *Boston Gazette* writer said on April 25, "While the ministry are dismissing the postmaster-general from his place, the Americans are dismissing the office forever."

[28] *Md. Journal*, Feb. 2, 1774, also 4 *American Archives*, I, 500–504.

[29] *Mass. Spy*, March 17, 1774, also the *Va. Gazette* (Purdie and Dixon), April 14, and 4 *American Archives*, I, 500 *n*.

[30] *Mass. Spy*, March 24, 1774; "Grotius" in the *Newport Mercury*, March 13, 1775; *N.–Y. Journal*, June 1, 1775, also 4 *American Archives*, II, 537 *n*.; *Va. Gazette* (Purdie and Dixon), June 30, 1774. The Williamsburg printers stated they seldom received more than a fourth of the newspapers sent them from the North.

By the time Goddard reached Boston on March 14 the "Constitutional Post" was already functioning between Baltimore and Philadelphia; New York City was about to join (with Holt's office as the headquarters), while numerous other places were only waiting on Massachusetts. Needless to say, the Boston Committee of Correspondence eagerly abetted the scheme. Chairman Samuel Adams, for example, urged it on the Marblehead Committee, emphasizing that Goddard was "engaged in this attempt, not only with a View of serving himself as a Printer, but equally from the more generous motive of serving the Common Cause of America." Similarly the *New-Hampshire Gazette* editorialized, "How cheerfully will every well wisher to his Country lay hold of the Opportunity to rescue the Channel of Public and Private Intelligence out of the Hands of a Power, openly inimical to its Rights and Liberties." [31]

In vain did the Tory press seek to stem the current. "A.Z." in Draper's *Massachusetts Gazette*, for instance, unkindly dug up Franklin's assertion at the House of Commons hearing in 1766 that the Americans did not consider the postal charges a tax, and the *Massachusetts Gazette and Boston Post-Boy* added that, if he subsequently changed his mind, how could he have honorably continued so long to "grasp the profits of oppression" instead of resigning? [32] The *New-York Gazetteer*, shifting the attack, branded as "an atrocious falsehood" a slight overstatement in the *New-York Journal* to the effect that Franklin's successor in office could "open all letters from Committees of Correspondence in this country." [33] Then, striking at public confidence in the patriot agency, Rivington revealed that a "Constitutional Post Rider" between Philadelphia and Baltimore had absconded with $558. [34] The *Journal*, while unable to deny this, vigorously contradicted the "industriously propagated" report that several prominent Philadelphians had deserted the un-

[31] *Mass. Spy*, March 17, 1774; Adams's letter of March 24, Samuel Adams, *Writings* (H. A. Cushing, ed., N. Y., 1904–08), III, 80–82; *N.-H. Gazette*, April 8.

[32] *Mass. Gazette and Boston News-Letter*, March 31, 1774; article from a London paper in the *Mass. Gazette and Boston Post-Boy*, May 9.

[33] *N.-Y. Gazetteer*, June 16, 1774, also the *N.-Y. Gazette and Weekly Mercury*, June 20. As has already been noted, this power resided only in the Secretary of State in London or in the Secretary of a province.

[34] *N.-Y. Gazetteer*, April 21, 1774. The *Mass. Spy*, April 28, took occasion to explain that the "Villain" in this affair was not the postrider but one of his underlings. Hoping to take advantage of the situation, the Crown authorities put on an additional rider of their own between the two cities. *Md. Journal*, July 16, also 4 *American Archives*, I, 504 *n.*

dertaking. Though this greatly exaggerated the fact, some Philadelphia patriots did in truth regret that so cantankerous a character as Goddard—a person "of very inconsiderable note," according to one, a "man who has not one well wisher," according to another—was heading the venture.[35]

Nevertheless the movement, reinforced by the resentment over the Intolerable Acts, swept all before it. By the time the Second Continental Congress met on May 10, 1775, the offices extended in a fairly complete chain from Portsmouth, N. H., to Williamsburg, Va. The newspaper editors, Thomas, Holt and Bradford, were among the original postmasters, with Goddard's sister Mary serving at Baltimore and Solomon Southwick a little later at Newport. That spring and early summer the Connecticut legislature together with provincial conventions in the other New England colonies and in New York gave the local branches quasilegal status. Then on July 26 the Continental Congress capped these moves by taking over the entire system and arranging to extend it as far south as Savannah, Ga. Unhappily for Goddard, however, he missed his anticipated reward, for the Congress made Franklin, now back in America, the Postmaster General, relegating Goddard to the inferior position of Surveyor of the establishment. The father of the "Constitutional Post" was too controversial a figure for some of the members, and in any event the returned luminary outshone him in all eyes. About a year later, in June, 1776, when Goddard petitioned the Congress for a military commission to repay him more adequately for his sacrifices and expenses, he suffered a further rebuff.[36] Resigning his surveyorship, he morosely resumed his duties on the *Maryland Journal*.

Despite these personal disappointments Goddard's extended labors had the intended effect of completely supplanting the "engine of Ministerial extortion, fraud, and revenge." As early as the spring of 1775 the Crown-appointed postmasters at New York and Boston

[35] *N.–Y. Journal*, May 19, 1774, also *Newport Mercury*, May 30, and 4 *American Archives*, I, 503 *n*.; Reed to Lord Dartmouth, June 10, W. B. Reed, *Life and Correspondence of Joseph Reed* (Phila., 1847), I, 69; an unnamed Philadelphian in the *Va. Gazette* (Rind), April 21, also 4 *American Archives*, I, 502 *n*.

[36] *Conn. Courant*, May 8, 1775, also 4 *American Archives*, II, 537–538; Samuel Ward, *Correspondence* (Bernhard Knollenberg, ed., Providence, 1952), 75; 4 *American Archives*, II, 802–803, 1802, 1892–1893, VI, 1012–1013, ser. 5, I, 442–443, 462; *Mass. Spy*, May 31; *N.–Y. Journal*, June 15; Oswald, *Printing in the Americas*, 255.

began discharging postriders for want of employment. On December 11 the Maryland Provincial Convention, to hasten the breakdown, barred the "parliamentary post" from that colony and seized the mail matter already in Baltimore. Two weeks later, on Christmas day, the British postal headquarters in New York, foreseeing the inevitable, canceled all its deliveries throughout the continent.[37] By audacious and timely intervention Goddard had thus safeguarded the channels of patriot communication.

V

Hand in hand with the assault on the imperial post went the offensive against the Intolerable Acts. This attained full momentum as Tuesday, June 1, 1774, the date for the blocking up of Boston Harbor, approached. Naturally the city slated to be "inhumanly murder'd in cold blood" took the lead, summoning the other colonies to its side.[38] As "An American" wrote in the *Evening-Post*, May 16, "It is not the Rights of Boston only, but of ALL AMER–ICA which are now struck at!—Not the Merchants only but the Farmer, and every order of Men who inhabit this noble Continent." The same day's *Boston Gazette*, after portraying the woes awaiting the Bostonians—*"the aged and the young, the widow and the orphan, the mother and the suckling"*—reiterated, *"Our sister colonies behold in this metropolis a specimen of what they may expect after we are subdued."* Newspapers far and wide eagerly responded with the slogans "UNITED WE STAND—DIVIDED WE FALL" and "JOIN OR DIE! !" [39]

"Tell it in Gath, publish it in Askelon," stormed the *Massachusetts Spy* on the day after the guillotine fell, ". . . Boston is thereby got into greater Distress, and is more insulted by an English arma-

---

[37] 5 *American Archives*, I, 442; *N.–Y. Journal*, May 4, 1775, also 4 *American Archives*, II, 506; *Mass. Spy*, May 10; *Md. Gazette*, Dec. 14, also 4 *American Archives*, IV, 234; *Pa. Ledger*, Dec. 30, also 4 *American Archives*, IV, 453.

[38] The quoted phrase is from the *Boston Evening-Post*, May 23, 1774.

[39] *Newport Mercury*, May 16, 1774; *Conn. Courant*, May 24; *Pa. Journal*, May 25; *Essex Gazette*, May 31; *N.–H. Gazette*, July 22. The form preferred by the *Mass. Spy*, May 12, the *Boston Gazette*, May 16, and the *S.–C. Gazette*, June 13, was "By UNITING we STAND, by DIVIDING we FALL," while the version of the *N.–Y. Journal*, June 23, was "UNITE OR DIE."

ment than she ever was by a French or Spanish fleet in the hottest war . . . ." [40] If the "tyrants" prevailed, avowed "An American" in the next number, "No man of honour or virtue will be safe—villains, robbers, murderers, and the vilest characters will be our *masters*, and tread the sons of honour in the dirt!" As for the weaker sex, "A Moralist" dwelt on *"the crafty wiles, as well as violent attacks,"* of the regulars "in almost every place, that has been so unhappy, as to have soldiers contained in it." "How will you feel," "Cato" adjured his countrymen in the *Newport Mercury*, "to see a ruffian's blade reaking from a daughter's heart, for nobly preserving her virtue." [41]

As the weeks dragged on, the Boston prints kept the other colonies fully apprised of the town's sinking state, picturing the "tyrants" as men who knew all evil, spoke all evil and did all evil. On August 1, for example, the *Boston Gazette* and the *Evening-Post* noted that "More than sixty days have now expired since Boston . . . has been besieged by a British Fleet and Army, and its trade annihilated," and they detailed "cruelties" exceeding any ever suffered from "the Savages of the American woods." A young student in John Adams's law office, John Trumbull, the later "Connecticut Wit," anonymously vented his resentment in a long poem, "An Elegy of the Times," in the *Massachusetts Spy*.[42]

From the newspapers elsewhere came pleas to the afflicted inhabitants to stand their ground. "Continue to bear up under your present Distress," "Hampden" (Samuel Ward) implored in the *Newport Mercury*. ". . . It is the cause of our King, our Country, and of God himself." "It's a cause worth dying in;" beseeched "Portius" in the *Connecticut Journal*, "a crown awaits the martyr that bleeds in defence of his country." [43] "A whole Community suffer for the Conduct of a few Individuals," wrote "A Philadelphian" in his press, ". . . and Thousands, accustomed to Affluence, are reduced to the lowest Species of Poverty." He too warned that "New-York,

[40] *Mass. Spy*, June 2, 1774, also *Boston Gazette*, June 6, and *Newport Mercury*, June 13.

[41] "A Moralist" in the *Mass. Spy*, May 12, 1774; "Cato" in the *Newport Mercury*, Aug. 29. See also "A Female American" in the *Spy*, Sept. 8.

[42] *Ibid.*, Sept. 22–29, 1774; Leon Howard, *The Connecticut Wits* (Chicago, 1943), 68–69.

[43] *Newport Mercury*, July 21, 1774; *Conn. Journal*, Aug. 25. The *Mercury* published like pieces by "Hampden" on May 2 and June 27. This author appears to have been former Governor Samuel Ward. See his *Correspondence*, 25.

Philadelphia and Charles-Town, cannot expect to escape the Fate of Boston. Our Doom is delayed only with a View to dividing and weakening us." [44]

John Dickinson, thinly disguised as "P.P.," elaborated the theme in a widely reprinted series of "Letters" in the *Pennsylvania Journal* addressed (like the earlier "Farmer's Letters") "To the Inhabitants of the British Colonies in America." Dismissing the Tea Party as only a pretext for punishing the Bay Colonists, he found the true reason in the earlier "Riots and weak Publications" of "a small Number of Individuals," and this notwithstanding the notorious fact that the homeland itself teemed with far more "enormous Riots" and "seditious, treasonable" publications. The punitive legislation, moreover, unmistakably disclosed Britain's sinister plan, long and "pertinaciously adhered to," to "sacrifice to a Passion for arbitrary Dominion the universal Property, Liberty, Safety, Honour, Happiness, and Prosperity, of us, unoffending, yet devoted Americans." All must combine against "so abject and so lasting a subjection": "The father of mercies never intended *us* for the slaves of *Britons*." [45]

To give visual expression to this sentiment, Holt in the *New-York Journal*, June 23, revived the famous Stamp Act emblem of the divided snake. Thomas followed in the *Massachusetts Spy*, July 7, with his serpent confronting an enraged dragon symbolizing Great Britain, and the Bradfords on July 27 introduced still another variant in the *Pennsylvania Journal*.[46]

In the South the press emitted similar heat. The two *Virginia Gazettes* in Williamsburg in fact charged the Ministry with "designedly" goading the Bostonians to violence as an excuse for applying "the Rod of Despotism" to "every Colony that moves in Defence of

---

[44] *Pa. Journal* and *Pa. Gazette*, May 18, 1774. For articles of similar tone, see "Philanthropos" in the *Journal*, June 22, and "An Old Man" in the *Gazette*, June 22.

[45] *Pa. Journal*, May 25–June 15, 1774. The *Mass. Spy* began the four articles on June 16, the *Boston Gazette* and the *Boston Evening-Post* on June 20, the *Va. Gazette* (Purdie and Dixon) on July 7, and the *Providence Gazette* on July 9. The *Boston Gazette* and the *Mass. Spy*, among others, identified the author as Dickinson. The complete text is in Dickinson, *Writings* (P. L. Ford, ed., Hist. Soc. of Pa., *Memoirs*, XIV, 1895), 469–501, where the quoted excerpts may be found on pp. 470, 473–474, 488–490, 495. The present version, however, follows the wording and form of the *Pa. Journal* text.

[46] For details, consult Albert Matthews, "The Snake Devices, 1754–1776, and the Constitutional Courant, 1765," Colonial Soc. of Mass., *Pubs.*, XI (1906–07), 446–452.

Liberty." "A Carolinian" in the *South-Carolina Gazette* emphasized that Parliament, "not contented with a claim to the right of
taxing us without our consent," had now assumed "the power of
breaking all our charters." Even some contributors in the *Georgia
Gazette* accused the Ministry of seeking to intimidate the entire
continent.[47]

The pro-British journalists sought unavailingly to undo the damage. A writer in the *Massachusetts Gazette and Boston Post-Boy*
jeeringly compared the Bay Colonists' efforts to implicate their sister colonies with "the fox that had lost his tail and who would have
persuaded his brethren to cut off theirs." [48] To underline the point,
these disputants strove to reformulate the issue in terms of the situation that had existed prior to the Intolerable Acts, maintaining
that the only thing at stake was the refusal of the Bostonians to pay
for private property lawlessly destroyed. Thus "A British American" in the *New-York Gazette and Weekly Mercury* admonished the
culprits as "constitutionally dutiful Subjects" to raise the money by
popular subscription, while others insisted that to make amends in
the circumstances was in no sense "a concession to authority" but
just a matter of "common equity." [49] Still others, though not with
Tory objectives in mind, urged that compensation be offered condi-
tionally in return for the repeal of all the revenue acts, or after Parliament had reimbursed the Americans for the many taxes it had
unconstitutionally levied.[50]

But the Whig scribes had ready answers for all such proposals. As
one of them summed up the patriot attitude, "There is not an argument offered for the payment of the tea, but what will operate
equally for the payment of the stamped paper, which was never paid
to this hour." [51] Moreover, they pointed out, knuckling under to

[47] "A Lover of the Constitution" in the two *Va. Gazettes*, June 20, 1774, simi-
larly "Benevolus" in the *Va. Gazette* (Rind), July 21; "A Carolinian" in the *S.–C.
Gazette*, June 20, also *Md. Gazette*, July 28; likewise an unsigned article in the
S.–C. Gazette, June 4, reprinted in the *Md. Gazette*, July 28, and another in the
S.–C. Gazette, June 13; "A Georgian" and "The Case stated" in the *Ga. Gazette*,
July 27.

[48] *Mass. Gazette and Boston Post-Boy*, Sept. 12, 1774.

[49] *N.–Y. Gazette and Weekly Mercury*, June 16, 1774, similarly "A New-York
Freeholder" on Sept. 25 and "Mercurius" in the *Ga. Gazette*, Aug. 10; "Mercator"
in the *Boston Evening-Post*, June 13; "A Philadelphian" in the *Mass. Gazette and
Boston News-Letter*, July 14.

[50] "Not a Massachusetts Man, tho' an American" in the *N.–H. Gazette*, May
20, 1774; "Rationalis" in the *Boston Evening-Post*, June 13.

[51] "Yet a Free Citizen" in the *Pa. Journal*, July 20, 1774. For other rebuttals,

Parliament would not remove the permanent disabilities fastened on Massachusetts. Then, like good propagandists, they magnified fear of the known with fear of the unknown. "J.L." in the *Boston Gazette* warned that the Bay Colonists must next expect the popular house of the legislature to be altered or abolished, and "Truth" in Mrs. Rind's *Virginia Gazette* reported from London ministerial designs to "take away from *every* colony the right of representation." [52]

Such a conditioning of the popular mind caused the Quebec Act, signed by the King on June 22, to be viewed not as a statesmanlike effort to assimilate the French Catholic population of that lately conquered province, but as an unmistakable foretaste of what awaited the thirteen colonies, in short, as another "Intolerable Act." The "diabolical" measure included provisions for a Crown-appointed legislature, direct taxation by Parliament and restrictions on trial by jury—all of which violated cherished American principles and supplied effective grist for the opinionmongers. The official establishment of the Catholic faith, the writers contended, was a bribe to the Canadians to side with Britain against the Americans and, even worse, portended that "We may live to see our churches converted into mass houses and our lands plundered by tythes for the support of the Popish clergy." One paper indeed solemnly alleged that Lord North had received papal absolution for sponsoring the law. The writers further accused the Ministry of extending Quebec's borders southward to the Ohio for the sake of hemming in the English colonists militarily.[53] The ill-timed "popery bill," however well intended by the framers, added critically to the disaffection.

The *Pennsylvania Journal* outdid all its contemporaries in sensationalism. On June 29 it issued a special supplement containing the text of what purported to be an imminent act of Parliament *"for the more effectual keeping of his Majesty's American Colonies depend-*

---

see "Dialogue" in the *N.-Y. Gazette and Weekly Mercury*, May 23; "Cincinnati" and "An American" in the *Mass. Spy*, June 16; "Consideration" in the *Mass. Gazette and Boston Post-Boy*, June 20; "A Bostonian" in the *Boston Evening-Post*, June 27, "Lex Talionis," July 18, and "A lover of Truth and Justice," Aug. 8.

[52] *Boston Gazette*, Aug. 18, 1774; *Va. Gazette* (Rind), July 14.

[53] *Pa. Packet*, Oct. 31, 1774; *Essex Gazette*, Sept. 13, also *N.-H. Gazette*, Sept. 16. For a detailed analysis of this journalistic propaganda, see C. H. Metzger, *The Quebec Act* (U. S. Cath. Hist. Soc., *Monograph Series*, XVI, 1936), 39–53, which contains excerpts from newspapers in all the New England colonies as well as in New York, Pennsylvania, Maryland and Virginia.

ent *on the* Crown." This law would tax every Briton thereafter settling in America £50 sterling; extort £15 for every male birth,
£10 for each female one and £50 for a bastard child; assess mar-
riages £20; and levy stiff export duties on colonial wheat and flour.
No reader could doubt Britain's fell purpose to choke the growth
of her unruly overseas population which, as the patriot propagandists had been boasting, would in due course exceed the number of
people at home. The proceeds, moreover, were to be applied to
"FORTS" and a "STANDING ARMY" to enforce the provisions.
The *Journal* importuned *"All the Printers of News Papers in the
British Colonies"* to republish the bill, which many of them did
without seeking to confirm its authenticity.[54]

If Franklin was the inventor of this cock-and-bull story, as the
Boston Tories believed, he obviously intended it as a travesty; but it
was not so regarded by the "deluded" masses who, according to a
loyalist observer, "would have rather suffered their Brains to be
beat out of their Heads, than to have their Faith in this Absurdity
beat out of their Brains." [55] Even the progovernment *Massachusetts
Gazette and Boston Post-Boy* credited the fiction, though it afterward apologized for spreading *"so daring a Libel."* Other Tory papers also tried to set the matter right. Thus a *New-York Gazetteer*
writer rebuked this unconscionable attempt to "alarm, inflame and
deceive," and the *Norwich Packet*—at the instance no doubt of the
Robertsons—disparaged the *Connecticut Gazette* for circulating the
"Effusion of a Lunatic's Brain." No Whig editor, however, had
the grace to retract the canard, and though it was not later repeated
in print, it undoubtedly helped materially to heighten popular fears
of Parliament's limitless power. As late as the spring of 1775 a
traveler reported "many deluded Germans" in the Pennsylvania
back country as devoutly believing the tale.[56]

[54] For example, the *Boston Gazette*, July 11, 1774, the *Mass. Spy*, July 15, the
Mass. Gazette and Boston Post-Boy, July 18, and the *N.-H. Gazette*, July 22.

[55] Peter Oliver, The Origin and Progress of the American Rebellion to 1776
(Gay Transcripts, Mass. Hist. Soc.), 149–150. Professor Crane has identified
Franklin as the author of an ironical piece of like tenor in the London *Public Ad-
vertiser*, May 21, 1774. Franklin, *Letters to the Press* (V. W. Crane, ed., Chapel
Hill, 1950), 262–264.

[56] *Mass. Gazette and Boston Post-Boy*, July 18, Aug. 8, 1774; "Veritas" in
the *N.-Y. Gazetteer,* July 14; *Norwich Packet*, Aug. 25; "An Englishman" in the
N.-Y. Gazetteer, March 30, 1775. "Massachusettensis" (Daniel Leonard) in the
Mass. Gazette and Boston Post-Boy, March 6, 1775, compared such gullible persons
to one of Addison's characters "that made it a practice to swallow a chimera every
morning."

Occasionally the verbal defiances blazed into talk of forceful resistance. "The country which our fathers purchased with THEIR BLOOD, we will defend with OUR BLOOD," screamed "A Countryman" in the *Massachusetts Spy*, June 22, 1774. "The man who arms himself in defence of his Life, Liberty, Fortune, Laws and Constitution of his Country, can never be accounted a Rebel by any but a Banditti of villains whose praise would be infamy, whose censure would be praise," echoed "Massachusettensis" in the *Boston Gazette*, August 29.[57] Nor was the saber rattling confined to New England. "An American Cato" advised against "all temporising Methods" in Purdie and Dixon's *Virginia Gazette*, July 28, reminding his readers that "with the Sword our Forefathers obtained their constitutional Rights, and by the Sword it is our Duty to defend them." And a Charlestonian avowed in the *South-Carolina Gazette*, June 4, that "the free-born colonists" would choose to see "these flourishing provinces deluged with the unnatural bloodshed of our brethren and fellow subjects" rather than "surrender the privileges of Englishmen."

VI

The journalistic uproar perturbed both friends and foes of the American cause. Could frenzied accusations and sheer gasconade promote a rational settlement of the dispute? Could an atmosphere surcharged with emotion foster a meeting of minds? "We seldom hear any solid reasoning," John Adams complained to his wife, and in the opposite camp Lieutenant Governor Colden used comparable language to the Ministry.[58] To the doctrinaire Whigs, however, the desire for *"Moderation, moderate men,* and *moderate measures"* cloaked a purpose "to charm us into a destructive supineness"; they would have none of it.[59] And pro-American letters and dispatches from London in the newspapers confirmed them in this conviction.[60]

---

[57] This writer was obviously not the "Massachusettensis" of the preceding footnote.

[58] John Adams to Abigail Adams, July 6, 1774, John and Abigail Adams, *Familiar Letters* (C. F. Adams, ed., Boston, 1875), 15–16; Colden to Lord Dartmouth, Aug. 2, British Papers Relating to the American Revolution (Sparks MSS., Harvard College Library), I, 312.

[59] "Anglus Americanus" in the *N.–Y. Journal*, July 7, 1774, also the *Providence Gazette,* Aug. 6; similarly, "C. M. Scævola" in the *Pa. Journal*, July 20.

[60] For examples, see the *Boston Gazette*, May 9, 1774; the *Mass. Spy*, May 12,

Despite the shrillness of the wordy battle, however, there occurred in some sectors of the press a reasoned examination of the underlying problem of imperial relations posed by the Intolerable Acts. "Camillus" undoubtedly exaggerated in stating in the *New-Hampshire Gazette*, May 13, 1774, that "even the Peasants" were becoming "versed in the Nature and Constitution of Government," but at the higher levels of discourse the scrutiny evidenced a surprisingly realistic grasp of the diverse aspects of the ancient connection.

Through all the discussion ran the presumption that the quarrel could somehow be amicably adjusted, since both parties had so much to gain from preserving the relationship. Typical of this attitude was "The Account between Britain and her Colonies candidly stated," in the *New-York Gazette and Weekly Mercury*, June 6, 1774. On the one hand, affirmed the unnamed author, the colonies were indebted to England for having planted them, for protecting their commerce against hostile powers, for opening foreign markets for commodities Britain itself could not absorb, and for helping to finance their civil and military establishments. On the other hand, he went on, the parent state was beholden to the colonies for "immense" revenues, for consuming its surplus manufactures, for serving as a "nursery of able mariners" and, in general, for making possible its commanding position in the world. So it followed that "Without the support of Britain, America must become tributary to some other nation; without America, Britain would cease to be an opulent, powerful nation." The solution of the difficulties, he concluded, lay in the mother country's restoring to the colonists their former "powers of distinct legislation and taxation, under the immediate controul of the Crown," and in the Americans' giving up smuggling, obeying the Acts of Trade and voluntarily paying their share of imperial costs.[61]

Though the proposal agreed with the patriot constitutional position, the writer's statement of the case contained the admission that

---

June 2; the *Pa. Gazette*, May 18, June 1, Aug. 10; the *Pa. Journal*, May 18, Aug. 17; the *Md. Gazette*, May 26; and the *N.–H. Gazette*, June 10. Governor Thomas Gage bitterly refers to the influence of such items in a letter to Lord Barrington, Gage, *Correspondence*, II, 649–650.

[61] This piece was reprinted in the *Va. Gazette* (Rind), June 23, 1774. For similar summations of mutual advantage, see "A Philadelphian" in the *Pa. Gazette* and the *Pa. Journal*, May 18, and "Brutus" in the same papers, July 12, as well as "Z" in the *N.–Y. Gazetteer*, Sept. 8.

both sides were in some degree at fault—which a Gaine contributor reiterated in a later article [62]—and this the majority of the Whig disputants denied. They saw the Ministry-dominated Parliament as the sole author of the troubles. As "A Philadelphian" put it, inasmuch as the Crown alone had *"supreme* Jurisdiction" over the colonies, "The Conduct of the British Parliament towards America, for several Years past, carried strong Marks of Insanity and Folly." [63] To *"restore* HARMONY *and perpetuate the* UNION *between* GREAT–BRITAIN *and* AMERICA," declared "Time and Judgment" (Samuel Adams) in the *Massachusetts Spy*, August 18, Parliament must straightway forgo taxing and legislating for the colonies (except as to minimum trade restrictions), in return for which the Americans would magnanimously "confirm Britain's sovereignty of the seas, by an act of their own." These spokesmen, of course, conceived of each province as linked to the Empire only through the King.[64] None dealt with the matter more learnedly or more uncompromisingly than "A British American" in a series in Mrs. Rind's *Virginia Gazette.* The writer, who revealed himself in the final installment as the Virginia lawyer-planter Thomson Mason, went so far as to deny Parliament's right even to regulate commerce and urged his countrymen to ignore all imperial legislation enacted since the founding of Jamestown.[65]

The colonists on this side of the argument turned a deaf ear to pleas "to compare their happy Situation with the Wretchedness of Nine Tenths of the Globe." [66] This good fortune had indeed been theirs, they retorted, and for that reason they must now stoutly defend it, especially since by so doing they could also come to the aid of the downtrodden masses in the old country. As "Anglo Americanus" remarked in the *New-York Journal*, July 7, "America must at present be considered as the principal, or indeed the only remaining seat of liberty." Corsica, Sweden and Poland, he pointed

[62] "Z." in the *N.–Y. Gazette and Weekly Mercury*, Aug. 15, 1774.

[63] *Pa. Gazette* and *Pa. Journal*, May 18, 1774.

[64] For a succinct formulation of this conception, see "Vox Vociferantis in Eremo" (probably the Rev. John Cleaveland of Ipswich) in the *Essex Gazette*, Aug. 2, 1774, also the *Boston Evening-Post*, Aug. 8, *Essex Journal*, Aug. 10, and *Pa. Journal*, Aug. 17.

[65] *Va. Gazette* (Rind), June 16, 30, July 7–28, 1774. All but the first installment are reprinted in 4 *American Archives*, I, 495–498, 519–522, 541–544, 620–624, 648–654.

[66] "Phileirenus" in the *N.–Y. Gazette and Weekly Mercury*, Aug. 22, 1774.

out, had already succumbed to tyranny, and Britain would certainly follow "unless propp'd by the virtue and spirit of the colonies."

In this discussion of imperial relations it was inevitable that the subject of Independence should crop up, but it was as yet only a meager interest, and the weight of opinion was decidedly against it. To be sure, a correspondent in the *Providence Gazette* argued that the colonists by setting up for themselves could save an annual £3,000,000 in duties and in outlays for English goods; and the *Massachusetts Spy*, singing an old tune, maintained that the people, already "millions strong" and destined in twenty-five years to outnumber the inhabitants of the British Isles, could defy "the hated tyrants of the earth." But neither paper actually espoused separation, and indeed another *Spy* contributor affirmed that the Americans were *"so connected by commerce, by language, by religion, by blood, &c."* with Britain that, if she but treated them justly, *"it is not only possible but highly probable her union with them might continue to the latest ages of the world."* [67] Still others contended that the colonies, even if able to win their freedom, would then be so exhausted in wealth and man power as to fall an easy prey to some other great power. The whole idea, exclaimed one, was "preposterous." [68] Some months were to pass and more desperate crises arise before the agitation for Independence would take a bolder line.

Instead of pinning their hopes on a will-o'-the-wisp solution, the propagandists worked for an intercolonial congress to implement the watchword "UNITED WE STAND—DIVIDED WE FALL." Such a conclave, as already noted, had been Samuel Adams's design in the *Boston Gazette* even before the dumping of the tea—so much so in fact that when the project finally came to fruition Hutchinson acridly remarked, "The whole Continent is ensnared by that Matchiavel of Chaos." [69] But the earlier proposals had contemplated

[67] "Solon" in the *Providence Gazette*, May 14, 1774; "A Christian" in the *Mass. Spy*, May 9, and "Consideration," July 15. An article in the *Boston Evening-Post*, March 14, calling for "A Grand Congress to complete the system for the American Independent Commonwealth," apparently stood alone except for the fact of its being reprinted in the *Newport Mercury*, March 21.

[68] "Patkul" in the *Pa. Journal*, April 27, 1774; "W.O." in the *Mass. Gazette and Boston Post-Boy*, June 13; "A Citizen of Philadelphia" in the *Pa. Packet*, June 20; "A zealous Friend to both Countries" in the *Pa. Gazette*, Aug. 31.

[69] Letter of Sept. 4, 1774, to unknown, Library of Congress transcript. Hutchinson doubtless had in mind also Adams's similar efforts as chairman of the Boston Committee of Correspondence and as leader in the Assembly. W. V. Wells, *The Life and Public Services of Samuel Adams* (Boston, 1865), II, 91; Richard Frothingham, *The Rise of the Republic of the United States* (Boston, 1872), 332 *n*.

concerted action in drafting a permanent charter or constitution defining America's rights; now the overriding purpose was "to plan and direct" measures specifically for "this great decisive day." [70]

Hardly had the Tea Party taken place when a *Boston Gazette* writer pleaded, "There is no time to be lost, a Congress or meeting of American states is indispensable." [71] But the cry did not become widespread until after the Intolerable Acts sent chills of horror through the continent. By early July, 1774, the Boston press reported, "The news-papers from all quarters, in every British American colony, so far as we have yet received intelligence, are chiefly filled with accounts of meetings and resolutions of towns and counties, all to the same purpose—complaining of oppression, proposing a congress, a cessation of intercourse with Great-Britain, and a contribution for the relief of Boston Poor." [72] The Rhode Island Assembly named its delegates on June 15, and in the ensuing weeks other colonies followed either by official or unofficial action. "It must revive the drooping Spirits of every desponding AMERICAN," exulted "Amicus" in the *New-Hampshire Gazette*, July 22, "to see all the Provinces *uniting* to withstand Oppression," and he urged that any persons who should disobey the injunctions of the prospective gathering be "stigmatized" with "Infamy to the latest Posterity."

The newspaper discussion concerned not the advisability of a congress—which every patriot favored along with many who hoped it might exert a moderating influence—but rather the mode of opposition it should adopt. As one of Holt's correspondents observed, "The Delegates must certainly desire to know the mind of the country in general. No rational man will think himself so well acquainted with our affairs as that he cannot have a more full and better view of them." [73] To this end the writers almost without exception demanded that, unlike the procedure of the Stamp Act Congress, trade restrictions be instituted to reinforce petitions for redress,[74] but within this

[70] Adams, writing as "Time and Judgment" in the *Boston Gazette*, Aug. 2, 1773; "Observation" in *ibid.*, Sept. 27, and "Z.," Oct. 10; "An American" in the *Mass. Spy*, June 2, 1774.

[71] "Union" in the *Boston Gazette*, Dec. 27, 1773.

[72] *Mass. Gazette and Boston News-Letter*, July 7, 1774; *Boston Gazette*, July 11; *Mass. Spy*, July 15.

[73] *N.–Y. Journal*, Aug. 4, 1774, also 4 *American Archives*, I, 635.

[74] The *N.–Y. Gazetteer* of course dissented, a "Virginian," for example, arguing on Aug. 22, 1774, that, inasmuch as Britain's trading connections were worldwide, America would be more hurt than helped by an interruption of commerce: though "We may teize the Mother Country, we cannot ruin her."

consensus existed sharp differences as to the most desirable kind. The chief matters at issue, in the words of a *New-York Journal* author on August 4, were:

> Shall we stop importation only, or shall we cease exportation also? Shall this extend only to Great Britain and Ireland, or shall it comprehend the West India Islands? At what time shall this cessation begin? Shall we stop trade till we obtain what we think reasonable, and which shall secure us for time to come; or shall it be only till we obtain relief in those particulars which now oppress us? Shall we first apply for relief and wait for an answer before we stop trade, or shall we stop trade while we are making application?

Some went on further to propose suspending debt payments to British merchants, arguing that the withholding of this estimated £3,000,000 would build a backfire that would quickly bring the Ministry to its senses.[75]

"We are variously affected," confessed "A Distressed Bostonian" in the *Boston Evening-Post*, September 5, "and as each feels himself more or less distres'd he is proportionately warm or cool . . . ." The predominant opinion, however, was for a combined nonimportation and nonexportation agreement against Great Britain, Ireland and the British West Indies, though this went beyond any of the members' instructions as framed by the bodies which had accredited them.[76] The measure would admittedly penalize many unoffending persons in the places involved, but its advocates contended that partial methods were useless, that a total boycott was necessary to produce maximum results.

The searching journalistic inquest did much to clarify both the constitutional and economic issues. The average citizen came to understand better the nature of the crisis, and by the same token those who must make the ultimate decisions gained a deeper insight into

---

75 "A Plain Dealer" in the *N.–Y. Journal*, July 21, 1774; anon. in the *Pa. Journal*, Sept. 28, also 4 *American Archives*, I, 811–814.

76 A Philadelphia correspondent in the *Mass. Spy*, June 18, 1774, and "A Connecticut Farmer," Aug. 25; "A Carolinian" in the *S.–C. Gazette*, June 20; anon. in the *N.–Y. Journal*, July 7, "A Plain Dealer," July 21, and "A Sincere Friend and Well-Wisher to America," July 28; "Camillus" in the *N.–H. Gazette*, Aug. 5; "A zealous Friend to both Countries" in the *Pa. Gazette*, Aug. 31, and "A Great Number of Mechanics," Sept. 7; "Juba" in the *N.–Y. Gazetteer*, Sept. 2; "A Distressed Bostonian" in the *Boston Evening-Post*, Sept. 5; unsigned article in the *Norwich Packet*, Sept. 15. For an analysis of the delegates' instructions, see A. M. Schlesinger, *The Colonial Merchants and the American Revolution* (N. Y., 1918), 396–400.

the problems as well as into the state of public opinion. When the delegates assembled in early September, they knew that the voice of the press demanded resolute action and were in turn assured that the great bulk of the editors would give their actions wholehearted support.

Chapter X

The
Pen Becomes the Sword

MANY CIRCUMSTANCES conspired to shape the course of the newspapers in the next seven months as the crisis with the motherland continued to deepen. One was the semiofficial role assigned the press by the First Continental Congress in the muting of opposition. Another was a sharp rise in the number of journals. A third was the ungovernable popular fury that swept through the colonies against Tory printers. Then came the collision of arms at Lexington and Concord, which placed the dispute in a wholly different setting.

I

The Congress met in Philadelphia from September 5 to October 26, 1774. Though it contained no newspaper editors, it included men like Dickinson and the Yankee Adamses, old hands at the game of political journalism. All agreed, however, that for the moment silence was the best propaganda, for, as John Adams observed, "Here is a diversity of religions, educations, manners, interests, such as it would seem almost impossible to unite in one plan of conduct," and silence made it possible to conceal from the public internal rifts of opinion. Accordingly, the only news releases consisted of bare factual bulletins on emergency matters. However, with an eye to a favorable popular response after the Congress should adjourn, the body adopted the unit rule of voting by delegations, so as to be able to record actions as having been taken unanimously even though large minorities might have been opposed to them.

208

Indeed, in the case of the debate over Galloway's proposed charter of union with Britain, the members went so far as to expunge every reference to it from the minutes.[1]

The pledge of secrecy was surprisingly well kept. The newspapers, though now and then proffering advice to the delegates, either knew nothing of what was going on or co-operated by saying nothing. Probably William and Thomas Bradford of the fiery *Pennsylvania Journal* felt under particular constraint as official printers to the Congress. Oddly enough, the only known leak to the press came from Samuel Adams, who wrote a letter to his old friend Joseph Warren in Massachusetts mentioning the choice of the Anglican minister Jacob Duché to offer prayer at one of the early sessions. Warren, seeing an opportunity to proselyte local Tories of that faith, inserted the relevant passage in the *Boston Gazette*, afterward telling Adams that, "although it was done without your permission, I know you will forgive it." [2] Adams's reply, though lost to posterity, could hardly have been very severe since he himself had been the original offender.

Proceeding behind closed doors the Congress hammered out its several theoretical pronouncements. It disavowed any desire for Independence, plighted undying fealty to the King, and rejected Parliament's right to do more than enact bona-fide trade regulations for the colonies. More explicitly, it demanded a restoration of the blessed posture America had enjoyed before the Sugar Act of 1764. Although the members joined in toasting "The Liberty of the Press" at a civic banquet, they did not see fit in their appeal to the King or in those to the peoples of Britain and America to so much as mention it. Evidently they felt that in this respect they had affairs well in hand. Only in their address to the inhabitants of Quebec (who, they may have forgotten, had never known a free press under the French) did they hold it up as one of the glories of Englishmen. This "grand" right, they proclaimed, safeguards the "advancement

[1] John Adams to William Tudor, Sept. 29, 1774, Adams, *Works* (C. F. Adams, ed., Boston, 1850–56), IX, 346; *Journals of the Continental Congress* (W. C. Ford and others, eds., Wash., 1904–37), I, 25–26, 43–51.

[2] *Boston Gazette*, Sept. 26, 1774, also Peter Force, comp., *American Archives*, ser. 4 (Wash., 1837–46), I, 802; Warren to Samuel Adams, Sept. 29, Richard Frothingham, *Life and Times of Joseph Warren* (Boston, 1865), 382. There is evidence that Galloway divulged some of the proceedings to the Ministry by way of Governor William Franklin of New Jersey. O. C. Kuntzelman, *Joseph Galloway, Loyalist* (Phila., 1941), 122–123.

of truth," the "ready communication of thoughts between subjects," and the "consequential promotion of union among them, whereby oppressive officers are shamed or intimidated, into more honourable and just modes of conducting affairs." [3] Intended purely for export, this declaration was presently to be flung back in their teeth by unfree dissidents at home.

Reinforcing political philosophy with concrete action, the Congress in a document known as the Continental Association declared a comprehensive boycott of Great Britain, Ireland and the British West Indies: a nonimportation and nonconsumption agreement to begin on December 1, 1774, and a prohibition of all exports to those places from September 10, 1775. To ensure compliance the Congress directed that "a committee be chosen in every county, city, and town" to "observe the conduct of all persons touching this association" and, in the event of any violations, to "cause the truth of the case to be published in the gazette," so that "all such foes to the rights of British-America" should be "universally contemned as the enemies of American liberty" and "all dealings" with them cease.[4]

The press, which had done so much to promote the policy of economic coercion, thus became in turn its principal means of enforcement. As a widely quoted newspaper writer said, "The Congress, like other legislative bodies, have annexed penalties to their laws. . . . They have held out no punishments but INFAMY, a species of infamy which sounds more dreadful to a freeman than the gallows, the rack or the stake. It is this, he shall be declared in the public papers to be an ENEMY TO HIS COUNTRY." [5]

This punitive function, it will be recalled, was not without precedent, for during the Townshend Acts newspapers had helped discipline the foes of nonimportation regulations. And even before the Continental Congress took action, New England editors had begun black-listing supporters of the Intolerable Acts, notably in Boston, where the *Massachusetts Spy* served warning that all "traitors" ac-

[3] *Journals*, I, 108. For the toast at the banquet, see the *Pa. Gazette*, Sept. 21, 1774, also the *Boston Gazette*, Sept. 26.

[4] Article 11 of the Continental Association, *Journals*, I, 79.

[5] Anon., "Political Observations, without order," *Pa. Packet*, Nov. 14, 1774, reprinted in the *N.–Y. Journal*, Nov. 24, the *Va. Gazette* (Purdie and Dixon), Nov. 24, the *Conn. Journal*, Nov. 25, the *Mass. Gazette and Boston Post-Boy*, Nov. 28, the *N.–Y. Gazetteer*, Dec. 1, the *Providence Gazette*, Dec. 7, the *Mass. Spy*, Dec. 8, and the *Essex Gazette*, Dec. 20. It is also in 4 *American Archives*, I, 976–977.

cepting posts under the Gage regime would face popular vengeance. A month later Thomas announced, "We have received the Recantations, Confessions, &c. of such a great number of Lawyers, Clerks, deputy Sheriffs &c. &c. &c. that we cannot publish them all unless we add a sheet extraordinary to this paper." [6] On October 21— nearly a week before the promulgation of the Continental Association—the Massachusetts Provincial Congress gave the practice quasilegal sanction, ordering the names of all officials still holding out to be "repeatedly published" in the press as "infamous Betrayers of their Country." [7]

The Continental Congress in effect universalized the system and vested it in patriot eyes with the highest possible authority. As a commentator in the *South-Carolina Gazette* phrased it, "We now know our Duty, happy for us, if we reduce our Knowledge into Practice. . . . The Wit of Man could not have devised any Thing more likely to obtain a Redress of our Grievances than the Plan concerted." But the opposition press, spearheaded by Rivington, raged at unlawful committees "clothed with the dangerous power" to "*post* in the public papers" anyone they might deem "an enemy to his country." "By heavens," this writer exploded, "I had rather submit to acts of Parliament implicitly, nay to the *will* of a King, than to the *caprice* of Committee-men." Out of fear of a distant and imaginary tyranny, so another put it, "we have created a dangerous and real one among ourselves." "The association," shrieked a third, ". . . is calculated for the meridian of a Spanish inquisition; it is subversive of, inconsistent with, the wholesome laws of our happy constitution." [8]

[6] *Mass. Spy*, Aug. 11, Sept. 17, 1774. For instances in other colonies, see the *N.-H. Gazette*, Oct. 7, the *Providence Gazette*, Sept. 17, the *Conn. Courant*, Sept. 19, and the *Norwich Packet*, Oct. 13. The *Packet*, for example, stigmatized the Anglican clergyman, Samuel Peters of Hebron, a Tory refugee in Boston, as "the most unnatural Monster" and "detestable Parricide to his Country that ever appeared in America, or disgraced Humanity."

[7] *Boston Gazette*, Oct. 24, 1774.

[8] "Vox Populi" in the *S.-C. Gazette*, Nov. 11, 1774, also *Pa. Gazette*, Nov. 30; "A Freeholder of Essex, and *real* Lover of Liberty" in the *N.-Y. Gazetteer*, Jan. 1, 1775, also 4 *American Archives*, I, 1094–1096; "Z" in the *N.-Y. Gazetteer*, Dec. 1, 1774; "America's Real Friend" in the *N.-Y. Gazetteer*, Feb. 16, 1775, also 4 *American Archives*, I, 1211–1213. For similar protests, see "An Anxious By-stander" in the *Pa. Gazette*, Jan. 4; a pamphlet quoted in the *Boston Evening-Post*, Jan. 23; "A Lover of Peace" in the *N.-H. Gazette*, Jan. 20; "Grotius" in the *Mass. Gazette and Boston Post-Boy*, Feb. 6, and "Massachusettensis" (Daniel Leonard) on March 21; "A Friend to Amity" (William Eddis) in the *Md. Gazette*, Feb. 16, reprinted in Eddis, *Letters from America* (London, 1792), 191–198.

But such outcries naturally went unheeded, and in the months that followed, the Committees of Observation and Committees of Inspection, as they were variously called, applied themselves to enforcing the regulations.[9] In addition, as the critics had accurately foretold, the tribunals inevitably exceeded their original assignment by going on to police all forms of political dissent whether banned by the Association or not. In some instances, moreover, town meetings anticipated the accredited agencies, while in still others mobs sprang into action. But whatever the means, the weapon of publicity proved basic to the proceedings.

In colony after colony the press blazoned the acknowledgments of guilt and pledges of reform of recreants who, like Andrew Leckie of Caroline County, Va., could not endure "the unsupportable Weight of publick Censure and publick Hatred." And by the same token editors held up impenitents to odium, with no exemption even for the clergy. In one case the Nansemond County Committee in Virginia advertised the Anglican minister John Agnew for disparaging the Continental Congress and declaring that "to resist the King and Parliament was rebellion." In another, at Baltimore, the Reverend William Edmiston, unlike his Virginia colleague, abjectly confessed his political errors and escaped further obloquy by promising "to avoid any just cause of offence" in the future.[10]

Sometimes the accused happily won vindication. Thus the Brunswick County Committee in Virginia, after sifting allegations against the merchant Allan Love, gave him a clean bill of health. Dr. Abner Beebe at East Haddam, Conn., however, came out less well. Being haled before the Committee of Inspection at the instance of "a great Number of the reputable Inhabitants," he flatly denied ever saying, *"I am a Tory"* or that *"the King and Parliament had a Right to Tax the Colonies,"* but as the hearing went into its second day, overwhelming evidence obliged him to admit his guilt. He even agreed to comply with the Continental Association, but the Committee nevertheless stigmatized him in the press, since he would not also endorse the Congress's constitutional declarations. At Petersham, Mass.,

    9 For details, see A. M. Schlesinger, *The Colonial Merchants and the American Revolution* (N. Y., 1918), 476–535.
    10 *Va. Gazette* (Purdie and Dixon), Nov. 3, 1774; *Va. Gazette* (Dixon and Hunter), April 8, 1775; letter of Andrew Miller, March 11, W. L. Saunders, comp., *Colonial Records of North Carolina* (Raleigh, 1886–90), IX, 1164; *Md. Gazette,* Jan. 26, also 4 *American Archives,* I, 1146–1147.

the town meeting, assuming the initiative, similarly branded fourteen "Incorrigible Enemies of America" for opposing what they had
termed "the pretended Authority of any Congresses, Committees of
Correspondence or other unconstitutional Assemblies"; and Marblehead for like reasons voted to *"break off all Connections in Commerce, and in every other Way,"* with six of its citizens. Lest these
avoid the penalty by flight, the town requested "every patriotic
Printer on the Continent" to take note so "that the Abettors of
Tyranny, and Parricides of their Country, may be universally
known and detested." [11]

Where vigilante groups intervened the victims stood in bodily
peril. Dr. Abrather Alden at Biddeford, Mass. (now Maine), for
example, made his amends under oath rather than defy mob fury;
and similarly John Taylor of Shrewsbury, after "being surrounded
by a number of Persons, armed with Clubs and Axes, . . . from
the Morning till the Evening," signed "a Confession and Promise,
which they had prepared for that Purpose." At the solicitation of
Marshfield Tories, Governor Gage sent a military detachment to
protect them from "Terrors of that Kind," but such assistance at best
could assure only temporary immunity.[12]

These incidents—a few out of legion—illustrate the zeal that
actuated the drive against dissidents. The offenders, having little
choice, generally found it prudent "to swim with the stream," but as
one protester inconsiderately reminded the Whigs, "if this be wise,
then were Hampden, Sidney, and Russel most unwise." A Tory
writer might well ask, "what man can suppose that any *promises,
declarations* and *engagements,* thus *extorted* can be *binding* upon
these unhappy victims to popular frenzy?" [13] But "the threats of
shame and infamy" at least had the merit of silencing voices which
might otherwise have had a divisive effect.

[11] *Va. Gazette* (Dixon and Hunter), March 25, 1775; *Conn. Gazette*, Oct. 27,
reporting an occurrence of Dec., 1774; *Boston Gazette*, Jan. 16, 1775; *Essex Gazette*, Feb. 7.
[12] *N.–H. Gazette*, Dec. 9, 1774; *Mass. Gazette and Boston News-Letter*, Dec.
29; Gage to Lord Dartmouth, Jan. 27, 1775, *N.–H. Gazette*, June 27, 1775.
[13] "Thomas Trueman" in the *Md. Gazette*, March 2, 1775; "Phileirene" in the
Mass. Gazette and Boston News-Letter, Jan. 12, similarly, "A Freeholder in the
County of Worcester" on April 13, "Philanthrop, jun.," in the *Mass. Gazette and
Boston Post-Boy*, Jan. 9, and "Agrippa" in the *N.–Y. Gazetteer*, March 30.

II

As the excitement waxed in the aftermath of the First Continental Congress, some noteworthy changes took place in newspaper ownership, and five new journals came into being. At Williamsburg on December 18, 1774, Alexander Purdie amicably parted company with John Dixon after nearly nine years, and on the following February 3 Purdie started his own *Virginia Gazette*, the third of that name in the provincial capital, taking as his motto: "ALWAYS FOR LIBERTY AND THE PUBLICK GOOD." Dixon meanwhile teamed up with William Hunter, Jr., son of a former owner of the paper, and they likewise assured their readers that "Whatever may be sent us in Favour of LIBERTY or for the PUBLICK GOOD will be published with Cheerfulness . . . ." [14] On April 6, 1775, John Hunter Holt, nephew of the editor of the *New-York Journal*, purchased the *Virginia Gazette or Norfolk Intelligencer*, allying it more firmly with the patriot party; [15] and at Annapolis, Frederick Green upon his mother's death on March 23 became with unchanged political allegiance sole publisher of the *Maryland Gazette*. A new paper now also appeared in Baltimore. Although Andrew Stewart's efforts toward that end in February had collapsed, John Dunlap, extending his operations as editor of the *Pennsylvania Packet*, stepped into the breach and on May 2 launched *Dunlap's Maryland Gazette*. [16]

The greatest activity, however, occurred in Philadelphia, recent seat of the Continental Congress and America's biggest city. There three additional newspapers sprang up in as many months. The *Pennsylvania Evening Post*, instituted on January 24 by Benjamin Towne, Goddard's unlamented short-time partner on the defunct *Chronicle*, was a triweekly which generally steered clear of politics. The *Pennsylvania Ledger*, which James Humphreys, Jr., sired four days later, professed to be "Free and Impartial," but it usually favored Whig news and views. The third, the *Pennsylvania Mercury*, signaled Joseph Galloway's re-entry into partisan journalism. "We only want, what you fortunately have," Galloway had written a

[14] *Va. Gazette* (Dixon and Hunter), Jan. 7, 1775.
[15] J. H. Holt's announcement of the transfer of ownership, *ibid.*, May 13, 1775.
[16] Stewart's proposals appeared in the *N.–Y. Gazetteer*, March 2, 1775, the *N.–Y. Journal*, March 9, and the *Va. Gazette* (Dixon and Hunter), April 1.

New York friend several weeks before, "a free Press, to recall the deluded people to their senses, and that I hope will be supplied in a very short time." Established by Enoch Story and Daniel Humphreys at (they stated) "the Solicitation and Encouragement of several Gentlemen of Reputation" or (as Joseph Reed put it) of "a little, dirty, despicable party endeavoring to sow dissension," the publication duly appeared on April 7.[17] Though more strongly Tory than the two other newcomers, it never lived up to Galloway's expectations, and a destructive fire in the printing plant at the very close of the year brought it prematurely to an end.

The thirst for news and yet more news revealed itself in other ways as well. At Savannah the Committee of Correspondence threatened James Johnston of the *Georgia Gazette* with starting a rival sheet unless he printed more Whig articles, which he thereupon grudgingly did. For a quite different reason John Holt apologized for omitting from the *New-York Journal* "many valuable pieces relating to our present controversy" and unavailingly suggested that to obviate this difficulty at a time "when so much art and assiduity is used to deceive the people" a fund be raised to enable him to enlarge his paper. At York, Pa., twelve new subscribers to the *Pennsylvania Journal* assured the Bradfords that "The Spirit of Liberty which appears in your Publication has gained you many Friends in this County." Isaiah Thomas had already met the enhanced reader interest by making the *Massachusetts Spy* "a third larger than any News-Paper published in this Province," and soon it attained "the greatest Circulation of *any News-Paper in New-England*." A group of Worcester patriots invited him to set up a journal in that place, and in February, 1775, he announced plans for doing so; but before they materialized, the outbreak of hostilities intervened. There had also been an earlier unsuccessful move to establish a paper at Falmouth (now Portland, Me.).[18]

Thirty-eight newspapers were going full blast on the eve of Lex-

[17] James Humphreys, Jr.'s, advance statement of editorial policy in the *Pa. Journal*, Jan. 11, 1775; Galloway to Samuel Verplanck, Feb. 14, *Pa. Mag. of History and Biography*, XXI (1897–98), 481; Story and Humphreys in the *Pa. Gazette*, Jan. 18; W. B. Reed, *Life and Correspondence of Joseph Reed* (Phila., 1847), I, 92; Isaiah Thomas, *The History of Printing in America* (rev. ed., Am. Antiquarian Soc., *Trans. and Colls.*, V–VI, Albany, 1874), I, 267–268.

[18] *Ga. Gazette*, Oct. 26, 1774; *N.-Y. Journal*, Feb. 23, 1775; letter of April 6, 1775, to the Bradfords, *Pa. Mag. of History and Biography*, XIV (1890–91), 445; *Mass. Spy*, June 2, Dec. 29, 1774, Feb. 10, 1775; Thomas, *History of Printing*, I, 180–181; *Salem Gazette*, Sept. 30, 1774.

ington and Concord in April, 1775, with Philadelphia supporting seven, Boston five, and New York, Williamsburg and Charleston three each.[19] Although the only aggressive Tory sheets were in Boston and New York—both garrisoned towns—the patriots nevertheless kept an eagle eye on the entire press for possible political waywardness. When an unsigned letter from Kent County, Del., in the *Pennsylvania Ledger*, February 11, 1775, averred that, "if the King's Standard were now erected, nine out of ten would repair to it," the Philadelphia Committee of Inspection (of which William Bradford was a member) referred the piece to the Kent County tribunal; and the terrified writer, one Robert Holliday, recanted the "malignant insinuation," promising to defend with his life and property "all the constitutional rights and privileges of America." Holliday's case had not been helped by the gleeful reprinting of his letter meanwhile by progovernment editors in New York and Boston.[20]

Correspondence from America in British newspapers also received sharp scrutiny. The Westmoreland County Committee of Observation in Virginia, for example, black-listed the schoolmaster David Wardrobe in the press for a mild criticism of political affairs appearing anonymously in the *Glasgow Journal*. The culprit after tasting for a time the husks of enforced unemployment publicly repented on his knees "for having traduced the good people of Virginia." In another instance the Anne Arundel County Committee in Maryland could not ferret out the local author of a "false, scandalous, and malicious" piece in the London *Public Ledger*, but it nonetheless denounced the unknown for seeking to foist on the people "the arbitrary decrees of a despotic ministry." [21]

This new-fledged censorship system turned upside down the common-law doctrine of seditious libel, since it was now seditious to asperse the Whigs' extralegal government and support constituted authority. Opposition spokesmen fumed with indignation. "Do you really mean to immure the colonies in Popish darkness . . . ?" a

[19] The often cited list in Thomas, *History of Printing*, II, 294–295, contains errors both of commission and omission.

[20] *Pa. Journal*, Feb. 22, May 17, 1775, also 4 *American Archives*, I, 1231, II, 466–467; *N.–Y. Gazetteer*, Feb. 16; *N.–Y. Gazette and Weekly Mercury*, Feb. 20; *Mass. Gazette and Boston News-Letter*, Feb. 23.

[21] *Va. Gazette* (Pinkney), Feb. 9, 1775, also 4 *American Archives*, I, 970–972; *Md. Gazette* (Annapolis), April 13.

loyalist group hotly demanded of the Suffolk County Committee in New York. "Are none to speak, write or print, but by your permission?" [22] To right the situation, the Tory argument continued, the Whigs needed but to practice what their Congress had so grandiloquently preached to the people of Quebec regarding freedom of discussion. Declared one writer ironically, *"the many advantages resulting therefrom to society, as pointed out in that address, cannot fail to* open *the press in America to the sentiments of all parties."* Indeed, chided another, unless the Congress had meant only to approve the liberty to criticize every species of rule save its own, then the suppressors of the freedom were themselves "enemies to their country, and the pests of society." [23]

But the popular party for the most part self-righteously ignored the devil quoting Scripture. The Newport Committee of Inspection, however, taking the now familiar patriot line, insisted that the Quebec declaration did not, of course, apply to newspapers "incessantly employed" in "exciting discord and disunion among the people." A facetious soul proposed to meet the Tory complaints by expressly setting apart one journal in each provincial capital "for the reception of *lyes* and *scurrility*." This, he contended, would satisfy the need and at the same time duly forewarn the public against attempts "by *hard words* to frighten us into a submission." [24]

III

Only in Boston and New York, as has been noted, did the Whigs face an alert and determined opposition press. In the Yankee metropolis the conduits of *"lyes* and *scurrility"*—the *Massachusetts Gazettes*, edited respectively by Margaret Draper and by Mills and Hicks—enjoyed the unwavering support of the military, thus intensifying the patriots' hatred of Gage as the army commander as

[22] Benjamin Floyd and others in the *N.-Y. Gazetteer*, April 6, 1775, similarly, "T.V.V." on Dec. 15, 1774, and a letter on Feb. 16, 1775, from an American in London; and "Freedom" in the *Mass. Gazette and Boston News-Letter*, Feb. 9, 1775.

[23] "A Freeholder in the County of Worcester" in *ibid.*, Feb. 2, 1775; "A Sailor" in the *N.-Y. Gazetteer*, Dec. 15, 1774. For examples of similar articles using the Quebec Address as a text, see "An Englishman" in *ibid.*, March 30, 1775, and Rivington on April 13; and "An Anxious By-stander" in the *Pa. Gazette*, Jan. 4, 1775.

[24] *Newport Mercury*, March 16, 1775, also 4 *American Archives*, II, 12–13; "A Lover of English Liberty" in the *Pa. Gazette*, March 8.

well as chief civil executive. Unexpectedly he seemed to be delivered into their hands when the *Boston Gazette*, the *Evening-Post* and the *Massachusetts Spy* lifted from a London paper a letter he had allegedly written to Lord Dartmouth, demanding unlimited authority and additional troops "to make some very severe examples" of the "deluded" popular leaders.[25] The Whig chieftains, remembering their machinations to unseat the two preceding Governors, now saw a chance to repeat the strategy, but the opportunity vanished when both the purported sender of the letter and the supposed recipient promptly published irate and convincing denials.[26] "Philo-Patriae" consoled Gage in Mrs. Draper's *Gazette* by assuring him that "humanity recoils at such malevolence" and that "a bad cause . . . thrives most in mire and filth." [27]

The patriot journalists achieved greater success in undermining whatever confidence the common folk still felt in the two pro-British newspapers. Flinging back Tory charges of "unbounded licence," they accused the "pensioned prostitutes" who "disgraced the Massachusetts Gazettes" of brandishing "scare-crows, raw-heads and bloody bones" to "*lessen* the continental congress in our esteem, or retard the measures they have recommended." [28] Then reviving the stories of a secret ministerial fund to bribe servile editors and writers, the *Spy* announced that the government had budgeted an estimated £10,000 for that object in Massachusetts alone.[29] Though the nonpartisan *Evening-Post* could scarcely have been aimed at, the Fleets unqualifiedly denied lending themselves to "such a base and mean Purpose," and Mrs. Draper, a much more obvious target, protested her innocence in wrathful italics.[30] Even

[25] *Boston Gazette* and *Boston Evening-Post*, Nov. 21, 1774; *Mass. Spy*, Nov. 24. Even the *Mass. Gazette and Boston Post-Boy*, Nov. 21, was taken in by the forgery, which had originally appeared in the *London Chronicle*, Sept. 13.

[26] *Mass. Gazette and Boston News-Letter*, Nov. 24, Dec. 1, 1774, the second reference being a reprint of Lord Dartmouth's disclaimer in the *London Gazetteer*, Sept. 20.

[27] *Mass. Gazette and Boston News-Letter*, Dec. 22, 1774, also *N.–Y. Gazette and Weekly Mercury*, Jan. 2, 1775. When Rivington reprinted this piece in his *Gazetteer*, Jan. 5, he attributed it to the *Boston Gazette*.

[28] *Mass. Spy*, Jan. 12, 1775. See "The Querist" in the *Mass. Gazette and Boston News-Letter*, Nov. 24, 1774, and "A Suffolk Yeoman" on Dec. 29 for examples of Tory characterizations of Whig journalistic methods.

[29] *Mass. Spy*, Feb. 9, 1775. The *Boston Gazette*, Feb. 27, suggested that "Good Mrs. Draper" was the particular recipient.

[30] *Boston Evening-Post*, March 6, 1775; *Mass. Gazette and Boston News-Letter*, March 9.

so, the allegation sowed suspicions that unequivocal disclaimers could hardly allay.

But the Whig printers despite their temerity realized that in a town overrun with redcoats they were operating only on sufferance. Time and again they received blunt warnings to that effect. A handbill by "A Friend of Gr. Brit. & America" called upon the troops, "the instant rebellion happens," to put to the sword certain named patriots, including "those trumpeters of sedition, Edes and Gill, and Thomas." [31] Thomas later reported in the *Spy* plans to assassinate him forthwith and assured his readers he was "taking PROPER CARE—to defend himself." Some months afterward a British regiment, halting at his office with the band playing "The Rogue's March," threatened to tar and feather him. As further notice both to him and his *Boston Gazette* colleagues, an anonymous broadside proposed that a tribunal of the army, navy and engineering corps should meet each week on the days their papers came out to take summary action against any "inflammatory, seditious, and treasonable" contributors. [32]

To lend aid and comfort to the harassed editors, Whig zealots outside Boston rallied to their side. Southwick of the *Newport Mercury* admonished the "ministerial hirelings" and "scribblers" that before long they would "be driven from this land of FREEDOM," [33] and a mob at Petersham in Worcester County, Mass., compelled one Ephraim Whitney to promise to write no more for the "Court Gazettes." [34] Several months later, on January 27, 1775, a convention of the patriots of the county added the weapon of economic duress. Bracketing the two *Massachusetts Gazettes* with Rivington's and Gaine's publications in New York, it enjoined all "good people" to boycott these "scandalous" sheets. [35] A crowd in Providence,

[31] *Boston Evening-Post*, Sept. 19, 1774, also *N.-Y. Gazetteer*, Oct. 17. Among others on the list were Samuel Adams, Thomas Young, Joseph Greenleaf and Josiah Quincy, Jr., all writers for these editors, though of course they had incurred Tory enmity on other grounds as well.

[32] *Mass. Spy*, Oct. 27, 1774; Thomas, *History of Printing*, II, 63–64 n.; *Mass. Gazette and Boston Post-Boy*, April 10, 1775, also *N.-Y. Gazetteer*, April 13.

[33] *Newport Mercury*, Sept. 26, 1774, similarly, "An American" in the *Essex Gazette* at Salem, Nov. 29.

[34] *Boston Evening-Post*, Oct. 17, 1774.

[35] *Ibid.*, Feb. 13, 1775, also *Mass. Spy*, Feb. 16, *N.-Y. Gazette and Weekly Mercury*, Feb. 20, and 4 *American Archives*, I, 1193. For outraged remonstrances against "this Effort to suppress the Liberty of the Press," see articles by the editors and others in the *Mass. Gazette and Boston News-Letter*, Feb. 16, March 2, and the *Mass. Gazette and Boston Post-Boy*, Feb. 13, March 6.

R. I., rising to the occasion, flung Mills and Hicks's paper along with Rivington's into a bonfire.[36]

This war of nerves, however, failed to yield the desired result, though it may explain why Mrs. Draper in reprinting an exceptionally violent polemic from Gaine's *New-York Gazette and Weekly Mercury* begged the townspeople not "to impute it to any particular fondness of the Publisher for such Things" but, rather, to a desire "to convey to the World, what is wrote and published in other Colonies, in these difficult Times." [37] But this was only a momentary reaction, for, besides continuing to cull articles from her Manhattan Tory contemporaries, she gave the public the disquisitions of such trenchant Boston partisans as "Phileirene" and "The Querist," while Mills and Hicks proved no less active.

Indeed, "Massachusettensis," who held forth in the *Massachusetts Gazette and Boston Post-Boy*, "spread alarms and terrors among the people" to such an extent that John Adams in the guise of "Novanglus" undertook to supply an "antidote against his poison" in the *Boston Gazette*.[38] Daniel Leonard, a former Whig, now Solicitor General to the Customs Board, besides hiding behind a pseudonym, further veiled his authorship by having the seventeen installments copied by another hand before sending them to the printers. So cogent was his reasoning and so impressive his parade of English legal and constitutional precedents that Adams could only suppose the writer to be his erstwhile friend Attorney General Jonathan Sewall, though others in the patriot circle guessed the identity of the writer more accurately.[39] Without advancing any novel views on the crisis the two gladiators traded wounding blows over such subjects as the Intolerable Acts, the lawfulness of the Continental Congress, the nature of America's constitutional dependence on the mother country, the underlying purpose of the patriots, and the liberty of the press. As to the last point, Leonard leveled the familiar

[36] *Boston Gazette*, March 13, 1775, also 4 *American Archives*, II, 15.

[37] *Mass. Gazette and Boston News-Letter*, Oct. 20, 1774.

[38] Letter to Jedidiah Morse, Nov. 20, 1815, Adams, *Works*, X, 179. The "Massachusettensis" series began on Dec. 12, 1774; that of "Novanglus" on Jan. 23, 1775. Both may be found in *Novanglus, and Massachusettensis* (Boston, 1819), for which Adams provided an introduction.

[39] Mellen Chamberlain, ed., "Memorial of Daniel Leonard," Mass. Hist. Soc., *Procs.*, ser. 2, VI (1890–91), 254; Adams to Morse, Adams, *Works*, X, 178–179, 194–195; John Eliot to Jeremy Belknap, April 11, 1775, Mass. Hist. Soc., *Colls.*, ser. 6, IV (1891), 8. Among others, John Trumbull in the first canto of *M'Fingal*, published early in 1776, assumed that Leonard was the author.

Tory charge that the Whigs "by playing off the resentment of the populace against printers and authors" had through the years become in reality "the licensers of the press." To this, Adams, drawing generously on his imagination, returned an unqualified denial and then, without citing authority, shot back that from £200 to £1500 a year "had been the constant reward of every scribbler" on the ministerial side. He even affirmed that John Mein's flight from Boston in 1769 had resulted not from the journalist's political obnoxiousness, but from his physical assaults on fellow townsmen and the importunities of his creditors.[40]

The protracted joust led a scattering of out-of-town newspapers to repeat one or the other of the series according to their political predilections. The *New-Hampshire Gazette,* leaning over backward, in fact published both, generally in parallel columns, advising its subscribers to *"read both Sides with an impartial Mind, without which we must unavoidably grope in a mazy Labyrinth of Error."* [41] In Boston meanwhile impassioned disputants hurried to the defense or the attack as the case might be. As the one group viewed "Massachusettensis," he deserved *"the approbation of every honest, wise, and good man, and above all, of Him, who looks to the heart."* To the other, the Tory's "Harrangues" revealed "a designing Man, in whose Breast Avarice and Ambition have extinguished the Love of God," while "Novanglus" shone "with the Abilities of the Statesman and Virtues of the Patriot." [42] With the issues still unresolved, the "shot heard round the world" in April brought the debate to an unanticipated conclusion.

---

[40] *Mass. Gazette and Boston Post-Boy,* Dec. 12, 1774; *Boston Gazette,* Feb. 6, 1775.

[41] *N.–H. Gazette,* March 10, 1775. In Salem the *Essex Gazette* carried "Novanglus," and the *Salem Gazette* "Massachusettensis"; the *N.–Y. Gazetteer,* beginning on Dec. 22, 1774, reprinted five installments of the latter.

[42] "A Fellow Citizen" in the *Mass. Gazette and Boston Post-Boy,* Jan. 2, 1775, "A British American" on Jan. 9, and "America Solon" on March 20. Apart from "Novanglus," the ablest sustained reply to Leonard's constitutional exposition came from a contributor who signed himself "From the County of Hampshire" (Joseph Hawley?) in the *Mass. Spy,* Feb. 9–March 9, March 23–May 10. The *Essex Journal* at Newburyport reprinted this series, beginning March 1. According to "X." in the *Boston Evening-Post,* March 13, "Massachusettensis and his Subalterns are fairly beat out of the field by Novanglus and the Writer from the County of Hampshire, &c."

IV

The Manhattan Tory editors, even more than the Boston ones, caused the Whigs sleepless nights. The *Massachusetts Gazettes* reached few readers outside New England, but Rivington with the largest circulation in the colonies carried his warfare to the remotest communities. Gaine's *New-York Gazette and Weekly Mercury*, though less pertinacious, ably seconded the *Gazetteer*, the two constituting in patriot eyes "Lord North's Press." These printers also turned out some of the most belligerent loyalist pamphlets in America. Holt's *Journal* despite the untiring zeal of that "crack-brained Republican"—a Tory viewpoint—could not singlehandedly offset the propaganda. Acting Governor Colden jubilantly reported that more was now being published in New York "against Measures which may be offensive to Parliament than in all the other Colonies put together." Rivington injected partisan bias even into his society items, remarking pointedly, for example, that "not a single whig" was among the forty-seven guests at a wedding in White Plains.[43]

Aided by the lack of Tory organs in most parts of America, he found moreover that his militancy richly paid off. In mid-October, 1774, he announced that he had added 500 subscribers in five months, bringing the total to 3600, "a number far beyond the most sanguine expectations of the Printer's warmest friends." Up and down the coast British adherents turned hungrily to the *Gazetteer* as their political bible. Joseph Galloway in the Pennsylvania Assembly acclaimed Rivington "an honour to his Country," the Anglican cleric Jonathan Boucher in Maryland styled him America's only "impartial" publisher, and Governor Josiah Martin of North Carolina feelingly told the Ministry that the New Yorker's courage was "really signal in the present times." In like spirit Governor Gage distributed 400 copies of each issue of the paper to the military personnel and Tory civilians in Boston.[44]

---

[43] Albany Committee of Correspondence in the *N.-Y. Journal*, Feb. 16, 1775, also 4 *American Archives*, I, 1097–1098; "A Real Churchman" in the *N.-Y. Gazette and Weekly Mercury*, Dec. 26, 1774; Colden to Lord Dartmouth, Oct. 5, 1774, Cadwallader Colden, *Letter Books* (N.-Y. Hist. Soc., *Colls.*, IX–X, 1876–77), II, 368; *N.-Y. Gazetteer*, April 20, 1775.

[44] *Ibid.*, Oct. 13, 1774; Jared Ingersoll to Jonathan Ingersoll, March 10, 1775, New Haven Hist. Soc., *Papers*, IX (1918), 454; Boucher to William Smith, May 4, *Md. Hist. Mag.*, VIII (1913), 240; Martin to Lord Dartmouth, March 23, *N. C.*

To stem the flood of pre-British pamphlets patriot gatherings at first resorted to burning and sometimes tar-and-feathering the more objectionable tracts.[45] Usually included were some of the ones anonymously written by the Anglican churchmen Myles Cooper (*The American Querist* and *A Friendly Address to All Reasonable Americans*) and Samuel Seabury (*Free Thoughts on the Proceedings of the Continental Congress* and *The Congress Canvassed*). The Whig press eagerly fed the resentment. Such "incendiary, prostituted, hircling scriblers," burst forth one writer, were indeed lucky not to "be return'd back to the land of poverty and bondage from whence they were sent!" [46] But Rivington only jeered at the frenzy, scoffing on one occasion, "Keep *yourself* out of the *fire*, Mr. Printer, says a Waggish Correspondent," and on another, "When you damn the Printer, and burn his Pamphlet, he laughs, reprints, triumphs and fills his Pocket." [47]

Meanwhile, week after week, the *Gazetteer* strove by fair means and foul to puncture the Whig claims of the solidarity of the opposition to Britain. Once, the New York Committee of Inspection posted Rivington for erroneously telling of discord among its own members. The editor grudgingly acknowledged that he had depended on *"common report"* without further verification, and while promising greater care for the future, he heatedly denounced "a reprehension highly savouring of *Legislative Authority*." Gaine likewise, though a lesser offender, drew down the wrath of the Albany County Committee for a similar misrepresentation.[48]

Not content with strewing seeds of distrust throughout his own

---

Colonial Records, IX, 1176; *Newport Mercury*, March 20, 1775, also *N.–Y. Journal*, March 30. The *N.–Y. Gazetteer* reprinted the Gage item without denying it on March 30. "A.B." in the *Pa. Journal*, April 5, disposed of the matter with an obscene reference.

[45] The *N.–Y. Gazetteer*, Nov. 17, 1774, recorded three local instances and one at Baltimore; the *N.–Y. Journal*, Nov. 24, reported three more in New York. Similar incidents occurred before the end of the year at Newtown and Elizabethtown, N. J., and doubtless elsewhere. *Ibid.*, Dec. 8; *N.–Y. Gazette and Weekly Mercury*, Dec. 19.

[46] "A Free American" in the *Newport Mercury*, Nov. 22, 1774, who evidently did not know that Seabury, unlike Cooper, was of colonial birth. An excited writer in the *N.–Y. Journal*, Dec. 8, even proposed legal action against the authors of such "treasonable writings."

[47] *N.–Y. Gazetteer*, Nov. 17, 1774; Charles Evans, comp., *American Bibliography* (Chicago, 1903–34), V, 19.

[48] *N.–Y. Journal* and *N.–Y. Gazetteer*, March 16, 1775, also *Newport Mercury*, March 27; *N.–Y. Journal*, Feb. 16, 1775. The items are also in 4 *American Archives*, I, 1097–1098, II, 50.

province, Rivington directed like tactics toward other colonies. The Philadelphia Committee in particular complained to its New York counterpart of the *Gazetteer*'s "holding out to the World Ideas of Dissensions here, which do not exist," and in retaliation it induced fifty fellow citizens to subscribe to Holt's *Journal*.[49] "We are astonished," reproached a Philadelphian in Holt's pages, "that your sons of liberty and committee, suffer that base fellow, Rivington, to continue publishing his vile calumnies of every province in America." In Philadelphia, the writer continued, "he would have been called on long ago to give up the authors of so much falshood." [50] From Annapolis, General Charles Lee expressed equal wonder "that the miscreant Rivington is suffer'd to heap insult upon insult on the Congress with impunity." Still farther away, in Orange County, Va., James Madison wrote to his former Princeton classmate William Bradford, son of the senior *Pennsylvania Journal* editor, "I wish most heartily we had Rivington & his ministerial Gazettes for 24 hours in this place," promising he "would meet with adequate punishment." A Tory testified that, when a wild report reached Philadelphia that "the mob had pulled down Mr. Rivington's house" and he "had broke his back" in escaping, the "Demagogues" exhibited "every mark of joy; approaching almost to rapture." [51]

Similar recriminations against the *Gazetteer*'s "Twistifications" and "false colourings" arose from the Virginia and New England journals, though sometimes the New Yorker's offense actually consisted in only disclosing the embarrassing truth.[52] The favorite Whig

[49] Letter to the New York Committee, Feb. 1, 1775, *N.–Y. Journal*, March 16, also *Newport Mercury* and *Boston Evening-Post*, March 27, and *Essex Gazette*, March 28; "An Englishman" in the *N.–Y. Gazetteer*, March 30, also 4 *American Archives*, II, 238–242. For examples of the kind of pieces the patriots objected to, see Philadelphia correspondence in the *N.–Y. Gazetteer*, Feb. 9, 23, March 15.

[50] *N.–Y. Journal*, March 2, 1775, also *Newport Mercury*, March 13, and 4 *American Archives*, I, 1233. For other Philadelphia denunciations of Rivington and sometimes also of Gaine, see "Queries" in the *Pa. Journal*, Oct. 19, 1774, "Jeffries, Junior" on Feb. 22, 1775, and "J. Parke" on March 8; "Philadelphus" in the *Pa. Gazette*, Jan. 25; and Philadelphia letters in the *N.–Y. Journal*, Feb. 16, March 9. "An Observer" in *ibid.*, Feb. 9, demonstrated that Rivington had for political reasons doctored two letters from England, originally appearing in the *Pa. Journal*. "Censor" in the *N.–Y. Gazetteer*, March 2, however, effectively countercharged the *Pa. Journal* with similarly mutilating one of his own letters.

[51] Lee to Benjamin Rush, Dec. 15, 1774, *Lee Papers* (N.–Y. Hist. Soc., *Colls.*, IV–VII, 1871–74), I, 143–144; Madison to Bradford, March, 1775, Bradford MSS. (Hist. Soc. of Pa.); *N.–Y. Gazetteer*, March 23, 1775, also 4 *American Archives*, II, 134.

[52] For examples of such charges, see the *Va. Gazette* (Pinkney), Feb. 17, 24,

epithet for Rivington's publication was the *Brussels Gazette*, after the newspaper which had gained notoriety in England during the Seven Years' War as the "lying Gazette." [53] Personal journalism of a sort never before known in America feathered these verbal shafts. "WHETHER OR NOT MR. RIVINGTON IS REALLY A PENSIONER FROM THE MINISTRY OR, HAS BEEN INFLUENCED BY HOPES OF THEIR FUTURE FAVOURS, EVERY ONE IS AT LIBERTY TO JUDGE FROM THE CONDUCT OF HIS PRESS," asserted a Manhattan handbill.[54] A rhymester addressing Rivington in the *New-York Journal* gibed,

> In politics your very self,
> An ign'rant, yet a treach'rous elf
>   The public now have found;
> For, trying metal as they shou'd,
> They, judging 'twixt the bad and good,
>   Condemn you from your *sound*.[55]

Edes and Gill more tersely labeled the Tory paladin "dirty" and "malicious," Thomas settled for "*that* JUDAS," while Solomon Southwick dubbed him "a most wretched, jacobitish, hireling *incendiary*." Rivington zestfully returned these favors in kind, calling the *Boston Gazette* "Monday's Dung Barge" from "Schism Lane," the *Massachusetts Spy* that "Boston Snake of Sedition," and the *Newport Mercury* editor "Solomon Saphead." [56]

The swelling popular wrath generated an unprecedented intercolonial campaign to force Rivington out of business. In the weeks following the First Continental Congress cancellations of subscriptions poured in from as far south as South Carolina, where indeed the Provincial Congress itself forbade the "scurrilous Sheets" to circulate. Then, in early December, 1774, certain self-styled "Friends

---

1775; the *N.–H. Gazette*, March 17, 1775; the *Mass. Spy*, Oct. 10, Dec. 29, 1774, Jan. 5, Feb. 16, 1775; the *Boston Evening-Post*, Feb. 27, March 13, 1775; and the *Newport Mercury*, Jan. 2, April 10, 1775; and for a revealing instance of Rivington's truth-telling, consult Appendix E of the present volume.

[53] *Boston Gazette*, Feb. 6, 27, 1775; *Mass. Spy*, Feb. 16; *Essex Gazette*, Feb. 21; *Boston Evening-Post*, Feb. 27; "Neoptolemus" in the *Pa. Journal*, March 8.

[54] Printed by John Holt, according to Evans, *American Bibliography*, V, 82; similarly, "An American" in the *Essex Gazette*, Nov. 29, 1774; "Neoptolemus" in the *Pa. Gazette*, March 8, 1775; and an unsigned article in the *Boston Gazette* and the *Boston Evening-Post*, Jan. 30, also the *Va. Gazette* (Pinkney), Feb. 24.

[55] One of four stanzas of "A Mirror for a Printer" in the *N.–Y. Journal*, Sept. 15, 1774.

[56] *Boston Gazette*, Jan. 16, 1775; *Mass. Spy*, Dec. 29, 1774; *Newport Mercury*, April 10, 1775; *N.–Y. Gazetteer*, Feb. 23, March 2, 30, 1775.

of America" in New York undertook to systematize the boycott, sending out letters to patriot committees far and wide to strike back at the "Pensioned Servile Wretch" together with all his advertisers and, while they were about it, to include every like-minded editor.[57] Rivington, however, continued to be the shining mark. Whig-inspired meetings, reviling the printer's newspaper and pamphlets as "fire-brands, arrows and death, in the hands of a madman," banned any further dealings with him. Before the close of January, 1775, thirteen communities in New York, New Jersey, Connecticut and Massachusetts were on record as so acting, and during the next two months eight more followed, including two in Rhode Island and Virginia.[58]

Rivington furiously denounced the persecution, avowing, as he had so many times before, that he was but the selfless champion of a free press and stating, correctly, that he had put out Whig pamphlets as well as Tory ones.[59] In his most elaborate vindication he caustically added that he no more regarded "the cry of a discontented party, than the howling of wolves"; and when a mob hung him in effigy on April 13, 1775, at New Brunswick, N. J., he mocked the "snarling curs"—the "very *Dregs of the City*"—by publishing a fanciful cut of the incident with his dangling figure garbed in the elegant attire of a gentleman.[60] An unusual feat of journalistic enterprise, it chalked up one more count against him.

Despite these defiant gestures the Tory war horse was rapidly nearing the end of his course. Deserted by subscribers, facing bankruptcy, fearing physical harm, he made a *"free and public declaration"* in the *Gazetteer*, May 4, that he would henceforth conduct

---

[57] *N.–Y. Journal*, Nov. 17, Dec. 12, 1774, and "An Observer" on March 2, 1775; "Friends of America" to the Hartford Committee of Observation, Dec. 5, 1774, Conn. Hist. Soc., *Colls.*, XXI (1924), 445–447.

[58] The quoted phrase was used by the Hartford County (Conn.) convention. *Conn. Courant*, Jan. 30, 1775. Acting prior to Jan. 31, 1775, were committees and other gatherings in Ulster and Morris Counties, Shawangunk, Hanover and Walkill, N. Y., Freehold, Elizabeth, Newark, Woodbridge and Middlesex County, N. J., Fairfield and Hartford Counties, Conn., and Worcester County, Mass.; and during February and March others in Suffolk County and New Windsor, N. Y., Hanover, N. J., New Haven, Fairfield and Litchfield Counties, Conn., Newport, R. I., and Orange County (James Madison's home), Va. This boycott movement can be conveniently followed in 4 *American Archives*, I–II, which, however, should be supplemented at a few points by the files of the *N.–Y. Journal* and Connecticut papers.

[59] *N.–Y. Gazetteer*, Nov. 10, Dec. 8, 29, 1774, March 30, 1775.

[60] *Ibid.*, Feb. 16, April 20, 1775.

himself *"upon such principles as shall not give offence."* The mob
nonetheless descended upon his home and printery six days later,
forcing him to flee to a naval vessel in the harbor. ("We hope the
Non-exportation Agreement to Great-Britain will always except
such traitors to the Liberties of America," quipped the *Pennsylvania
Journal*.) From this ark of refuge he then "humbly" petitioned the

Laſt Thurſday was hung up by ſome of the lower claſs
of inhabitants, at New-Brunſwick, an effigy, repreſenting
the perſon of Mr. Rivington, the printer at New-York,
merely for acting conſiſtent with his profeſſion as a free
printer.

Second Continental Congress for pardon, assuring it that, "however
wrong and mistaken he may have been in his opinions, he has always meant honestly and openly to do his duty." That body, however, referred the plea to the New York Provincial Congress, which
on June 7, taking note that the culprit had now signed the Continental Association, decreed that he could resume business without
further molestation of "his person or property." Doubtless the members felt with Gouverneur Morris that the printer had been mis-
guided rather than wicked-hearted and that in the circumstances
magnanimity would work a lasting conversion.[61] In this expectation,
however, they were doomed to disappointment.

[61] For Rivington's abasement, see 4 *American Archives*, II, 679, 726, 836–
837, 899–900, 1284; *Pa. Journal*, May 17, 1775; *Lee Papers*, I, 178–179. Oddly

V

At the level of abstract constitutional discussion the opposing parties, as in the case of "Massachusettensis" and "Novanglus," hardly did more than rehash the old arguments as to whether the colonies were attached to the Empire through the Crown or Parliament. The principal shift in the Whig analysis was the tentative chipping away at the idea that the King could not be blamed for the "hideous calamities" perpetrated by his Ministers. "Put thine own hands to the helm of government, and no longer trust your *state villains*," one spokesman entreated George III. "GOOD GOD! Sir," implored another, "awake from your lethargy, and recede from the measures you have taken!" [62] An even bolder voice, anticipating Tom Paine by more than a year, maintained that the Almighty had given mankind kings "ONLY in his anger," with the corollary that "A good King is a miracle." Though apparently he alone advanced so daring a thesis, the press widely reprinted his tirade, thereby indicating a growing receptivity to the idea.[63] To British partisans, however, it was *"Such treason as few villains have ever had the opportunity of committing."* [64]

Tory penmen, seizing on such intimations, accused the patriot leaders of plotting Independence. One of Rivington's contributors stated categorically that this had been the "deep laid scheme" of "the republican part of the Congress," who had desisted only on finding the majority immovable. These sowers of alarm spared no pains to depict the awful consequences of the step: "intestine broils" and "anarchy" within the country or, alternatively, a dictatorship of the strong, and in either event the loss of external trade and the fish-

enough, Rivington despite his warfare against the Continental Association had nevertheless acceded to it in Dec., 1774, by handing over a consignment of imported books to the New York Committee of Inspection. *N.–Y. Gazetteer*, Dec. 19, 1774.

[62] "Truth" in the *Providence Gazette*, Oct. 29, 1774; "Scipio" in the *Pa. Journal*, Oct. 5, also *Mass. Spy*, Oct. 20. For similar sentiments, see "Queries" in *ibid.*, Oct. 19, also the *N.–Y. Journal*, Oct. 27; and a letter to Gage's troops in the *Va. Gazette* (Pinkney), Feb. 9, 1775.

[63] Anon., "Political Observations, without order," in the *Pa. Packet*, Nov. 14, 1774, reprinted in the *N.–Y. Journal*, Nov. 24, *Va. Gazette* (Purdie and Dixon), Nov. 24, *Conn. Journal*, Nov. 25, *Mass. Gazette and Boston Post-Boy*, Nov. 28, *Providence Gazette*, Dec. 7, *Mass. Spy*, Dec. 8, *Essex Gazette*, Dec. 20; also 4 *American Archives*, I, 976–977.

[64] "Nestor" in the *N.–Y. Gazetteer*, Dec. 1, 1774.

eries attended by foreign pillaging of American territory and other "aggravated miseries." [65]

Whether these disputants actually sensed an unconscious drift of opinion or desired merely to distract attention from the constitutional issues at stake is not clear. But, whatever their motive, the Whig protagonists almost to a man repudiated every thought of so vile a purpose, and none was firmer in this regard than John Adams as "Novanglus." [66] As one writer put it, "I do not . . . aspire at an independence of the crown. My most ardent hope is for a continuance of the connection between the mother country and the colonies, on the true principles of the constitution; and though I scorn to acknowledge allegiance to a British house of commons, or crouch to an East India director, I glory in being the subject of a British king." In the words of another, "Even that future independency, which, in the course of human affairs, these colonies must arrive at, cannot for our true interest be too long delayed." [67] Quite out of step were the few who predicted that this "decisive Blow" would nevertheless surely follow if Britain herself first drew the sword.[68]

Talk of armed resistance centered, rather, on the advisability of employing force to obtain redress without leaving the Empire. The Tory prints naturally condemned such a course both as *"High Treason"* and "the most terrible Calamity (abject Slavery excepted) that can befal a Community." Besides, they insisted, there was no sufficient cause, since the British form of government was "the nearest to Perfection, of any that now is, or ever has been, in the World." Those blowing "the trumpet of rebellion through the land," they continued, desired merely to seize the property of the industrious

[65] "M." in *ibid.*, Dec. 1, 1774, also 4 *American Archives*, I, 978–979; "Phileirene" in the *Mass. Gazette and Boston News-Letter*, Jan. 26, March 2, 1775; "Massachusettensis" in the *Mass. Gazette and Boston Post-Boy*, Jan. 30, April 3; London correspondence in the *N.-Y. Gazetteer*, Feb. 2, 16.

[66] "Millions of Loyal Americans" in the *Boston Evening-Post*, Sept. 19, 1774; "A Citizen" in the *N.-Y. Journal*, Jan. 5, 1775; *Mass. Spy*, Jan. 12; *Conn. Courant*, Jan. 23; "Novanglus" in the *Boston Gazette*, Feb. 13; "Camillus" in the *Pa. Gazette*, Feb. 22, also *Va. Gazette* (Pinkney), March 24, and 4 *American Archives*, II, 8–9; "A Lover of English Liberty" in the *Pa. Gazette*, March 8.

[67] "Americanus" in the *Va. Gazette* (Purdie), Nov. 11, 1774; "Rusticus" in the *Pa. Packet*, Jan. 2, 1775, also *Norwich Packet*, Feb. 2, and *N.-Y. Gazette and Weekly Mercury*, Jan. 16.

[68] "Time and Judgment" in the *Boston Evening-Post*, March 6, 1775, also *Essex Gazette*, March 14; similarly, the *Newport Mercury*, Sept. 12, 1774, a pamphlet of General Charles Lee reprinted in the *Mass. Spy*, Jan. 5, 1775, and the *Essex Gazette*, Jan. 17; and a writer in the *Conn. Courant*, April 17.

and the frugal in the resulting chaos. At any rate there was not "the slightest Reason to hope for Success, in a War, with a Nation, whose invincible Arms so lately carry'd Conquest to every Quarter of the Globe." [69]

But the Whig journalists vindicated domestic insurrection as sanctioned by some of the most glorious moments of English history and contended that the only true rebels against the constitution were the rulers who violated it, not their injured subjects: "Hence, Loyalty itself, justifies us in opposing such men and such measures." Moreover, as "Novanglus" among others asserted, in an "unnatural, horrid war" of this kind the "hardy, robust" Americans, inured to firearms and able to fashion their own, could hold out, if need be, "against all the world." In any event, they prophesied, France and Spain would cripple Britain's striking power by pouncing on her the minute she undertook to subdue the colonists. Explicitly or implicitly, however, these swashbucklers made it clear that the patriots would embark on civil strife only in case the British began it. Then, as a Yankee jingo put it, the "*only* Way left" would be "to sacrifice every New-England *Tory* among us," offer inducements to the redcoats to join "the Cause of American Liberty" and open "all our Ports" to trade with Europe.[70]

VI

This arresting discussion possessed a special urgency for the Boston patriots, who had the military in their midst and the navy at their door. The townsfolk and the "Bloody-Backs" eyed each other

[69] "The Querist" in the *Mass. Gazette and Boston News-Letter*, Nov. 24, 1774, and "Philo-Libertas" in the *N.–Y. Gazetteer*, Oct. 20; similarly, "Z" in *ibid.*, Dec. 1, 1774, and "A Yeoman of Suffolk County" on Feb. 16, 1775; "A Friend to New-England," in the *Mass. Gazette and Boston Post-Boy*, Jan. 16, 1775, and "Americanus" on Feb. 20; "A Freeholder in Worcester County," *Mass. Gazette and Boston News-Letter*, Feb. 9; and the *Md. Gazette*, Feb. 23, quoting "Liberty and Licentiousness" from the *Mass. Gazette and Boston Post-Boy*.

[70] "Pacificus" in the *Pa. Gazette*, Sept. 14, 1774; "Millions of Loyal Americans" in the *Boston Evening-Post*, Sept. 19, "Senex" on Oct. 3, "Meanwell" and "An American" on Oct. 24; "Caius" in the *Pa. Journal*, Oct. 5, and "Queries" on Oct. 19; "Solon" in the *Mass. Spy*, Oct. 20; "A Free American" in the *Newport Mercury*, Nov. 22; "A Son of New-England" in the *Mass. Gazette and Boston Post-Boy*, Jan. 2, 1775; "A Watchman" in the *N.–H. Gazette*, Jan. 13; "Novanglus" in the *Boston Gazette*, Feb. 6; "Essex" in the *N.–Y. Journal*, April 6; "Johannes in Eremo" (the Rev. John Cleaveland) in the *Essex Gazette*, April 18.

with daily increasing rancor, while martial preparations proceeded through the New England countryside. "From Appearances no People are more determined for Civil War . . . ," Gage glumly wrote the Ministry. The Whig press kept the public abreast of the activities while spurring the inhabitants to greater exertions. One correspondent urged them "forthwith to raise an Army of Observation" for deployment "near the expected Scene of Action." Another pointed out that *"Nature* and *Convenience"* made it possible to defend the New England terrain "almost inch by inch," since "every *stone wall* and *logg fence"* would serve as "a breast work." [71]

In Boston itself the editors continued to excite the citizens with stories of "the more than savage barbarity of the soldiers, encouraged and often joined and headed by the officers." A single issue of the *Evening-Post* recounted three "flagrant" instances in as many days, one involving the firing "without any Provocation" upon two small boys. To add to the tension, a letter from London to Holt at New York ("Send this to Boston immediately") alleged that the officers had already partitioned John Hancock's lands among themselves.[72]

The pressures steadily built up toward an explosion. At dawn on September 1, 1774, a surprise expedition of the British confiscated the powder and two field guns at Charleston and Cambridge. The patriots thereupon became more watchful lest "the tyrants" seize what a newspaper writer grandiosely called "all their forts, castles, arms, ammunition and warlike stores." [73] They were therefore on the alert when the regulars set out at daybreak on April 19, 1775, for Concord via Lexington on a similar mission. Minutemen at Lexington offered the first resistance. Which side began the shooting is a moot question that continues to baffle historians,[74] but the contem-

---

[71] Gage to Lord Barrington, Sept. 25, Oct. 3, 1774, Gage, *Correspondence with the Secretaries of State* (C. E. Carter, ed., New Haven, 1931–33), 654–656; "A Correspondent" in the *Norwich Packet*, Sept. 15, 1774, also *N.–H. Gazette*, Oct. 10; "A Military Countryman" (William Heath of Roxbury) in the *Boston Gazette*, Sept. 26. For the identification, see William Heath, *Memoirs* (Boston, 1798), 9.

[72] A Boston correspondent in the *Newport Mercury*, April 3, 1775, also *Pa. Journal*, April 12; *Boston Evening-Post*, Jan. 23, also *Mass. Spy*, Jan. 26; *N.-Y. Journal*, April 22, also *Conn. Journal*, April 26.

[73] "A Watchman" in the *Mass. Spy*, Feb. 23, 1775.

[74] See, for example, Harold Murdock, *The Nineteenth of April 1775* (Boston, 1923), 25–34; Allen French, *General Gage's Informers* (Ann Arbor, 1932), 47–69; W. M. Wallace, *Appeal to Arms* (N. Y., 1951), 18–20; Christopher Ward,

porary Whig version unequivocally pinned the guilt on the redcoats along with the onus of alleged atrocities committed in the fighting there and at Concord. As in the case of the Boston Massacre, the popular leaders exploited to the full the propaganda value of the bloodshed, but now the stake was vastly greater and their audience stretched from New Hampshire to Georgia. "O! what a glorious morning is this!" Samuel Adams is reported to have cried as he slipped away from Lexington just ahead of the British.[75]

The patriots sped the tidings in every direction either by ship or, more usually, by overland couriers riding day and night, whom towns along the way helped out with messengers of their own. Everywhere the newspapers rushed the news into print, at least five publishers anticipating their regular issues with handbills. Thomas, who had himself joined in peppering away at the foe, exhorted his countrymen:

> AMERICANS! forever bear in mind the BATTLE of LEXING–TON! where British Troops, unmolested and unprovoked, wantonly and in a most cruel manner fired upon and killed a number of our countrymen, then robbed them of their provisions, ransacked, plundered and burnt their houses! nor could the tears of defenceless women, some of whom were in the pains of childbirth, the cries of helpless babes, nor the prayers of old age, confined to beds of sickness, appease their thirst for blood!—or divert them from their DESIGN of MURDER and ROBBERY! [76]

Other accounts tended to be of the same pattern, though the very earliest ones, especially in places at a distance, were often purely factual. The *New-Hampshire Gazette* headed its original notice "BLOODY NEWS" and followed it up in the next number with a fuller and more lurid write-up set off with heavy black rules. The *Essex Gazette* railed that the "Cruelty" was "not less brutal than what our venerable Ancestors received from the vilest Savages of the Wilderness." In the sarcastic words of the *New-York Journal*, "The kind intentions of our good mother—our tender, indulgent

---

The War of the Revolution (N. Y., 1952), I, 38–39; J. R. Alden, *The American Revolution* (N. Y., 1954), 22–23.

[75] W. V. Wells, *The Life and Public Services of Samuel Adams* (Boston, 1865), II, 294.

[76] *Mass. Spy*, May 3, 1775; Thomas, *History of Printing*, I, 169. Murdock, *Nineteenth of April*, 101–132, after thoroughly sifting the evidence pro and con, dismisses these and similar charges as having little basis in fact.

mother—are at last revealed to all the world," for she had indubitably shown herself "a vile impostor—an old abandoned prostitute —crimsoned o'er with every abominable crime, shocking to humanity!" Even Dickinson, though questioning some of the extreme atrocity stories, was nevertheless convinced that "the butchery of unarmed Americans at Lexington" had inaugurated this "impious war of tyranny." [77]

Against this barrage Governor Gage could make little headway. Locally, popular fury paralyzed the two government organs. Indeed, the *Massachusetts Gazette and Boston Post-Boy* quit publishing permanently, while the *News-Letter* did so temporarily after explaining on April 20 that its terse cautious report of the "unhappy Affair" was due to inability to "collect any Thing consistent" from information "so various." As for the press elsewhere, Gage apprised Lieutenant Governor Colden in New York that "the Faction" had closed the mails to all outgoing letters save "those that would inflame the Minds of the People." Consequently he encountered difficulty in acquainting the public outside Massachusetts with his view of the engagement which, of course, represented the Americans as the aggressors. When he finally got his account into Colden's hands early in May and the latter sought to insert it in the *New-York Gazette and Weekly Mercury*, Gaine demurred and then refused— which Colden attributed to the presence in New York of Adams and Hancock on their way to the Second Continental Congress.[78] Rivington, already the object of popular resentment, displayed similar circumspection, ostentatiously lamenting the clash of arms and praying that "the Almighty" would avert "the impending miseries" by restoring peace "upon principles of liberty and the constitution!" [79]

---

[77] *N.–H. Gazette*, April 21, 28, 1775; *Essex Gazette*, April 25; letter of April 26 in the *N.–Y. Journal*, May 25; Dickinson to Arthur Lee, April 29, R. H. Lee, *Life of Arthur Lee* (Boston, 1829), 307–310. For the reporting of the news throughout the colonies, see F. L. Mott, "The Newspaper Coverage of Lexington and Concord," *New England Quar.*, XVII (1944), 489–505, and J. H. Scheide, "The Lexington Alarm," Am. Antiquarian Soc., *Procs.*, L (1940), 49–79.

[78] Thomas Gage to Cadwallader Colden, May 4, 1775, Colden, *Letters and Papers* (N.–Y. Hist. Soc., *Colls.*, L–LVI, 1917–23), VII, 291; Colden to Gage, May 31, Colden, *Letter Books*, II, 414. Gaine, having meanwhile drenched his readers with reports of the redcoats' "shocking barbarities," finally printed Gage's narrative on June 5, with the notice to the public: *"For the Provincial Account of the above unhappy Affair, see several of our late Papers."*

[79] *N.–Y. Gazetteer*, April 27, 1775.

On the other hand some Whig editors carried Gage's communiqué, no doubt figuring that the highly colored patriot versions would more than offset its effect.[80]

The sorely tried commander, finding himself caged in Boston by a formidable rebel army, proclaimed martial law on June 12 with an offer of amnesty to all repentant "incendiaries" excepting only Samuel Adams and John Hancock. "The authors of the present unnatural revolt," he stormed, ". . . have uniformly placed their chief confidence in the suppression of truth." With particular venom he assailed "the flagitious prints," which with "indefatigable and shameless pains" had perpetrated "the grossest forgeries, calumnies and absurdities that ever insulted human understanding." But the day of reckoning had now arrived: he would forthwith show the "rebels and traitors" that the British "do not bear the sword in vain." [81] "Your late *infamous Proclamation*," a Whig propagandist lashed back, "is as full of notorious Lies, as a Toad or Rattle-Snake of deadly Poison," for "a defensive War" such as had been forced upon the Americans "is warranted by a first Principle of Nature, self-preservation, hence by the God of Nature." [82]

The long controversy thus entered a new and more perilous stage.

[80] Among these papers were the *Md. Gazette* at Annapolis, the *Va. Gazette* (Dixon and Hunter), the *Cape-Fear Mercury* and the *S.–C. and American General Gazette*. Philip Davidson, *Propaganda and the American Revolution* (Chapel Hill, 1941), 172, 306.

[81] The *Mass. Spy*, June 12, 1775, published this "infamous thing" full of the "most abominable lies" and "daring expressions of tyranny."

[82] "Johannes in Eremo" (the Rev. John Cleaveland) in the *Essex Gazette*, June 17, 1775, also the *New-England Chronicle*, July 13, *Boston Gazette*, July 17, and *N.–H. Gazette*, July 18.

Chapter XI

The Drift Toward Independence

THE ONSET of civil insurrection profoundly affected the newspapers, reducing their number and vitally altering their function. The editors, whether on the one side or the other, perforce enlisted for war. The few Tory journals waged a losing struggle for existence, while the Whig organs, being far more numerous, could better stand casualties without notable injury to their cause. They concentrated on ceaselessly fueling the martial spirit and sustaining civilian morale, a task requiring constant adaptation to swiftly changing conditions.

These alarums and excursions, as pictured by a pro-American commentator at the close of 1775, included the following:

I. GREAT BRITAIN resolved to hold three millions of People, at 3,000 miles distance from her, by the tenure of her power, after having enjoyed a supremacy over them for 200 years, by the tenure of affection.

II. Great Britain risqued the loss of three millions a year, in trade, for taxes, the amount of which would not more than defray the expence of collecting them.

III. A British Parliament voted an army to enforce British laws upon America. . . .

VI. Thirteen Colonies, differing from each other in laws, religion, manners and interests, *united* to oppose the British troops by arms. . . .

X. An army of Americans, commanded by a VIRGINIA

FARMER, blocked up 10,000 British troops commanded by three of the ablest generals in the British service. . . .

XIV. Great Britain called upon Hanoverians,—Hessians—Russians—Irish Roman Catholics—Canadians—Savages and Negroes to assist her in enslaving the Americans.[1]

The patriot press not only mirrored these and related developments but influenced popular thinking as to their import. It rendered its most lasting service, however, in helping to prepare the public for the revolutionary creed of Tom Paine's pamphlet *Common Sense*, which appeared just after the turn of the year.

I

Wartime exigencies disposed of nine newspapers in six provinces during the remainder of 1775, sent several others beyond British reach, and brought two new ones into being. Tory losses included not only the *Massachusetts Gazette and Boston Post-Boy* but also the *Salem Gazette*, both of which, along with the neutral *Boston Evening-Post*, succumbed immediately after the Lexington clash. Nathaniel Mills of the *Post-Boy*, whose patriot father had fallen in the fight, duped the Whigs for a time into believing that he too had now come to see the light, but after gathering valuable information for Gage regarding the American forces at Cambridge, he "traiterously" rejoined the "tyrants." [2] Thomas and John Fleet of the *Evening-Post*, though expecting to revive their paper when the dust settled, never did so. Continuing as job printers, however, they issued an edition of Paine's *Common Sense* shortly after the British abandoned Boston.[3]

Isaiah Thomas and Edes and Gill, the "Trumpeters of Sedition," pursued a different course. Thomas fled Boston on the morning of the battle, having smuggled out his printing equipment at dead of night forty-eight hours before, and with a stock of paper supplied by the Provincial Congress he re-established the *Massachusetts Spy* in Worcester on May 3, reaffirming his political faith by adding *Amer-*

---

[1] "REMARKABLE EVENTS *in the year* 1775," *Pa. Packet*, Jan. 1, 1776, also *Essex Journal*, Feb. 2.

[2] John Boyle, "Journal of Occurrences in Boston," *New England Hist. and Genealogical Register*, LXXXV (1931), 26; *New-England Chronicle*, Oct. 26, 1775; Peter Force, comp., *American Archives* (ser. 4, Wash., 1837–46), III, 326.

[3] *Boston Evening-Post*, April 24, 1775; *Boston Gazette*, April 8, 1776.

ican Oracle of Liberty to his title with the bellicose motto: "Americans!—Liberty or Death!—Join or die!" [4] His flight cost him 2000 of his 3500 subscribers, but he still fared better than John Gill of the *Boston Gazette* who, seized by the British, was locked up for some weeks with Peter, the son of his partner Benjamin Edes, until they gave bail not to leave town.[5] Meanwhile, however, the elder Edes with the help of an antiquated press and types resumed the *Gazette* alone on June 5 at Watertown, the seat of the Provincial Congress. Thus both these fearless Whig organs managed to survive, though the famous team of Edes and Gill after years of valiant service came to an unseasonable end. Samuel and Ebenezer Hall of the *Essex Gazette* at Salem also hunted safer quarters, settling in Cambridge, the American army headquarters, and rechristening their vehicle the *New-England Chronicle or Essex Gazette* upon its first issue there on May 12.

Boston, only recently a bear pit of five newspapers, now had only one: the *Massachusetts Gazette and Boston News-Letter*, published, according to the patriots, *"by permission of ministerial butchers."* Margaret Draper, however, walked a thorny path. Disheartened by the dropping off of subscribers as well as by the problem of securing outside news, she suspended publication for weeks at a time and finally took on a young printer John Howe to share her woes. The editors in exile treated Mrs. Draper with studied contempt, a typical instance being the *New-England Chronicle* which reprinted some of her items only to sneer, "The Impudence they contain is so gross, and the Falshood so notorious, as to render any Remark or Contradiction unnecessary." [6] It need hardly be said that her paper did not outlast the British evacuation of Boston.

In the neighboring colonies as well, wartime vicissitudes posed trials for the press. The burning of Falmouth (Portland) by the enemy in the autumn of 1775 caused the *New-Hampshire Gazette* in nearby Portsmouth to shift to the little town of Greenland for a

[4] *Mass. Spy*, May 3, 1775, Dec. 1, 1780; John Hancock to the Mass. Committee of Safety, April 26, 1775, and Thomas to Daniel Hopkins, Oct. 2, Thomas Papers (Am. Antiquarian Soc.); Annie R. Marble, *From 'Prentice to Patron* (N. Y., 1935), 92–99, 118–121.

[5] 4 *American Archives*, III, 175, 712, V, 168; S. L. Boardman, *Peter Edes, Pioneer Printer in Maine* (Bangor, 1901), 93–95, 99, 109.

[6] *Mass. Spy*, Nov. 13, 1775; *Mass. Gazette and Boston News-Letter*, May 19, Aug. 17, Nov. 30; *New-England Chronicle*, Sept. 28, also *Mass. Spy*, Sept. 29, and *N.-H. Gazette*, Oct. 3.

month while the Continentals fortified Portsmouth, where the editor then resumed publication on December 5. With similar acts of *"hellish* tyranny, oppression and plunder" threatening Newport, Southwick, unsure of what the future held in store, brought out the *Mercury* during November in reduced size and under camouflaged titles.[7] For a different reason—the "utter *Impossibility* of obtaining a Supply of Paper"—the *Connecticut Courant* at Hartford suspended for a few weeks in December until a local paper mill could be completed.[8]

Farther to the south the distractions and uncertainties of the times made other inroads on the newspapers. Indeed, the mortality proved greater than nearer the fighting front. Charles Crouch's *South-Carolina Gazette and Country Journal* closed down on August 1, 1775; and Peter Timothy, whose multiple duties with patriotic organizations had probably left him little time or taste for office work, discontinued his *South-Carolina Gazette* in mid-December. As a result Charleston, the South's largest city, found itself for the first time in many years with but a single publication, the *South-Carolina and American General Gazette*. Fortunately one of its two owners, Robert Wells, a Tory, departed permanently for England in May, thus making it possible for his son and partner John to take over alone and align it definitely with the American cause.[9] The *Cape-Fear Mercury* at Wilmington, N. C., flickered out sometime during the fall, and early in January, 1776, its printer, Adam Boyd, joined the Continental forces.[10] The *Pennsylvania Mercury* gave up the ghost when a conflagration of unknown origin destroyed its plant on the last day of 1775. Considering the tenseness of feeling in Philadelphia this mild Tory sheet may well have been the victim, as one of its editors alleged, of "the infatuated Populace." [11]

The most sensational developments outside New England occurred, however, in Virginia and New York. In these colonies the

[7] *Newport Mercury*, Oct. 16, 1775; *An Occasional Paper*, Nov. 6; *Freshest Advices, Foreign and Domestic*, Nov. 13–27.

[8] *Conn. Courant*, Dec. 11, 1775.

[9] Isaiah Thomas, *The History of Printing in America* (rev. ed., Am. Antiquarian Soc., *Trans. and Colls.*, V–VI, Albany, 1874), I, 351, II, 172; Clarence Brigham, ed., *History and Bibliography of American Newspapers, 1690–1820* (Worcester, 1947), II, 1036.

[10] *Ibid.*, II, 779.

[11] Testimony of Enoch Story, supported by others, in Transcripts of the Manuscript Books and Papers of the Commission of Enquiry into the Losses and Services of the American Loyalists (N. Y. Public Library), L, 514–518, 522.

violence was open and aboveboard and, as it happened, inflicted by opposite parties. Following the Lexington encounter the Virginia press busied itself in what the Governor, Lord Dunmore, bitterly called "poisoning the minds of the people" against his efforts to quell the Old Dominion's fast mounting resistance. He took particular umbrage at John Hunter Holt who published the *Virginia Gazette or Norfolk Intelligencer* under the very guns of the British fleet, where Dunmore had taken refuge. On one occasion Captain Matthew Squire of the *Otter* threatened to kidnap Holt if the printer went on accusing him of "negro-catching" and like "falsities." Finally, on September 30, 1775, after Holt ran a disparaging genealogy of Dunmore, a landing party carried off the type, part of the press and two of the journeymen, Holt himself only barely escaping. The *Gazette* thereafter appeared sporadically on shipboard under direction of the Governor's principal secretary, Hector M'Alester.[12] By one stroke Dunmore had wreaked revenge and secured an organ of a sort of his own. In lieu of other redress the dispossessed editor collected partial damages by stealing several of Dunmore's horses, but the burning of Norfolk on New Year's day, 1776, ended his hopes of "sounding the alarm" against the enemy's "black designs" in a new journal.[13]

Fortunately for the patriots, the three Williamsburg *Virginia Gazettes* lay beyond the Governor's reach, and they kept up the agitation. When Purdie showed signs of succumbing to business difficulties, the House of Burgesses in June, 1775, appointed him official printer to help him out. Dixon and Hunter's *Gazette* also functioned full blast, and on December 6 Pinkney's, perhaps with an eye on Dunmore's captive publication, began putting out two issues a week. Thus, despite the Governor's highhanded action, the Virginians continued to enjoy "a speedy circulation of intelligence of the highest importance." [14]

In New York, where the Crown authorities lacked Dunmore's decision, Rivington at last met the fate that had long been in the

---

[12] *Va. Gazette* (Purdie), Sept. 22, Oct. 6, 13, 1775, April 26, 1776; Dunmore to Lord Dartmouth, cited in F. L. Berkeley, Jr., *Dunmore's Proclamation of Emancipation* (Charlottesville, 1941), unpaged; *Va. Gazette or Norfolk Intelligencer,* Sept. 13, 1775; *Va. Gazette* (Dixon and Hunter), Oct. 7, 14, 1775. See also F. S. Siebert, "The Confiscated Revolutionary Press," *Journalism Quar.,* XIII (1936), 179–181.

[13] *Va. Gazette* (Purdie), Oct. 13, 20, 1775.

[14] *Ibid.,* June 9, 1775; *Va. Gazette* (Pinkney), Dec. 6.

cards. Following his restoration to public favor by the Provincial Congress in June, 1775, he had for a time avoided offending the patriots, but then, emboldened by appointment as His Majesty's printer in New York at £100 a year, he gave his contributors a freer hand.[15] As a writer in the *New-York Journal* saw it, "these tory vermin begin to creep out again, one after another, and, according to their natures, renew their works of mischief." [16] But Nemesis was stalking the printer in the form of Isaac Sears, a mob captain since Stamp Act days, whom the *Gazetteer* had called a "*tool* of the lowest order," a "*political cracker*" and, perhaps most irritating of all, "the *laughing-stock* of the whole town." [17] "King" Sears, a fugitive from justice because of recent riotous acts, had decamped to New Haven, Conn., whence on Monday, November 20, he set forth for New York like an avenging angel, attended by seventy-five Connecticut Light Horse who were "joined by great numbers of sons of liberty in the towns through which he passed." Arriving at Thursday noon, the raiders demolished Rivington's press and carried away the type, tendering in mock payment "an order on Lord Dunmore." [18]

This "notorious enemy to the rights of the Colonies" thus vanished from the journalistic world, sailing for England in January not to return till more than a year after Independence when the British army held New York.[19] A mouthpiece and pacemaker for the whole Tory party in America, the *Gazetteer*'s demise left a void no substitute could fill. Gaine still remained at his post, but his sheet sounded

[15] The appointment was retroactive to the beginning of the year. John Pownall to Rivington, April 5, 1775, E. B. O'Callaghan and Berthold Fernow, comps., *Documents Relating to the Colonial History of the State of New York* (Albany, 1856–87), VIII, 568.

[16] "An Occasional Remarker," *N.–Y. Journal*, Nov. 16, 1775, also 4 *American Archives*, III, 1552–1554.

[17] "A Merchant of New-York" in the *N.–Y. Gazetteer*, Aug. 18, 1774. See also an exchange of insulting letters between Rivington and Sears in *ibid.*, Sept. 2 and 8.

[18] *Conn. Courant*, Nov. 27, 1775; *Pa. Gazette*, Nov. 29; Governor William Tryon of New York to Lord Dartmouth, Dec. 6, *Documents Relating to the Colonial History of New York*, VIII, 645–646; Jonathan Mix, *A Brief Account of the Life and Patriotic Services of Jonathan Mix* (W. P. Blake, ed., New Haven, 1886), 14–21. The New York Congress, though admitting the Tory editor's manifest "demerits," formally protested this lawless interposition from a neighboring colony, but the Connecticut Governor suavely rejoined that the expedition's ringleader, being a New Yorker, could be punished by that province alone. 4 *American Archives*, IV, 393, 400–401, V, 354, VI, 1398–1399.

[19] The quoted phrase is from the *Mass. Spy*, Dec. 1, 1775.

a faint and fluctuating note.[20] Consequently the *New-York Journal* dominated the Manhattan field; and the founding of the semiweekly *Constitutional Gazette* on August 2, 1775, by the patriot John Anderson, who had once served on the old *New-York Gazette or Weekly Post-Boy*, meant that Holt for the first time since James Parker's death had a faithful ally.

II

Upon the devoted editors of the patriot press fell the duty of convincing a people proud of their English heritage that rebellion was both right and practicable; and the Committees of Observation and Inspection—now frequently called Committees of Safety—assisted by advertising the names of avowed obstructionists, with other Whig groups sometimes also assuming that function. As the Philadelphia Committee succinctly put it, "no person has the right to the protection of a community or society he wishes to destroy." [21] The *Connecticut Courant*, mixing patriotism with profits, began after a time to charge penitents a dollar for inserting their pledges of reformation.[22]

The transgressions ranged all the way from the petty to the portentous—from drinking to British success at a tavern, disregarding the Continental Fast Day and "cursing the Hon. Continental Congress," to such graver offenses as discouraging enlistments, refusing the Continental currency and sending food or information to the enemy.[23] The newspapers in their zeal sometimes even pilloried the innocent. One such case, coming to the attention of the West Augusta County Committee in Virginia, involved William Trent, a frontier trader and land speculator, whom a Maryland paper had

[20] "An Occasional Remarker" in the *N.-Y. Journal*, Nov. 16, 1775, makes it evident that the Whigs nevertheless kept a sharp watch on Gaine.

[21] *Pa. Evening Post*, Sept. 23, 1775, also 4 *American Archives*, III, 731–732; similarly, "A. Z." in the *N.-H. Gazette*, Aug. 29, a resolution of the New York Provincial Congress in the *N.-Y. Gazetteer*, Sept. 9, and "A Son of Liberty" in the *Conn. Gazette*, Sept. 29.

[22] *Conn. Courant*, April 8, 1776.

[23] These and many like instances may be conveniently found in 4 *American Archives*, II–III, and W. L. Saunders, comp., *Colonial Records of North Carolina* (Raleigh, 1886–90), X.

accused of harboring £ 40,000 of ministerial funds to be used in inciting the Indians against the colonists. Convinced by conclusive evidence that this was not true, the Committee sharply admonished editors henceforth "to be cautious how they suffer publications in their papers against any persons without good and sufficient reasons." [24]

In any event the system of supervision proved highly effective, and as the war fever heightened, so also did the nature of the reprisals. The culprits had to endure not only ruinous publicity, but oftentimes such additional punishment as surrendering their weapons or going to prison or into exile. In November, 1775, the Rhode Island Assembly even decreed death and the forfeiture of all property in flagrant cases. Because of the increasingly severe penalties the Continental Congress on January 2, 1776, bade the Committees act with the utmost circumspection and, whenever possible, to temper justice with mercy.[25] This injunction, however, came too late to have any noticeable result.

Meanwhile the press in a parallel campaign blackened the characters of British partisans by printing such specimens of their correspondence as it could unearth, a device which the Bay Colonists had earlier employed against hated governors. The incriminating evidence came from a variety of sources: captured ships, prisoners of war, files of London newspapers, the looted homes of loyalist refugees. Another recourse was Goddard's "Constitutional Post," which was now rapidly displacing the British mail system. As a Virginia Tory complained toward the end of 1775, "It is now, and has been for a long time past, an established rule to break open all letters either going from or directed to any officer in the service of the crown." [26]

Some of those culled from the London press seem to have been sheer fabrications by British well-wishers of America, but they proved no less telling for that reason so long as they went uncontradicted or the contradictions went unbelieved. The disclaimers, however, generally bore the ring of truth. For example, Oliver De

24 *Pa. Journal*, Nov. 29, 1775, also *Pa. Evening Post*, Nov. 30, and 4 *American Archives*, III, 1204–1205.

25 *Providence Gazette*, Nov. 11, 1775, also 4 *American Archives*, III, 1376–1377; *Pa. Ledger*, Jan. 6, 1776.

26 Intercepted letter of Walter Hatton of Norfolk, Nov. 21, 1775, to N. Coffin at Boston in the *Va. Gazette* (Purdie), Feb. 2, 1776; similarly, an intercepted letter of George Munro of Bladensburg, Md., June 18, 4 *American Archives*, III, 52.

Lancey of the New York Executive Council hotly disowned a purported letter which represented him as gloating over expected defections from the patriot movement, and two of the province's delegates to the Second Continental Congress publicly vouched for his good faith.[27] Similarly, the *Massachusetts Gazette and Boston News-Letter* repudiated on General John Burgoyne's behalf certain ill-natured reflections he had allegedly sent his family regarding the Continentals at the Battle of Bunker Hill.[28] In Philadelphia, Joseph Galloway, to scotch reports that he too had written to England observations "inimical to America," defied anyone to prove it. (Rumor had probably confused him with Stephen P. Galway, a transient in that city who, on getting wind that one of his letters was about to be published, "took horse with the utmost haste" for parts unknown.) [29]

Embattled Massachusetts naturally afforded the best opportunity for intercepting enemy mail. Before the close of 1775 its newspapers made public at least twenty-eight such communications and summarized an indefinite number of others. A few excerpts will indicate their help in spurring the war effort.[30] One of Gage's soldiers scored the Americans for being "as bad as the Indians for *scalping and cutting the Dead Men's Ears and Noses off,*" while an amorous comrade sniggered, "Tell Bill if he will come to Boston he may have a Wife in every House . . . ." Different in tenor but equally potent as propaganda were the unguarded admissions of certain British officers that they were "fighting in a bad cause" and willing "to treat and sell out." The discovery of more than a hundred letters of ex-Governor Hutchinson—now in England—at his former Milton residence near Boston enabled the press also to turn its fire once more against "that arch-traitor" for his "diabolical plans" to "enslave the country." [31] But this flogging of a dead horse apparently did not long hold the attention of a people beset with more exigent dangers.[32]

---

[27] *N.–Y. Gazette and Weekly Mercury,* May 1, 1775. De Lancey, though evidently innocent of this offense, later fought on the British side in the Revolutionary War.

[28] *Mass. Gazette and Boston News-Letter,* Nov. 30, 1775.

[29] *Pa. Evening Post,* May 13, 1775; *Pa. Journal,* April 19, May 3.

[30] *New-England Chronicle,* May 12, 1775; *Pa. Ledger,* June 17.

[31] *Boston Gazette,* May 1, 1775.

[32] Dr. William Gordon anonymously edited the correspondence for the Massachusetts Provincial Congress. For the circumstances, see Mass. Hist. Soc., *Procs.,*

Of greater effect were the revelations from the secret correspondence of Governors still holding office: Tryon of New York, Eden of Maryland, Lord Dunmore of Virginia and Martin of North Carolina.[33] Though the texts were usually allowed to speak for themselves, one of Dunmore's dispatches "most grossly misrepresenting the good people of this colony" aroused the Committees of four Virginia counties to scathing rejoinders.[34] The newspapers of that province stirred up another hornets' nest by publishing the letters of nine Norfolk and Portsmouth merchants who were clandestinely infringing the Continental Association.[35] Next to Massachusetts, the Old Dominion displayed the greatest diligence in indicting British adherents out of their own inkpots.

The dying Tory press had few chances to reverse the strategy, so it was with evident relish that the *Massachusetts Gazette and Boston News-Letter* printed two indiscreet letters from John Adams at the Second Continental Congress to his wife and his friend James Warren, which a naval patrol had captured. Adams had railed against the "Fidgets, the Whims, the Caprice, the Vanity," of some of the more cautious delegates, singling out a "certain great Fortune and piddling Genius whose Fame has been trumpeted so loudly"—his newly formed opinion of Dickinson.[36] The British party undoubtedly hoped to breed bad blood among the members as well as to dis-

---

XIII (1873–75), ser. 1, 223–225, and LXIII (1929–30), 313–314. The letters, interlarded with the editor's caustic comments, appeared in first instance in the *Boston Gazette*, beginning June 5, 1775. On Sept. 4, Edes, having then published 54, announced he would "desist for the present" since the people were now fully apprised of Hutchinson's machinations; but, probably at the behest of the Provincial Congress, he printed 66 more, concluding with the issue of March 8, 1776. Other newspapers publishing some or all of the original run of these letters included nine in New England as well as the *Pa. Journal* and *Pa. Ledger*. "Cosmopolitan" in the *Mass. Spy*, Feb. 16 and March 26, 1776, did his best to keep alive public interest in the "detestable" correspondence.

[33] For Tryon, see the *N.-Y. Journal*, Jan. 4, 1776, and the *Conn. Journal*, April 3, 17, 1776; for Eden, the *Va. Gazette* (Purdie), April 12, 1776; for Dunmore, *ibid.*, Jan. 26, 1776; for Martin, the *Pa. Ledger*, Sept. 30, 1775.

[34] *Va. Gazette* (Dixon and Hunter), May 13, June 10, July 29, 1775; *Va. Gazette* (Purdie), July 7.

[35] *Va. Gazette* (Purdie), Dec. 22, 29, 1775. For other Virginia examples, see *ibid.*, Dec. 6, 1775, Jan. 2, March 15, April 26, 1776; and, for additional ones in other colonies, the *N.-H. Gazette*, May 26, 1775, the *Conn. Journal*, May 31, 1775, the *Pa. Journal*, Oct. 11, 1775, the *Pa. Packet*, Nov. 27, 1775, and the *Md. Gazette*, July 4, 18, Aug. 10, 17, 1775.

[36] *Mass. Gazette and Boston News-Letter*, Aug. 17, 1775, also John Adams, *Works* (C. F. Adams, ed., Boston, 1850–56), I, 178–180. Adams alleged that the letters were printed "with a little garbling," though he did not deny their essential correctness. *Ibid.*, II, 412.

credit them with the public, but Adams himself, wishfully perhaps, thought that the net effect was to increase outside interest in a final break with Britain. For a time, however, so Dr. Benjamin Rush tells us, his fellows treated him with "nearly universal scorn and detestation"; and when Dickinson next encountered Adams on the street, he "haughtily" ignored him. And, indeed, the two were never afterward on cordial terms.[37]

III

Besides exposing foes of the appeal to arms, the press undertook to justify the recourse to force on rational grounds. The Americans, even in open rebellion, had to feel they were acting lawfully, that they were only exemplifying their historic and natural rights as Englishmen. The groundwork for this had been laid before Lexington and Concord, but, as then envisaged, a civil conflict had been only a future possibility. Now, with the grim reality at hand, the newspapers refurbished the old arguments and devised new ones.

"Let no man be dismayed at being proclaimed a *Rebel* . . . ," adjured a Virginian. "We have taken up arms, it is true; but this we have an undoubted right to do, in defence of the British constitution" and "on the principles of the glorious revolution." Though all subjects of the King had sworn allegiance to him, observed a New Yorker, the King in his coronation oath had also sworn allegiance to his subjects, and now that he had let Parliament ravish their liberties, it followed that they were "absolved *ipso facto,* from their obligations of obedience." "REBELLION," agreed a Pennsylvanian, "is the resisting the *just* and *lawful* power of government," not "an *unjust* and *usurped* power; for it would then be rebellion to resist rebellion." A Connecticut spokesman, pleading divine sanction for essaying "the rough ocean of civil war," reasoned that "the liberty our

---

[37] *Ibid.,* II, 410, 412–413, 423, 513 *n.,* IX, 552. Adams had also made a slighting allusion to General Charles Lee who, however, took it good-naturedly. Lee to Benjamin Rush, Sept. 19, 1775, and to Adams, Oct. 5, *Lee Papers* (N.-Y. Hist. Soc., *Colls.,* IV–VII, 1871–74), I, 207–209. Along with Adams's two letters Mrs. Draper also published one from Benjamin Harrison of Virginia (the father and great-grandfather of United States Presidents) to General Washington in Cambridge, which the British appear to have doctored by interpolating a bawdy reference to a washerwoman's daughter, probably with the hope of besmirching the characters of both sender and recipient. For this incident, see Allen French, "The First George Washington Scandal," *Mass. Hist. Soc., Procs.,* LXV (1932–36), 468–474.

Creator has given us" was "a sacred deposit which it would be treason against Heaven to betray." [38]

In any case, the propagandists went on, Britain, not America, had commenced the bloodletting—"a CRISIS, which none of our eyes desired to see," and which confronted the people with "the hard necessity of either taking up arms, or of surrendering life, liberty and every valuable privilege, into arbitrary hands." [39] Events moreover had now proved what earlier had been only a matter of conjecture, namely, that the colonists were more than a match for the redcoats. "If 300 undisciplined Yankeys . . . can vanquish and drive before them 1800 of the best ministerial veterans," the writers argued in the light of the initial hostilities, "can even the ministry think of sending a sufficient force to effect their wicked purposes?" Subsequent engagements at Ticonderoga, Crown Point and Bunker Hill only reinforced the patriots' favorite thesis that America's teeming man power and expert marksmanship plus the advantages of fighting defensively ensured victory over an enemy handicapped by having to cross the ocean and the likelihood of being attacked by the French or Spanish.[40]

To enhance the spirit of resistance the journalists, profiting by the success of their inflammatory reporting of Lexington and Concord, accused the "wicked and depraved Ministry" of seeking to crush the colonists with

Base Wretches, who fight for Pay and Plunder; Caitiffs devoid of all Principles of Tenderness, Humanity and Honour! . . . What may we not expect from such merciless Ravagers?—Alas! must

[38] *Va. Gazette* (Purdie), Dec. 8, 1775, similarly, "Americanus" in the *N.-H. Gazette*, Aug. 1, and "The Monitor" in the *N.-Y. Journal*, Nov. 16; "Americus Constitutionalis" in the *N.-Y. Journal*, Oct. 19, also *Conn. Gazette*, Oct. 27; "A Freeman" in the *Pa. Evening Post*, June 27, similarly, "Johannes in Eremo" (the Rev. John Cleaveland of Ipswich) in the *Essex Gazette*, June 17, "Cosmopolitan" in the *Mass. Spy*, Nov. 3, "The Monitor" and an unsigned poem in the *N.-Y. Journal*, Nov. 16, 23, and a *Conn. Courant* article, Feb. 5, 1776; "Fabricius" in the *Norwich Packet*, Nov. 6, 1775, similarly, a writer in the *Essex Journal*, Nov. 17, 1775, and "X" in the *New-England Chronicle*, Feb. 8, 1776.

[39] "Fabricius" in the *Norwich Packet*, Nov. 6, 1775; "X" in the *New England Chronicle*, Feb. 8, 1776.

[40] "Unanimity" in the *Providence Gazette*, May 27, 1775; "S. Sp. Skinner" in the *N.-Y. Gazetteer*, July 6; *Conn. Gazette*, Aug. 4; *Va. Gazette* (Purdie), Sept. 22; "Cosmopolitan" in the *Mass. Spy*, Oct. 27, Nov. 17, 24, Dec. 1, 8. The press circulated similar assurances from British sources—from persons whom the *N.-Y. Gazette and Weekly Mercury*, Oct. 16, called "false Friends." See the *Va. Gazette* (Purdie), June 9, the *Pa. Mercury*, Aug. 1, the *N.-Y. Journal*, Oct. 26, and the *Constitutional Gazette*, Nov. 4.

we see our flourishing Country pillaged and laid waste, our Houses fired, our Fathers massacred, our Wives, our Mothers, our Sisters, and our Daughters, fall a Prey to brutal and inhuman Ravishers; our tender Infants torn from the Breast, the Walls and Fences sprinkled with their Blood, whilst Cries and Groans transpierce the yielding Air! . . . Forbid it Heaven! [41]

Tidings from the mother country heaped fuel on the blaze. In March and April, 1775, Parliament passed the "Black Acts" forbidding New England and five other provinces to trade with any country but Britain and the British West Indies and barring them from the fisheries.[42] "They will doubtless next," exploded the *New-York Journal*, "make an act to restrain us from rain and sunshine, which they have an equal right to do and we shall equally regard." [43] As though to confirm such apprehensions, the editors passed on from English sources that "the general talk upon London exchange is, *Reduce the American rebels, and hang up the dogs*," and further that the Ministry planned to finance the war by carrying off all the Negro slaves and selling them in the foreign West Indies.[44] On top of these reports came the alarming word that the Ministry was casting about for German mercenaries to throw into the fight. According to the *Massachusetts Spy* and other papers, the number sought was 10,000, each of whom after seven years would be given a farm with a house and implements at the expense of the colonies. This meant, the advices darkly continued, that if America lost the struggle there would by the year 1800 be "no less than a million of that nation, including their offspring, within the four New England provinces alone." [45]

Such terrors, however well or ill-founded, enabled the press to help steel public opinion against Parliament's offer in February, 1775, to settle the troubles by exempting the Americans from im-

[41] "Cariolanus" in the *Providence Gazette*, June 24, 1775, similarly, "Johannes in Eremo" in the *Essex Gazette*, June 17, "A Friend to His Country" in the *Conn. Gazette*, Sept. 1, "Cosmopolitan" in the *Mass. Spy*, Nov. 17, and "A Freeman" in the *New-England Chronicle*, Nov. 23.

[42] *Essex Gazette*, April 25, 1775, and *Pa. Mercury*, May 19, also 4 *American Archives*, I, 1691–1696, 1716–1720.

[43] *N.-Y. Journal*, May 11, 1775, also *Mass. Spy*, May 17.

[44] *Va. Gazette* (Purdie), July 14, 1775; *Cape-Fear Mercury*, June 26, also *N.-C. Gazette*, July 7, *N.-Y. Gazette and Weekly Mercury*, July 31, and *Pa. Ledger*, Aug. 19.

[45] *Mass. Spy*, Oct. 13, 1775; *Va. Gazette* (Dixon and Hunter), Oct. 14; *Mass. Gazette and Boston News-Letter*, Oct. 19.

perial taxation in case they should voluntarily tax themselves to Parliament's satisfaction. Some of the agitators rejected out of hand a peace tender accompanied by the sword.[46] Others, penetrating to the core of the proposal, showed that, far from meeting the demand for self-taxation, it would permit the colonists neither to fix the amount nor determine how the money should be spent, and this despite the probability that it would be devoted to their further "enslaving": "What is this but taxing us in the gross, instead of the detail?" [47] "The dispute is become too serious," exhorted others, "to think of temporizing accommodations, or partial contracted negociations," which would establish only a "patched up peace" with "latent seeds of discord" that in a few years would "spring up in more violent convulsions." [48]

Nonetheless, just as in the earlier stages of the controversy, the overwhelming majority repudiated the slightest wish for Independence except, of course, independence from the "unconstitutional" encroachments of Parliament.[49] The *"very idea"* was *"amazingly absurd,"* asserted a contributor in the *New-Hampshire Gazette,* who estimated that *"scarcely ten Men in America"* desired an *"unconnection with Great Britain."* Like the Second Continental Congress, which convened on May 10, the propagandists demanded simply a return to the relations subsisting before Grenville's "tyrannical" innovations of 1764. This, in the words of the *Providence Gazette* editor, would ensure "a full Restoration of our Liberties, and the Confusion of all who have aimed at an Abridgement of them." [50]

News columns reflected the same limited goal. When a Philadelphia visitor in Manhattan alleged in August, 1775, that the Continental Congress had fixed on March 1, 1776, for the act of separation unless Parliament meanwhile backed down, the report "gave a Shock like an Earthquake," and the press with obvious approval re-

[46] For example, "S. Sp. Skinner" in the *N.–Y. Gazetteer,* July 6, 1775.
[47] *Newport Mercury,* May 8, 1775; "The Monitor" in the *N.–Y. Journal,* Dec. 14, 1775, Jan. 4, 1776.
[48] "Cosmopolitan" in the *Mass. Spy,* Oct. 27, 1775; "The Monitor" in the *N.–Y. Journal,* Feb. 22, 1776.
[49] "Unanimity" in the *Providence Gazette,* May 27, 1775; "An American" in the *New-England Chronicle,* June 1; "S. Sp. Skinner" in the *N.–Y. Gazetteer,* July 6; "An American" in the *N.–H. Gazette,* July 11; *Md. Gazette,* July 20; "Philo-Patriae" in the *Boston Gazette,* Sept. 11; "The Monitor" in the *N.–Y. Journal,* Nov. 16.
[50] "Coloni" in the *N.–H. Gazette,* Aug. 8, 1775; John Carter in the *Providence Gazette,* April 26.

corded the New York Committee's branding of the *"malicious"* tale-bearer as *"an Enemy to this Country."* In Hanover County, Va., according to two of the *Virginia Gazettes*, a resident escaped a similar penalty in September only by abjectly retracting his avowal that the Americans "aimed at a state of independence more than opposition to parliamentary taxation." When the lone Tory organ in Boston reported a rumor in December that the Congress had actually taken the step, the Whig papers contemptuously reprinted the item without comment save to note its irresponsible source.[51]

IV

Yet, as the year 1775 lengthened, a dissonant note crept into the discussions. Some commentators, though spurning as mere "Tory-jargon" and a "scare-crow" any present thought of Independence, nevertheless admitted the possibility if the situation continued to worsen.[52] In particular, the notion—hitherto almost unchallenged—that the King stood above the strife and hence was more sinned against than sinning showed signs of weakening. According to one correspondent, "if he is determined to support the ministry who have almost ruined his affairs, the time may not be far distant when he will cease to be considered even as the *nominal* Sov-----n of America." Others—and history in large degree bears them out—indicted George himself as "the infernal author" and "most strenuous supporter of all those diabolical measures which had been adopted and pursued against America." [53] But, whether his responsibility was primary or secondary, the critics injected the troubling query whether so wicked a monarch deserved to hold the direct relationship to the colonial legislatures which patriot theory assigned him. Without "kingly virtues," declared a Virginia contributor, he

[51] William Smith, *Historical Memoirs* (W. H. W. Sabine, ed., N. Y., 1956), 250; *N.-Y. Gazette and Weekly Mercury*, Aug. 7, 1775; *Va. Gazette* (Purdie), Oct. 6, and (Dixon and Hunter), Oct. 7; *Mass. Gazette and Boston News-Letter*, Dec. 14, *New-England Chronicle*, Dec. 28, and *Boston Gazette*, Jan. 1, 1776.

[52] "Antoninus" in the *Pa. Journal*, Oct. 11, 1775; "A Virginian" in the *Va. Gazette* (Purdie), Nov. 10.

[53] "Decius" in the *New-England Chronicle*, Oct. 12, 1775, also the *Md. Gazette*, Nov. 23; "Cato" in the *Va. Gazette* (Pinkney), Oct. 19. See likewise "Lucius" in the *Constitutional Gazette*, Sept. 27; "Americus Constitutionalis" in the *Conn. Gazette*, Oct. 27; a Petersham correspondent in the *Boston Gazette*, Jan. 15, 1776; and "An American" in the *Va. Gazette* (Purdie), Jan. 26, 1776.

must be regarded as simply another man. A Massachusetts fire-eater, going the whole way, cried, "King George the third adieu!," your acts "have DISSOLVED OUR ALLEGIANCE to your crown and government!" [54]

Others urged their countrymen on added grounds as well to lay aside their crippling "fondness for Britain" and *"cut the Gordian knot."* [55] "I wish, from my very soul," exclaimed one, "to be forever separated from . . . . a people whose cruelty in the East and West Indies lately, in Africa annually, and now throughout America, is unparalleled in the history of mankind." The time had come, in the words of a second, to form "a GRAND REPUBLIC of the AMERICAN UNITED COLONIES," for "if tyranny should prevail in this great country, we may expect LIBERTY will expire through the world." Victory, moreover, would crown the struggle, for, as some of the correspondents confidently predicted, not only would France gladly intervene against her ancient foe, but other nations would jump at the chance to share for the first time in America's trade.[56]

Although such voices were very much the exception, their boldness nevertheless helped to condition the public mind for Thomas Paine's resounding call to Independence at the turn of the year. Of humble birth, Paine after a feckless career in England had arrived in Philadelphia early in the winter of 1774–75 with a rooted aversion for the British ruling class and credentials from Franklin as "an ingenious worthy young man." Finding employment with a bookseller and printer, he soon won the friendship of leading Whigs. Like most of these, he too at first regarded the dispute "as a kind of law-suit" which "the parties would find a way either to decide or settle," but the "fatal nineteenth of April, 1775," caused him to reconsider his attitude. On August 12, under the pen name of "Atlanticus," he celebrated "The Liberty Tree" in verse in the *Pennsylvania Ledger* as a symbol of the colonists' undying determination to

---

[54] "The Whisperer" in the *Va. Gazette* (Pinkney), Feb. 9, 1775; "Johannes in Eremo" in the *Essex Gazette*, April 25, 1775, and the *New-England Chronicle*, Jan. 18, 25, 1776.

[55] "An American" in the *Va. Gazette* (Purdie), Jan. 5, 1776, also the *N.–Y. Journal*, Jan. 25. See likewise "Independent Whig" in the *Pa. Journal*, Nov. 29.

[56] Unsigned article in the *Va. Gazette* (Purdie), Dec. 15, 1775, also the *N.–Y. Journal*, Jan. 4, 1776; "A Freeman" in the *New-England Chronicle*, Nov. 23, 1775; a Rhode Islander in the *Pa. Journal*, Dec. 13; a letter from England in the *N.–H. Gazette*, Dec. 5; "Lycurgus" in the *N.–Y. Journal*, Dec. 21.

withstand the tyranny of "Kings, Commons, and Lords"; and on October 18, as "Humanus" in the *Pennsylvania Journal*, he flayed London's "horrid cruelties" toward the people of India and the red and black races of the New World, warning that "The Almighty will finally separate America from Britain." [57]

Then, on January 9, 1776, his ideas fully matured, Paine anonymously published *Common Sense*, the most influential piece of Whig propaganda since the "Farmer's Letters," but penned with a different purpose and in a quite different style. He had originally planned to follow Dickinson's example of first serializing the pamphlet in the press, but knowing, as he admitted in the Preface, that his views were "not *yet* sufficiently fashionable," he feared he might not get it "generally inserted." [58] This very realization probably stirred him to all-out vehemence; if people were deaf he must scream at them.

Professing to offer only "simple facts, plain arguments, and common sense," Paine first reviled the institution of the monarchy from Scriptural times onward as "the most prosperous invention the devil ever set on foot for the promotion of idolatry. . . . Of more worth is one honest man to society, and in the sight of God, than all the crowned ruffians that ever lived." In particular, George III, who had callously imbrued his hands with American blood, was a "royal brute," a "hardened, sullen-tempered Pharaoh," the "greatest enemy this continent hath." [59] Nor would Paine concede that the colonists had ever earlier derived any benefit from the imperial tie, or even that Britain was in a real sense their mother country since "This new world hath been the asylum for the persecuted lovers of civil and religious liberty from *every part* of Europe." All reason pleaded for dissolving the connection. "Even the distance at which

[57] "The Forester" (Thomas Paine) in the *Pa. Evening Post*, April 30, 1776; Paine, *Complete Writings* (P. S. Foner, ed., N. Y., 1945), I, pp. xi, 25, 143, II, 20, 1091–1092.

[58] Advertisement of *Common Sense* in the *Pa. Evening Post*, Jan. 30, 1776, and the *Pa. Packet*, Feb. 5; Paine, *Complete Writings*, I, 2. Paine had finished "nearly the first part" in October. Dr. Benjamin Rush asserted in 1809 that he had prior knowledge of the contents and had suggested the title; but his further statement that Franklin and probably also Samuel Adams saw the manuscript in advance belies Paine's own assertion in 1777 that he had deliberately kept Franklin in the dark in order to surprise him and that at that time he did not know Adams. Rush to James Cheetham, July 17, 1809, Rush, *Letters* (L. H. Butterfield, ed., Princeton, 1951), II, 1008; "The American Crisis, III," April 19, 1777, Paine, *Complete Writings*, I, 88–89 *n.*

[59] *Ibid.*, I, 10, 16, 17, 25, 29.

the Almighty hath placed England and America is a strong and natural proof that the authority of the one over the other, was never the design of heaven," not to mention that there was "something absurd, in supposing a Continent to be perpetually governed by an island." To make matters worse, the relationship implicated America in "European wars and quarrels" contrary to her "true interest" to "steer clear of European contentions." [60]

Like previous patriot spokesmen, he also asserted that the colonies had the man power and the military potential "to repel the force of all the world" and that by flinging open their commerce to all countries and declaring Independence they would obtain the almost certain help of France or Spain as well as perhaps of other states. He went on to sketch a confederated republican government for the prospective nation, rejecting every thought of a king in favor of a president to be named by a popularly elected Congress. "All plans, proposals, &c. prior to the nineteenth of April," he said, ". . . are like the almanacks of the last year . . . . As well can the lover forgive the ravisher of his mistress, as the continent forgive the murders of Britain." In truth, "The sun never shone on a cause of greater worth. . . . The blood of the slain, the weeping voice of nature, cries, 'TIS TIME TO PART." [61]

V

Common Sense notably fortified the case for Independence, presenting the grounds for it with a bluntness and cogency that arrested both friend and foe. No doubt John Adams was right in believing that its author had picked the brains of Dr. Rush and others and that "the phrases, suitable for an emigrant from Newgate, or one who had chiefly associated with such company, such as 'The Royal Brute of England,' 'The blood upon his soul,' and a few others of equal delicacy, had as much weight with the people as his arguments." [62] But the arguments too were adapted to the masses, for

---

[60] *Ibid.*, I, 19, 20, 21, 24, 30.

[61] *Ibid.*, I, 17, 18, 21, 28–29, 30, 31.

[62] Adams, "Autobiography," *Works*, II, 507, 509. At the time it appeared, however, Adams praised the "clear, simple, concise and nervous style," though he considered the author "a better hand in pulling down than building." Letter to Abigail Adams, March 19, 1776, John Adams, *Letters Addressed to His Wife* (C. F. Adams, ed., Boston, 1841), I, 90.

they cut through the cobwebs of constitutional dialectics to the clear "common sense" of the matter. The unthinking as well as the thinking could thrill to his sentiment: "The cause of America is in great measure the cause of all mankind." [63]

The pamphlet was promptly reissued far and wide, with a translation for the Pennsylvania Germans and another for the New York Dutch. Paine reported 120,000 sold in three months.[64] "I never saw such a masterly, irresistible performance," General Charles Lee wrote Washington from Connecticut, and the latter learned from his own colony that it was "working a powerful change there in the minds of many men." [65] Some admirers, however, regretted that it had not first appeared in the public prints, for though "Common Sense has been read by many, yet the news papers are read by many more." [66] Paine himself probably concurred, for when writing "The Forester's Letters," a sequel to the tract, he chose the press as his medium, as he did later when inditing his memorable summons to valor, "The American Crisis."

The newspapers, however, did everything possible to make up for the lack. They pushed sales of local editions with glowing advertisements, and some, including the *Connecticut Journal*, the *Norwich Packet* and Purdie's *Virginia Gazette*, reprinted the text in whole or part. Many, moreover, carried panegyrics of the "incomparable pamphlet" by correspondents. A sampling of these will suffice to convey their general tone. "This animated work dispels, with irresistable energy, the prejudices of the mind against the doctrine of independance . . . ." It "introduces a new system of politics, as widely different from the old, as the Copernican system is from the Ptolemaic." It is "like a ray of revelation." It has "worked miracles, made TORIES WHIGS, and washed Blackamores white." It is "of more worth than its weight in gold." In fact the author "deserves a

[63] Paine, *Complete Works*, I, 3.

[64] *Conn. Courant*, Feb. 19, 1776; "The Forester" (Paine) in the *Pa. Gazette*, April 10.

[65] Lee to George Washington, Jan. 24, 1776, *Lee Papers*, I, 259–260; Washington to Joseph Reed, April 1, Washington, *Writings* (J. C. Fitzpatrick, ed., Wash., 1931–44), IV, 455.

[66] "Aristides" (the Rev. John Witherspoon) in the *Pa. Packet*, May 13, 1776. For the identification, see Witherspoon, *Works* (rev. ed., John Rodgers, ed., Phila., 1802), IV, 315. For a similar comment, see James Bowdoin to Mercy Warren, Feb. 28, John Adams and others, *Warren-Adams Letters* (W. C. Ford, ed.; Mass. Hist. Soc., *Colls.*, LXXII–LXXIII, 1917–25), I, 209.

Statue of *Gold*." [67] Little wonder that, as the editors widely proclaimed, "A favourite toast, in the best companies, is 'May the IN–
DEPENDENT principles of COMMON SENSE be confirmed
throughout the United Colonies.' " [68]

The very toast, however, constituted an admission that "the IN–
DEPENDENT principles," despite all the incense burning, were not
yet confirmed. The Virginia patriot Landon Carter indeed considered that Paine's "rascally & nonsensical" effusion "disgraces the
American cause." A Pennsylvania commentator confessed that,
though upon a first reading he had "soar'd aloft" with the author
"into the wilds of fancy" to "a republic in the stars," a second reading had persuaded him that the wiser and more promising course
was to persevere in seeking "a firm basis of liberty" within the Empire. Even less did the pamphlet convert those with Tory leanings.
"Could it be expected that all America would instantly take a leap
in the dark? Is this *Common Sense*, or common *Non-Sense*?" raged
the Reverend Dr. Smith of the College of Philadelphia, who deemed
the performance an "*ignis fatuus* to draw the unwary into untried
regions, full of precipices and quagmires." His fellow citizen Edward Shippen, while acknowledging the arguments to be "artfully
presented," declared they "might be easily refuted," an opinion
which Maryland's Daniel Dulany fully shared. According to Shippen, an influential member of the Continental Congress (John
Dickinson?) earnestly hoped that to end all question the "various public bodies might somehow or other signify their disapprobation." [69]

Paine's tour de force by dramatizing the issue of Independence
compelled an anxious searching of hearts and heads, but further in-
doctrination was "necessary to most minds," as a Williamsburg cor-

[67] "An Independent Whig" in the *N.–Y. Journal*, Feb. 22, 1776; *Constitutional
Gazette*, Feb. 24; "F.A." in the *Boston Gazette*, April 29; *Pa. Evening Post*, Feb.
13; "Z.F." in the *N.–Y. Packet*, March 7; Charleston letter in the *Pa. Journal*,
March 27.

[68] *New-England Chronicle*, April 4, 1776; *Conn. Courant*, April 8; *Mass. Spy*,
April 12; *Va. Gazette* (Purdie), April 26.

[69] Carter, "Diary," Feb. 14, 24, 1776, *William and Mary College Quar.*, ser. 1,
XVI (1907–08), 149, 152; "Moderator" in the *Pa. Ledger*, April 27; "Cato" (Wil-
liam Smith) in *ibid.*, March 30, April 27; Shippen to Jasper Yeates, Jan. 19, *Pa.
Mag. of History and Biography*, VII (1883), 25–26; Maryland letter in the *Pa.
Evening Post*, Feb. 13.

respondent reluctantly admitted.[70] Even within the Whig party substantial segments still remained to be convinced, including, most important of all, a majority of the Continental Congress. In this unfinished business of propaganda the press would play a notable part.

[70] Williamsburg letter in the *Pa. Packet*, April 8, 1776, also the *Essex Journal*, April 26.

Chapter XII

The Great Debate

A<small>T SUCH A</small> D<small>AY AS THIS</small>," wrote a colonist, "where is the Man, that is not anxious for himself, and all his Connections, and from Week to Week is uneasy till he receives his News-Paper . . . ." Unhappily, these reports underscored Britain's determination to win at almost any cost. Among other acts the burning of port towns displayed her disregard for civilian life and property. "A few more of such flaming arguments, as were exhibited at Falmouth and Norfolk, added to the sound doctrine and unanswerable reasoning contained in the pamphlet '*Common Sense*,' " said George Washington at the close of January, 1776, "will not leave numbers at a loss to decide upon the propriety of a separation." [1] Even the enemy's evacuation of Boston on March 17, "after suffering an ignominious blockade of nearly eleven months," occasioned almost as much anger as joy, for the departing "Banditti" looted the town, "breaking & destroying every thing they could not carry off," and—so the press further alleged—"diabolically" mixed arsenic with the medicines they left in their hospital. [2]

The Ministry's longer-range preparations heightened the resentment. Parliament's "piratical, or plundering Act," as the patriots called it, banned American trade with all the world from March 1

---

[1] *N.–H. Gazette* (Exeter), July 6, 1776; Washington to Joseph Reed, Jan. 31, Washington, *Writings* (J. C. Fitzpatrick, ed., Wash., 1931–44), IV, 297.

[2] *Boston Gazette*, March 14, 25, April 15, 1776, also *Newport Mercury*, March 25, April 22. The reports of the looting were well founded, but an investigation by the Massachusetts Council indicated that the British in the excitement of departure had without malice aforethought scattered the arsenic with other medicines promiscuously on the floor. Allen French, *The Siege of Boston* (N. Y., 1911), 423–427; *Boston Gazette*, April 22, 1776.

onward,[3] while official confirmation of the intended employment of German soldiers climaxed the bitterness. And presently military moves against the Carolinas and a threatened advance from Canada into New York provided further terrors.

The great debate precipitated by *Common Sense* reflected these developments and reactions, hardening the will of some, weakening that of others, and compelling a thorough examination of the pros and cons of the crisis.

I

The stepped-up hostilities created fresh problems of survival for the press, though they as yet had little effect on New York and Philadelphia, the principal journalistic centers, and the British withdrawal reopened Boston to Whig newspapers. In Manhattan, indeed, Samuel Loudon, a book dealer, established the *New-York Packet* on January 4, 1776, at the instance of "a numerous circle of warm friends to our (at present much distressed) country," thus providing an ally for the *Journal* and the *Constitutional Gazette*. Within a few months, however, Loudon quite innocently found himself in hot water for agreeing to print a pamphlet in reply to *Common Sense*. Since at the time the Continental Congress itself was opposed to Independence, he had, as he stated, absolutely "no consciousness of guilt in the affair." But some of the more radical townsfolk thought otherwise, and even though he agreed to hold up the publication, a mob on the night of March 19 invaded his office and burned the entire edition of 1500 copies on the Common. Loudon, notwithstanding, retained the confidence of the Whig higher-ups, and toward the end of the year the New York Committee of Safety granted him an annual £200 for carrying its releases in the *Packet*.[4]

The abandonment of Boston by the enemy, while decidedly improving that city's journalistic position, failed to restore its earlier leadership. The evacuation dealt a final blow to the *Massachusetts Gazette and Boston News-Letter*, the only outspoken Tory organ

[3] John Adams to Horatio Gates, March 23, 1776, E. C. Burnett, *The Continental Congress* (N. Y., 1941), 297.

[4] Loudon's prospectus in the *N.-Y. Journal*, Dec. 14, 1775; Peter Force, comp., *American Archives* (ser. 4, Wash., 1837–46), V, 438–440, 1389, 1441–1442; A. J. Wall, "Samuel Loudon," N.-Y. Hist. Soc., *Bull.*, VI (1922), 75–92.

then left in the colonies as well as the oldest American newspaper; and its proprietors, Mrs. Draper and John Howe, along with Mills and Hicks of the defunct *Massachusetts Gazette and Boston Post-Boy*, prudently accompanied the British forces to Halifax.[5] With the way thus cleared for the patriot press, the *New-England Chronicle* in a few weeks forsook Cambridge for Boston, deeming the latter a more promising field than Salem, its original abode; and on May 30, 1776, John Gill, formerly of Edes and Gill, started a second Boston paper, the *Constitutional Journal*, at "the solicitation of his Friends." The *Boston Gazette*, however, because of a smallpox epidemic in the capital, did not return from Watertown until four months after the Declaration of Independence;[6] and the *Massachusetts Spy* remained permanently at Worcester. Meanwhile, in Salem, Ezekiel Russell, lately of the short-lived and unmourned *Salem Gazette*, sought to make a comeback with the *American Gazette or Constitutional Journal*, which he founded on June 18 in the name of John Rogers, a journeyman printer. Though the fledgling piously professed unreserved devotion to the "GLORIOUS CAUSE," it barely managed to survive six issues. Salem went without another newssheet until 1781.

In Portsmouth, Daniel Fowle of the *New-Hampshire Gazette* ran into trouble in January, 1776, as the result of publishing a forceful argument by "Junius" against Independence—an offense comparable to Loudon's in New York. Although no mob attacked Fowle, the Provincial Congress reprimanded him so severely for the "ignominious, scurrilous, and scandalous piece" that he forthwith stopped the paper until his nephew Robert L. Fowle in effect revived it on May 22 at Exeter. The first number of this *New-Hampshire Gazette* advertised *Common Sense* for sale at the printer's office. Benjamin Dearborn, one of the elder Fowle's former apprentices, also entered the New Hampshire field, setting up the *Freeman's Journal* on May 25 at Portsmouth "to promote the grand cause."[7] Elsewhere in

[5] Transcripts of the Manuscript Books and Papers of the Commission of Enquiry into the Losses and Services of the American Loyalists (N. Y. Public Library), III, 124 (hereafter cited as Loyalist Transcripts); *Freeman's Journal*, July 6, 1776; E. A. Jones, *The Loyalists of Massachusetts* (London, 1930), 214.

[6] *Boston Gazette*, Oct. 7, 1776.

[7] "Junius" in the *N.–H. Gazette*, Jan. 9, 1776; 4 *American Archives*, V, 11; A *N.–H. Gazette*, May 25, one of the two handbills which preceded Robert Fowle's regular publication on June 1; Dearborn's prospectus in the *Essex Journal*, April 26; *Freeman's Journal*, May 25.

New England the press underwent no significant change except in Connecticut, where Alexander and James Robertson of the *Norwich Packet* sold out to their Whig partner John Trumbull in May upon finding "they could no longer carry it on without making it subservient to the Cause of Rebellion." The pair crustily went off to Albany, N. Y., where as job printers "they imagined they could be of more immediate Service to Government," only to remove to New York City, however, after the British occupied it in September.[8]

In the Southern colonies three journals now disappeared permanently from the scene, all in February. Lord Dunmore's offshore *Virginia Gazette* had never had more than an intermittent existence, and since its circulation was confined "to such tools as he would choose to work with," it had now outlived any further usefulness. James Johnston's mildly Tory *Georgia Gazette* had aroused the increasing ire of the Whigs, and a few weeks after the royal Governor fled the province in January, it too closed down.[9] The third one, Pinkney's ardently patriotic *Virginia Gazette* at Williamsburg, probably succumbed to the increasingly formidable difficulties of publication.

These difficulties—the scarcity of newsprint owing to the cutting off of imports, the spiraling cost of the domestic variety, and the shortage of journeymen due to wartime demands and distractions—beset the press in greater or less degree throughout America. Printers continually entreated the public to save linen, cotton and canvas rags for the American mills, or else the country "will soon be destitute of Paper of all kinds."[10] Many met the stringency by skipping issues—the *South-Carolina and American General Gazette*, Charleston's one surviving journal, suspended entirely from May 31 to August 2—or by publishing in reduced size, as did Dixon and Hunter's *Virginia Gazette* from June 1 through the rest of the year. The resulting "want of room" forced editors repeatedly to apologize for omitting articles and advertisements.[11] And because of the "in-

---

[8] Their testimony in Loyalist Transcripts, XLI, 453–454; *Norwich Packet*, May 20, 1776, the first number to be conducted by Trumbull alone.

[9] Interview with a Mr. Watkins of Halifax, who had recently talked with Dunmore, in the *Va. Gazette* (Purdie), March 22, 1776; L. T. Griffith and J. E. Tallmadge, *Georgia Journalism, 1763–1950* (Athens, 1951), 6.

[10] For example, the *New-England Chronicle*, Feb. 1, 1776; the *Mass. Spy*, Feb. 9; the *Essex Journal*, March 15; the *Pa. Ledger*, April 6; the *American Gazette*, July 2; the *N.–H. Gazette*, July 20.

[11] For example, the *Va. Gazette* (Purdie), Jan. 26, 1776; the *Pa. Evening Post*, Feb. 29, May 21; the *N.–Y. Journal*, March 7.

creased Price of Paper (the chief Article of a Printer's Stock) and of almost every Necessary of Life," practically all newspapers raised their subscription rates.[12]

Despite these conditions the total number of journals on July 4, 1776, was thirty-two, precisely the same as at the beginning of the year. Though five had vanished in the interval, in nearly every instance they had been replaced by stronger publications, and with a single unimportant exception the new ones actively supported the Whig party. A commentator could still speak of "the incredible number of news-papers," whose influence "could never have been so great in any community, yet known, as in these *pantaplebeian* colonies." A project for the establishment in some central province of "a periodical paper, in manner of the Spectator," to be edited by "persons of genuine COMMON SENSE, of serious and 'continental minds,' " failed to catch hold, but obviously not because the proponent intended it to demonstrate that the American cause stemmed "as much from God, as the descent of the Holy Ghost on the day of the Pentecost." [13]

Even in face of the higher subscription rates an editor testified that "a much greater Number" were taking papers "than was ever before known throughout the whole Continent," the demand in some cases exceeding the supply.[14] Most important of all, the six sheets in Philadelphia—the *Journal*, the *Gazette*, the *Packet*, the *Evening Post*, the *Ledger* and the *Staatsbote*—stood intact; and in that city, the seat of the Second Continental Congress and the cynosure of all eyes, the most notable discussions of Independence took place.

II

The "terrible wordy war," as Joseph Reed, a member of the Congress, called it, was not, however, waged between Whigs and Tories, for the Tories had lost all standing with the public and in any event

[12] Notice of John Carter, the editor, in the *Providence Gazette*, May 27, 1776. The *Pa. Evening Post* on March 31 apparently set the example by boosting its subscription charge 50 per cent—from 10 to 15 shillings a year.

[13] "Demophilus" in the *Pa. Packet*, Feb. 12, 1776, quoting from a pamphlet; "Massachusettensis" in the *New-England Chronicle*, June 6.

[14] Robert L. Fowle in the *N.-H. Gazette*, July 6, 1776. See also later, Appendix A on the circulation of newspapers.

had little or no access to the press.[15] Instead, the contending groups were three species of Whigs: the disunionists or separationists, who held that the mother country had sinned beyond redemption; the reunionists or reconcilers, who sought a solution short of Independence; and the fence sitters, who had not yet made up their minds. In the language of one of the participants, "We all agree in this, that Great Britain is unjust and arbitrary," and only disagree over "the mode of opposition." [16] Moreover, as Reed remarked, "the city seems desirous they should all have fair play." [17] In this spirit the Philadelphia editors freely presented the conflicting points of view, and their brethren up and down the coast avidly repeated the principal articles while injecting others of their own. Editorial tolerance, however, did not ensure sobriety of discussion; rather the reverse. In the stress of the combat the disputants resorted to hyperbole, misrepresentation and vilification along with cool and rational argument. "Opprobrious names can prove nothing . . . ," protested one of the contestants only to be himself rebuked for his "personal and private innuendoes." [18]

The disunionists for their part damned those who were "sobbing and whining after their darling dependence" as "puling pusilanimous cowards" and—crowning insult—"disguised Tories." [19] To justify this epithet one of them observed, with a backward look over the long decade of controversy,

It is remarkable that the Tories in every colony have *affected* to differ from the Whigs only in *small matters*. . . . Have not the Tories followed them in every step except the last? Thus when the Whigs proposed non-importation and non-exportation agreements, the Tories urged petitions to the King only, and when the Whigs proposed making military preparations, the Tories urged them to adhere to the non-importation and non-exportation agreements.—

[15] Reed to Charles Pettit, March 30, 1776, W. B. Reed, *Life and Correspondence of Joseph Reed* (Phila., 1847), I, 182.

[16] "A Friend to Posterity and Mankind" in the *Pa. Packet*, Feb. 12, 1776.

[17] Abigail Adams upon receiving a batch of Philadelphia newspapers from John similarly attested to the "full liberty of the press." Letter to John Adams, April 21, 1776, *Familiar Letters* (C. F. Adams, ed., N. Y., 1876), 162.

[18] "Cato" (the Rev. Dr. William Smith) in the *Pa. Ledger*, March 30, 1776; "The Forester" (Thomas Paine) in the *Pa. Packet*, April 1.

[19] "Some Queries offered to the Freeholders and People of Virginia at large" in the *Va. Gazette* (Purdie), April 19, 1776; "Z.F." in the *N.-Y. Packet*, March 7; "Candidus" (Samuel Adams) in the *Pa. Evening Post*, Feb. 3. For the Adams identification, see W. V. Wells, *The Life and Public Services of Samuel Adams* (Boston, 1865), II, 360–363.

And now when a declaration of independence is absolutely necessary for our safety and future welfare, they tell us to rely upon our
arms and Great Britain will soon come to our terms.[20]

To such dedicated souls a desire for reconciliation or a pose of neutrality was criminal: "He that is not for us, is against us." [21]

The reunionists hotly rejected so spurious a political lineage. Denying that "a *Whig* and an *Independant* are convertible terms," they
retorted that the only "true Whigs" were those who, having "first
set on foot the present opposition," were still intent on "preserving
the constitution, as well as against the secret machinations of ambitious innovators, as against the open attacks of the British parliament." Their defamers, they warned the people, "are attempting to
hurry you into a scene of Anarchy; their scheme of Independence is
visionary, they know not themselves what they mean by it." [22]

Behind such acerbities, however, the debate searched deeply into
the practical consequences, political, military and economic, of the
alternative courses of action, with only incidental mention of the
constitutional aspects of imperial relations. Paine's *Common Sense*
provided the frame as well as the springboard for the exchanges. In
Philadelphia, where the controversy centered, the two foremost
champions of separation were James Cannon, a mathematics tutor
in the College of Philadelphia, who took up his pen as "Cassandra"
in the *Pennsylvania Evening Post*, March 2, 1776, and Paine himself, who resumed his labors as "The Forester" in the *Packet*, April
1, after anonymously smiting the reconcilers in a supposed colloquy with the ghost of General Richard Montgomery, the recently
fallen hero in the ill-fated assault on Quebec.[23] Among their comrades in arms were President John Witherspoon of Princeton

20 "A Watchman" in the *Pa. Packet*, June 10, 1776; similarly, "Hector" in
the *N.-Y. Packet*, April 11.
    21 "B.A." in the *Va. Gazette* (Dixon and Hunter), May 6, 1776.
    22 "R." (John Dickinson?) in the *Pa. Packet*, April 8, 1776; "Civis" in the *Pa.
Gazette*, May 1. For Dickinson's probable authorship, see footnote 25 of the
present chapter.
    23 The "Cassandra" series is reprinted in 4 *American Archives*, V, 41–43,
431–434, 921–926, 1092–1094. For Cannon's identity, see the letter of John Adams
to his wife Abigail, April 28, 1776, Adams, *Letters Addressed to His Wife* (C. F.
Adams, ed., Boston, 1841), I, 105; and for the "Dialogue between the Ghost of
General Montgomery Just Arrived from the Elysian Fields; and an American
Delegate, in a Wood near Philadelphia," see the *Pa. Packet*, Feb. 19, also Paine,
Complete Writings (P. S. Foner, ed., N. Y., 1945), II, 88–93. Foner reprints "The
Forester's Letters" in II, 60–87.

("Aristides"); Samuel Adams who as "Candidus" and "A Religious Politician" took time out from his heavy duties in the Congress to contribute an occasional piece; and doubtless many like Paine's intimate, Dr. Benjamin Rush, who, as he said, "wrote under a variety of signatures, by means of which an impression of numbers was made." [24] Elsewhere on the continent outstanding advocates on the same side were "Essex," "An Independent Whig" and "Spartanus" in the *New-York Journal* and "A Planter" in Dixon and Hunter's *Virginia Gazette*, whose identities remain hidden.

Opposing these zealots the major figure was the Reverend William Smith, Provost of the College of Philadelphia, who entered the lists as "Cato" in the *Pennsylvania Ledger*, March 9. With allies not now known but almost certainly including John Dickinson, he strove valiantly to refute the dogmas of *Common Sense* whose proponents, "like true quacks, are constantly pestering us with their additional doses," and to administer the healing potion of reconciliation instead. [25] There was, finally, a small number of spokesmen for the uncommitted middle group, who shot probing questions at both sets of disputants.

III

The crusaders for Independence, as a preliminary to their positive argument, set about to discredit the Continental Congress's demand for a return to the paradise lost of 1763. They raucously de-

[24] Witherspoon, *Works* (rev. ed., John Rodgers, ed., Phila., 1802), IV, 309–316; Wells, *Samuel Adams*, I, 445; Rush, *Autobiography* (G. W. Corner, ed., Princeton, 1948), 110, 112, 115.

[25] "Cato" in the *Pa. Ledger*, March 16, 1776. The entire series is reprinted in 4 *American Archives*, V, 125–127, 188–190, 443–446, 514–517, 542–546, 839–843, 850–853, 1049–1051. According to Jared Ingersoll writing to his nephew Jonathan Ingersoll, April 13, Dickinson was believed to have penned the article by "R." in the *Pa. Packet*, April 8, flaying "The Forester" and defending "Cato." New Haven Colony Hist. Soc., *Papers*, IX (1918), 465–466. Smith, an Anglican clergyman, had in the moderates' sense of the term been a "true Whig" ever since Stamp Act days. In a sermon he had recently vindicated the American resistance at Lexington as an act of self-preservation, "the first great law of Nature as well as Society." In addition to the "Cato" series, he probably wrote the pamphlet *Plain Truth*, published on March 14, a reply to *Common Sense* designed to show that the scheme of Independence was "ruinous, delusive, and impracticable." When later faced with the actuality of separation, however, he quietly acquiesced. A. F. Gegenheimer, *William Smith, Educator and Churchman* (Phila., 1943), 159–182; P. L. Ford, "The Authorship of 'Plain Truth,'" *Pa. Mag. of History and Biography*, XII (1888–89), 421–424.

rided "the lullaby of our having been a very happy and flourishing people during our dependance upon the parent state." Granted that the mother nation had helped the colonies militarily on occasion, the colonies had borne their own due share of the burden and, alas, had in addition been dragged into Britain's chronic wars. Granted further that the people had prospered somewhat materially, they owed this not to London's beneficence, but exclusively to "the fertility of the soil, and the sobriety, industry and equality of the inhabitants," which had overcome trade restrictions "worth ten times the protection, besides the sums we pay in customs and other duties to the amount of a million annually." Even from a strictly political standpoint those "former golden days" had conferred "not *freedom, but merely not slavery*." [26]

In any case, these tribunes went on, "Can we condescend to accept of a peace, that, however proper it might have been a few years ago, in our present circumstances, can have no colour of equity?" When the Congress had declared for the status of 1763, "our towns were not burnt, our people were not murdered, nor our property stolen from us, nor had we been put to such extraordinary expenses as we since have." Indeed, "What device to ruin us, though never so mean, barbarous, and bloody, such as no heart but that of a Devil or a tyrant can refrain from shuddering at, have they not pursued?" "A Planter" estimated the financial cost to the colonists as already £7,850,000: £4,000,000 for the cutting off of trade; £2,400,000 for military outlays; £1,400,000 for the damages to Boston, Charlestown, Norfolk and other places; and £50,000 for the losses arising from piracies, looting and sheepstealing. The "former declarations of Congress," these commentators chorused, are "out of date. Times and things are altered." [27]

But, even if the outrages had not occurred, "We would ask the *bugbear sticklers for colony dependency*, what one good thing the

[26] "Candidus" in the *Pa. Gazette*, March 6, 1776; "Salus Populi" in the *Pa. Journal*, Feb. 14, and "A.B." on Feb. 28; "C.D." in the *Va. Gazette* (Purdie), May 3, and "An American" on March 29; "A British American" in the *Va. Gazette* (Dixon and Hunter), Feb. 17; "A Pennsylvania Countryman" in the *Pa. Packet*, May 13.

[27] "A Planter" and "B.A." in the *Va. Gazette* (Dixon and Hunter), May 6, 1776, and "A British American" on Feb. 17; "Honest, Sensible, and Spirited Farmer" in the *Pa. Journal*, Feb. 28, "Queries" on March 20, and "The Forester" on April 10; "Independent" in the *Pa. Packet*, March 18; "Americanus" in the *Md. Journal*, March 20; "A Watchman" in the *Pa. Evening Post*, June 13; "Plain Dealing" in the *Freeman's Journal*, June 18.

people of these colonies could now depend upon from Great-Britain, governed by *such a King,* and *such a majority* of Parliament, as the present?" As the writers variously expounded the thesis, Britain is "tottering on the brink of ruin"; "From the King on the throne to the meanest freeman in the nation, all is corrupt"; "venality and corruption has pervaded the whole mass"; "the electors are bought, and the majority of the Commons are kept in pay by the minister"; "the junto, who have usurped a tyrannic power, want provinces to drain of their wealth, as their patterns, the debauched Romans, had." [28] At all events, "the present Parliament can make no laws which shall bind any future one." Hence "the sun that rises on a reconciliation and dependance, such as we enjoyed before the year 1763 will see . . . new schemes concerted for enslaving us, which will be concealed only until more certain of success than at present." "America can never be safe in being dependent on such a foe." [29]

The issue assumed acute form when the news reached the press in February, 1776, that Parliament had authorized the appointment of commissioners to grant pardons to "all well-disposed" persons, colonies and communities in America. The reunionists, eagerly grasping at the straw, insisted that it was "the soundest policy, as well as the honestest, to hear what the Commissioners have got to say" and charged the opposition with being so mad for Independence as to be "inimical to whatever carries the appearance of peace." [30] In reply the latter, fearing the effects of war weariness on the public, demonstrated from the wording of the act that the envoys would have no power to make concessions, only to pardon cravens who acknowledged Parliament's omnipotence. "Now, Sir," sneered one of the commentators, "if any men, idiots and lunatics excepted, can imagine any good, is to be expected from such Commissioners, I am myself deprived of reason." At any rate, said another, "It is no time to parley with a robber about your purse when

---

[28] "Argus" in the *Providence Gazette*, March 23, 1776; "Probus" in the *Boston Gazette*, March 11; "A Religious Politician" in the *Pa. Journal*, Feb. 7; a Virginia letter in the *Pa. Evening Post*, April 9; "Hector" in the *Md. Journal*, May 1; "Candidus" in the *Pa. Gazette*, March 6; "R." in the *Conn. Courant*, May 1.

[29] "Cassandra" in the *Pa. Ledger*, April 27, 1776; "Salus Populi" in the *Pa. Journal*, Jan. 24; "Candidus" in the *Pa. Gazette*, March 6; "A Friend to Posterity and Mankind" in the *Pa. Packet*, Feb. 12, and "A Pennsylvania Countryman" on May 13; "F.A." in the *Boston Gazette*, April 29.

[30] "T . . . L" in the *Pa. Evening Post*, March 26, 1776; "Cato" in the *Pa. Packet*, March 11; "A Settled Citizen" in the *Pa. Ledger*, May 4; "A Lover of Liberty" in the *Va. Gazette* (Dixon and Hunter), May 18.

he has his pistol at your breast." [31] The Ministry's real object, these arguers maintained, was to gain time to raise more troops and, in the interval, to *"tempt towns, counties, and colonies, into a defection from the American union, by bribes of trade and pardon"* on the principle of *"divider et imperare."* [32] For this purpose, the press reported from London, each emissary would have at his disposal £4000 "as a Douceur for transacting the Business." "Cassandra" enjoined the Continental Congress to arrest the agents immediately upon their arrival, then speed them back to the enemy unless they could produce instructions to withdraw the British army and navy from America.[33]

The newspapers cast further disbelief on the Ministry's pacific intentions by printing the texts of the treaties made in January, 1776, with Brunswick, Hesse-Cassel and other German states for the use of mercenaries in the war. The "sceptered savage of Great-Britain," they shuddered, "thirsteth for the blood of America. Hessians, Hanoverians, Brunswickers, Canadians, Indians, Negroes, Regulars and Tories are invited to the carnage." [34] According to London advices, the Teuton hirelings would number at least 17,000 or 20,000— which came very close to the truth.[35] "Oh George! Are these thy Commissioners of peace and conciliation?" the writers stormed. Let no one be duped by the *"stale trick* of *pretending peace* while *war* was carrying on with the utmost diligence against us." In a British officer's opinion, it was, "above all, the hiring foreign troops to desolate their country" that made the Americans "fierce, frantic and invincible." [36]

---

[31] *N.–Y. Journal*, April 25, 1776; "A Planter" in the *Va. Gazette* (Dixon and Hunter), April 13.

[32] *Pa. Journal*, Feb. 28, 1776; *Va. Gazette* (Purdie), April 19, May 3; "Independent" in the *Pa. Packet*, March 18, and "The Forester" on April 1; "Sincerus" in the *Pa. Evening Post*, Feb. 13, "Cassandra" on March 2, and "Dialogus" on March 9; "Somers" in the *Md. Journal*, March 20; "A Planter" in the *Va. Gazette* (Dixon and Hunter), March 23.

[33] *Boston Gazette*, March 4, 1776; *Pa. Ledger*, March 9; "Cassandra" in the *Pa. Evening Post*, March 2.

[34] *Norwich Packet*, July 8, 1776; "Armatus" in the *Conn. Courant*, June 17; "Honest, Sensible, and Spirited Farmer" in the *Pa. Journal*, Feb. 28.

[35] *Conn. Journal*, April 24, 1776; *Pa. Packet*, May 6; *Pa. Journal*, May 29. The total number, at this time 17,775, became 29,875 before the end of the war. Christopher Ward, *The War of the Revolution* (J. R. Alden, ed., N. Y., 1952), I, 209.

[36] *Pa. Packet*, May 6, 1776, similarly, "A Card" in the *Pa. Journal*, May 8, "An Elector" in the *Pa. Gazette*, May 15, and a Philadelphia correspondent in the

Actually the furor over the commissioners, whatever its propaganda effects, was decidedly premature. The Ministry did not make the anticipated move till a few weeks after the Declaration of Independence and then, as was to be expected, the emissaries met a stern rebuff.[37]

IV

The reunionists, besides striving for a peaceful adjustment on "constitutional principles"—a term rarely defined but which seemed loosely to coincide with the Congressional goal of the status of 1763—maintained both that Independence would not be in America's interest and that in any case it would be impossible to achieve. The arguments had a familiar ring, for many of them had been advanced earlier. Now, however, they had a more immediate bearing on the crisis, and their exponents were Whigs, not Tories.

These contestants, while freely conceding that Britannia of late had been "a cruel Step-dame" rather than "a fostering Parent," insisted that a severance of the bonds would fatally worsen matters. Consider, they pleaded, the many benefits of the ancient connection. The British constitution was "the admiration of the world" and, "at this moment, gives birth to the only freemen in the habitable globe!" The institution of the kingship, far from being condemned by the Bible, as Paine and others alleged, wholly accorded with its teachings: "JESUS CHRIST left all the potentates of this world and their subjects, to decide their several rights by the temporal laws of each nation, and never *intimated* WHAT FORM OF GOVERNMENT WAS MOST CONVENIENT OR ELIGIBLE." Under the "gentle" sway of England's limited monarchy "political liberty never existed in greater perfection" than in the thirteen colonies. "Some abuses indeed we had reason to be uneasy under, but they were rather complained of, as establishing precedents for future violations, than as severely felt." [38]

In any case, the reconcilers contended, Britain had more than

---

N.-Y. Gazette and Weekly Mercury, May 13; letter of a British officer, March 25, reprinted from the London *Evening Post* in *Freeman's Journal*, Oct. 5.

[37] W. A. Brown, *Empire or Independence: a Study in the Failure of Reconciliation* (Baton Rouge, 1941), chaps. v–vi.

[38] "Cato" in the *Pa. Ledger*, March 23, 1776, and "Civis" on April 6; "Cato" in the *Pa. Packet*, April 8, 15; "Rationalis" in the *Pa. Gazette*, Feb. 28.

atoned for these errors by serving America "as an outwork of defence against the ambitious and potent nations of Europe," as well as by acting as "a guide and a governor, to prevent and heal those civil dissensions which mutual jealousy and emulation are too apt to excite in colonies growing up in each other's neighborhood." [39] She had, moreover, subsidized certain agricultural undertakings, protected the colonists' foreign commerce, and sold them her manufactures vastly cheaper than any other country would. The Ministry would faithfully abide by any concessions it might now make because "Great-Britain by this dispute will be taught that her true interest lies in a friendly connexion with us and a few years hence a similar attempt will be impracticable from our increase in numbers and strength." One sanguine soul even perceived signs of magnanimity in the "late remarkable event of the British troops evacuating Boston, with the circumstances attending." [40]

The Americans, these spokesmen continued, had no conceivable chance of wresting Independence from the mightiest country on earth. Hitherto they had encountered only "a Part of British Power, 6000 land Forces," whereas a struggle for liberation would entail "a tedious and expensive war; the blood of thousands bedewing the ground, and the whole wealth of the continent, the whole labour of a century, vanish'd in air," with final defeat unavoidable.[41] The colonists' hope for French and/or Spanish intervention was a snare and a delusion, for how probable was it that "both branches of the *Bourbon Family,* so long the terror of *Protestants and Freemen,* should now join as their protectors!" Besides, France "in the present ruinous state of her finances" would not "rush into a new and expensive war" after her catastrophic losses in the last one, nor would Spain aid a revolt that might incite her own dependencies to emulation. At all events history showed that foreign allies were likely to end up the masters of those whom they helped. Then the Americans would face the cruel alternative of submitting to "POPISH PRINCES . . . who are strangers to *Liberty*" or of abjectly suing to recover the benison of British rule. If it should ever become neces-

[39] "Hampden" in the *Pa. Packet,* May 18, 1776, similarly, "Cato" in the *Pa. Ledger,* March 23, and a pamphlet, *The Sentiments of a Foreigner,* quoted in the *Norwich Packet,* Feb. 19.

[40] "Junius" in the *N.–H. Gazette,* Jan. 9, 1776; "Civis" in the *Pa. Ledger,* April 6, and similarly "Cato" on March 23; "A Settled Citizen" in *ibid.,* May 4.

[41] "Junius" in the *N.–H. Gazette,* Jan. 9, 1776; "Moderator" in the *Pa. Ledger,* April 27.

sary to disown the mother country, it would obviously be wiser to wait until we could "protect our commerce and coasts by our own fleets, without looking to any nation upon earth for assistance." [42]

But, these journalists triumphantly pointed out, the Continental Congress, the official voice of America, had "never lisped the least desire for independency or republicanism; all their publications breathe another spirit . . . ." [43] Those seeking to "explore the dark and untrodden way" were either "adventurers who have nothing to lose" or "men exalted by the present confusions into *lucrative* offices, which they can hold no longer than the continuance of the public calamities." [44] Should they by some miracle accomplish their purpose, they would tragically "burst asunder the bands of religion, of *oaths,* of laws, of language, of *blood,* of interest, of commerce; of all those habitudes, in fine, which hold us united among ourselves, under the influence of the common parent"; or, as another expressed it, I should as soon "believe that those were my friends who would advise me to renounce my family, as I could believe them to be such who would seperate me from my near connections in the land that gave birth to my ancestors." Independence, on the other hand, would turn Britain, once America's undeviating well-wisher, into her "perpetual enemy." [45]

Domestically as well, this "leap in the dark" held for the reconcilers an utterly dismal prospect, since in their view a "Country of Farmers, Planters and Fishermen" could neither produce the necessary manufactured goods nor "Trade with any Foreign Power sufficiently to reimburse them for their Protection." Still worse, "He that reads the state of the Grecian or Roman Republics, what doth he read, but scenes of domestic violence and rapine, war and bloodshed?" In the case of the Americans "the ambition and desperation" of their leaders would set colony against colony:

> our fertile fields will be deluged with blood, our wives & children be involved in the horrid scene; foreign powers will step in and share in the plunder that remains, and those who are left to tell

---

[42] "Cato" in *ibid.*, March 23, 30, April 6, 1776; "Hampden" in the *Va. Gazette* (Dixon and Hunter), April 20, 27; "Civis" in the *Pa. Gazette,* May 1.

[43] "Plan of the American Compact" in the *N.–Y. Packet,* April 4, 1776.

[44] "Civis" in the *Pa. Ledger,* April 6, 1776, and "Cato" on March 23; similarly, "People of America!" in the *Md. Gazette,* May 9.

[45] "Hampden" in the *Va. Gazette* (Dixon and Hunter), April 27, 1776; "A Settled Citizen" in the *Pa. Ledger,* May 4; "Cato" in the *Pa. Gazette,* April 6.

the story will be reduced to a more abject slavery than that which you now dread.[46]

And even if it were possible to escape these calamities, how could the far-strewn "little commonwealths" with their "diversity of laws" and "inequality of riches" ever compose their differences and cement a permanent national government? The existing harmony of purpose, based upon common opposition to Britain, would dissolve with the emergency, reviving ancient jealousies and freeing the stronger states to exploit the weaker.[47] Plainly, internal as well as external security lay in preserving the imperial relation.

But the reunionists pleaded a cause which both the thrust of events and the adroitness of the opposing propaganda rendered a losing one. Moreover, they weakened their own case by betraying doubt as to the Ministry's willingness to grant the requisite concessions, some of their ablest spokesmen acknowledging that despite their dire warnings Independence might prove necessary as a "dernier resort." In this spirit "Cato" himself declared, "When it shall clearly appear, that we can be no longer *free,* nor secure in our *rights* and *property* in connection with Britain, . . . the author of these letters shall not then lisp a word against whatever measures the sense of the majority of this country, fairly taken, shall adopt for the common good," and in that event he pledged "his best assistance for carrying them into execution." Being Whigs rather than Tories, probably most of these disputants also believed, as one of them wrote, that time was working in America's behalf, so that without an internecine struggle "nature must, at last, have its course, and a total separation take place." [48] But for a people already embroiled in war such a philosophical view carried cold comfort.

V

The disunionists, seizing upon the admission that British obstinacy might justify separation, branded reconciliation "a phan-

---

[46] "Civis" in the *Pa. Ledger,* April 6, 1776, and *Pa. Gazette,* May 1; "Junius" in the *N.–H. Gazette,* Jan. 9; "Z.Z." in the *Mass. Gazette and Boston News-Letter,* Jan. 11; "Hampden" in the *Va. Gazette* (Dixon and Hunter), April 20.

[47] "Hampden" in *ibid.,* April 27, 1776, put this case most succinctly.

[48] "Rationalis" in the *Pa. Gazette,* Feb. 28, 1776, and "Cato" on April 24; "Moderator" in the *Pa. Ledger,* April 27.

tom," "a *lure*," "a painted dream," "a pitfall to catch you in." The vain hope reminded one critic of "the old proverb, 'After death call the doctor,' " which in the present context meant, he said, "fight for an accommodation till all your brave men, who have courage to fight, are slain, then set up independency" when it would be "too late." In fact, declared another, reconciliation, not Independence, was the "untrodden path; for where can we find an instance of a people's returning to their allegiance to a tyrant, after he has violated every political and moral obligation to them?" A third held it "disgraceful and scandalous" that any gentleman or Christian in America should be only "a moderate lover of his country" and evidence only "a moderate concern for the rights and liberties of mankind." [49]

The most desperate foes of Independence, these protagonists asserted, were the affluent merchants, notably the Pennsylvania variety, who, having "gotten the whole trade into their hands," were "making immense fortunes at the expence of the people. . . . What is the *ruin of their country* to men who make from 15 to 20,000 pounds per month profit?" Let every such person remember, however, "that a freeman worth fifty pounds is entitled by the laws of our province to all the privileges of the first Nabob in the country." [50] Others, they went on, opposed the step from such ignoble motives as:

1. I shall lose my office.
2. I shall lose the honor of being related to men in office.
3. I shall lose the rent of my houses for a year or two.
4. We shall have no more rum, sugar, tea, nor coffee, in this country, except at a most exorbitant price.
5. We shall have no more gauze, nor fine muslins, imported among us.
6. The New-England men will turn Goths and Vandals, and overrun the southern colonies. . . .
7. The church will have no King for a head.
8. The Presbyterians will have a share of power in this country. . . .

[49] "An Elector" in the *Pa. Packet*, April 29, 1776; *N.–Y. Journal*, May 9; "Remarks" in the *N.–Y. Packet*, April 18; "Serious Questions addressed to the advocates for Dependance" in the *Pa. Evening Post*, May 14; "American Patriot" in the *N.–Y. Packet*, April 11.

[50] Unsigned article in the *Pa. Evening Post*, April 30, 1776; "A Watchman" in the *Pa. Packet*, June 24.

9. I shall lose my chance of a large tract of land in a new purchase.

10. I shall want the support of the first officers of government, to protect me in my insolence, injustice, and villainy.

11. The common people will have too much power in their hands. . . .[51]

Such Americans, the disunionists raged, while "suffering from real calamities," shivered at "the contemplation of imaginary ones," or else callously placed self-interest above the common interest. Out of thin air they conjured up "terrifying ideas," painted Independence as a "dreadful chimera" and "the bugbear of the day." [52] But what lover of freedom could "hesitate in the choice?" "The evils of war are both tolerable and temporary, while the miseries of slavery are intolerable and endless." "Have the *Dutch* repented, or the *Swiss,* that *they shook off the yoke of their tyrants?*" "The day in which the colonies declare their independence," avowed the alleged shade of General Montgomery, "will be a jubilee to Hampden, Sidney, Russell, Warren, Gardiner, Macpherson, and the other heroes who have offered themselves as sacrifices upon the altar of liberty." [53] Invoking still higher sanction, these arguers proclaimed that God Himself had "placed this rich and fruitful continent at a great distance from all other parts of the inhabited world" as "the secure asylum of religion and morality when they had been driven from every other part of the earth"; the Almighty never intended America to be forever "subject to an island not so large as the four New-England colonies." As long ago as 1633 "that venerable and learned Divine," Thomas Hooker, had preached that "*England* hath seen her best Days," and she "shall be abased and brought down to Hell." [54] The colonists had outgrown their "non-age," their "infantile dependence," and only demanded the right to stand on their own feet. "And from the justice and equity of the cause, America may appeal to the world, yea to the Sovereign of all worlds for a decision . . . ." [55]

51 "Hutchinson, Cooper, Cato, &c. &c." in the *Pa. Evening Post,* June 1, 1776.

52 "A.B." in the *Va. Gazette* (Purdie), April 12, 1776; "Salus Populi" in the *Pa. Journal,* March 6; "Cassandra" in the *Pa. Packet,* April 8.

53 "Phil-Americus" in the *Va. Gazette* (Purdie), March 8, 1776; "Cassandra" in the *Pa. Ledger,* April 8; "A Dialogue between the Ghost of General Montgomery and a Delegate" in the *Pa. Packet,* Feb. 19.

54 "Juvenis" in the *Conn. Courant,* April 22, 1776; anon. in the *N.–H. Gazette,* June 8.

55 "Candidus" in the *Pa. Gazette,* March 6, 1776; a member of the Virginia

In reality, some of the writers maintained, Britain herself had already declared the colonies independent, for "the nineteenth of April, A.D. 1775 made them so" upon the first American's being "killed by an English soldier, by orders from his officer." [56] At all events, the British were fighting "as hard as though we had declared for independency. Why then in the name of *common sense,* should we decline it, and lose the advantages that may result from doing it?" Indeed, whether or not we strike for freedom, the "proud tyrants," if they won, would vengefully "keep us poor and weak" and "insult us on every occasion"; hence, since "we cannot make our affairs worse; we may make them better." [57] A complete and irreparable break, moreover—and here the disunionists cocked an eye particularly at their Quaker compatriots—would ensure "peace for ever. We are tired of contention with Britain, and can see no real end to it but in a final separation." And, by the same token, it would rid America internally of "the disorders which arise from the unlimited, undescribed, and *sometimes* arbitrary powers of Conventions, Committees of Safety, and Committees of Inspection." [58] A parting of the ways, in short, was the best guarantee of lasting peace and order both within and without.

The propagandists poured endless scorn upon defeatists who questioned America's military ability to win Independence. They cited not only the successes already gained, but also the fact that Britain, whose "power once made all Europe to tremble," had in her feebleness now found it necessary to summon the help of foreign mercenaries. [59] And, just as in earlier discussions, practically every forecaster of victory pledged that France and probably Spain would spring to America's support. [60] Ridiculing the doleful predictions of

---

Convention in the *Pa. Journal*, April 3; a resident of Chester County in the *Pa. Packet*, March 18.

[56] "Philanthropy" in the *Essex Journal*, June 7, 1776; similarly, a member of the Virginia Convention in the *Pa. Journal*, April 3.

[57] "An Independent Whig" in the *N.-Y. Journal*, Feb. 22, 1776; "A Pennsylvania Countryman" in the *Pa. Packet*, May 13; "The Watchman" in the *Pa. Ledger*, April 20.

[58] "To the Representatives of the religious society of the People called Quakers" in the *Conn. Courant*, March 18, 1776; "Reasons for a Declaration of the Independence of the American Colonies" in the *Pa. Evening Post*, April 20.

[59] A Chester County resident in the *Pa. Packet*, March 18, 1776; Casper Guttenburg and J. W. Leo in the *Pa. Journal*, March 20; "Americanus" in the *Freeman's Journal*, June 1, and "Orthodoxus" on June 29; "Juvenis" in the *Conn. Courant*, April 22; "Candidus" in the *Pa. Gazette*, March 6.

[60] Typical examples of such writers are "Questions and Answers" in the *Pa.*

popish armies "ravaging up and down the country" and terrorizing liberty-loving Protestants, they promised that, "As long as the wide Atlantic ocean rolls between us and Europe, so long will we be free from foreign subjection were we once clear of Great-Britain . . . ." [61]

With equal conviction they asserted America's capacity to finance the struggle as well as to prosper in freedom. "Our dependancy costs us as much in twenty years now, as would enable us with Divine assistance to finish the present war with success, and protect our trade in a state of independancy for five hundred years to come." Furthermore, "the vacant and ungranted land may be made a fund for paying off a part of this debt." In Virginia alone, a severing of the bonds would save the people an estimated £5,987,300 annually in import taxes, restrictions on exports, profits of British factors and like impositions. "If we aim *only* at *interest* in the present contest, it appears plainly what part we ought at once to resolve upon." [62] In the longer view, Independence would in addition ensure

> a proportionable rise in the value of land; the establishment, gradual improvement and perfection of manufactures and science; a vast influx of foreigners, encouraged by the mildness of a free, equal, and tolerating government to leave their native countries, and settle in these colonies; an astonishing encrease of people from the present stock.[63]

With like confidence the separationists dismissed the bogy of domestic turmoil in the wake of victory. As one writer put it, "To see a society of farmers, tradesmen and merchants, quit their peaceful employments, and make war upon one another, would be a phenomenon which the world has not yet beheld, and I will venture to say never will." [64] They even outlined possible forms that the new

---

Evening Post, Feb. 17, 1776, "Reasons for a Declaration of the Independence of the American Colonies" on April 20, and "Republicus" on June 29; "A British American" in the *Va. Gazette* (Dixon and Hunter), Feb. 17; "An American" in the *Va. Gazette* (Purdie), March 29; unsigned piece in the *Boston Gazette*, April 15.

[61] "The Forester" in the *Pa. Journal*, March 24, 1776, and "Salus Populi" on Feb. 14.

[62] "Salus Populi" in *ibid.*, Feb. 14, 1776; "Questions and Answers" in the *Pa. Evening Post*, Feb. 17; "A Planter" in the *Va. Gazette* (Dixon and Hunter), April 13, May 6; similarly, "Aesculapius" in the *Conn. Courant*, April 8, and "Hector" in the *Md. Gazette*, May 1.

[63] "Questions and Answers" in the *Pa. Evening Post*, Feb. 17, 1776.

[64] "Salus Populi" in the *Pa. Journal*, March 6, 1776.

federal republic might take—with some pressing for action while "the terrors of the common enemy" underlined the need [65]—and they argued that a representative system such as America's vast extent required would avert the disasters that had beset the turbulent little democracies of old. Moreover, they held, inexperience in self-government, hampered by persisting aristocratic principles, had handicapped those earlier experiments, whereas the colonists, thanks to long practice in managing their own affairs, were "aptly circumstanced to form the best of republicks, upon the best terms that ever came to the lot of any people before us." [66]

On this high note they closed their case.

VI

Midway between the disunionists and the reconcilers stood the irresolute. A correspondent, appropriately signing himself "Seek Truth," best expounded their attitude. Warning that "Men must be *convinced* before they become *converted*," he excoriated the "passion" and "intolerable abuse" that befogged much of the debate and insisted that "the grand political question" be "sifted to the bottom" by "sober argument." [67] As elaborated by "A Common Man," this involved a detailed ledger account of the assets and liabilities of the alternative courses of action.[68]

Confessing unconcern as to whether he lived "under an Emperor, a Pope, a Bashaw, a King of England, or a Republick," this champion of the undecided declared he only sought "*irrefutable arguments,* that such or such a state contained the greatest quantity of happiness for the people at large, and for individuals in particular."

[65] "Proposals for a Confederation of the United Colonies" in the *Pa. Evening Post*, March 5, 1776; "J.R." in the *Conn. Courant*, April 22; "An Independent Whig" in the *N.-Y. Journal*, Feb. 29, March 14, 28, April 18, "Essex" on March 7, April 4, anon. on May 9, and "Spartanus" on May 30, June 13, 20.

[66] "Demophilus" in the *Pa. Packet*, Feb. 12, 1776; "Salus Populi" in the *Pa. Journal*, March 13; "E.F." in the *Va. Gazette* (Purdie), May 17.

[67] *Pa. Packet*, April 22, 1776.

[68] His article was addressed "To Cato, Cassandra, and all the Writers on the Independence Controversy," in the *Pa. Ledger*, March 30, 1776. "A Planter" in the *Va. Gazette* (Dixon and Hunter), April 13 (see the preceding section of this chapter), had indeed ventured some general figures of this sort in the case of Virginia, only to have them disputed, however, by "A Virginian" in the same pages, April 27.

This, too, he said, was the aspiration of "99 out of every 100 in the world, who have no expectations of ever ascending into office, and riding upon the top of the machine," but who desired that the machine be "so constructed, as to move with as little labour as possible" and "be the least liable to get out of order in the variety of rough and smooth roads through which we must inevitably pass."

Of the separationists he demanded,

> State the advantages of an Independence,—the benefits to be derived from a new mode of government, how it will affect *individuals;* the additional happiness and freedom it will produce, *particularized* in a number of *plain, clear* instances . . . . tell them, also, of the particular *new trades,* which will be opened to us; the prices our goods will bear *at home* to the farmer, and what they will bring at *such* and *such* ports, and how much those prices *exceed* what we have been used to get for them, at the markets we were allow'd to trade to; in this you must *name* the articles, the prices, and the places; you must then tell us, the advantages of buying linens, woolens, cottons, silks and hard ware in France, Spain and Portugal, . . . and whether those places will take in exchange, our lumber, our naval stores, our flax seed &c &c and what prices they will give; what credit it is customary for those several places to allow to foreigners on what we commonly call dry goods . . . . Next you must shew, that the charge of supporting government will be less in a state of Independence, than it hath been heretofore.[69]

Next, turning to the reunionists, he bade them answer at equal length and with equal concreteness a parallel questionnaire regarding the economic benefits the colonies had derived from British rule "before the present rupture." In addition, he went on, it behooved them to prove "that by a reconciliation on constitutional principles, we shall return to the free money-getting trade we formerly enjoyed, and that we shall have it enlarged to us upon a grand national scale . . . without our paying any taxes for the support of government more than what we have been used to (the debts arising from the present dispute only excepted)." Then, if the balance sheet demonstrated that it was better "to cut the Gordian Knot," he would give that course his "hearty concurrence."

Such voices, however, made little or no impression on either set of propagandists. Both dealt in the currency of denunciation, ex-

[69] "Moderator" in the *Pa. Ledger,* April 27, 1776, also queried the separationists, though more briefly, along these same lines.

hortation and prophecy rather than in that of business accounting. Granted that "Men must be *convinced* before they become *converted*," they well knew that the art of effective persuasion lay in stirring the deeper human emotions of fear and hope. In any event they could hardly have supplied the plethora and particularity of data which the "Common Man" and his like insisted on having. The disunionists, however, doubtless feeling more vulnerable to this species of interrogation, alone deigned to notice the "Common Man." "Under a thin and silly pretence of impartiality," jeered "Aristides," "he takes it upon him to tell us what a number of things must be all previously settled before we proceed to fix upon a regular plan of government . . . . Are our understandings to be so insulted?" "This unparalleled contention of nations," exploded "The Forester," "is not to be settled like a school-boy's task of pounds, shillings, pence, and fractions. . . . For the first and great question, and that which involves every other in it, and from which every other will flow, is *happiness*," and America can be as happy under a government of her own choosing "as she please; she hath a blank sheet to write on." "Cassandra," heartily agreeing, thundered that "of infinitely more importance" than all the "Common Man's" queries was *an absolute security for the enjoyment of our liberties.*" [70] And there, so far as the separationists were concerned, the matter rested.

VII

While the great debate over Independence raged in the press, the division over the question behind the closed doors of the Second Continental Congress grew ever sharper. On July 6, 1775, the Congress in justifying the resort to civil war had solemnly told the British people, in language drafted by John Dickinson, that "we mean not to dissolve that Union which has so long and so happily subsisted between us . . . . We have not raised armies with ambitious designs of separating from Great Britain, and establishing independent states"; and even nine months later, on March 23, 1776, John Adams complained to a friend that the thought of disunion

[70] "Aristides" in the *Pa. Packet*, May 13, 1776; "The Forester" in the *Pa. Gazette*, April 24; "Cassandra" in the *Pa. Ledger*, April 13.

was still "a Hobgoblin of so frightful Mien" as to throw a majority of the delegates "into Fits to look it in the Face." [71]

Nevertheless, under the spur of circumstance and the ceaseless journalistic prodding, the members moved steadily if unwittingly toward a final breach. As a writer gibed in the press, the very ones who quailed "at the *name* of independance" supported measures embodying "all the *spirit* of it," and he cited as evidence that the Congress had "made laws, erected courts of judicature, established magistrates, made money, levied war, and regulated commerce, not only without his Majesty's intervention, but absolutely against his will." [72] And hardly had his article appeared when the delegates on April 6 committed themselves further by throwing open America's trade to all the world but the British Isles. The specific object was to obtain outside supplies for waging the hostilities, but the action had been advocated in the newspapers, as well as on the floor, as also a means of engaging "the interest of foreigners" in a favorable outcome. [73] Then, on May 10 and 15, the Congress bade the respective colonies suppress all vestiges of British authority and establish governments emanating from the people. In John Adams's mind, though still not in that of most of his colleagues, this amounted to "a total absolute independence" of both King and Parliament. [74]

Meanwhile newspaper writers urged on Congress the culminating step. As one affirmed, "Many honest persons two years ago, would have trembled at the thought of such a thing, who are now fully convinced of the expediency, the safety and necessity of this measure, as our only security." According to another, "independence is now become the universal cry; all ranks and conditions of men seem to be waiting in silent and anxious expectation of a formal declaration," which among other advantages would "give vigor to our military operations." [75] "Suppose," darkly suggested a third, "France

[71] Continental Congress, *Journals* (W. C. Ford and others, eds., Wash., 1904–37), II, 155; letter of Adams to Horatio Gates, E. C. Burnett, ed., *Letters of Members of the Continental Congress* (Wash., 1921–38), I, 406.

[72] A member of the Virginia Convention in the *Pa. Journal*, April 3, 1776.

[73] "Questions and Answers" in the *Pa. Evening Post*, Feb. 17, 1776; "A British American" in the *Va. Gazette* (Dixon and Hunter), Feb. 17; "Philanthropy" in the *Essex Journal*, June 17.

[74] John to Abigail Adams, May 17, 1776, Burnett, *Letters of Members*, I, 453.

[75] *Constitutional Gazette*, May 8, 1776; *Boston Gazette*, April 14.

should grow weary in listening to our *whining* cries after our MOTHER COUNTRY, and instead of striking a blow to draw off the British armies and fleets from our coasts, should accept of Canada as a condition of neutrality," or, alternatively, that "the southern Colonies should be offered to Spain on condition of her neutrality, or assistance in the reduction of them?" The colonists, this writer exhorted, must not "neglect the present critical moment of asserting and securing their freedom." In the importunate words of others, the people "wait with impatience for our Honourable Continental Congress to cut the Gordian Knot"; they "humbly pray your Honours to cause a Manifesto to go out" immediately "declaring the United Colonies a free State." [76]

With joy unconfined the *Newport Mercury* on April 8 announced that the New Jersey Provincial Congress had named a pro-Independence man to the Continental Congress: *"A striking proof that those people, as well as all other true Americans, are ripening fast for that state, short of which they cannot long be either* happy *or* safe." Although for two months more the New Jersey delegation as a whole opposed separation, the press reported the adhesion of a number of other colonies to the standard, led by North Carolina on April 12 and Virginia on May 15. Nevertheless John Adams read his own hopes into the developments when writing from the Congress, "Every Post and every Day rolls in upon Us, Independence like a Torrent." [77] Even on Friday, June 7, when Richard Henry Lee with Adams as his seconder submitted his famous motion "that the United Colonies are, and of right ought to be, free and independent States," the delegates remained of two minds. After a hot debate on the next day and another on the 10th they postponed final consideration till July 1 so as to give the still reluctant Middle Colonies further opportunity to weigh their course. To what extent these secret transactions became known to the public it is impossible to say, but at least one newspaper, Purdie's *Virginia Gazette* on June 21, correctly reported the date that had been "fixed upon to decide the grand question." When the time arrived, the discussion went on so long that the decisive vote was deferred to the following day,

[76] "Serious Questions addressed to the Congress and all other Legislative Bodies in America" in the *Pa. Evening Post*, April 16, 1776; "Z.F." in the *N.-Y. Packet*, March 7; "Common Sense" in the *Conn. Gazette*, April 12.

[77] Letter to James Warren, May 20, 1776, Burnett, *Letters of Members*, I, 460.

July 2.[78] Then the members without recorded dissent passed Lee's resolution, and on Thursday, July 4, adopted the Declaration of Independence setting forth "to a candid world" the principles of human rights and the "repeated injuries and usurpations" that had impelled them to their decision.

Many factors and forces had brought affairs to this extremity. The journalistic agitation for Independence, however important, was but one of a complex of influences and derived much of its potency from the fact that the mounting crisis had rendered the popular mind increasingly receptive. If hardy souls like the brace of Massachusetts Adamses had prevailed, the Congress would have acted at least six months earlier; but when obliged to wait in spite of themselves, both men frankly acknowledged that "The Colonies were not then all ripe for so momentous a Change." Much more needed yet to be done, in Samuel Adams's words, "to remove old prejudices, instruct the unenlightened, convince the doubting and fortify the timid." It was the incessant discussion in newspapers and pamphlets, John Adams stated, which, along with the canvassing of the question in public bodies and informal private groups, had "gradually and, at last, totally extinguished" the rushlight of reconciliation, for the delay enabled "the whole people"—and, he might well have added, the majority of the Congress—"to ripen their judgment, dissipate their fears, and allure their hopes." [79] In this campaign, as none knew better than these two veterans at propaganda, the press had played a crucial part.

[78] J. H. Powell, "The Debate on American Independence, July 1, 1776," *Delaware Notes*, XXIII (1950), 37–62.

[79] Samuel Adams to Benjamin Kent, July 27, 1776, Samuel Adams, *Writings* (H. A. Cushing, ed., N. Y., 1904–08), III, 304–305; John Adams to Abigail Adams, July 3, John Adams, *Works* (C. F. Adams, ed., Boston, 1850–56), IX, 419–420.

Chapter XIII

The
Tally Sheet

W AS THERE EVER a Revolution brot about, especially so important as this without great internal Tumults & violent Convulsions!" exulted Samuel Adams. The people, he said, looked on the Declaration of Independence "as though it were a Decree promulgated from Heaven." [1] But five harrowing years lay ahead before freedom would finally be won. In these "times that try men's souls," as Tom Paine immortalized them, the newspapers would serve the cause as valiantly as they had in the past. The press indeed had come a long way since 1763 when its voice was small and unsure. It now held an essential place in the community, and by the same token it could look confidently to the future. The puling infant had come of age. Moreover, in the process it had wrought changes in newspaper methods that would have profound effects on all later American journalism.

I

The public at large first learned of the decision for separation when it read reports of the fateful action the Congress had taken preparatory to the formal Declaration. "Yesterday," both the *Pennsylvania Journal* and the *Pennsylvania Gazette* tersely announced on July 3, 1776, "the CONTINENTAL CONGRESS declared the UNITED COLONIES FREE and INDEPENDENT STATES,"

[1] Letter to Benjamin Kent, July 27, 1776, Samuel Adams, *Writings* (H. A. Cushing, ed., N. Y., 1904–08), III, 304.

and the *New-York Gazette and Weekly Mercury* on July 8 and the
Boston Gazette a week later repeated the news with equal brevity.
To the modern reader this way of handling so momentous an event
would seem unenterprising, but the printers, evidently thinking
that the six months of debate had only yielded the expected conclu-
sion, felt no need to elaborate the obvious. Even before issues of the
Philadelphia papers reached Worcester the *Massachusetts Spy* on
July 10 had broadcast a rumor that the Congress had abjured "that
Monster of imperious domination and cruelty—Great Britain!
Which we hope is true." The thrilling news of the July 2 resolution
indeed sped through the land faster than mere print could carry it.
To cite one other instance, Purdie's *Virginia Gazette* on July 12 re-
ported it in Williamsburg on the strength of a letter from the Freder-
icksburg postmaster who had it from "a gentleman just arrived from
Philadelphia" who in turn had seen it in the *Pennsylvania Evening
Post*.

After the official Declaration was adopted on the evening of
Thursday, July 4, the Congress on Friday and Saturday sent off
printed copies to all the legislative assemblies, conventions and
similar bodies as well as to the military commanders. As a result,
couriers bore the document to most centers before the editors, hampered by publication dates, could present it to their readers. Probably for this reason, too, few papers got out "Extraordinaries." The
regular issues, however, almost invariably displayed the unabridged
text on the first page. There the great instrument usually appeared
without comment, for it spoke with matchless eloquence for itself.
It was the ablest piece of propaganda born of the long controversy,
a resounding exposition of "unalienable rights" which ever since
has reverberated through the country and the world.

Distance from Philadelphia and facilities of transmittal generally
determined the promptness with which the newspapers printed the
Declaration. The *Pennsylvania Evening Post* on July 6, thanks to
being a triweekly, scooped all the local press. Outside the city *Dunlap's Maryland Gazette* at Baltimore followed on the 9th, and the
New York *Constitutional Gazette* on the 10th. In New England the
New London *Connecticut Gazette* outstripped all its contemporaries
on the 12th, with the *Providence Gazette* leading the way on the
13th in Rhode Island, the Salem *American Gazette* on the 16th in
Massachusetts, and the Exeter *New-Hampshire Gazette* on the same

day in its state. South of Maryland, because of poorer communications, Dixon and Hunter's *Virginia Gazette* was first in the Old Dominion on July 20, and the *South-Carolina and American General Gazette* (which, however, had not published since May 31) trailed along on August 2.

Pa. Evening Post, July 6
Pa. Packet, July 8
Philadelphische Staatsbote, July 9
Dunlap's Md. Gazette, July 9
Pa. Gazette, July 10
Pa. Journal, July 10
Md. Journal, July 10
Constitutional Gazette, July 10
N.–Y. Packet, July 11
N.–Y. Journal, July 11
Md. Gazette (Annapolis), July 11
Conn. Gazette, July 12
Pa. Ledger, July 13
Providence Gazette, July 13
N.–Y. Gazette and Mercury, July 15
Conn. Courant, July 15
Norwich Packet, July 15
N.–H. Gazette, Extraordinary, July 16

American Gazette, July 16
Mass. Spy, July 17
Conn. Journal (New Haven), July 17
Continental Journal (Boston), July 18
New-England Chronicle, July 18
Newport Mercury, Extraordinary, July 18
Essex Journal (Newburyport), July 19
Freeman's Journal (Portsmouth), July 20
Va. Gazette (Dixon and Hunter), July 20
Boston Gazette (Watertown), July 22
Va. Gazette (Purdie), July 26
S.–C. and American General Gazette, August 2

FIRST PRINTING OF THE FULL TEXT OF THE DECLARATION OF INDEPENDENCE

Based on C. S. Brigham, *Journals and Journeymen*
(Phila., 1950), 58–59

The press joyfully returned to the subject in depicting the celebrations that everywhere marked the public reading of the Declaration. It told of the dignitaries present, the cheering crowds, the military paraders flaunting the banner of the new nation, the roll of drums, thunder of cannons and pealing of bells, the civic banquets with their inspirational toasts, the bonfires and illuminations. A single number of Purdie's *Virginia Gazette* described such festivities at Williamsburg, Trenton, N. J., and New York City. In Manhattan, the *Gazette* jubilantly reported, the "sons of freedom," improving on the usual proceedings, demolished "the equestrian statue of George III, which Tory pride and folly raised in the year 1770," and melted it into bullets "for our infatuated adversaries, who to gain a pepper corn have lost an empire. *Quos deus volt perdere prius dementat.*" The article further noted that "A general jail delivery to debtors took place yesterday. One of the first fruits of independence —the oppressed are set free." [2]

Up and down the coast, newspaper readers learned of the populace sweeping away all visible symbols of British rule, of the Bostonians destroying tavern signs—like the Lion and Crown and the Heart and Crown—that jarred republican sensibilities, and of a Baltimore mob burning the King in effigy "to the no small mirth of the numerous spectators." The Virginia Convention in similar spirit removed all references to the monarch from the Anglican service, and on pain of heavy fine the Rhode Island General Assembly forbade that state's clergymen to acknowledge him in any "Way and Manner" as "our rightful Lord and Sovereign." [3]

II

No contemporary could doubt the part of the press in bringing matters at length to this pass. "It was by means of News papers," John Holt of the *New-York Journal* boasted to Samuel Adams, who hardly needed to be told, "that we receiv'd & spread the Notice of the tyrannical Designs formed against America, and kindled a Spirit that has been sufficient to repel them." And in the opposite camp Ambrose Serle, private secretary to Admiral Lord Richard Howe, apprised the Ministry, "Among other Engines, which have raised the present Commotion next to the indecent Harangues of the

[2] *Va. Gazette* (Purdie), July 26, 1776.
[3] *Md. Gazette* (Annapolis), Aug. 3, 1776; *Boston Gazette*, July 22; *Va. Gazette* (Dixon and Hunter), July 20; *Newport Mercury*, July 22.

Preachers, none has had a more extensive or stronger Influence than the Newspapers of the respective Colonies." Probably most observers, however, would have rejected the secondary role thus assigned to the press. For example, a patriot commentator with far greater knowledge of the facts than the recently arrived Briton unhesitatingly testified that "more attention is paid by many to the *News Paper* than to Sermons." [4]

Doubtless a fair over-all judgment would be that, although a multitude of factors from the Sugar Act onward pushed the colonists along the road to Independence, the movement could hardly have succeeded without an ever alert and dedicated press. At every crisis the patriot prints fearlessly and loudly championed the American cause, never yielding ground as did some of the politicians. Moreover a number of editors, as we have seen, participated firsthand in subversive activities. Outstanding among the militants were Edes and Gill, Isaiah Thomas and Solomon Southwick in New England, James Parker and John Holt in New York, William Bradford in Philadelphia, Peter Timothy in Charleston and the peripatetic William Goddard in towns all the way from Providence to Baltimore. However unwittingly, Thomas and John Fleet of Boston also rendered valuable assistance. Though they conscientiously and consistently opened their columns to both parties, their attitude of detachment in fact aided the Whigs more than the Tories, since the Whigs by and large wielded the abler pens.

Luckily, the patriots enjoyed the additional advantage of a generally spineless opposition press, a condition which the representatives of the Crown despite all their efforts could do little to cure. Editors like Richard Draper in Boston, Hugh Gaine in New York and James Johnston in Savannah privately rejected the Whig program, but, save when pressed by royal authorities who had the power to grant them official favors and a measure of protection, they trimmed their journalistic sails to the prevailing wind. John Mein and "Jemmy" Rivington, the exceptions, paid for their temerity by being run both out of business and out of the country. This proved an object lesson which their more timid brethren could not well disregard.

[4] Holt to Adams, Jan. 29, 1776, V. H. Paltsits, "John Holt—Printer and Postmaster," N. Y. Public Library, *Bull.*, XXIV (1920), 494; Serle to Lord Dartmouth, Nov. 26, Hugh Gaine, *Journals* (P. L. Ford, ed., N. Y., 1892), I, 57; "A Friend to Decency" in *Freeman's Journal* (Portsmouth), Nov. 12.

As for other considerations that may have influenced an editor's course, both sides to a degree received subsidies from the government in the form of public printing, the Tories usually from the executive department and the Whigs from the popularly elected legislative branch. Many if not most of the latter, however, supported the American cause without such emoluments. Nor was their place of birth a significant determinant. Though Mein, Rivington, Gaine, Johnston and other loyalist publishers hailed from the mother country, their fellow partisans such as Richard and Margaret Draper, Nathaniel Mills, John Hicks and Ezekiel Russell sprang from colonial stock. By the same token, all the leading patriot editors were American-born, yet their auxiliaries in the struggle like Samuel Loudon, John Dunlap and Alexander Purdie came from the British Isles. The two German-language printers afford interesting further evidence, though neither was a major factor in the contest. Both were German immigrants and hence presumably disinterested spectators. Yet Henry Miller dedicated his *Philadelphische Staatsbote* wholeheartedly to the Whig cause, copying most of his controversial articles from likeminded English contemporaries, while Christoph Sower appears to have devoted his *Germantowner Zeitung* just as stoutly to the British side. As a Dunker and religious pacifist Sower naturally disapproved of any lawless disturbance of the status quo, but, beyond that, he was a Tory by conviction.[5]

The sex of the newspaper owners seems to have had no more bearing. Not only did the men divide politically, but so also did the handful of women. Margaret Draper after her husband's death simply kept to the pro-British course he had set for the *Massachusetts Gazette and Boston News-Letter*. Although the four others backed the patriots, the reasons at bottom were much the same. Sarah Goddard of the *Providence Gazette* and Mary K. Goddard of the *Maryland Journal* were respectively mother and sister of William Goddard, who had founded both papers, and Anne Catherine Green of

[5] The *Zeitung* was a biweekly until April 20, 1775, when it began to appear weekly. Christopher Sower III, who joined his father on the paper sometime in 1776, testified to the elder's politics when he told the postwar parliamentary commission on Tory losses that he had "inherited Loyalty from his father and was attached to the British Government both from a sense of duty and a thorough conviction of its excellence." J. O. Knauss, "Christopher Saur the Third," Am. Antiquarian Soc., *Procs.*, n.s., XLI (1931), 235–238; J. J. Stoudt, "The German Press in Pennsylvania and the American Revolution," *Pa. Mag. of History and Biography*, LIX (1935), 76–78.

the *Maryland Gazette* and Clementina Rind of Rind's *Virginia Gazette* took over the responsibilities of their deceased spouses. In all these cases, then, the family connection sufficiently accounts for the editorial policies.

III

The newspaper offensive which began with the Sugar and Stamp Acts pursued a varying course as new emergencies reshaped the issues. Throughout, however, the patriot journalists sought to activate popular resentment while keeping several paces ahead of it. Playing upon both fears and hopes, they dissected the measures, imputed satanic motives to the opposition, and endlessly vaunted the colonists' time-honored right to manage their affairs with a minimum of outside interference.

When the Tory protagonists were at last disposed of and the journalistic strife took the form of a Whig family quarrel over the question of Independence, both factions ventured pronouncements which future events were to put to the test. The success of propaganda obviously does not depend upon the soundness of the arguments it advances; but in this culminating stage of the controversy, when opposing groups vied desperately for the public mind, history may well ask which side displayed the greater prescience.

From this vantage point it is clear that the disunionists proved right in predicting the people's fortitude, their ultimate military triumph, the intervention of France and Spain against Britain, and also the general postwar well-being, the absence of armed strife among the states, and the erection of a stable national government. The reconcilers, though they misjudged all these matters, could nevertheless take credit for correctly foretelling the long and wasting struggle and the difficulties—which they, however, deemed insurmountable—of creating a durable federal union. They also mistakenly warned that the establishment of Independence would render the mother country America's undying enemy. Probably the most sanguine colonist, however, could not then have foreseen that, thanks to the shifting power situation in Europe, George III in little more than a score of years would acclaim President Washington the greatest of living men, or that British officers would march in the

memorial procession in New York upon Washington's death.[6]
Whether by prevision or chance, the advocates of separation turned
out to be the truer prophets.

IV

Oddly, neither party to the debate exhibited any evident concern
over the disruptive effects that a protracted war would have on the
press.[7] Doubtless both believed that the journalists, having weath-
ered many a past gale, would somehow be able to outride any future one. That at all events proved generally to be the case. A goodly
number of the publishers, as had recently happened in beleaguered
Boston, fled the advancing British arms to resume their activities
elsewhere until it should be safe to return; others suspended their
papers during periods of stress; while still others, being outside the
fighting zone, operated without interruption. Only a very few gave
up altogether. Moreover, of the entire roster of editors in 1776,
only three afterward betrayed the patriot cause by changing their
sheets into enemy mouthpieces and, of these, one executed a double
somersault back to the Americans. The Whigs, however, temporarily lost two other organs when the printers abandoned them to
join the British. Besides the case of William Hunter, Jr., later to be
noticed, Robert L. Fowle at Exeter thus discontinued the *New-
Hampshire Gazette* in July, 1777, on suspicion of complicity in
counterfeiting the new paper currency. Within seven months, how-

6 Bradford Perkins, *The First Rapprochement: England and the United States,
1795–1805* (Phila., 1955), 18, 125.

7 Data regarding these effects on the press, both Whig and Tory, are strewn
through Isaiah Thomas, *The History of Printing in America* (rev. ed., Am. Antiquarian Soc., *Trans. and Colls.*, V–VI, Albany, 1874), and C. S. Brigham, ed.,
History and Bibliography of American Newspapers, 1690–1820 (Worcester, 1947).
For New York, see, in addition, Gaine, *Journals*, I, 54–64; S. I. Pomerantz, "The
Patriot Newspaper and the American Revolution," R. B. Morris, ed., *The Era of
the American Revolution* (N. Y., 1939), 305–331; C. M. Thomas, "The Publication of Newspapers during the American Revolution," *Journalism Quar.*, IX
(1932), 358–373; and A. J. Wall, "Samuel Loudon," N.-Y. Hist. Soc., *Quar. Bull.*,
VI (1922), 75–92; and, for other cities, A. M. Lee, "Dunlap and Claypoole,"
Journalism Quar., XI (1934), 160–178; Mills and Hicks, "Letter Book" for 1781–
84, R. E. Moody and C. C. Crittenden, eds., *N. C. Hist. Rev.*, XIV (1937), 39–83;
and three articles by R. A. Brown: "The Newport Gazette, Tory Newssheet,"
R. I. History, XIII (1954), 97–108, XIV (1955), 11–20, "New Hampshire Editors
Win the War," *New England Quar.*, XII (1939), 35–51, and "The Pennsylvania
Ledger: Tory News Sheet," *Pa. History*, IX (1942), 161–175.

ever, his brother Zechariah atoned for the defection by setting up the patriot *Exeter Journal or New-Hampshire Gazette.*

Newspaper fortunes by and large reflected the ups and downs of the fighting. As the foe approached New York in August, 1776, Anderson stopped his *Constitutional Gazette* forever, while his three fellow editors fled to less exposed locations. Loudon, with assistance from the Provincial Congress at Fishkill, took his *Packet* there for the rest of the war. Holt, on the other hand, licked his wounds in nearby Connecticut until, being commissioned state printer, he started afresh at Kingston (then Esopus), N. Y. In his first number, on July 7, 1777, he bitterly explained, "After remaining for ten months past, overwhelmed and sunk, in a sea of tyrannic violence and rapine, The New-York Journal, just emerging from the waves, faintly rears its languid head . . . ." But rough waters still lay ahead. Several months later the enemy burned Kingston, causing him to decamp to Poughkeepsie, where, despite long suspensions due to lack of supplies and subscribers, he managed to keep the *Journal* afloat until peace finally restored it to New York City. Similarly, Gaine bore one of his presses across the Hudson to Newark, N. J., there to issue the *New-York Gazette and Weekly Mercury* for the patriots. But in little more than a month, presumably convinced he had backed the wrong horse, he betook himself and his sheet back to Manhattan and the British.

By contrast, the seizure of Newport, R. I., by the enemy in December, 1776, affected only a single publication, but that, the *Mercury*, had long been a particular trial to the Crown authorities. Southwick, after hastily burying his press and types, dramatically escaped with his wife and eldest son in an open boat under gunfire from the shore. Living successively in Rehoboth and Attleboro, Mass., and finally at Providence in his native state, he did official printing for the Rhode Island government on a press he had meanwhile obtained. When the foe withdrew in October, 1779, he joyfully returned to Newport to help re-establish the *Mercury*. Fortunately in the interval patriotic Rhode Islanders had enjoyed uninterrupted access to the *Providence Gazette.*

The hostile occupation of Philadelphia from September, 1777, to June, 1778, produced comparable results. William Bradford, who as an officer in the militia had fought to turn back the British advance at Princeton and Trenton, suspended the *Pennsylvania Jour-*

nal to devote full time to the army, and Miller likewise halted the *Staatsbote*. Of the three other papers, two resumed elsewhere with subsidies from the American authorities in the shape of public printing or otherwise. Dunlap, also betimes a soldier, thus moved his *Packet* to Lancaster, the seat of the refugee state government, while Hall and Sellers carried the *Gazette* to York, the haven of the Continental Congress. Only Towne, whose *Evening Post* had led the American press in publicizing the Declaration of Independence, elected to shift his politics rather than his place of business. In fact, he accomplished the remarkable feat of apostatizing twice, for after the British quit the city he managed so to ingratiate himself with the restored administration that it suffered him to continue his sheet.

At Charleston, John Wells stopped his *South-Carolina and American General Gazette* for some weeks in 1776 and again in 1779 because of threatening enemy operations; but when the city fell in May, 1780, Wells, like Towne, chose to preserve his property rather than his principles and renamed his paper the *Royal Gazette*. With the evacuation in December, 1782, he hurriedly took ship for the Bahamas. By contrast, doughty old Peter Timothy, who amidst his political involvements had resumed newspapering with the *Gazette of the State of South-Carolina* in April, 1777, terminated it shortly before the fall of Charleston and was sent a prisoner to St. Augustine with Christopher Gadsden and other patriot leaders.[8] Exchanged after some months Timothy died in 1782, but his widow loyally helped to resuscitate his journal a year later.

Wartime straits caused other newspaper casualties in the South as well. The *Maryland Gazette* in Annapolis suspended from December, 1777, to April, 1779, as did *Dunlap's Maryland Gazette* in Baltimore from January, 1779, to May, 1783. At New Bern the *North-Carolina Gazette*, at this time the state's only newspaper, ceased altogether in November, 1778. The Virginia press also suffered difficulties. At Williamsburg, Dixon and Hunter's *Virginia Gazette* breathed its last in December, 1778, when Hunter unexpectedly deserted to the foe, but Dixon within a few months set up another *Virginia Gazette* in association with Thomas Nicolson, a beginner at the trade. In 1780 the two transplanted the sheet to the new state capital at Richmond, where, however, nearby fighting in May,

---

[8] Edward McCrady, *The History of South Carolina in the Revolution* (N. Y., 1901), 716–726.

1781, ended further publication. But Nicolson seven months later established still another and more enduring *Virginia Gazette* in Richmond. Meanwhile, at Williamsburg, Purdie's *Virginia Gazette* passed to other hands upon his death in 1779, only to expire itself in December of the next year, probably from failure to follow the political center of news to Richmond.

V

Such were the blows of the hammer of war on the Whig editors. The resurgence of British power, however, also drew the former Tory journalists out of hiding.[9] Almost certainly the Crown authorities helped finance their undertakings. This at any rate was the earnest recommendation of Ambrose Serle, Admiral Howe's secretary, who urged on the Ministry that "The Expence of allowing Salaries (if needful) to some able Superintendants of the Press in different Colonies" was "too trifling to mention, considering the almost incredible Influence these fugitive Publications have upon the People."[10] Serle at the moment was himself acting in somewhat that capacity in New York City.

Be that as it may, these men, so recently on the run, swarmed into the occupied towns, stridently resuming their activities while fortune permitted. John Howe of the defunct *Massachusetts Gazette and Boston News-Letter* fathered the *Newport Gazette*, giving the British their solitary organ in all New England. Alexander and James Robertson, lately of the *Norwich Packet*, augmented the New York Tory press with the *Royal American Gazette* on which, appropriately enough, Mills and Hicks of the whilom *Massachusetts Gazette and Boston Post-Boy* joined them a few years later. James Robertson, meanwhile extending his operations, availed himself of further British successes to establish the *Royal Pennsylvania Gazette* in Philadelphia and help launch the *Royal South-Carolina Gazette* in Charleston.

James Humphreys, who had dropped his *Pennsylvania Ledger* under popular pressure and fled to the countryside in November, 1776, resurrected the paper in Philadelphia during the British oc-

---

[9] See footnote 7.
[10] Letter to Lord Dartmouth, Nov. 26, 1776, Gaine, *Journals*, I, 58.

cupation; and the Sowers, having found it too dangerous to remain any longer in Germantown, gladly added the *Pennsylvanische Staats-Courier* to the Tory battery. Left in the lurch by the British withdrawal, Christopher Sower III next went to New York to serve the Crown as an adviser and translator, and in due course he there set up still another Tory sheet, the *New-York Evening Post*. In Georgia meanwhile, after the British seized Savannah at the end of 1778, James Johnston of the quondam *Georgia Gazette* re-entered the arena with the *Royal Georgia Gazette*.

New York, the city longest under British control, was naturally their principal newspaper as well as military center. Overshadowing the Robertsons, Mills and Hicks, Sower and the William Lewis who in 1779 started the *New-York Mercury* stood two veterans of the local journalistic scene, Hugh Gaine and James Rivington. Though Gaine had momentarily strayed from the fold by removing his *Gazette and Weekly Mercury* to Newark, he had doubtless watched enviously from that patriot outpost while Serle, taking advantage of his flight, issued a Tory vehicle of the same name on one of Gaine's abandoned presses. In any event—and there may well have been more specific inducements—Gaine, as we have seen, soon returned to Manhattan, where from November 11, 1776, onward he himself blithely conducted the paper in the Crown's behalf. Then some months later, in September, 1777, Rivington showed up from London with the lucrative appointment of "Printer to the King's Most Excellent Majesty" to found the *New-York Loyal Gazette*, which he shortly renamed the *Royal Gazette*. In Gaine's welcoming words,

> Rivington is arriv'd—let ev'ry Man
> This injur'd Person's Worth confess;
> His loyal Heart abhor'd the Rebel's Plan
> And boldly dar'd them with his *Press*.[11]

Even though the Tory publishers had few or no readers outside British-held territory, the reappearance of these "servants of the servants of the abandoned servile profligate ministry of an infatuated Prince" incensed a people struggling desperately for freedom.[12] Patriots of a literary bent sharpened their quills on Towne,

[11] *N.-Y. Gazette and Weekly Mercury*, Sept. 29, 1777.
[12] "O" in the *N.-Y. Journal* (Kingston), Sept. 15, 1777.

Gaine and Rivington in particular.[13] When Towne, having pirouetted back to the American side, asked John Witherspoon to write for the *Pennsylvania Evening Post* again, the learned doctor with tongue in cheek assented on condition that the editor publish a "humble confession, declaration, recantation, and apology" of Witherspoon's own composing. But Towne understandably declined to admit, among other things, that he had never "pretended to be a man of character" and that, as some citizens believed, "instead of being suffered to print, I ought to be hanged as a traitor to my country." This, however, did not prevent the skit from making the merry rounds of the Whig press.[14]

Though Philip Freneau, the bard of the American cause, directed his keenest shafts at Rivington, he found time to impale "*honest Hugh Gaine*" for petitioning the New York legislature to remain in the state after the provisional treaty of peace in 1781. According to this apocryphal rendering, Gaine explained that

> Like the rest of the dunces I mounted my steed,
> And galloped away with incredible speed

to Newark, but acknowledged that he had then acted even more foolishly in scurrying back to the British:

> As matters have gone, it was plainly a blunder,
> But then I expected the Whigs must knock under,
> And I always adhere to the sword that is longest,
> And stick to the party that's like to be strongest.[15]

Against Rivington, Freneau loosed a whole quiver of barbs. In "Rivington's Reflections" the Tory defender was made to exclaim,

> If I offered to lie for the sake of a post,
> Was I to be blamed if the king offered most?
> The King's Royal Printer!—Five hundred a year!
> Between you and me, 'twas a handsome affair.

[13] John Trumbull had earlier set the example in the first canto of *M'Fingal*, published in Philadelphia in Jan., 1776, by mocking the Boston Tory editors "Mills and Hicks and mother Draper" for their thrusts " 'gainst Sons of Freedom, All for your good and none would read 'em." *M'Fingal* (B. J. Lossing, ed., N. Y., 1857), 40; *Pa. Journal*, Jan. 31, 1776. Among other newspapers the *Essex Journal* (Newburyport) serialized the canto, beginning on April 26.

[14] Thomas, *History of Printing*, I, 265–266; John Witherspoon, *Works* (rev. ed., John Rodgers, ed., Phila., 1802), IV, 397–401.

[15] "Hugh Gaine's Life," Freneau, *Poems* (F. L. Pattee, ed., Princeton, 1902), II, 201–208, also in *Freeman's Journal* (Phila.), Jan. 8, 1783, and later.

In "Lines on Mr. Rivington's new engraved King's Arms to his
Royal Gazette," Satan commended the editor,

> Since under my banners so bravely you fight,
> Kneel down!—for your merits I dubb you a knight,
> From a passive subaltern I bid you to rise
> The Inventor as well as the Printer of lies.

And "Rivington's Last Will and Testament" began,

> IMPRIMIS, my carcase I give and devise
> To be made into cakes of moderate size,
> To nourish those tories whose spirits may droop
> And serve the king's army with Portable soup.

Listed among his other bequests were bound volumes of the *Royal
Gazette* for George III, Benedict Arnold and Satan.[16]

When the printer, like Gaine, sought at the war's end to continue
in New York, the poet with equal venom satirized the about-face in
"Rivington's Confessions." [17] Even earlier, however, Witherspoon,
anticipating that Rivington when the time came would sue the Continental Congress for pardon, had thoughtfully provided him with a
cringing "Supplication," and Francis Hopkinson in Philadelphia
supplied still another one after the surrender at Yorktown. Both
were members of the Congress. In Witherspoon's version the editor
pleaded that no one could say he had ever injured America since no
one had ever believed him; in Hopkinson's he vowed he would
thereafter devote "his eminent talents in the art of political devia-
tion from truth in support of a *bad cause*" to "defending a *good
one*." Hopkinson further published a supposed advertisement of the
sale of Rivington's effects, an extensive inventory containing such
items as "*The political Liar:* a weekly Paper, published by the Subscriber," an "*elegant Map* of the British empire in North America,
upon a very small scale," and "*Tears of Repentance:* or, the present
state of the loyal Refugees in New York, and elsewhere." [18]

[16] Freneau, *Poems*, II, 190–195, also in two numbers of the *Freeman's Journal*,
Dec. 1782; Freneau, *Poems*, II, 125, also in *Freeman's Journal*, March 27, 1782;
Freneau, *Poems*, II, 120–123, also in *Freeman's Journal*, Feb. 27, 1782.

[17] Freneau, *Poems*, II, 229–238, also in *Freeman's Journal*, Dec. 31, 1783.
For still other flings of Freneau at Rivington, see his *Poems*, 116–117, 124, 143–
146, 169–171, all originally published in *Freeman's Journal*.

[18] Witherspoon, *Works*, II, 387–396, also *U. S. Mag.* (Phila.), I (1779), 34–
39; Hopkinson, *Miscellaneous Essays and Occasional Writings* (Phila., 1792),
159–169, 175–177, also *Pa. Packet*, Nov. 10, 20, 1781.

Tory journalists, however, suffered more than verbal harassment. The Americans would have made short shrift of the culprits if they could only have laid hands on them. Even Governor William Livingston of New Jersey could write half seriously to Gouverneur Morris, "If Rivington is taken, I must have one of his ears; Governor Clinton [of New York] is entitled to the other; and General Washington, if he pleases, may take his head." [19] As it was, most of the legislatures proscribed loyalist printers and expropriated their property. The Robertsons, for example, estimated their losses at £650, and Mrs. Draper and Christopher Sower III respectively set theirs at £2093 and £9606. These confiscations, of course, had no effect while the British retained control, and a postwar parliamentary commission on Tory hardships awarded many of the editors partial damages. The Robertsons thus received a lump sum of £350; Mrs. Draper, £940 plus a pension of £100; and Sower, £3361 with a £40 pension.[20]

Meanwhile most of the unfortunates had fled to Britain, Canada and elsewhere, though some ultimately returned to the United States after the wartime passions had cooled. James Johnston, however, was the only one ever again to publish an American newspaper, the Georgia government permitting him to do this after the peace upon payment of a fine.[21] The most egregious offenders, Rivington and Gaine, somehow succeeded in escaping any official retribution and unobtrusively lived out the rest of their lives in New York. Rivington's name, though, long continued to be a byword and a reproach. As late as the Civil War, when the editors of the *Boston Journal* rebuked the antiadministration *New York World* for "intemperate party warfare," they pointedly remarked, "Rivington lives in history as well as Arnold." [22]

[19] Theodore Sedgwick, Jr., *A Memoir of the Life of William Livingston* (N. Y., 1833), 247; similarly, a letter to Robert Livingston, April 22, 1782, *William and Mary Quar.*, ser. 3, XIII (1956), 397.

[20] Transcripts of the Manuscript Books and Papers of the Commission of Enquiry into the Losses and Services of the American Loyalists (N. Y. Public Library), III, 124, XI, 262, XLI, 453–461, XLIX, 446–452. For the cases of James Humphreys, Enoch Story, Robert Wells and William Hunter, Jr., see *ibid.*, XI, 312, XLIX, 163–169, L, 514–525, LVI, 534, 542–551, LIX, 536–539.

[21] L. T. Griffith and J. E. Talmadge, *Georgia Journalism, 1763–1950* (Athens, 1951), 8–9.

[22] Letter of March 6, 1863, to Manton Marble, cited in J. M. Bloch, The Rise of the New York *World* during the Civil War Decade (Harvard doctoral thesis, 1941), I, 216.

VI

The newspaper offensive unleashed by the Sugar Act, aside from its political consequences, made a permanent impress on American journalism. For one thing the prolonged agitation enormously enhanced the influence of the press, instilling a newspaper-reading habit which has characterized all succeeding generations. Public prints had increased but slowly in the three-score years following John Campbell's *Boston News-Letter* in 1704 and had existed only in populous centers. Then, thanks to the heightened demand for news and views, the number in the brief span from 1764 to the outbreak of hostilities in 1775 jumped more than sixty per cent—from twenty-three to thirty-eight—and they throve in communities that had never before possessed any.

Moreover, some of the newer journals, breaking sharply with tradition, came out two or three times a week instead of just once, thus nourishing an appetite for still greater frequency. As a result, Towne's *Pennsylvania Evening Post*, which had experimented with both triweekly and semiweekly issues, evolved after the war into America's pioneer daily. Starting on May 30, 1783, the ill-run sheet managed to maintain its exacting schedule for only a month, but the next year another Philadelphia venture under different auspices showed that the daily newspaper had come to stay. This was the *Pennsylvania Packet*, which John Dunlap and his partner David C. Claypoole converted from a triweekly to a daily on September 21, 1784. Doubtless its most illustrious subscriber was George Washington of Mt. Vernon, Va. Under various names and ownerships the *Packet* survived for nearly half a century.[23] By 1790 like undertakings were flourishing in New York, Baltimore and Charleston, a harbinger of what the future held in store for sizable cities throughout the nation.

The quarrel with the mother country also established with finality the opinion-making function of the press. The newspapers, as they had before the dispute, purveyed commercial and personal intelligence, but now nearly every one had a partisan ax to grind as

[23] On these beginnings, see three accounts by A. M. Lee: "First American Daily," *Editor & Publisher*, March 17, 1934, pp. 12, 40; "Dunlap and Claypoole," *Journalism Quar.*, IX (1934), 160–178; and *The Daily Newspaper in America* (N. Y., 1937), chap. iii.

well. Although editorial columns in the modern sense were still lacking, the printers nevertheless struck out boldly on occasion in signed statements, they sometimes inserted pungent italicized or bracketed comments in news reports, and they also advertised their sentiments in large-type mottoes adjoining their name plates. Increasingly, too, as the tension mounted, they deliberately colored supposedly factual accounts of public affairs. Their principal and most potent editing, however, lay in playing up contributors of their own political stripe.

With similar intent they developed ingenious typographical devices—another augury of later journalistic practice. Headings in capital letters occasionally appeared over articles, though never longer than a single line. Far more important, the publishers overcame mechanical obstacles to feature emotion-charged symbols, such as mourning borders, coffins, skulls and crossbones, and the divided snake. Curiously, however, the Tory Rivington was the only one to pictorialize an actual incident—in the spoofing caricature of himself hanging from a tree—and even he did this but once.

The opinion-making role of the newspapers inescapably involved them in the issue of freedom of the press. As long as the Crown wielded effective control, the Whig journalists endlessly extolled the virtues of unfettered discussion, calling in witness such notables of the past and present as the authors of *Cato's Letters*, John Wilkes and Zenger's attorney, Andrew Hamilton. And though the common-law doctrine of seditious libel ran squarely to the contrary, the patriots actually succeeded by hook or crook in preventing a single editor or contributor from suffering the judicial consequences of defaming the government. As the crisis deepened, however, and the Whigs gradually gained the upper hand, they unblushingly invoked for their own purposes the murky distinction between the liberty and license of the press which, when it was advanced by their adversaries, they had earlier so passionately rejected. Their idea of license, though, was diametrically the opposite: not defiance of royal authority, as the Tories held, but defiance of popular authority, that is, of the agencies working to cripple royal authority. Lacking legal means, they necessarily resorted to intimidation, boycotts and violence. Even John Adams in an angry moment offered as one reason for renouncing Britain that "The [opposition] presses will produce no more seditious or traitorous speculations." [24] The great and honorable exception to this reign of intolerance, though affording no relief to Tories, was the free and open debate within the Whig party itself during the first half of 1776 over the question of Independence.

When the erection of state governments passed the levers of power to the people's representatives instead of the Crown's and thus offered official possibilities of suppression, Francis Hopkinson for his part restated the patriot case in language which Governor Hutchinson in his heydey could not have bettered. "The liberty of the press," he roundly affirmed,

> hath been justly held up as an important privilege of the people. . . . But when this privilege is manifestly abused, and the press becomes an engine for sowing the most dangerous dissensions, for spreading false alarms, and undermining the very foundations of government, ought not that government, upon the plain principles of self-preservation, to silence by its own authority, such a daring violator of its peace, and tear from its bosom the serpent that would sting it to death.[25]

Hopkinson undoubtedly spoke for many; yet, despite the excesses that had marked the treatment of Tory editors and writers, the predominant opinion reflected an older and profounder conviction. All save two of the states framing new constitutions asserted in words resembling those of the Virginia Bill of Rights: "the freedom of the press is one of the great bulwarks of liberty, and can never be restrained but by despotic governments." In Maryland's succinct version, "the liberty of the press ought to be inviolably preserved." And John Adams himself took the lead in demanding a forthright declaration in his state's basic law.[26]

[24] Letter to John Winthrop, June 23, 1776, John Adams, *Works* (C. F. Adams, ed., Boston, 1850–56), IX, 409.

[25] Hopkinson in an article signed "A Tory" in the *Pa. Evening Post*, Nov. 16, 1776. For the same piece somewhat revised, see his *Miscellaneous Essays*, I, 132–136.

[26] Dixon and Hunter's *Virginia Gazette* took the Virginia declaration for its motto, beginning on Nov. 15, 1776. The New York and New Jersey instruments lacked such provisions, and two of the other original states, Connecticut and Rhode Island, continued their colonial charters, which said nothing on the matter. On the other hand, Vermont, not one of the thirteen, inserted a free-press clause in its constitution of 1777. L. R. Schuyler, *The Liberty of the Press in the American Colonies before the Revolutionary War* (N. Y., 1905), 77; C. A. Duniway, *The Development of Freedom of the Press in Massachusetts* (Cambridge, 1906), 132–136.

Nor were these mere pious professions. In Maryland the question of whether a newspaper could voice unpopular sentiments quickly came to a test. The veteran printer, William Goddard, so often a stormy petrel in the past, now returned to that role. On February 25, 1777, he published a piece in the *Maryland Journal* in which Samuel Chase, the later Justice of the United States Supreme Court, using the pen name of "Tom Tell-Truth," satirically counseled acceptance of recent British peace proposals. When the outraged Whig Club of Baltimore demanded that the contributor repudiate the "clumsy irony," Goddard "with *brutal impoliteness*" refused to divulge his name, and the Club thereupon ordered the editor to leave the vicinity. The lower house of the legislature exonerated him, however, under Maryland's Bill of Rights. Two years later, on July 6, 1779, Goddard once more gave offense with an anonymous screed against General Washington by the lately court-martialed General Charles Lee. This time a mob terrified him into identifying the writer and into temporarily disowning Lee's views, but again the state authorities rallied to his defense. Thus, even in the midst of war, the constitutional guarantee twice vindicated Goddard's right to editorial independence.[27]

When the Federal Constitutional Convention assembled in 1787, however, the question received scant attention. Though Charles Pinckney of South Carolina sought to place a free-press clause in the nation's organic law, a slight majority rejected the proposal on the ground that in view of the division of authority between the state and central governments Congress would have no control over newspapers—a not unreasonable position before the Federalist party upon taking office developed the doctrine of implied powers. But members of the state ratifying conventions, as well as many of their constituents, took alarm at the omission of this and other guarantees of civil liberties. Jefferson, for example, declared that "The few cases wherein these things may do evil, cannot be weighed against the multitude wherein the want of them will do evil." Sam-

---

[27] W. B. Terwilliger, "William Goddard's Victory for the Freedom of the Press," *Md. Hist. Mag.*, XXXVI (1941), 139–149; L. C. Wroth, *A History of Printing in Colonial Maryland* (Balt., 1922), 135–140. A similar instance in another state was that of Eleazer Oswald of the Philadelphia *Independent Gazetteer*, John Holt's son-in-law, whom a grand jury declined to indict in 1782 for publishing attacks on certain decisions of Judge Thomas McKean. J. T. Wheeler, *The Maryland Press, 1777–1790* (Balt., 1938), 28–29. It goes without saying that in the throes of war like immunity was not granted an enemy organ.

uel Adams, as might be expected, displayed particular concern over the failure to safeguard "the just liberty of the press." Accordingly, Congress in 1789 in its first session under the new instrument formulated a national Bill of Rights for incorporation in the Constitution, which contained the injunction that Congress shall make no law "abridging the freedom of speech, or of the press." [28]

Even so, the question remained unresolved at both the state and federal levels as to whether an unrestricted but undefined liberty of the press superseded the traditional English doctrine. Was it intended that the principles of the Zenger acquittal or those of the common law of seditious libel should prevail? This was a point upon which laymen and a precedent-minded bench could well disagree.[29] Unfortunately, only Pennsylvania and Delaware in their respective constitutions of 1790 and 1792 declared categorically that truth might be offered as evidence and that the jury should determine both the law and the facts. Surprisingly enough, the repressive Sedition Act, passed by the Federalist Congress in 1798, contained a comparable provision.[30] Nonetheless some years were to elapse before the courts, which had the final say, put this enlightened concept fully into effect.[31]

The sober second thought of the Revolutionary generation thus in the end conferred a priceless boon on American journalism and the democratic process: the rooted conviction that freedom of utterance ranks unique among human rights as the protector and promoter of all the others. And to this conviction Alexander Hamilton, remembering the dangers to political discussion during the quarrel

[28] Zechariah Chafee, Jr., *Free Speech in the United States* (Cambridge, 1941), 4–6; R. A. Rutland, *The Birth of the Bill of Rights* (Chapel Hill, 1955), 119–189; Thomas Jefferson to James Madison, July 31, 1788, Jefferson, *Writings* (P. L. Ford, ed., N. Y., 1892–99), V, 46; W. V. Wells, *The Life and Public Services of Samuel Adams* (Boston, 1865), III, 267.

[29] For the popular view that the common-law doctrine had been supplanted, see J. C. Miller, *Crisis in Freedom* (Boston, 1951), 83–84. J. M. Smith, *Freedom's Fetters* (Ithaca, 1956), 427–431, and Chafee, *Free Speech in the United States,* 16–22, agree that this was the intent of the framers of the First Amendment.

[30] J. M. Smith, "Alexander Hamilton, the Alien Law, and Seditious Libels," *Review of Politics,* XVI (1954), 305–333, takes issue with the statement of some historians that Hamilton was responsible for this ameliorative clause; and the same author shows in *Freedom's Fetters,* 421–424 and *passim,* that the clause was interpreted by the courts in such a way as virtually to perpetuate the common-law doctrine.

[31] Charles Warren, *A History of the American Bar* (Boston, 1911), 236–239; Duniway, *Freedom of the Press in Massachusetts,* 141–162; Smith, *Freedom's Fetters,* 200–218, 431–432 n.

with Britain, added the admonition that "its security, whatever fine declarations may be inserted in any constitution respecting it, must altogether depend on public opinion, and on the general spirit of the people and of the government." [32] That indeed is the durable lesson which posterity has ignored at its peril and never for long. Next to Independence itself, it was the Revolutionary generation's greatest legacy to the American people.

[32] In no. lxxxiv of *The Federalist* (H. C. Lodge, ed., N. Y., 1888), 537–538.

Appendix A

CIRCULATION figures of colonial newspapers, though fragmentary and unverifiable, possess an inherent credibility and indicate a steady upward trend. In 1719 the *Boston News-Letter*, then New England's only organ, had fewer than 300 subscribers after fifteen years as a going concern. By 1754, however, when Boston alone had four journals, each averaged nearly 600. According to James Parker of the *New-York Gazette or Weekly Post-Boy* in 1766, a subscription list of 500 or 600 was by that time a normal expectation.[1]

But already the Anglo-American dispute was stepping up the number. In 1765 the *New-York Journal* had 1500; in 1768 the *Boston Chronicle*, a Tory publication, 1500; in 1770 the *Pennsylvania Chronicle*, 2500. In 1771, during the period of political calm, there may have been a falling off, for the *New-York Gazette or Weekly Post-Boy* reported only "near 1000," and the newly established *Massachusetts Spy* in Boston, "about 500" though with 300 more in the offing. If a decline actually occurred, the renewal of the difficulties in 1774 repaired the damage. In that year the *Massachusetts Gazette and Boston News-Letter* and the *New-York Gazetteer*, both Tory papers, possessed 1500 and 3600 respectively; and in 1775 the *Constitutional Gazette* in New York mustered over 2000, while the *Boston Gazette* and the *Massachusetts Spy* (before the outbreak of war forced them from Boston) boasted 2000 and 3500 each.[2] If these figures are representative, circulations in the major towns in the period from the Stamp Act onward averaged 1475 per newspaper until the climactic events of 1774 and 1775 raised the number to 2520. As for smaller places, the *Providence Gazette* in 1766 had 800 subscribers; Salem's *Essex Gazette* in 1770, about 700; Hart-

---

[1] Isaiah Thomas, *The History of Printing in America* (rev. ed., Am. Antiquarian Soc., *Trans. and Colls.*, V–VI, 1874), II, 8, 17; Parker to William Bradford, Dec. 4, 1766, Bradford Papers (Hist. Soc. of Pa.), II, 74.

[2] *Ibid.* (regarding the *N.–Y. Journal*); *Boston Chronicle*, June 6, 1768; *Pa. Chronicle*, Jan. 22, 1770; *N.–Y. Gazette or Weekly Post-Boy*, Aug. 19, 1771; *Mass. Spy*, Jan. 21, 1771; E. A. Jones, *The Loyalists in Massachusetts* (London, 1930), as to the *Mass. Gazette and Boston News-Letter*; *N.–Y. Gazetteer*, Oct. 13, 1774; R. D. Morris, ed., *The Era of the American Revolution* (N. Y., 1939), 320, for the *Constitutional Gazette*; *Boston Gazette*, Jan. 2, 1797; *Mass. Spy*, Dec. 21, 1780.

ford's *Connecticut Courant* in 1775, 700; and Purdie's *Virginia Gazette* at Williamsburg in 1775 indicated something of its total by complaining that "upwards of ONE THOUSAND" had failed to remit.[3]

From a strictly business standpoint, Isaiah Thomas of the *Massachusetts Spy* stated, "It has always been allowed that 600 customers, with a considerable number of advertisements, weekly, will but *barely* support the publication of a news-paper." Thomas himself in 1775 asked a guarantee of 700 before starting the *Worcester Gazette or Oracle of Liberty,* while Andrew Stewart at Baltimore the same year similarly sought 1000 for his projected *Maryland Gazette and Baltimore Advertiser.*[4] In neither case, however, was the desired response forthcoming.

In view of the smallness of colonial towns the circulations were sizable, especially when it is remembered that some places supported as many as four or five sheets and that the readers always greatly outnumbered the purchasers. The publisher of the *New-York Gazetteer* said of his list of 3600 that "the presses of very few, if any of his brethren, including those in Great Britain, exceed it." The comparison, however, was misleading, for, so far at least as London was concerned, its papers were dailies rather than weeklies. But, if allowance be made for this, it is worth noting that the *Public Advertiser* had upward of 2000 subscribers in 1765 and over 3000 in 1770 and that the *Gazetteer and New Daily Advertiser*, the foremost journal, numbered 5000 in 1769.[5]

---

[3] *Providence Gazette,* Aug. 15, 1766; Harriet S. Tapley, *Salem Imprints* (Salem, 1927), 20; J. E. Smith, *One Hundred Years of Hartford's Courant* (New Haven, 1949), 11; *Va. Gazette* (Purdie), Aug. 9, 1776.

[4] *Mass. Spy,* Feb. 10, 1775, Dec. 21, 1780; *N.-Y. Gazetteer,* March 2, 1775 (for Stewart).

[5] Benjamin Franklin, *Letters to the Press, 1758–1775* (V. W. Crane, ed., Chapel Hill, 1950), p. xvii; F. J. Hinkhouse, *The Preliminaries of the American Revolution as Seen in the English Press* (N. Y., 1926), 27.

Appendix B

THE AMERICAN manufacture of paper started about 1690 at German-town, Pa. Gradually other mills were established; New England's first one was at Milton, near Boston, in 1728. Since the output was not sufficient, however, to satisfy the demand, printers depended on England for the vast bulk of their supply. The hard times dogging the Seven Years' War emphasized the need to save the money thus "sunk to us in the Pockets of European Merchants" and brought about further mills, at Providence in 1764 and Norwich in 1766.[1] Thanks to these increasing facilities, the *Massachusetts Gazette and Weekly News-Letter* from May 2, 1765, onward got its paper from Milton; the *New-Hampshire Gazette* followed suit on February 27, 1767; the *New-York Gazette and Weekly Mercury* used Pennsylvania-made paper;[2] and the *New-London Gazette*, commencing on December 12, 1766, obtained its stock from Norwich—"a proof that this colony can furnish itself with one very considerable article which has hitherto carried thousands of pounds out of it." Other newspapers may have done likewise.

The Townshend legislation, 1767–1770, though taxing paper imported into America from Britain, did not forbid the colonists to make it for themselves. In fact, as a Connecticut resident observed, "the Dutys laid on Paper may be justly reputed a premium upon the very branch of Manufacture in this Country, & I am amazed," he added, referring to the Ministry, "at their Stupidity, when I reflect."[3] The patriots themselves spurred the domestic production by including the British article in their nonimportation agreements of 1768 and 1769,[4] and the Connecticut legislature in the latter year went so far as to offer bounties to the same end.[5]

[1] Dard Hunter, *Papermaking in Pioneer America* (Phila., 1952), chaps. iii–xi; L. C. Wroth, *The Colonial Printer* (N. Y., 1931), 116–117, citing William Goddard's *New-England Almanack for 1765* (Providence, 1764).

[2] Bradford Papers (Hist. Soc. of Pa.), I, 162.

[3] Benjamin Gales to Ezra Stiles, Oct. 15, 1767, Stiles, *Itineraries and Other Miscellanies* (F. B. Dexter, ed., New Haven, 1916), 493. See also *ibid.*, 470.

[4] Whig groups in all the provinces but New Hampshire took such action. A. M. Schlesinger, *The Colonial Merchants and the American Revolution* (N. Y., 1918), chap. iii, *passim*.

[5] Hunter, *Papermaking*, 57.

Naturally the press gave its wholehearted support. "This paper is the manufacture of this colony;" declared the *Newport Mercury,* November 16, 1767, "and if the inhabitants would be careful in preserving rags, we might soon be furnished with a sufficiency of paper, of all kinds, without sending out of the government for it." Save your rags, echoed the *New-London Gazette,* December 18, "if you really love your country." To facilitate collections from householders, the *Boston Gazette* and the *New-Hampshire Gazette* acted as agents for the "Manufacturers of Paper at Milton"; within two months one of the producers reported that he was receiving more tons of rags than he formerly had hundredweights.[6] When the *New-Hampshire Gazette* reduced the size of its number for January 6, 1769, the publishers laid this to a temporary shortage of domestic paper, since they were "determined to make use of as little as possible on which the Duties must be paid." Even the Tory *Boston Chronicle* consumed between £300 and £400 worth of the Milton commodity from December, 1767, to August, 1769.[7]

The newspapers in the Middle colonies meanwhile displayed comparable zeal. As "Philo-Patriae" sounded off in the *Pennsylvania Chronicle,* December 2, 1767,

> The manufacturing of Paper, upon which so exhorbitant a Duty has been laid, now demands our particular Attention. . . . The City of *Dublin,* . . . by small Premiums, . . . procured in a very short Time a sufficient Quantity [of rags] for their own Consumption. And if the same Measure was pursued by the Inhabitants of *Pennsylvania,* and the neighbouring Provinces, the Linen Rags of which great Quantities are destroyed in every City, it would soon enable us to keep within ourselves, the great Sums of Money which are annually exported for that Article.

The *Pennsylvania Journal,* February 2, 1769, likewise implored "every one who thinks his own interest, or the liberty and prosperity of this province and country worth his notice," and particularly all housewives, to co-operate in stopping the payments "annually torn from us to maintain in voluptuousness our greedy task masters." New York, which had hitherto relied wholly upon outside sources, in 1768 acquired its pioneer paper mill. By 1770, according to one student of the subject, there were forty in Pennsylvania, Delaware and New Jersey.[8]

In the absence of statistics of production the net effect of these ef-

---

6 *Boston Gazette,* Nov. 30, 1767, Jan. 25, 1768.

7 *Boston Chronicle,* Aug. 17, 1769.

8 E. B. O'Callaghan, comp., *The Documentary History of the State of New York* (Albany, 1849–51), I, 736; Joel Munsell, *Chronology of the Origin and Progress of Paper and Paper-Making* (Albany, 1876), 43.

forts is difficult to determine. Indirect light is perhaps thrown on the matter, however, by the imperial customs receipts for the Townshend years. The total duties paid by all the colonies for imported paper amounted to only about £500 as compared, in the single instance of New York, with £490 for glass and £4644 for tea.[9] Had the printers been getting most of their stock from Britain as they had earlier when it was untaxed, the figure would have been many times higher.

The repeal of the duties on paper in 1770 removed the question as a political issue but not as a practical problem. Despite the increasing American output the demand still outran the supply, and the press continued to cry up the economic benefits of aiding the infant industry. Remember, too, one editor added, that "Paper was a main article in the late *unconstitutional Taxes,* which have been so nobly parried by the AMERICANS." [10] Though few new mills resulted, Hugh Gaine of the *New-York Gazette and Weekly Mercury* in 1773 helped set up one at Hempstead Harbor, Long Island, and Ebenezer Watson of the *Connecticut Courant* in 1775 helped start another near Hartford. Before Watson's was in operation, however, he had to suspend publication for a month because of lack of paper.[11] Scattered evidence indicates that, as earlier, printers regardless of politics used the domestic commodity when available. Isaiah Thomas, for example, launched the patriot *Massachusetts Spy* in 1770 on "good Paper manufactured in this Province," and James Rivington, who instituted the Whig-baiting *New-York Gazetteer* in 1773, stated that he annually spent nearly £1000 for "the manufacture of Pennsylvania, New-York, Connecticut and Massachusetts." [12]

The patriotic motive did not have full play again until the Intolerable Acts in 1774 inflamed American sentiment. "The present alarming situation of the colonies renders it entirely needless to point out the utility of establishing this and every other kind of manufactory among us, as soon as possible," so one writer put it, "this being the safest and most efficacious method of convincing the ministry of Great-Britain of their error, and securing opulence to ourselves." [13] Accordingly, the Continental Association shut out the imported product along with all other articles from Britain; Whig conventions and allied groups in 1775 and

[9] Letter of O. M. Dickerson to the author, Dec. 29, 1953. See also Dickerson's *The Navigation Acts and the American Revolution* (Phila., 1951), 198.

[10] *Pa. Packet,* March 16, 1772.

[11] *N.-Y. Gazette and Weekly Mercury,* Dec. 13, 1773; J. E. Smith, *One Hundred Years of Hartford's Courant* (New Haven, 1949), 11.

[12] *Mass. Spy,* July 17, Dec. 10, 1770; Morton Pennypacker, *General Washington's Spies on Long Island and in New York* (Brooklyn, 1939), 6.

[13] *N.-Y. Gazette and Weekly Mercury,* July 7, 1774.

1776 exhorted the colonial public to step up the supply of rags; and the patriot congresses in Maryland and the Carolinas offered financial inducements for building new mills.[14] The additional paper thus provided rendered possible the flood of printed matter which at this critical juncture helped sweep the country into the War for Independence.

[14] L. H. Weeks, *A History of Paper-Manufacturing in the United States* (N. Y., 1916), 37–40, 62–64.

Appendix C

British Policy Toward Overseas Freedom of the Press

By LETTING the lawbreaking printers get off scot-free at the time of the Stamp Act the British government foreshadowed a course from which it never afterward departed. This hands-off policy did not stem from ignorance of the "licentious" utterances, for the governors and other Crown officials repeatedly advised the Ministry of them. Governor Francis Bernard, especially active in this regard, usually backed up his complaints with offending copies of the *Boston Gazette* and the *Boston Evening-Post*. He reported that one of the contributors, upon "being admonished by a Friend that if they went on as they were going, they would probably incur a Censure from G Britain, answered 'that is what we want.'" [1]

The only noteworthy discussion of the situation in Parliament occurred in 1767. In April, Lord Shelburne suggested to the Earl of Chatham (William Pitt) that Parliament should declare it misprision of treason for a colonist to write, say or print that Britain did not possess the full right to bind America, but the proposal was not submitted to the Cabinet. In November, however, George Grenville, then out of power but still smarting from the colonial newspaper attacks on him for having fathered the Stamp Act, demanded in the House of Commons that it summon Edes and Gill to England to inform against the perpetrators of "Infamous libels" that "tended to stir up the People of that Country to sedition & rebellion." He particularly cited two writers in the *Boston Gazette*, August 31, who had contended that Parliament's suspension of the New York legislature for disregarding part of the Quartering Act was unconstitutional. One, "A.F.," had avowed that, "Tho' the Press . . . be *threatened with the summary proceedings of the Star Chamber,* and our righteous opposition to slavery be called rebellion, yet will a true Englishman pursue his duty with firmness, and leave the event to Heaven." The other, "Sui Imperator," had implored his countrymen, "tho' wading thro' seas of blood," to "defend your Liberties and maintain your Rights." The House, however, remained

[1] Letter to Lord Shelburne, Oct. 30, 1767, Bernard Papers (Sparks MSS., Harvard College Library), VI, 248–249.

unmoved. Henry S. Conway insisted that the action would violate all established procedure and that, in any event, the Commons should first stop libelous publications at home before calling to account printers and authors on the other side of the ocean. As the debate proceeded, it became evident that the members, though deeming the articles "of very Ill Tendency," agreed with the Ministry that it would be "below the dignity of Parliament to pay any regard to angry newspaper writers." Hence "with a laugh"—so Horace Walpole reported—they shelved further consideration of the matter for six months in the expectation that by that time Parliament would be dissolved.[2]

Governor Bernard, convinced by bitter experience that he could not silence the obnoxious editors by his own means, came increasingly to share Grenville's belief that the home government must itself intervene. After all, he wrote the Ministry on March 5, 1768, "these Printers are answerable to Great-Britain, an Hundred Times more" than to the colonial Crown representatives. Some months later, on January 25, 1769, he specifically urged that Edes and Gill be seized and compelled to identify their "treasonable & seditious" contributors. These two, he pointed out, wielded more than a local influence, being "the apparent Instruments of raising that Flame in America, which has given so much Trouble & is still like to give more to Great Britain & her Colonies." On further thought, on March 25, he added the publishers of the *Boston Evening-Post*, the *Providence Gazette* and the *New-York Journal* as others who were "continually directing Daggers to the Heart of their Mother Country." Again, on May 25, he insisted that the responsibility for curing the evil lay with London, "where the precise Distinctions of Law are much better understood than they can be here."[3]

Bernard's importunities did not wholly fail, for the Privy Council on July 6, 1770, asserted in a formal complaint against Massachusetts that "seditious and libellous publications are encouraged, and go unpunished," with "a design to stir up the people to acts of violence and opposition to the laws." It recommended that the King lay the matter

[2] C. R. Ritcheson, *British Politics and the American Revolution* (Norman, 1954), 91; *Boston Gazette*, March 7, 14, 1768; *Pa. Chronicle*, March 14, 1768; W. S. Johnson in London to Jared Ingersoll, Nov. 20, 1767, New Haven Colony Hist. Soc., *Papers*, IX (1918), 418–419; W. S. Johnson to William Pitkin, Dec. 26, 1767, Mass. Hist. Soc., *Colls.*, ser. 5, IX (1885), 247–248; Horace Walpole, *Memoirs of the Reign of King George the Third* (G. F. R. Barker, ed., London, 1894), III, 82–84. Bernard believed that one of the pieces had been written by Dr. Benjamin Church, the later turncoat. Letter to Lord Hillsborough, Jan. 24, 1768, Papers Relating to the American Revolution (Sparks MSS., Harvard College Library), 196.

[3] Letters to Lord Shelburne, John Pownall and Lord Hillsborough in Bernard and others, *Letters to the Ministry* (Boston, 1769), 10, and Bernard Papers, VII, 126–127, 158–159, 273–274.

before the next session of Parliament. The Massachusetts Council self-righteously denied the charge and demanded in return to know why the London authorities had not suppressed subversive writers at home. "If we have any amongst us," they gibed, "there are fifty in England to one here." [4]

The Ministry, so far as is known, did not act upon the recommendation of the Privy Council either then or later, preferring to leave the problem to the officials on the spot and blithely ignoring the circumstances which rendered the local efforts hopeless.[5] Conway in his remarks in Parliament in 1767 and the Massachusetts Council in its retort of 1770 hinted at what was probably the true reason for the inaction: the government's lack of success in coping with similar and more formidable conditions in the mother country. John Wilkes, the unidentified "Junius" and a host of other writers were flouting constituted authority to such an extent that Lord North burst out in Parliament, "Can any man recollect a period when the press groan'd with such a variety of desperate libels? Such is their number, that one would imagine there is not a single pen made, a single standish used, or a single scrap of paper bought, but in order to manufacture a libel." [6] Yet every attempt to curb the offenders merely gave their writings the greater publicity and thus backfired against the government. That would almost certainly have been the effect in America also if Parliament or the Ministry had directly intervened to restrict the liberty of the press. From this point of view, then, the hands-off policy justified itself. On the other hand, the struggle in Britain for the right to criticize public men and measures served to invigorate the parallel efforts in the colonies.

[4] State Papers (Gay Transcripts, Mass. Hist. Soc.), XIII, 39–43; *Acts of the Privy Council, Colonial Series* (J. B. Munro, ed.), V (London, 1912), 262; Alden Bradford, ed., *Speeches of the Governors of Massachusetts . . . and Other Public Papers* (Boston, 1818), 273–276.

[5] The King's speech at the next session of Parliament, Nov. 13, 1770, contained nothing about the journalistic abuses, only referring in general terms to "unwarrantable practices" in Massachusetts arising from "lawless violence." *The Parliamentary History of England* (T. C. Hansard), XVI (London, 1813), 1032.

[6] Speech of Dec. 27, 1770, reported in the *Mass. Gazette and Boston Post-Boy*, April 22, 1771. For the background of his remarks, see F. S. Siebert, *Freedom of the Press in England, 1476–1776* (Urbana, 1952), 355–363, 368–380, 384–389.

Appendix D

THIS daily chronicle of garrisoned Boston appeared first in John Holt's *New-York Journal* at intervals from October 13, 1768, to November 20, 1769. Harbottle Dorr, a Boston Son of Liberty, jotted on his copy of the *Boston Evening-Post*, December 12, 1768 (now in the library of the Massachusetts Historical Society), that the author was William Cooper, town clerk and brother of the patriot clergyman, Dr. Samuel Cooper of the Brattle Street Church.[1] Internal evidence, however, renders it unlikely that a single hand was responsible. This surmise is strengthened by the fact that Hutchinson spoke of "the author or authors," and that Bernard more specifically ascribed the "Journal" to Samuel Adams and "his Assistants, among which there must be some one at least of the Council as every thing that is done or said in Council which can be made use of is constantly perverted, misrepresented and falsified."[2] Subsequent speculation has added the name of John Adams because of resemblances between one passage in the "Journal" and certain memoranda in Adams's papers, but Adams himself stated on June 22, 1771, that he had not written "one line in a newspaper" for two years, a period which covered in part the preparation of the series.[3] Be that as it may, the probability of plural composition gains further credence from the fact that the New York Sons of Liberty, with whom Holt was intimately associated, offered a toast at their dinner on October 25, 1769, to "The Authors of the Boston Journal of Occurrences."[4]

[1] J. S. Loring in *The Hundred Boston Orators* (Boston, 1852), 9–10, makes the same attribution, though without citation of authority, and some later writers have followed his lead.

[2] Thomas Hutchinson, *The History of the Province of Massachusetts Bay*, III (London, 1828), 225; Bernard to Lord Hillsborough, Feb. 25, 1769, Bernard Papers (Sparks MSS., Harvard College Library), VII, 148. The Council member may very well have been James Bowdoin, as F. G. Walett argues in "James Bowdoin, Patriot Propagandist," *New England Quar.*, XXIII (1950), 336.

[3] Josiah Quincy, Jr., *Reports of Cases Argued and Adjudged in the Superior Court of Judicature of Massachusetts* (S. M. Quincy, ed., Boston, 1865), 457; John Adams, *Works* (C. F. Adams, ed., Boston, 1850–56), II, 282.

[4] *N.-Y. Gazette and Weekly Mercury*, Nov. 2, 1769, also *Boston Gazette*, Nov. 13.

Apart from the *Boston Evening-Post*, the American newspapers copying the "Journal" in whole or part included the *Essex Gazette* at Salem, Mass., the *New-London Gazette*, the *Connecticut Courant*, the *New-York Gazette or Weekly Post-Boy*, the *Pennsylvania Chronicle*, the *Pennsylvania Journal*, the *Pennsylvania Gazette*, the *Maryland Gazette*, the two *Virginia Gazettes*, the *South Carolina Gazette and Country Journal* and the *Georgia Gazette*. This is probably not a complete list. In addition, English readers became acquainted with the series through the pages of the *Oxford Magazine* and of the London newspapers: the *Gazetteer and New Daily Advertiser*, the *St. James's Chronicle* and the *American Gazette*.

Appendix E

THE WHIG REPORTING OF A QUAKER TESTIMONY

AN INSTRUCTIVE sidelight is thrown on patriot methods of propaganda by the journalistic reporting of a "Testimony" adopted by a Meeting of the Friends of Pennsylvania and New Jersey in Philadelphia on January 24, 1775. This pacifist religious sect, capping earlier resolutions, declared its "entire Disapprobation" of "many of the late political Writings" and recent popular proceedings as threatening "the Subversion of the constitutional Government," and it unqualifiedly denounced "all Combinations, Insurrections, Conspiracies, and illegal Assemblies" against "the Laws and Government." Rivington's *New-York Gazetteer* led in publishing the item, whence it spread to the newspapers in other parts of America.[1]

The Whigs faced the problem of how to blunt its effect, for Quaker influence was potent in Pennsylvania, and the patriots had for some time been worrying over the efforts of "that damn'd slow heavy quakering Nag" to temper their opposition.[2] At Philadelphia the *Pennsylvania Journal* insisted that the pronouncement could not possibly be intended to apply to "the present Congresses and Committees," since the Meeting's own chairman (James Pemberton) along with others of his coreligionists had themselves participated in such organizations. The purpose, the writer blandly suggested, was merely "to preserve the general cause from being sullied by the violence, or caprice of rash and turbulent minds."[3]

In Boston, on the other hand, the Whig scribes, taking advantage of their remoteness from Philadelphia, contended that "the *American Brussels* Gazette" in New York and its local counterpart, the *Massachusetts Gazette and Boston News-Letter,* had duped the public with a declara-

---

[1] *N.-Y. Gazetteer,* Jan. 26, Feb. 2, 1775; *Pa. Journal,* Feb. 1, 8; *Mass. Gazette and Boston News-Letter,* Feb. 2, 9; *Boston Evening-Post,* Feb. 2; *Md. Gazette,* Feb. 2; *Mass. Gazette and Boston Post-Boy,* Feb. 13; *Pa. Gazette,* Feb. 22; *N.-H. Gazette,* April 7; also Peter Force, comp., *American Archives* (ser. 4, Wash., 1837–46), I, 1176–1177.

[2] Charles Lee to Robert Morris, Jan. 27, 1776, *Lee Papers* (N.-Y. Hist. Soc., *Colls.,* IV–VII, 1871–74), I, 168.

[3] "B.L." in *Pa. Journal,* Feb. 1, 1775, also *Pa. Gazette,* March 8, and 4 *American Archives,* II, 80–81.

tion actually adopted during the Stamp Act ten years before, for they asserted that in fact "the FRIENDS, to the Southward and elsewhere, are as much against the measures now pursuing by the crown as any set of men whatever." In some indignation "Good Mrs. Draper" denied the charge of deceit, offering to show any inquirer a copy of the resolutions to compare with the 1765 text. Rivington raucously commented that the "Republican Printers" in the Yankee city had so brazenly inverted "the order of nature and reason" as to call truths lies.[4] The patriot papers thereupon dropped the matter, but neither then nor ever did they retract the canard.

[4] *Mass. Spy*, Feb. 9, 1775, also *Boston Evening-Post*, Feb. 13; *Boston Gazette*, Feb. 27; *Mass. Gazette and Boston News-Letter*, March 2; *N.-Y. Gazetteer*, March 23, also 4 *American Archives*, II, 134.

Bibliographical Note

PHILIP DAVIDSON'S pathbreaking study, *Propaganda and the American Revolution, 1763–1783* (Chapel Hill, 1941), in its earlier chapters covers much of the same subject matter as Part I of the present volume, but does so from a different point of view. Information regarding colonial journalism is to be found in many sources, though the only extensive over-all accounts are Clarence S. Brigham, ed., *History and Bibliography of American Newspapers, 1690–1820* (2 v., Worcester, 1947), an invaluable mine of data on ownership, places and duration of publication, changes of title and the location of surviving files; Isaiah Thomas's semiautobiographical *The History of Printing in America* (rev. ed., Am. Antiquarian Soc., *Trans. and Colls.*, V–VI, Worcester, 1874), which has the virtues and failings of this type of work; and Sidney Kobre, *The Development of the Colonial Newspaper* (Pittsburgh, 1944), a more unified narrative than either of the others but marred by numerous inaccuracies. Supplementary treatments include Clarence S. Brigham, *Journals and Journeymen* (Phila., 1950); John C. Oswald, *Printing in the Americas* (N. Y., 1937), chaps. i–xxix; Elizabeth C. Cook, *Literary Influences in Colonial Newspapers, 1704–1750* (N. Y., 1912); Lawrence C. Wroth, *The Colonial Printer* (rev. ed., Portland, Me., 1938), and *A History of Printing in Colonial Maryland* (Balt., 1922); Livingston R. Schuyler, *The Liberty of the Press in the American Colonies before the Revolutionary War, with Particular Reference to Conditions in the Royal Colony of New York* (N. Y., 1905); Clyde A. Duniway, *The Development of Freedom of the Press in Massachusetts* (Cambridge, 1906); Edward W. Hocker, *The Sower Printing House of Colonial Times* (Norristown, Pa., 1948); John J. Stoudt, "The German Press in Pennsylvania and the American Revolution," *Pa. Mag. of History and Biography*, LIX (1935), 74–90; Christopher C. Crittenden, *North Carolina Newspapers before 1790* (Chapel Hill, 1928); Jarvis M. Morse, *Connecticut Newspapers in the Eighteenth Century* (New Haven, 1935); J. Eugene Smith, *One Hundred Years of*

316

Hartford's Courant (New Haven, 1949), chaps. i–iii; and Hennig Cohen, *The South Carolina Gazette, 1732–1775* (Columbia, S. C., 1953). The standard histories of American journalism by Frank Luther Mott, William G. Bleyer, Edwin Emery and Henry L. Smith, Frederic Hudson and others also devote chapters to the colonial era. The only guide to the contents of any of the papers is the *Virginia Gazette Index, 1736–1780* (Lester J. Cappon and Stella F. Duff, comps., 2 v., Williamsburg, 1950), which covers the various Williamsburg journals bearing that title.

Biographical studies are scarce. Three of the best deal with editors whose careers fell mainly or wholly prior to the period of Revolutionary agitation: Livingston Rutherfurd's *John Peter Zenger* (N. Y., 1904), the publisher who made his historic stand for freedom of the press in the 1730's; Anna J. DeArmand's *Andrew Bradford, Colonial Journalist* (Newark, Del., 1949), who died in 1742; and John C. Oswald's *Benjamin Franklin, Printer* (N. Y., 1917), who ended his connection with the *Pennsylvania Gazette* shortly before the repeal of the Stamp Act. Other lives of Franklin also throw light on his journalistic activities. Of later figures the only extended accounts are John W. Wallace, *An Old Philadelphian, Colonial William Bradford, the Patriot Printer of 1776* (Phila., 1884); Charles F. Dapp, *The Evolution of an American Patriot, Being an Intimate Study of the Patriotic Activities of John Henry Miller* (Po.-German Soc., *Procs.*, XXXII, 1924); James O. Knauss, Jr., "Christopher Saur the Third," Am. Antiquarian Soc., *Procs.*, n. s., XLI (1931), 235–253; Annie R. Marble, *From 'Prentice to Patron, the Life Story of Isaiah Thomas* (N. Y., 1935); and Clifford K. Shipton, *Isaiah Thomas, Printer, Patriot and Philanthropist* (Rochester, 1948). In addition, useful sketches of these and other editors appear in the *Dictionary of American Biography* (Allen Johnson and Dumas Malone, eds., 21 v., N. Y., 1928–37).

Apart from such evidence as is afforded by the newspapers themselves, original sources on the internal workings of the press are few and fragmentary. The Historical Society of Pennsylvania possesses manuscript records of William and Thomas Bradford; the New York Public Library, of John Holt, Hugh Gaine and James Rivington; the New-York Historical Society, of Holt and Rivington; the American Antiquarian Society, of Isaiah Thomas; and the Alderman Library at the University of Virginia, of William Rind and Joseph Royle. Available in published form are *Account Books Kept by Benjamin Franklin: Ledger, 1728–1739*, and *Journal, 1730–1737* (George S. Eddy, ed., 2 v., N. Y., 1928–29); *A Work-Book of the Printing House of Benjamin Franklin & David Hall, 1759–1766* (George S. Eddy, ed., N. Y.,

1930); James Parker, "Letters to Benjamin Franklin, 1747–1770," Mass. Hist. Soc., *Procs.*, ser. 2, XVI (1902), 189–227; and Hugh Gaine, *Journals* (Paul L. Ford, ed., 2 v., N. Y., 1892). Portraits may be found of William Bradford in the *Pa. Mag. of History and Biography*, XV (1891), opp. 385; of John Carter in the R. I. Hist. Soc., *Colls.*, XI (1918), opp. 101 and 108; of William Goddard in *ibid.*, XII (1919), opp. 56; of Hugh Gaine in his *Journals*, I, frontispiece; of James Rivington in the N.–Y. Hist. Soc., *Quar.*, XXV (1951), opp. 30; and of Isaiah Thomas in Marble, *From 'Prentice to Patron*, frontispiece and opp. 264. Pictures of Franklin are too common to need listing.

The footnotes in the present volume cite many other manuscript and printed sources and secondary works adjacent to the relevant subject matter.

Index

A NOTE ON THE AUTHOR

Arthur Meier Schlesinger *was born in Xenia, Ohio, on February 27, 1888. After studying at Ohio State University (B.A., 1910) and Columbia University (Ph.D., 1917), he joined the history department of Ohio State in 1912. Leaving there in 1919, he became professor of history and head of the history department at the University of Iowa, moving on in 1924 to Harvard, where he was Francis Lee Higginson Professor from 1939 until his retirement in 1954. He has served as visiting professor in European universities and has been awarded numerous academic and other honors. His published books include* The Colonial Merchants and the American Revolution *(1918),* The Rise of the City *(1933),* Paths to the Present *(1949), and* The American as Reformer *(1950). He was also co-editor of* A History of American Life *(13 vols., 1927–44). Professor Schlesinger died in 1965.*

A NOTE ON THE TYPE

The text of this book was set on the Linotype in a face called TIMES ROMAN, *designed by* STANLEY MORISON *for* The Times *(London), and first introduced by that newspaper in 1932.*

Among typographers and designers of the twentieth century, Stanley Morison has been a strong forming influence, as typographical adviser to the English Monotype Corporation, as a director of two distinguished English publishing houses, and as a writer of sensibility, erudition, and keen practical sense.

In 1930 Morison wrote: "Type design moves at the pace of the most conservative reader. The good type-designer therefore realises that, for a new fount to be successful, it has to be so good that only very few recognize its novelty. If readers do not notice the consummate reticence and rare discipline of a new type, it is probably a good letter." It is now generally recognized that in the creation of Times Roman *Morison successfully met the qualifications of this theoretical doctrine.*